AGUR'S WISDOM AND THE
COHERENCE OF PROVERBS 30

ANCIENT ISRAEL AND ITS LITERATURE

Corrine L. Carvalho, General Editor

Editorial Board:
Andrew R. Davis
Alphonso Groenewald
Shuichi Hasegawa
Elaine James
Naomi A. Steinberg

Number 50

AGUR'S WISDOM AND THE COHERENCE OF PROVERBS 30

Alexander T. Kirk

SBL PRESS

Atlanta

Copyright © 2024 by Alexander T. Kirk

All rights reserved. No part of this work may be reproduced or transmitted in any form or by any means, electronic or mechanical, including photocopying and recording, or by means of any information storage or retrieval system, except as may be expressly permitted by the 1976 Copyright Act or in writing from the publisher. Requests for permission should be addressed in writing to the Rights and Permissions Office, SBL Press, 825 Houston Mill Road, Atlanta, GA 30329 USA.

Library of Congress Control Number: 2024935659

For Meghan.
We did it, babe.

לאדני
הקיצתי ועודי עמך
Ps 139:18

Contents

Acknowledgments ix
Abbreviations and Sigla xiii

1. Introducing Agur Ben-Yakeh: The Coherence of Proverbs 30
   and the Voice of Agur 3
   1.1. An Incoherent Text or an Eccentric Sage?   3
   1.2. Voice, Coherence, and the Anthological
        Nature of Proverbs   8
   1.3. The Argument and Structure of This Study   25

2. Agur and His Interpreters: Wisdom Literature, Form Criticism,
   and the Hermeneutical Potential of Proverbs 30 29
   2.1. How Has Agur Been Read?   29
   2.2. How Might We Read Agur?   47

3. Reframing Agur's Words: Reading Proverbs 30:1 as the
   Superscript of a Collection 61
   3.1. Burdened with Many Problems   61
   3.2. Invoking Agur   62
   3.3. What Might משא Mean?   69
   3.4. Toward a Reading of Proverbs 30:1b   95
   3.5. Proverbs 30:1 as the Superscript of a Collection   107

4. Agur's Wisdom: Voice, Tone, and Theology in Proverbs 30:2–10 109
   4.1. Will the Real Agur Please Stand Up?   109
   4.2. Reading Proverbs 30:2–10   110
   4.3. Finding Agur's Voice   143

5. Agur's Beastly Ethics: The Numerical Saying, Animal Imagery,
   Humor, and Coherence in Proverbs 30:11–33 147
   5.1. Coherence, Form, and Content in Proverbs 30:11–33   147

5.2. The Numerical Saying, Animal Imagery, and Humor: Hermeneutical Perspectives	148
5.3. Reading Proverbs 30:11–33	165
5.4. Satirizing Pride and Greed: Tone, Ethics, and Coherence in Proverbs 30:11–33	198

6. Agur in His Own Words: Coherence, Genre, and Philology in Proverbs 30 201
    6.1. Aspects of Coherence in Proverbs 30 — 201
    6.2. Agur's Words and the Question of Genre — 204
    6.3. Reading Agur's Words as Wisdom Literature within Proverbs — 208
    6.4. Philology, Reading, and Hermeneutics — 215

Appendix: Translation and Philological Notes 221
    Translation of Proverbs 30 — 221
    Philological Notes — 223

Bibliography 251
Ancient Sources Index 281
Modern Authors Index 299

Acknowledgments

If you start counting from when I first began working on Prov 30, this volume has been over ten years in the making. My long journey was filled with circles and doubling back, yet I have received better than I deserved, and I have gathered many debts of gratitude on my way.

Bruce Waltke first suggested to me, in my final semester of seminary, that the unity of Prov 30 would make a good topic for research. But more than that, with quiet passion Dr. Waltke introduced me to the beauty and awe of the Old Testament through his lectures, commentaries, and conversation. He is the reason I set out to try to be a scholar of the Hebrew Bible in the first place.

I was immensely privileged to study with both Walter Moberly and Stuart Weeks. Walter's postgraduate module, "Bible and Hermeneutics," not to mention his famous informal seminar, taught me to read with charity, precision, and faith. His invested reading of my own writing slowly and steadily improved it and consistently encouraged me. Stuart, on the other hand, did me the honor of never quite being satisfied with my work. In many long sessions at various pubs around Durham, Stuart apprenticed me in philology and set a high bar for the work I was attempting. Later, as I drafted chapters, Stuart sent me back to rewrite them again and again. He kept insisting that I didn't quite have my whole argument worked out yet. He was, of course, right. If Walter and Stuart had not guided and challenged me, I cannot imagine how impoverished this work would be. I am now proud to call myself both a philologist and a theologian.

Many other friends, colleagues, and mentors aided me on my journey. I would not have managed the transition from seminary to PhD studies without Mark Futato, Scott Swain, Scott Jones, and Scott Redd. Special credit is also due to Robert Holmstedt, who introduced me to the philological tools that made this study possible. I am further thankful to Rob for challenging me to publish my first papers, for bracing me with his hard-won perspective on academia, and for readily providing bits of syntactic guidance over the years. Bernd Schipper welcomed me to two consecutive years of his phenomenal Berlin-Oxford Summer School and has continued to support my research. Chris Ansberry kindly invited me to present an early paper and has championed my work ever since. Andrew Judd generously shared his own unpublished research and gave me reassuring notes on my treatment of genre. Will Kynes and Katherine Southwood have been valuable mentors, particularly generous with much-needed advice and encouragement about wisdom literature, biblical humor, and the various foibles and vagaries of trying to make one's way in academia. Suzanna Millar and David Janzen posed helpful questions, spotted many typos, pushed me toward sharper definitions in key places, and offered advice toward publication.

Without the support of Training Leaders International and our many generous and faithful partners—I cannot possibly list all the names—my research simply would not have been financially possible. It has been an honor—you have my deepest thanks. At Training Leaders International, Daren Carlson, Jim Jordan, Paul Smith, Jonathan Worthington, and Joost Nixon were particularly supportive, understanding, and encouraging. When we transitioned to Durham, Richard Rohlfing Jr. welcomed us and helped us find a home to live in, which—as much as anything else—made this research and writing possible through both the COVID-19 pandemic and the birth of two little girls. I am lucky to have friends like Robb Coleman, Joseph Justiss, and Hannah Bash, who all read bits of my work and made helpful comments. Michael Morgan's generosity and encouragement know no bounds. Pierre-Yves Koenig helped with French translations. Demetrios Alibertis infiltrated some of the world's best libraries to send me critical editions of the Peshitta when I could not access them. Jesse Schumann helped advance my Hebrew skills and became a great friend in the process. Jesse Peterson was my faithful companion as we both studied at a distance from Durham, offering me the gift of endless debate and critical moral support. Jacques Boulet and Rony Kozman—great friends since Toronto—have not stopped encouraging me and walking with me from afar. John Screnock has been like an older brother. From viewing apartments in Toronto, to providing excellent, detailed feedback on the most technical parts of this volume, to helping navigate academia and creating opportunities for me, John has been unflaggingly supportive. Brandon and Brittany Hurlbert, Dan and Megan York, and Luke and Bekah Irwin—fellow pilgrims in Durham—supported and encouraged us with their friendship in ways that I cannot summarize or repay.

My wonderful in-laws, Jeff and Rebecca Kiel, have always opened their home and their hearts to me. They never questioned or stopped supporting our work through their generosity and prayers, even when the life-choices Meghan and I made probably left them scratching their heads. My mom and dad, Larry and Connie Kirk, gave me my earliest and, in many ways, best education. Through dad's faithful preaching and mom's unflinching conviction that all truth is God's truth, they set me on this path. I am forever indebted to their example, their prayers, and their sacrificial love.

My little girls, Rue, Willa, and Janie—all three of whom were born during the course of my PhD—have been God's gift of perspective. I will cherish our Saturday daddy-daughter-days as long as I live. My wife, Meghan, has supported our quest for me to become a biblical scholar no matter what. More importantly, she has helped me keep that quest in perspective when it threatened to consume me. She is my best friend, and this book is for her.

Finally, though some may sneer, I would be remiss in my own conscience if I did not acknowledge the Lord my God. Ultimately, his incongruous grace enabled this work, from the natural gifts and inclinations he placed in me, to the parents he placed me with, to the woman he placed beside me, the scholars he placed me under, and the resources he placed at my disposal. What do I have that I did not receive?

Durham, 14 July 2023

Abbreviations and Sigla

Sigla
√	Semitic root
{}	translation of reconstructed Hebrew text that deviates from MT
§	section number

Greek Letters for Hexaplaric Sources
α′	Aquila
θ′	Theodotion

Abbreviations
1cs	first-person common singular
2ms	second-person masculine singular
3fs	third-person feminine singular
3mp	third-person masculine plural
3ms	third-person masculine singular
AB	Anchor (Yale) Bible
ABD	Freedman, David Noel, ed. *Anchor Bible Dictionary.* 6 vols. New York: Doubleday, 1992.
Avod. Zar.	Avodah Zarah
Avot R. Nat.	Avot of Rabbi Nathan
AIL	Ancient Israel and Its Literature
A.J.	Josephus, *Antiquitates judaicae*
AJSL	American Journal of Semitic Languages and Literatures
ANEM	Ancient Near Eastern Monographs
ANET	Pritchard, James B., ed. *Ancient Near Eastern Texts Relating to the Old Testament.* 3rd ed. Princeton: Princeton University Press, 1969.
AnOr	*Analecta Orientalia*
AOAT	Alter Orient und Altes Testament

AOTC	Abingdon Old Testament Commentaries
ArBib	Aramaic Bible
ATD	Das Alte Testament Deutsch
AuOr	*Aula Orientalis*
b.	Babylonian Talmud
BBRSup	Bulletin for Biblical Research Supplement
BDAG	Danker, Frederick W., Walter Bauer, William F. Arndt, and F. Wilbur Gingrich. *Greek-English Lexicon of the New Testament and Other Early Christian Literature*. 3rd ed. Chicago: University of Chicago Press, 2000.
BDB	Brown, Francis, S. R. Driver, and Charles A. Briggs. *A Hebrew and English Lexicon of the Old Testament*. Oxford: Clarendon, 1907. Repr., Peabody, MA: Hendrickson, 1997.
Ber.	Berakot
BHBib	Bibliotheca Hispaña biblica
BHS	Elliger, Karl, and Wilhelm Rudolf, eds. *Biblia Hebraica Stuttgartensia*. Stuttgart: Deutsche Bibelgesellschaft, 1983.
BHQ	Biblia Hebraica Quinta
BHRG	Merwe, Christo H. J. van der, Jacobus A. Naudé, and Jan H. Kroeze. *A Biblical Hebrew Reference Grammar*. 2nd ed. London: Bloomsbury T&T Clark, 2017.
Bib	*Biblica*
BibInt	*Biblical Interpretation*
BibInt	Biblical Interpretation Series
BibOr	Biblica et Orientalia
BJRL	*Bulletin of the John Rylands University Library of Manchester*
BJS	Brown Judaic Studies
BKAT	Biblischer Kommentar, Altes Testament
BLS	Bible and Literature Series
BSOAS	*Bulletin of the School of Oriental and African Studies*
BT	*The Bible Translator*
BTB	*Biblical Theology Bulletin*
BWANT	Beiträge zur Wissenschaft vom Alten und Neuen Testament
BZ	*Biblische Zeitschrift*
BZAW	Beihefte zur Zeitschrift für die alttestamentliche Wissenschaft

CAD	Gelb, Ignace J., et al., eds. *The Assyrian Dictionary of the Oriental Institute of the University of Chicago*. 21 vols. Chicago: Oriental Institute of the University of Chicago, 1956–2010.
CAL	The Comprehensive Aramaic Lexicon. http://cal.huc.edu.
CBET	Contributions to Biblical Exegesis and Theology
CBQ	*Catholic Biblical Quarterly*
CBQMS	Catholic Biblical Quarterly Monograph Series
CD	Cairo Genizah copy of the Damascus Document
ConBOT	Coniectanea Biblica: Old Testament Series
ConcC	Concordia Commentary
COS	Hallo, William W., and K. Lawson Younger Jr., eds. *The Context of Scripture*. 4 vols. Leiden: Brill, 1997–2016.
CrStHB	Critical Studies in the Hebrew Bible
CurBR	*Currents in Biblical Research*
DBSup	Pirot, Lous, and André Robert, eds. *Dictionnaire de la Bible: Supplément*. Paris: Letouzey & Ané, 1928–.
DCH	Clines, David J. A., ed. *The Dictionary of Classical Hebrew*. 9 vols. Sheffield: Sheffield Academic, 1993–2016.
DCLS	Deuterocanonical and Cognate Literature Studies
DDD	Toorn, Karel van der, Bob Becking, and Pieter van der Horst, eds. *Dictionary of Deities and Demons in the Bible*. 2nd ed. Leiden: Brill; Grand Rapids: Eerdmans, 1999.
DJD	Discoveries in the Judaean Desert
DMOA	Documenta et Monumenta Orientis Antiqui
DNWSI	Hoftijzer, Jacob, and Karen Jongeling. *Dictionary of North-West Semitic Inscriptions*. 2 vols. Leiden: Brill, 1995.
DSD	*Dead Sea Discoveries*
DULAT	Olmo Lete, Gregorio del, and Joaquín Sanmartín. *A Dictionary of the Ugaritic Language in the Alphabetic Tradition*. Translated and edited by Wilfred G. E. Watson. 3rd ed. HdO 112. Leiden: Brill, 2015.
EBR	Klauck, Hans-Josef, et al., eds. *Encyclopedia of the Bible and Its Reception*. Berlin: de Gruyter, 2009–.
ET	English translation
FOTL	Forms of the Old Testament Literature
FRLANT	Forschungen zur Religion und Literatur des Alten und Neuen Testaments
fs	feminine singular

G	The Greek version of the Hebrew Bible commonly known as the Septuagint
G^A	The Greek version of the Hebrew Bible according to Codex Alexandrinus
GKC	Gesenius, Wilhelm. *Gesenius' Hebrew Grammar*. Edited by Emil Kautzsch. Translated by Arthur E. Cowley. 2nd ed. Oxford: Clarendon, 1910.
GöMisz	*Göttinger Miszellen*
HALOT	Koehler, Ludwig, Walter Baumgartner, and Johann Jakob Stamm. *The Hebrew and Aramaic Lexicon of the Old Testament*. Edited and translated under the supervision of Mervyn E. J. Richardson. 2 vols. Leiden: Brill, 2001.
HAT	Handbuch zum Alten Testament
HBAI	*Hebrew Bible and Ancient Israel*
HBCE	The Hebrew Bible: A Critical Edition
HBM	Hebrew Bible Monographs
HCS	Hellenistic Culture and Society
HdO	Handbuch der Orientalistik
HS	*Hebrew Studies*
HTR	*Harvard Theological Review*
HUCA	*Hebrew Union College Annual*
IB	Buttrick, George A., et al. *Interpreter's Bible*. 12 vols. New York: Abingdon, 1951–1957.
IBC	Interpretation: A Bible Commentary for Teaching and Preaching
IBHS	Waltke, Bruce K., and Michael Patrick O'Connor. *An Introduction to Biblical Hebrew Syntax*. Winona Lake, IN: Eisenbrauns, 1990.
ICC	International Critical Commentary
Int	*Interpretation*
ITQ	*Irish Theological Quarterly*
JANES	*Journal of Ancient Near Eastern Studies*
JAOS	*Journal of the American Oriental Society*
JBL	*Journal of Biblical Literature*
JBW	*Jahrbücher der biblischen Wissenschaft*
JCS	*Journal of Cuneiform Studies*
JETS	*Journal of the Evangelical Theological Society*
JHS	*Journal of Hebrew Scriptures*
JNSL	*Journal of Northwest Semitic Languages*

Joüon	Joüon, Paul. 2011. *A Grammar of Biblical Hebrew*. Translated and revised by Takamitsu Muraoka. 2nd ed. SubBi 14. Rome: Pontifical Biblical Institute, 2011.
JPSV	Jewish Publication Society Version
JQR	*Jewish Quarterly Review*
JSem	*Journal of Semitics*
JSJSup	Journal for the Study of Judaism Supplement
JSOT	*Journal for the Study of the Old Testament*
JSOTSup	Journal for the Study of the Old Testament Supplement
JSS	*Journal of Semitic Studies*
JSSSup	Journal of Semitic Studies Supplement
JTS	*Journal of Theological Studies*
KAI	Donner, Herbert, and Wolfgang Röllig. *Kanaanäische und Aramäische Inschriften*. 2nd ed. 3 vols. Wiesbaden: Harrassowitz, 1966–1969.
Ketub.	Ketubbot
Klio	*Klio: Beiträge zur Alten Geschichte*
KTU	Dietrich, Manfried, Oswald Loretz, and Joaquín Sanmartín, eds. *Die keilalphabetischen Texte aus Ugarit, Ras Ibn Hani und anderen Orten*. 3rd ed. AOAT 360. Münster: Ugarit-Verlag, 2013. Cited according to Smith and Pitard 2009.
LD	Lectio Divina
LEH	Lust, Johan, Erik Eynikel, and Katrin Hauspie, eds. *Greek-English Lexicon of the Septuagint*. Rev. ed. Stuttgart: Deutsche Bibelgesellschaft, 2003.
Let. Aris.	Letter of Aristeas
LHBOTS	Library of Hebrew Bible/Old Testament Studies
LSAWS	Linguistic Studies in Ancient West Semitic
LSJ	Liddell, Henry George, Robert Scott, and Henry Stuart Jones. *A Greek-English Lexicon*. 9th ed. with revised supplement Oxford: Clarendon, 1996.
Menah.	Menahot
Midr.	Midrash (+ biblical book)
M^L	Masoretic text as witnessed to by Leningrad Codex
mng.	meaning
MT	Masoretic text of the Hebrew Bible
NAC	New American Commentary
NCB	New Century Bible

NETS	Pietersma, Albert, and Benjamin G. Wright. *New English Translation of the Septuagint*. New York: Oxford University Press, 2007.
NIB	Keck, Leander E., ed. *The New Interpreter's Bible*. 12 vols. Nashville: Abingdon, 1994–2004.
NICOT	New International Commentary on the Old Testament
NJPS	*Tanakh: The Holy Scriptures; The New JPS Translation according to the Traditional Hebrew Text*
NMES	Near and Middle Eastern Series
NRSV	New Revised Standard Version
NS	new series
NTG	Neue Theologische Grundrisse
OBO	Orbis Biblicus et Orientalis
OLA	Orientalia Lovaniensia Analecta
Or	*Orientalia* NS
OSHT	Oxford Studies in Historical Theology
OTL	Old Testament Library
OTM	Oxford Theological Monographs
OTP	Charlesworth, James H., ed. *Old Testament Pseudepigrapha*. 2 vols. New York: Doubleday, 1983–1985.
OTS	Old Testament Studies
OtSt	*Oudtestamentische Studiën*
OTWSA	*Oud Testamentiese Werkgemeenskap in Suid-Afrika*
P.Amh.	Papyrus Amherst
P.Ins.	Papyrus Insinger
PEQ	*Palestine Exploration Quarterly*
Pesah.	Pesahim
PHSC	Perspectives on Hebrew Scriptures and Its Contexts
PSB	*Princeton Seminary Bulletin*
PTMS	Princeton Theological Monograph Series
Qidd.	Qiddušin
R-H	Rahlfs, Alfred, and Robert Hanhart, eds. *Septuaginta: Editio Altera*. Stuttgart: Deutsche Bibelgesellschaft, 2006.
Rab.	Rabbah (+ biblical book), i.e., midrashic works
RB	*Revue biblique*
Rhet.	Aristotle, *Rhetoric*
RSO	*Rivista degli studi orientali*
S	The Syriac version of the Hebrew Bible, or the Peshitta
Shabb.	Shabbat

Sanh.	Sanhedrin
SCS	Septuagint and Cognate Studies
Sef	*Sefarad*
SJT	*Scottish Journal of Theology*
SPIB	Scripta Pontificii Instituti Biblici
SStLL	Studies in Semitic Languages and Linguistics
STDJ	Studies on the Texts of the Desert of Judah
StPohl	Studia Pohl
SubBi	Subsidia Biblica
SymS	Symposium Series
T	The Targum, or the Aramaic version of the Hebrew Bible
Tanh.	Tanhuma
TDOT	Botterweck, G. Johannes, Helmer Ringgren, and Heinz-Josef Fabry, eds. *Theological Dictionary of the Old Testament*. Translated by John T. Willis et al. 17 vols. Grand Rapids: Eerdmans, 1974–2021.
Text	*Textus*
Tg. Neof.	Targum Neofiti
Tg. Onq.	Targum Onqelos
THB	Textual History of the Bible
TLOT	Jenni, Ernst, and Claus Westermann, eds. *Theological Lexicon of the Old Testament*. Translated by Mark E. Biddle. 3 vols. Peabody, MA: Hendrickson, 1997.
TOTC	Tyndale Old Testament Commentaries
TUGAL	Texte und Untersuchungen zur Geschichte der altchristlichen Literatur
TWOT	Harris, R. Laird, Gleason L. Archer Jr., and Bruce K. Waltke, eds. *Theological Wordbook of the Old Testament*. 2 vols. Chicago: Moody Press, 1980.
V	The Vulgate, or Jerome's Latin version of the Hebrew Bible
VT	*Vetus Testamentum*
VTSup	Vetus Testamentum Supplement
WBC	Word Biblical Commentary
WeBC	Westminster Bible Companion
WLAW	Wisdom Literature from the Ancient World
WOO	Wiener Offene Orientalistik
WZKM	*Wiener Zeitschrift für die Kunde des Morgenlandes*
YJS	Yale Judaica Series
ZAW	*Zeitschrift für die alttestamentliche Wissenschaft*

Agur ... may aptly be termed the Hebrew Voltaire.
—E. J. Dillon, *The Skeptics of the Old Testament*

"Ah! you are a happy fellow," said Mr. Farebrother, turning on his heel and beginning to fill his pipe. "You don't know what it is to want spiritual tobacco—bad emendations of old texts, ... or a learned treatise on the entomology of the Pentateuch, including all the insects not mentioned, but probably met with by the Israelites in their passage through the desert; with a monograph on the Ant, as treated by Solomon, showing the harmony of the Book of Proverbs with the results of modern research. You don't mind my fumigating you?"
—George Eliot, *Middlemarch*

1
Introducing Agur Bin-Yakeh:
The Coherence of Proverbs 30 and the Voice of Agur

1.1. An Incoherent Text or an Eccentric Sage?

The thirtieth chapter of the book of Proverbs is one of the more obscure texts in the Hebrew Bible. Nestled between Solomon's collections of sayings in chapters 10–29 and the famous ode to the strong woman in chapter 31, these words are attributed to a sage named Agur Bin-Yakeh, about whom we know nothing. No other ancient text mentions him, and he has no clear provenance. It is not clear just what role Agur plays in this chapter, nor, indeed, how much of the chapter ought to be attributed to him. Many scholars argue that 30:1–3 or 30:1–4 encapsulate the words of Agur, a skeptic, to whom an orthodox voice responds in verses 5–9 (Scott 1965, 180–82; McKane 1970, 643; Perdue 2000, 253). Other scholars argue that Agur's voice unites verses 1–9 (Franklyn 1983; Moore 1994; Fox 2009, 850) but that verses 10–33 are a miscellaneous collection of formally similar material that grew through accretion (Whybray 1994b, 150; Murphy 1998, 234). It is not at all obvious that any line of thought connects one stanza to the next. According to William McKane (1970, 643), the material in Prov 30 is arranged according to the catchword principle and affinity of theme, but these connections are merely "superficial links" and do not suggest a coherent message. Likewise, Norman Whybray (1994b, 150–51) argues that verses 15–33 have been arranged "apparently at random," and "no attempt has been made to maintain a unity of style or a logical sequence of content." Michael Fox (2009, 849) suggests the material in 30:10–33 resulted from a scribe simply filling up empty space at the end of a scroll with leftover material "that seemed appropriate." "The term 'editor,'" he argues, "is somewhat misleading" when applied to the final two chapters of Proverbs because it implies a level of intention in shaping the whole. To make matters worse, the Greek text of Proverbs has the chapter split apart and relocated within the book.[1] Departing radically from the Hebrew, Prov 30:1 contains no proper names and makes no mention of Agur in the Greek. Not only does the Greek witness to a different edition of Proverbs, but Agur himself is erased from the record. Many scholars find the Greek division conclusive and consider 30:1–14 a discrete unit, which they feel amounts to decisive evidence that there is no unifying principle in Agur's words (von Rad 1972, 15 n. 1; Gemser 1963, 103; Murphy 1998, 226–27). In short, the general consensus on the coherence of the chapter as a whole among critical scholars is that there is none.

Speaking broadly for a moment, there are, perhaps, two reasons interpreters tend not to find coherence in the chapter. The first has to do with the nature of the text itself and the second with trends in scholarship over the last several hundred years. First, the text itself is challenging both philologically and hermeneutically. Raymond Van Leeuwen (1997b, 250) calls the words of Agur "one of the most difficult and controverted sections in Proverbs;" and Leo Perdue (2000, 251) writes, "The first four verses of this chapter are among the most difficult to translate not only in the book of Proverbs but, indeed, in the entire Old Testament." This text is broken up by static, as if transmitted through fog from a radio tower that stands just out of range, and at times its sense seems to cut out altogether. These thirty-three verses have more than their fair share of intractable text-critical dilemmas. The second half of verse 1 is one of the most baffling jumble of letters in the whole Hebrew Bible. The state of verse 31 is hardly better and verses 3a and 15a each have their own serious problems. Moving beyond the challenge that simply deciphering the text presents, the language of the chapter is itself difficult to comprehend. Twenty-seven lexical forms in these thirty-three verses occur five times or less in the entire Hebrew Bible.[2] Eight forms occur only in this chapter. We find animals that are referred to nowhere else in ancient Hebrew: the עלוקה (leech?) in verse 15, the שממית (lizard? spider?) in verse 28, the זרזיר (rooster? sparrow? greyhound? warhorse?) in verse 31. Accordingly, the imagery can be obscure—what does the word חפן (palms?) in

---

1. In §1.2.4, I address the issues posed by the Septuagint in detail.

2. This is a blunt measurement for attempting to describe the difficulty of the Hebrew quantitatively. For the sake of comparison, this is more than any chapter in Proverbs, it is more than any chapter except ch. 30 in the notoriously difficult Hebrew of Job, and it is more than all but five chapters in Isaiah (3, 10, 28, 30, 44).

verse 4 picture? Just how vulgar is צאה (filth?) in verse 12? What action is being punned with מיץ (churning?) in verse 33? And the idioms are often abstruse—what does נאם הגבר ("the oracle of the man") entail in verse 1? What is the tone of כי תדע ("for you know") in verse 4? How are we meant to understand חכמים מחכמים ("exceedingly wise," NRSV) in verse 24 or יד לפה ("hand to mouth") in verse 32?

The many philological challenges, which I have only sampled here, contribute to the broader hermeneutical complexity of the chapter as a whole. As indicated above, the ideas in 30:1–6 seem dissonant enough that many scholars have posited a change of speakers. Does Agur—a sage—truly repudiate wisdom in 30:2–3? Is verse 4 meant to show us the way to wisdom or to deny categorically its availability to humanity? Are verses 5–6 meant to ground the ideas in verses 2–4, or do they stand as a rebuttal? Who is praying in verses 7–9 and does this prayer have any connection to what precedes it? In the second half of the chapter, verses 10–33 feature short stanzas with vivid imagery but no transitions, summaries, or applications to draw connections or develop ideas from one stanza to the next. Proverbs 30:11–14 develops a repulsive description of the generation "who curses its father," culminating in verse 15's leech; verse 17 presents a chilling picture of unburied children with carrion birds pecking out their eyes. A collection of four awe-inspiring images in verses 18–19 is juxtaposed with a vulgar snapshot of a sexually adventurous woman in verse 20 and followed by a list of four class-reversals that threaten the very foundations of the world in verses 21–23. Then, verses 24–28 catalog four animals that succeed despite weakness, followed in verses 29–31 by four animals who know how to strut their stuff. Arranging such evocative imagery merely by juxtaposition leaves the text hermeneutically underdetermined. There is a deeply enigmatic yet intriguing nature to this material that suggests a complex and esoteric way of looking at the world. It feels like there is a surplus of meaning but its overarching significance remains elusive. For many scholars, finding coherence in such material amounts to a self-administered Rorschach test.

The second reason interpreters have not seen coherence in Prov 30 has to do with broader trends in the history of biblical studies. For much of the last two hundred years, scholarship has prioritized questions that encourage mining the biblical texts for historical data rather than constructing readings for their theological and ethical significance. Starting in the mid-nineteenth century, *wisdom literature* came to be associated with a worldview in ancient Israelite religion that was gradually distinguished from and opposed to the priestly and prophetic traditions rooted in the particularity of Israel's revealed torah. *Wisdom theology*, by contrast, was grounded in the observation of the natural world and human society, philosophical in its outlook and universalistic in its ethics. But Prov 30 contains material that does not readily conform to this understanding of a wisdom text. Proverbs 30:1–9 seem to downplay wisdom and make theologically distinctive claims for revelation. Proverbs 30:1 uses terms associated with prophecy like "utterance" (משא) and "oracle" (נאם) to describe Agur's words. Proverbs 30:5 and 6 appear to contain quotations from covenantal traditions found in 2 Sam 22:31 // Ps 18:30 (31 ET) and Deut 4:2. Proverbs 30:7–9 feature a prayer that is unique in the book of Proverbs and highly unusual for wisdom literature. By contrast, verses 10–33 look like the least theological kind of natural reflections. There is no mention of God past verse 9; instead, we find some eleven different animals and the enigmatic numerical sayings that are found almost exclusively in wisdom literature. Under the influence of form criticism, twentieth-century scholarship on the numerical saying focused on analyzing its formal features as a window on its origins. In the case of Prov 30, such research deflected interest away from the collection as a whole in favor of interpreting the individual sayings in isolation. Accordingly, the occasion for their association was often assumed to be their common form rather than their content. For much of the last two hundred years, then, scholarly assumptions surrounding wisdom literature and form criticism encouraged separating out the various elements of this chapter since their origins were clearly to be found in disparate traditions and social settings. Given the philological and hermeneutical complexity of the material, wisdom literature, as a conceptual grid, and form criticism, as a critical method, largely precluded finding coherence in the chapter.

As scholarly assumptions have shifted, it is worth paying sustained attention to the philological and hermeneutical complexity of this text. The goal of this study is to offer a fresh reading of Prov 30 as a coherent text that takes the philology of the chapter seriously in light of shifting hermeneutical assumptions around wisdom literature and form criticism.[3]

---

3. I am unaware of any monograph-length study dedicated to Prov 30. Its fullest treatment exists in commentaries such as Delitzsch 1875; Waltke 2005; and Fox 2009. I discuss Georg Sauer's (1963) *Die Sprüche Agurs* in ch. 2. Rudolf Stier's (1850) *Die Politik der Weisheit in den Worten Agur's und Lemuel's Sprüchwörter Kap. 30 und 31* dedicates some eighty pages to Prov 30, but much of that discussion is pitched for

As a heuristic to facilitate this reading, I propose we reanimate the persona of Agur as an ancient eccentric genius and the instructor within the text. If we class Agur with Vladimir Nabokov and Fyodor Dostoevsky, William Faulkner and Flannery O'Connor, or, less anachronistically, Socrates and Qohelet, we can begin to understand him on his own terms—to hear his message as it is presented to us in the Masoretic Text of Proverbs. These figures were all masters of tradition *and* creative thinkers who were not at all afraid to take a trope and reimagine it, to blend genres, or to confront existing ideas. Imagining someone as an eccentric genius yields two interpretive benefits. First, we imagine that person to be unusually intelligent, wise, or insightful. This means that we assume there is something to learn and that it makes sense even if it is complex and mysterious. Second, because of the eccentric's gifts, we are willing to bear with more than the usual amount of strangeness. Perhaps their quirks somehow empower their gifts? What if we approached Agur's words as the teaching of a sage whose wisdom and theological insight exceeds our own, and therefore someone that we should endeavor to understand before we critique? To be clear, I am not making an argument about a historical sage named Agur.[4] Rather, I am inviting the reader to consider Agur as he is presented within the literary world of Proverbs. Agur is nothing if not the persona of an eccentric sage mediated to us by this one brief anthology of his wisdom. Perhaps, if nothing else, we can use the self-presentation of the text as a hermeneutical key and the attribution of the whole chapter to this unknown sage as a reading strategy.

In the remainder of this chapter, I will attempt to lay a foundation for my reading of Prov 30 by developing its warrant. To do this, I will consider the anthological nature of Proverbs, the role of Agur's voice within the chapter, the unity and coherence of anthological texts, and the different arrangement of the chapter in the Greek. First, I will address the presen-

---

"everyman," with a short "appendix for scholars." This work has recently been digitized, but I have not interacted with it substantially because it was unavailable to me during the research for this volume.

4. In interpreting Proverbs, as with many biblical texts, the authors have been largely lost to us, so we are forced into a sort of new critic's position whether we want it or not. In other words, only by using internal criteria can we reconstruct the author, but then we must allow that this is a *reconstruction* rather than a historical portrait. I will further develop my approach to the persona of Agur based on the attribution of 30:1 in ch. 3.

tation of the chapter within Proverbs. Does the anthological nature of a text like Proverbs preclude a reading that seeks any real coherence? On the contrary, I argue that Proverbs presents the chapter as a discrete collection and encourages us to look for literary coherence even where it is not obviously present. Second, attending to the way Proverbs frames the chapter encourages us to take Agur's voice seriously as a unifying feature of the text. Here, I will consider the dynamics of voice within Prov 30 and compare this with the pervasive role of voice in ancient didactic literature. Third, I will turn to consider the broader issue of coherence in anthological texts. After all, just because a text is a collection and is voiced by a particular sage does not mean that it must be coherent in any deeper sense. Yet we find again and again that ancient texts hold together diverse materials in ways that tend at first to seem cacophonous to moderns. This feature of the texts that have come down to us ought to push us toward more careful attention to the "ways of the text," to use a phrase from Alexander Samely (2013, 24), before we dub them *in*coherent. Finally, considering coherence naturally leads me to address the shape of Prov 30 in Greek. Perhaps counterintuitively, I will argue that the differences in the Greek might actually encourage us to attempt reading the chapter as a coherent collection. I will close this chapter by sketching the argument of the rest of this study.

1.2. Voice, Coherence, and the Anthological Nature of Proverbs

1.2.1. Proverbs as an Anthological Composition

First, we must consider the nature of anthological compositions and how the book of Proverbs frames chapter 30. As we have received the Hebrew text of Proverbs from antiquity, seven headings apportion the book into sections, each with its own designation attributing it to a sage or a cohort of sages. There is Solomon in 1:1 and 10:1, "the wise" in 22:17 and 24:23, "the men of Hezekiah" in 25:1, Agur Bin-Yakeh in 30:1, and Lemuel, a king, in 31:1.[5] These headings and collections have long been the starting point

---

5. Although there are certainly seven headings (1:1; 10:1; 22:17; 24:23; 25:1; 30:1; 31:1), scholars vary in terms of how they describe the internal arrangement of the book. Waltke (2005, 9) believes the seven headings delineate seven sections. In a similar manner, Fox (2000, 5) finds six "parts" by treating chs. 30 and 31 as appendices. Schipper (2019, 9) emphasizes the seven headings and speaks of seven parts, but also allows for "a fivefold division of the book as a whole" by treating 22:17–24:34 and

for historical-critical study of Proverbs (Smend 1995, 261). Scholars hold varying views on the level of organization and intention in these collections (e.g., Weeks 1994, 20–40; cf. Heim 2001), but it is universally acknowledged that the different sections of the book have distinctive characteristics. So, for example, the first Solomonic collection (10:1–22:16) famously contains almost exclusively contrastive couplets, so-called antithetical parallelism, in chapters 10–15. Proverbs 16–22 shift toward comparative couplets, so-called synonymous parallelism, and contain many sayings that deal with God and king. We find few proverbial couplets in "the sayings of the wise" (22:17–24:22) where the format is rather more instructional, stringing together short discursive stanzas of advice on loosely related topics (cf. Prov 1:8–9:18; see Weeks 2007, 33–66). The sayings in the second Solomonic collection (25:1–29:27) largely return to the proverbial couplet but exhibit more diversity of form and complexity of theme. While the internal organization of these sections may appear random, they are not interchangeable. The collections are carefully arranged to lead the student on a pedagogical journey and the text is designed to instill the virtues it commends (Brown 2002; 2014, 29–66; Schipper 2019, 8–11).[6] The broader structure of the book of Proverbs and the precise system of superscripts within the book suggest that the redactors of MT Proverbs saw 30:1–33 as one of the discrete units that comprise the book and contribute to its overall pedagogical goals (Kuntz 2001; Brown 2002, 175–78; Yoder 2009a).

Glancing over the chapter itself confirms at once that Prov 30 has a set of internal features that give it a distinctive character vis-à-vis the rest of Proverbs in a way similar to the other collections (e.g., 10:1–22:16; 22:17–24:22; 25:1–29:27).[7] If one rationale for collections within the book of Proverbs is

---

30–31 as units. For a helpful discussion of how the headings structure the book consult further Schipper 2019, 6–11. One potential outlier to this system of headings is the poem celebrating the strong woman in 31:10–31. By dint of its acrostic form and its placement at the end of the book scholars often allow that it is its own literary unit without a title or heading (Balentine 2021, 496). These varying construals are largely inconsequential, but the plot thickens when we factor in the arrangement of the material in the Greek, as I will explore below.

6. Anne Stewart's (2016, 2, 203–19) nuanced study of Proverbs' poetry deepens our appreciation of the affective role that the form of the book plays in character formation, even as she helpfully challenges the narrative framework that William Brown and others have proposed for Proverbs.

7. The reader may find it helpful throughout the book to follow along with my translation of Prov 30, which is included in the appendix.

poetic form, then Prov 30 clearly exhibits this. Like 22:17–24:34, Prov 30 contains slightly longer sayings that form short stanzas. As for structure, these stanzas often use anaphora, repetition, numbered lists, and numerical sayings. Thematically, key words build bridges across the chapter (e.g., "wisdom," חכם, in vv. 3 and 24; "to be sated," שבע, in vv. 9 and 15–16; "father/mother," אב/אם, in vv. 11 and 17; "to eat," אכל, in vv. 14 and 20; and "destructive man/to be destructive," גבל, in vv. 22 and 32). Creation language and a preponderance of animal imagery round out its distinctive flavor. These observations do not on their own suggest that the collection exhibits any deeper coherence, but their presence might encourage us to probe for it.

The unit labeled "the words of the wise" (דברי חכמים) in 22:17–24:22 presents an instructive analogy. While the material in this collection is notably different from the material that flanks it in the two Solomonic collections (10:1–22:16 and 25:1–29:27), topical and thematic considerations alone would not provide strong enough warrant for delineating the unit. Its small blocks of material move from topic to topic without transparent logical progression. However, its superscript, specifying *thirty* sayings (22:20), a more discursive style with longer blocks of teaching, and clear dependence on the Egyptian text known as the Instruction of Amenemope, all conspire to make clear that this is a discrete section within the book.[8] Comparison with Amenemope brings further insight into the compositional logic of the passage. In an impressive study, Fox (2014b) argues that the author of 22:17–23:11 worked through a scroll of Amenemope in five "sweeps," pulling out successive source material each time. The resulting composition has drawn on and reworked Amenemope thematically to develop a central thesis: "trust in God and rely on his justice" (90). Without Amenemope this material could look like a rather ad hoc development of topics traditionally associated with wisdom literature, but in comparison with Amenemope a compositional logic emerges that gives a deeper level of coherence to the material.[9] To cite a similar analogy from a different

---

8. The emendation to "thirty" sayings is broadly accepted by the commentators, e.g., Fox 2009, 710; Waltke 2005, 219 n. 113. However, there are dissenting voices, e.g., Whybray 1994b, 133.

9. There are, of course, other ways of construing the relationship between Amenemope and Proverbs. For an authoritative English translation with bibliography see Lichtheim 2006b, 146–63. For an argument supporting the dependence of Proverbs on Amenemope, see Shupak 2005. For a different construal of the relationship between the texts that still supports dependence, see Emerton 2001.

book and genre, scholars largely accept that Lev 19 is a discrete collection of laws within the Holiness Code. Arranged without an obvious organizing principle, however, these laws initially strike the reader with their range and diversity. Yet the introduction in 19:1, the refrain "I am YHWH" (אני יהוה), and key phrasing at the beginning, middle, and end of the collection mark it off. Careful analysis of this material has resulted in a general consensus—although questions about the specifics remain—that the chapter presents a microcosm of diverse laws, offering expanded permutations on the Ten Commandments, that extends the demand of holiness to the moral life of all the people of Israel (Milgrom 2000, 1598, 1715; Levine 1989, 124–25). Proverbs 22:17–24:22 and Lev 19 present examples of discrete collections that were likely composed through processes of anthological composition and that exhibit a certain unity *despite* their apparent diversity.

On analogy with texts such as Prov 22:17–24:22 and Lev 19, there is warrant for entertaining the entirety of Prov 30 as a discrete collection. Particularly when one accounts for the structure of Proverbs and its subunits, this amounts to taking the superscript with full seriousness as an ancient editorial frame that already grants the chapter a certain external unity (Steinberg 2018, 182; cf. Samely 2013, 24–25).[10] We should press on to ask whether there is any deeper coherence to the material beyond the frame itself. If we find the argument compelling that Proverbs is developing a pedagogical program that takes the reader on a journey of moral formation (Brown 2002), then the idea that Prov 30 might have a distinctive theme or message that plays a role in this program gains still more credence.

1.2.2. Agur's Voice in Proverbs 30

As we have already seen, the delineation of voice(s) is one of the more significant interpretive decisions concerning Prov 30. Scholars who see

---

10. *Pace* Whybray (1994b, 148) who writes, "it is clear that these [two headings at 30:1 and 31:1] were not intended to cover the whole of the subsequent material." For ch. 30, his argument appears to depend to some extent on the break at 30:15 in the Greek. However, I would argue that this is not as clear as he suggests. There is no clear boundary marking the end of the text before the superscript of 31:1. Indeed, scholars have posited breaks after 30:6, 9, and 14. Consider here Samely's (2013, 24–25) caution, "The text's boundaries must be allowed to define and limit the meaning options, in particular for the reader who is unfamiliar with the ways of the text. The factuality of boundaries is what permits the text to make sense in unexpected ways, but only if the reader takes them seriously."

no coherence in the chapter tend to see multiple conflicting voices. If we allow that the superscript at 30:1 appears to frame the chapter as a discrete collection within Proverbs, then the role of Agur's voice takes on new significance, potentially giving coherence to the whole. In literary criticism, the concept of voice relates to whom the reader identifies as speaking and being addressed. When applied to poetry, voice is a metaphor for conceptualizing the vocal presence in a poem (Richards 2012, 1525). Whatever role we assign to the author, "voice is not simply individual but compound,… since the speaker anticipates the listener and vice versa. They meet in the poem" (1525). A speaking voice within a text suggests a hearer—the implied audience. The audience may exist within the world of the text but also necessarily includes readers down through the centuries. Paying sustained attention to voice within Prov 30—as well as how voice functions within Proverbs and ancient sayings collections more broadly—encourages us to read the whole chapter with reference to Agur as the speaker. At this stage, I merely want to walk through the text and note the dynamics of voice that are at work.

The issue of voice surfaces at the start of verse 1 with the introduction of our sage, Agur Bin-Yaqeh, but immediately encounters significant difficulties in the text-critical challenges of verse 1b. Most scholars allow that Agur is speaking in the first person and many identify an addressee in the letters לאיתיאל ואכל ("to Ithiel and Ukal," NJPS). In verses 2–4 there is no question that Agur is speaking in the first person. At the start of verse 4, however, five rhetorical questions stack up to pivot the discourse toward the second person. The rhetorical questions evoke an audience, but the emphatic clause כי תדע ("Surely you know!") makes the shift to second person explicit and pointed. Proverbs 30:5 is stated in the third person, but verses 6 and 10 bring the discourse back to the second person with similarly structured negative imperatives. In between these two negative commands, the prayer in verses 7–9 weaves first- and second-person speech in a tight "I-Thou" mode. The next seven verses (vv. 11–17) are taken up with impressionist object lessons reported in the third person. No first- or second-person dynamics intrude. It is all the more striking, then, when a speaking voice reemerges with "I" in verse 18: "There are three things that are extraordinary to me [ממני], / And four that I cannot comprehend [ידעתי]." After this brief intrusion, however, the speaking voice recedes again; the remainder of the numerical sayings are relayed in the third person in verses 19–31. The last saying in the chapter (vv. 32–33), however, marks a return to second-person admonition and closes an open loop back to verse 10, which itself connects to verses 4 and 6. To sum up then, first-person speech occurs in 30:1b–3, 7–9, and 18, while second-person speech occurs in 30:4, 6, 7–9, 10, and 32. Throughout the bulk of the chapter (30:11–31), however, third-person discourse predominates and the speaker and addressee are not clearly in view.

This survey of the dynamics of voice within the chapter raises several questions. While the *I* of verses 1b–3 clearly ought to be equated with the figure of Agur, Who is the *I* of verses 7–9 and even more elusively of verse 18?[11] And how does this *I* relate to the *you* of verses 4, 6, 10, and 32? If Agur's words only extend to verse 4 or to verse 9 then this potentially leaves verses 6, 7–9, 10, 18, and 32 without a defined speaker. But if we allow for Agur's voice animating the whole chapter, then the first-person language has a clear reference and the *you* in question becomes the addressee, either the idealized reader or, perhaps, an addressee identified in verse 1. These questions cannot be decided at this stage. I merely want to point out that the dynamics of voice in the text suggest, or at a minimum allow for, Agur to be speaking throughout and this might encourage us to look for coherence in the text.

Associating the collection as a whole with a particular speaking voice is in keeping with ancient Near Eastern instructions and sayings collections and with biblical anthologies, particularly those associated with wisdom literature (Weeks 2010a, 4). The Sumerian text, The Instructions of Šuruppak, for example, is one of the world's oldest known poetic compositions. Although it is almost entirely a collection of sayings, it is framed as instructions that "the man from Šuruppak" gave to his son, Ziusudra (lines 6–10; Alster 2005, 57). "My son, let me give instructions; let my instructions be taken! / Ziusudra, let me speak a word to you; let attention be paid to them!" (lines 9–10; Alster 2005, 57). This introduction finds its parallel in the concluding lines of the instruction: "(this) gift of many words, [like] the stars [of heaven], is instructions that the man from Šuruppak, son of Ubartutu, gave as instructions" (lines 286–287; Alster 2005, 100). The double frame is significant since it underscores that the entire composition is understood as spoken by "the man from Šuruppak." Egyptian instructions and sayings collections are also attributed to speaking voices. The prologue to the Instruction of Ptahhotep says, "The mayor

---

11. This is the fraught question of how far Agur's words extend. By rephrasing it more broadly in terms of the overall issue of voice within the chapter, I hope to bring a fresh dimension to the question.

of the city, the vizier Ptahhotep, said" (Lichtheim 2006c, 62). Likewise, the Instruction of King Amenemhet begins: "Beginning of the Instruction made by the majesty of King Sehetepibre, son of Re, Amenemhet, the justified, as he spoke in a revelation of truth, to his son the All-Lord. He said" (I, 1; Lichtheim 2006c, 136). The Instruction of Any is framed as the speech of the scribe Any to his son, Khonshotep (9, 10–15; Lichtheim 2006b, 144). The Instruction of Amenemope is presented as the speech of that sage (II, 11–13; Lichtheim 2006b, 149), and all four of its sections contain first-person speech, which is naturally understood as the voice of the sage in the text. To these examples, I would add the Aramaic instruction of Ahiqar, which presents a large collection of fables and sayings inside one of the most elaborate narrative frames we possess. Although the texts are badly damaged, the proverbial material contains first-person speech clearly presented as the "words of Ahiqar" (מלי אחיקר), "which he taught his son" (זי חכם לברה; Porten and Yardeni 1993, 27; C1.1.1.). In sum, it is a mainstay of ancient instructions and sayings collections that they are attributed to a speaking voice—an idealized instructor—within the text.[12]

Similar Jewish literature continues the pattern we observed in the broader ancient Near Eastern material. Tobit voices an instruction for his son, Tobias (Tob 4:3–21), while Ben Sira and Baruch are presented as written instructions, preserving the voice of Ben Sira's grandfather, Jesus, and the voice of Baruch in perpetuity (Sir Prologue; Bar 1:1–4). Ecclesiastes is a long monologue in the first person, which is framed by the commentary of an unnamed narrator who attributes it to an eccentric and mysterious sage dubbed Qohelet. All of the instruction in the book of Job is placed in the mouths of sages from the East, with none other than God delivering the climactic speeches. While there is sometimes a question about who is meant to be speaking, as in, for example, Job 28, there is never any question that *someone* is speaking. As laid out in the previous section, the book of Proverbs is itself carefully divided into collections that are attributed to named sages or subsumed under the attribution to Solomon in 1:1. Yet as

---

12. Vayntrub (2019, 192, and see 209–10 n. 32) asserts, "Looking at over a dozen Sumerian, Akkadian, Egyptian, Aramaic, and Greek instruction collections, dating from the third millennium BCE to the end of the first millennium BCE—all of the texts whose opening lines were reasonably preserved—one observes that with only one notable exception, these collections are all framed by a narrative of transmission, a narrative of speech performance, or both." She does not clearly identify the "notable exception," although I presume on the basis of her larger argument that it is Proverbs.

Jacqueline Vayntrub has carefully shown, the book of Proverbs is distinctive among ancient instructional literature for *not* framing its instructions and sayings collections within a narrative where they are explicitly spoken by a character. But this lack of a narrative frame does not displace the importance of voice. The text itself becomes the perpetual voice of Solomon, the wise, Lemuel's mother, and, of course, Agur Bin-Yakeh (Vayntrub 2019, 205). "In this literary culture, then," concludes Vayntrub, "the human voice is uniquely privileged, or authorized, to articulate claims. This speaking voice is understood as an extension of the self, and this voice is attached to the name and biography of legendary characters" (218). An unvoiced, floating instruction or collection of wisdom sayings would be unusual.[13]

1.2.3. Unity and Coherence in Anthological Texts

If the book of Proverbs, then, is an anthological composition that presents chapter 30 as a discrete collection and frames it as the voice of Agur, this raises the question of how such apparently disparate material can be meaningfully held together. Ancient and biblical texts seem to combine material that is both thematically and formally diverse within broader frameworks. The early fourth-century Aramaic text in demotic script, also known as Papyrus Amherst 63, offers a striking example (Steiner 1997, 309–27).[14] This pagan text weaves together a cornucopia of genres, including prayers, hymns, *Heilsorakel*, erotic lyrics, myths, and propagandistic narratives within "the liturgy of the New Year's festival of an Aramaic-speaking community in Upper Egypt" (Steiner 1997, 310). The various borrowed and adapted elements, such as a paganized hymn with striking resemblance to Ps 20 (P.Amh. 11.11–19) and narrative traditions about Assurbanipal (P.Amh. 17.5–22.9), underscore the anthological nature of the text (Quick 2019, 108). A different kind of example that also comes

---

13. We do have collections of sayings, principally from Mesopotamia, that lack framing devices or attribution. Some of these texts are fragmentary and lack their headings or introductions (e.g., Papyrus Insinger; Lichtheim 2006a, 184–217). With others, however, it is less than clear what literary purpose they served in the form that we have received them. The Sumerian proverb collections seem to be arranged topically and may have served particular scribal purposes, such as writing practice or as stock collections to draw on when composing other texts (see Lambert 1996, 222–24; and Alster 1997, xiii–xxix).

14. Thanks to Laura Quick for bringing this text to my attention.

from Egypt is Papyrus Insinger (Lichtheim 2006a, 184–217). This demotic instruction is formally consistent. It is made up of chapters of sentence literature arranged under thematic headings such as gluttony and poverty (P.Ins. 5.12), fools (7.20), and instructing your son (8.21). The chapters then compile wise advice on these topics: "Poverty does not take hold of him who controls himself in purchasing" (6.17; Lichtheim 2006a, 190). Ultimately, however, Insinger juxtaposes contradictory statements, and each chapter ends by relegating weal and woe to the whim of the gods: "Nor is it the one who spends who becomes poor. The god gives a wealth of supplies without an income" (7.16–17; Lichtheim 2006a, 191). When this pattern is repeated chapter by chapter, it becomes clear that these contradictory statements have been juxtaposed to serve a larger literary agenda that elevates divine control over human agency (Weeks 2020, 101; cf. Schipper 2019, 24). On a formal rather than a thematic level, we might note that the Sayings of Ahiqar combines a large collection of diverse types of sayings within an elaborate narrative framework. The collection of sayings is so extensive that it is hard to imagine it could have been read out within a performance of the narrative. Conversely, if the collection is meant as a repository of wit and wisdom, the narrative is an unwieldy setting for accessing this material. Ancient audiences, however, seem to have tolerated or even preferred this mixing of genres since they composed and transmitted them together intentionally.

Turning now to consider a number of Jewish compositions, the Dead Sea Scrolls are notorious for blending generic elements, perhaps particularly when it comes to so-called wisdom texts (Goff 2019). A text like 4QMysteries (4Q27, 4Q299, 4Q300, 4Q301[?]), for example, bears affinities to both Ben Sira and Daniel, leading Samuel Thomas (2017, 329) to conclude, "Mysteries mixes elements of sapiential, prophetic and priestly perspectives, and these together make up a text whose date and provenance are difficult to determine." Similarly, Wisdom of Solomon moves seamlessly from long poems on the nature of wisdom to poems reflecting on Israel's history in the exodus. In the midst of this, the speaking voice suddenly shifts to the first person and takes up the persona of Solomon (6:22–9:18). There's an autobiographical reflection (7:1–22a), an ode to Wisdom (7:22b–8:1), and ultimately a prayer (9:1–18) all woven into the broader discourse. Likewise the book of Tobit begins as a first-person narrative that shifts unexpectedly to the third person after the prayer in 3:2–6. Tobit goes on to deliver an extended instruction to his son, Tobias, in 4:3–21 and the various prayers of the characters are located in situ, which to the modern reader seems repeatedly to break up the flow of the narrative (Weeks 2020, 12). The book of Daniel combines a series of independent narratives with apocalyptic visions and it does this in two languages. Most surprisingly, the transitions from Hebrew to Aramaic and back do not align with the seams between literary units. The book of Psalms, itself an anthological collection, sets much diverse material side by side. At times, the material within a single psalm presents a spectacular mixing as when Ps 19 combines a paean to creation with a reflection on the perfections of torah, or Ps 34 envelops proverbial material within a hymn of praise (see Weeks 2013). Reflecting on the significance of such examples, Stuart Weeks (2020, 12) wrote, "Rather than try to explain all such examples in terms of diverse sources or problems in transmission, it seems easier to accept that ancient audiences tolerated, and probably even enjoyed, such variations and shifts of tone."

As a particularly instructive final example we might sit with Qohelet for a moment. On a formal level, after a short introduction (1:1–3) the material opens with a sort of prose poem (1:4–11) that gives way quickly to an autobiographical reflection (1:12–2:26). This reflection then transitions to another prose poem (3:1–8) which is followed by further reflection (3:9–22). Any semblance of autobiographical narrative then drops away and from chapters 4–11 we encounter short topical reflections that circle around several key themes (time, death, work and profit, wisdom and folly, righteousness and wickedness, joy) without sustaining any one line of argument. There are, of course, two blocks of proverbial material set within this loose discourse (7:1–12; 9:17–11:4). Finally, there is a third kind of prose poem (12:1–8) and an epilogue presented in a different editorial voice (12:9–14). Nevertheless, this formal diversity has clear unifying features. The speaking voice stays in the first person and the whole thing is framed by the famous refrain: "vanity of vanities, all is vanity" (הבל הבלים הכל הבל, 1:2 // 12:8). Thus it seems fitting to describe the vast core of the book as a monologue (Weeks 2020, 9–13). However, the book resists all attempts to discern its structure and this "has encouraged rather atomistic readings of Ecclesiastes, as a loose assemblage of different sayings or poems" (12). Indeed, many scholars find the text at best incoherent and at worst rife with irreconcilable contradictions. Scholars of this persuasion have often posited a composite text with multiple viewpoints. Weeks (2020, 47) outlines the major approaches: "(1) the book actually contained from the outset a dialogue, or an interplay between several different characters; (2) the book includes quotations of other viewpoints, to which Qohelet reacts; or (3) the book began with the expression of a single viewpoint, but has been supplemented with material that expresses other views." The hypothesized interlocutor or redactional elements tend to enter the text right at "the limits of our tolerance for its formal and ideological inconsistencies" (48). In the original text there is no punctuation, nor are there marked quotations. No other speaker is introduced and we do not have any other recensions of the text that preserve it before, say, a zealous scribe intercalated an opposing viewpoint.

> Without such external criteria available, therefore, all three of these approaches present the same methodological difficulty: commentators who wish to separate the various viewpoints that they find are obliged first to define them, and then to apply their pre-determined templates to the text—which is no more scientific a procedure than Michaelangelo removing the stone that was not David. Even if one of the many attempts to isolate separate voices did actually stumble upon original distinctions, we should have no way to know it or to prove it, and if the book really is composite, then we have no agreed basis for distinguishing separate voices or recovering an original version. (Weeks 2020, 47–48)

The way out of this dilemma is not to suggest that there are no tensions or contradictions within the book. Nor is it to suggest that Qohelet ultimately agrees with all the ideas voiced therein. The book seems rather to revel in paradox and even to employ contradictions—or at least apparent contradictions—as part of its overall rhetorical strategy (Weeks 2020, 46–47).[15] Indeed, one could argue that the use of such contradictory statements encapsulates something about how Qohelet views the world and thinks about the human condition.

Ancient texts commonly hold together incredible formal and thematic diversity. In light of these examples—to which we could add many more—we have to think seriously about what constitutes a coherent text and whose standards of coherence we are working with. For the purposes of this study, a text is coherent if it exhibits literary and thematic unity.[16]

---

15. Weeks elucidates several helpful instances; in Proverbs the parade example is 26:4–5.

16. Teeter and Tooman (2020, 94–101) offer an up-to-date entry point on the literature surrounding coherence. On one level, coherence is a necessary component of all meaningful communication. Indeed, it has been described as "a constitutive feature of textuality" and defined as "the compatibility between constituents of a text"

In other words, a discrete composition or collection should be considered coherent if it can be demonstrated to have an internal logic or design driving a purpose or a message.[17] Of course, describing coherence this way raises questions about authors/editors versus readers. As Andrew Teeter and William Tooman (2020, 100) argue, it is a false dichotomy to pit "inherent textual properties" against the "contribution of the reader" in the search for coherence. Coherence is rather a collaborative effort between author/editors and readers. Authors and editors imbue texts with a certain amount of coherence, or at least they attempt to, and readers discern the coherence present in texts. Readers can construct coherence where there is none, but they can also fail to discern coherence where an author may have intended it or where early audiences may have discerned it. Still, readers seek coherence. Marc Brettler (2010, 419) argues that the authors/editors of biblical texts knew this and actively sought to bring coherence to materials they shaped. The examples just surveyed above suggest that ancient readers may have had different instincts in constructing coherence than

---

(94, 100). But in the technical literature, particularly within linguistics and literary theory, definitions abound: "Within text-linguistic research, for example, the concept of 'coherence' has been understood in a wide variety of ways and with diverse applications, ranging from the very narrow (closely approximating the notion of grammatical and lexical cohesion) to the very broad ('coherence' as a comprehensive category of understanding that applies to all essential aspects of a text)" (Teeter and Tooman 2020, 95–96).

17. Texts can, of course, exhibit different degrees of coherence. To take examples from Proverbs, the coherence of the first Solomonic collection in 10:1–22:16 is much looser than the coherence of the instruction concerning the adulterous woman in ch. 7. Proverbs 7 is an extended first-person narration with an introduction and conclusion that draw a clear moral relating to the plot of the narration. Proverbs 10:1–22:16, on the other hand, contain hundreds of proverbial sayings with no immediately obvious connection one to another. However, scholars tend to see this collection as broadly coherent on the basis of formal features (the proverbial couplet and the superscripts in 10:1 and 22:17) as well as a thematically consistent portrait of wisdom and righteousness over against foolishness and wickedness. If some of the sayings appear contradictory, this does not frustrate the fundamental coherence of the collection because a certain amount of wrestling with life's contradictions is inherent to wisdom and to the proverbial genre. Similarly, as already noted, Qohelet and Papyrus Insinger incorporate paradox and contradiction as part of coherent literary strategies. Such apparent incoherence does not affect the overall coherence of these texts because through close reading and comparative analysis it can be shown to contribute to the message of the whole.

modern readers, and anthology, as a compositional principle, seems to have exploited this. The question at issue is discerning coherence in texts, particularly when those texts hail from cultures distant in space and time from the reader's own. In my view, the only way of demonstrating coherence in ancient texts is through close reading and comparative analysis.

Scholarship of the Hebrew Bible is only just beginning to engage research on coherence self-critically. In an important programmatic essay, Teeter and Tooman (2020, 94) argue that "modern standards of literary (in)coherence are not necessarily appropriate to ancient Jewish literature, and we propose that these issues can only be properly approached after undertaking an inductive, comprehensive analysis of the ancient Jewish literature itself, in effect, learning the 'ways of the text.'"[18] Samely sketches a manifesto:

> For a limited period all close reading, including that of ancient sources by the modern critical scholar, has to invest up front in the coherence of the text. For the reader, in particular the reader encountering a text across a historical and cultural depth yet to be plumbed, must first acquire sufficient experience in the ways of the text before she or he has the "right," so to speak, to stop looking for the text's unity. The ways of the text cannot even be explored adequately without first investing in the text's unity. Small linguistic units like the single word or the single sentence do not have a definite meaning without a larger whole, that is, without something with boundaries into whose economy they can be placed. So the ways of the text do not become visible without the expectation that it forms an internally complex but bounded whole, without investment in coherence. This is true in particular for texts whose ways are unfamiliar to the reader—the situation of the modern scholar reading ancient sources. The alternative, namely giving up on coherence too soon, is hard to remedy. Just as the expectation of coherence can be self-fulfilling for uncritical readers, so the expectation of incoherence can be self-fulfilling for readers who give up too early. (Samely 2013, 24)

---

18. One important attempt to begin such work is the "Typology of Anonymous and Pseudepigraphic Jewish Literature of Antiquity, c. 200 BCE to c. 700 CE," a large-scale research project conducted from 2007 to 2011 as a collaboration between the Universities of Manchester and Durham. This project produced the Database for the Analysis of Anonymous and Pseudepigraphic Jewish Texts of Antiquity (http://literarydatabase.humanities.manchester.ac.uk/) as well as notable publications (Samely et al. 2013).

If there is good warrant for treating the entirety of Prov 30 as a discrete collection that may exhibit genuine coherence, even though the chapter has more than its fair share of philological and hermeneutical challenges, then perhaps what is needed is a reading that sticks with the text, "investing in the text's unity" as Samely puts it.[19] Such a reading, as Teeter and Tooman (2020, 127) insist, will not necessarily conclude the text is coherent, nor will it "assume the coherence of a text as an act of faith" that then attempts a post-hoc justification (Samely 2013, 27). It does, however, treat the text we have as a historical artifact that reflects the intentions of at least one tradition of writers and readers.[20] Again, drawing on the idea that the persona of Agur might be imagined as an eccentric genius—a sage whose idiosyncratic musings do not at first hang together—I want to argue that we ought to give him his due. Before we write off or pull apart his words, we ought to present the most generous reading of them available. In light of the remarkable formal and thematic diversity of didactic material both inside and outside the Hebrew Bible, I will contend that no incoherence has overtaken Agur but that which is common to ancient texts.

1.2.4. The Septuagint and the Unity of Proverbs 30

Finally, then, we must contend with the shape of the chapter in the Greek (G). It is generally thought that G witnesses to a recension of the book of Proverbs that is different from what we find in MT (Tov 1990; Aitken and Cuppi 2015; although Cook 1997 dissents). The arrangement of the

---

19. Vayntrub (2019, 10) also affirms this impulse in her work when she writes, "This is not to discount the value of a purely diachronic study of the texts and their development, but rather to assert the need to first generate a basic synchronic description of the texts and their configurations before we might be able to trace their changes over time."

20. What Samely, Teeter, and Tooman are suggesting has a certain affinity with the canonical approach associated with Brevard Childs (see Seitz 2005 for a clear and concise summary). The difference, however, is that a canonical approach sees the final form as "a kind of commentary on the text's prehistory" that "has a claim to our greatest attention" (Seitz 2005, 100, 102). While for Samely, Teeter and Tooman the concern is more of a methodological prolegomenon to doing proper historical and diachronic work (Samely 2013, 24; Teeter and Tooman 2020, 128–29). If we don't adequately follow through on the assumption of a text's coherence, then our diachronic work has no more claim to historical plausibility for its skepticism than a synchronic reading that clings naively to the self-presentation of the text.

first twenty-four chapters is largely identical, although G has significant variants and a large number of expansions, many the result of double translations.[21] After 24:22, however, there are major structural changes. The chart below shows the arrangement of units following 24:22 according to G (first column, using the versification of MT), with MT and G headings for comparison.

	Unit heading in MT	Unit heading in G (NETS)
30:1–14	"The words of Agur"	"My son, fear my words"
24:23–34	"These also are sayings of the wise"	"Now these things I also say to you who are wise"
30:15–33	None (numerical sayings?)	None (numerical sayings?)
31:1–9	"The words of King Lemuel"	"My words have been spoken by God"
25:1–29:27	"These also are proverbs of Solomon, which the men of Hezekiah king of Judah edited"	"These are the miscellaneous systems of education of Salomon, which the friends of Hezekias, king of Judea, copied."
31:10–31	None (acrostic paean to the strong woman)	None (paean to the courageous woman)

Greek Prov 30 and 31 are both divided in half and earlier units are placed between the halves. Thus 24:23–34 is placed in between 30:1–14 and 30:15–33, while 25:1–29:27 is placed between 31:1–9 and 31:10–31. Since G may sometimes represent an earlier stage of textual transmission than the MT, many have taken G's arrangement as decisive, prima facia evidence that the text is not unified (Gemser 1963, 103; von Rad 1972, 15 n. 1; Plöger 1984, 356; Crenshaw 1995, 372 n. 5; Murphy 1998, 226–27; Schipper 2021, 269). But assuming that G Proverbs is determinative for the unity of the chapter is reductive. The questions posed by G Proverbs are far too complex to decide the issue so simply. At this juncture I will not

---

21. Together Waard 2008, 6*–8*; Fox 2015, 36–61; and Aitken and Cuppi 2015 offer a comprehensive and authoritative introduction to Greek Proverbs.

deal with the issues G Proverbs poses, but merely attempt to frame their import to this study.

First, although we clearly possess two editions of the book of Proverbs, scholars are at an impasse as to the precise relationship between them (Schipper 2019, 40–43; Waltke 2004, 3; Whybray 1994b, 148; and cf. Cook 1997 with Tov 1990). It is not at all clear that MT Proverbs gave rise to G Proverbs nor that the MT Proverbs represents the *Vorlage* of G Proverbs. The situation appears to be more complex, with both editions sharing a common ancestor. As Lorenzo Cuppi (2011, 207) is at pains to emphasize, each variant must be assessed on its own merits. Even if it could be proved that G or MT was certainly earlier, this would not necessarily make it "better," nor would it be clear what such a designation was meant to denote. Instead a literary argument would need to be made for each edition, allowing for the possibility that different emphases or nuances of the material emerged in different contexts as the text developed. Second, the headings of G Proverbs are consistently different from MT Proverbs. In fact, every reference to an authorial voice other than Solomon's is obscured in G (Waltke 2004, 4). Whether this difference existed already in a Hebrew *Vorlage* or occurred at the moment of translation, the material has not merely been rearranged—its framing and presentation have been reinterpreted.[22] Third, the ancient division of G Prov 30 flies in the face of the seams that many modern scholars *do* find in the text. There is a general consensus among interpreters that Prov 30:1–9 is a subunit within the chapter.[23] Generally, scholars who identify verses 1–14 as a unit do so on the basis of the Greek with a loose sense that verses 15–33 were once an independent collection of numerical sayings (e.g., Schipper 2021, 269). In fact, verses 11–17 actually hold together quite tightly on the level of vocabulary, tone, and theme (Davis 2000, 142–44; Fox 2015, 38). This creates a certain kind of problem for those scholars who use G as evidence

---

22. To my knowledge, this has not been adequately explored, but it can be correlated with the rabbinic trend to interpret all the names in MT Proverbs as cyphers for Solomon; see, e.g., Midrash Tanhuma, Vaera 5 (Berman 1996) and Midrash Mishle (Visotzky 1992).

23. Many studies dedicated to "the words of Agur" have confined themselves to the first nine verses, and major commentaries recognize these verses as a unit whether or not they are ambivalent about the unity of the whole chapter (Franklyn 1983; Moore 1994; Van Leeuwen 1997b, 251; Waltke 2005, 464; Fox 2009, 850–51; Saur 2014; O'Dowd 2018).

for the lack of unity in MT. These scholars are simply faced with different collections to analyze. It is not just that the tradents behind G or its *Vorlage* did not consider 30:1–33 a collection, but rather that they *did* consider 30:1–14 + 24:23–34 + 30:15–33 a collection.[24] Literary analysis of G Proverbs would thus entail detailed study of the Greek material that parallels MT Prov 24:23–34 in the midst of the Greek material that parallels Prov 30:1–33. In short, the differences between G Proverbs and MT Proverbs run deeper than is commonly acknowledged even by those scholars who prioritize the break between 30:14 and 15 over MT's arrangement of the chapter. Greek Proverbs presents a complex series of questions for the interpreter at both the micro and the macro level. As an appendix to this study, I include philological notes on MT Proverbs where I deal carefully with many questions posed at the micro level. However, we cannot begin to adequately deal with macro-level questions of redaction and comparison until a close reading of each text as a literary composition has been accomplished. Without attending to the voice of each text on its own terms we cannot hope accurately to compare their distinctive emphases, ethics, or theologies. So, although scholars have taken G Proverbs as evidence of the disunity of Prov 30, this cannot be simply assumed but must rather be demonstrated through close reading.[25] The brute fact that the book of

---

24. Or perhaps the literary seams of G Proverbs delineate other units of text that we would need to take seriously. On the other hand, Fox (2015, 38) believes the arrangement we have in G resulted from a large-scale scribal error where a copyist accidentally skipped over a large chunk of material, "perhaps by rolling up his scroll then reopening it too far along," before going back and adding in the missed material. He sees no editorial logic in G's arrangement and believes it obscures the logic of MT. Tov (1990, 55), on the other hand, finds the arrangement of G and MT "equally good."

25. In fact, we possess empirical evidence—although not as much as we might like—that ancient Near Eastern scribes redacted, expanded, and rearranged sayings collections down through the centuries in the three major versions of the Instructions of Šuruppak. The so-called classical Sumerian version (dated to the beginning of the second millennium BCE) expands on and in a few cases rearranges proverbial material from the so-called archaic Sumerian version (dated to the mid-third millennium BCE; Samet 2021, 211; Alster 1975b, 71–81). In a recent study, Nili Samet (2021, 219–22) identifies four tendencies in how Šuruppak was updated: (1) the proverbial collections were expanded with additional material, (2) opening/concluding formulas were added or altered, (3) religious content was added, and (4) there is a tolerance for *dis*harmonious material existing side-by-side. This suggests that scribes felt at some liberty to "improve" their source material as they transmitted it, thereby creating a distinctive literary work. For analysis of transmission and versions of Šuruppak,

Proverbs exists in two editions does not therefore invalidate my project, it rather demonstrates the need for it by urging us to listen all the more closely to Agur's words.[26]

1.3. The Argument and Structure of This Study

For many scholars, Prov 30 is self-evidently an incoherent text. Agur's is a dissonant voice in the tradition, which is confined to the first four to nine verses, and the anthological nature of the composition has often been treated as a de facto argument against coherence. In the present chapter, I have attempted to show that these conclusions are well worth questioning. I base this on the framing of the chapter within the broader structure of Proverbs, the voiced nature of biblical poetry and collections of Proverbs, the diverse and anthological nature of ancient texts more broadly, and the arrangement of the material in the Greek. In different ways, all these factors commend the attempt to read Prov 30 as a coherent text. I contend that we ought seriously to attempt such a reading before we decide that it is incoherent on the basis of formal features or thematic dissonance.[27] In this study, I will undertake just such a project and argue that MT Prov 30 is best read as a coherent collection with a unifying theme that is animated by the voice of Agur. I will argue my case by means of philological analysis and close reading that attempts to attend to the "ways of the text," as Samely puts it. Since the persona of Agur as the speaker animating the text will be my controlling framework, I will be particularly attuned to issues of voice and tone throughout my reading.

Before I take up my own reading, I will consider how Agur has been read and what interpretive opportunities remain. This is the burden of

---

see Alster (1975b and 2005), Sallaberger (2018), and Samet (2021). The differences between MT and G Proverbs surely witness such a literary agenda and, no matter which gave rise to the other, each is worthy of literary analysis in its own right.

26. Note that "Agur's words" is a meaningless construct in G Proverbs since there is no persona "Agur" animating the collection and there is no discrete collection marked off that contains MT Prov 30:1–33.

27. Indeed, some scholars have read the chapter as a unified collection (e.g., Sauer 1963; Davis 2000; Yoder 2009a, 2009b; Waltke 2005; Steinmann 2009; Ansberry 2011; O'Dowd 2017), but these attempts remain a minority report and largely lack rigorous critical and philological grounding (Waltke 2005 and Steinmann 2009 being exceptions). I will engage some of this work more fully in ch. 2 and in my own constructive readings.

chapter 2, "Agur and His Interpreters." Through a selective history of interpretation, I hope to deepen and substantiate my claim that wisdom literature, as a conceptual grid, and form criticism, as a critical method, have largely precluded finding coherence in the chapter. In conclusion, I will suggest that recent skepticism surrounding these ideas, together with insights from more literary and theological approaches, encourage a fresh reading that takes account of voice, tone, and themes.

In chapters 3–5, I develop my reading proper. Chapter 3, "Reframing Agur's Words" is devoted to three intractable philological problems in verse 1: the significance of the name Agur Bin-Yakeh, the meaning of the lexeme *maśśā'* (משא), and the text-critical hurdle posed by verse 1b (לאיתיאל לאיתיאל ואכל). Because of their complexity and the hermeneutical significance of verse 1 as a superscript, these issues warrant an entire chapter's discussion. Making careful use of philological tools, I will argue that verse 1 encourages us to read Prov 30 as something of a sardonic warning, animated by the voice of an eccentric sage, and opening on a note of emotional and spiritual exasperation. The reader should be warned that this chapter contains the most sustained, technical argumentation in the book.

Chapter 4, "Agur's Wisdom," looks at verses 2–10. Because the questions concerning Agur's voice and theology are focused here, these verses are worth examining as a unit. Through a close reading that pays particular attention to intertextuality and philological questions, I endeavor to tease out the theology of verses 2–10 in order to help delineate voice in the chapter. On my reading, Agur is not an atheist, nor yet a skeptic, but is rather styled as a faithful if unconventional sage, who warns his readers off pride and greed while commending a stance of humility and contentment in relationship to God. I argue for a consistent, orthodox theological position in these verses and find no reason to posit a change of speaker.

Chapter 5, "Agur's Beastly Ethics," treats 30:11–33. There is no overt theology here and the sayings are arranged in short stanzas with no apparent connection between them, so the hermeneutical issues are distinct from verses 2–10. To set up my reading, I consider the form of the numerical saying, which has often been seen as the pretext for the collection, the function of animal imagery in the Hebrew Bible, and the role of humor. I argue that the numerical saying is merely a rhetorical device and that together with the prevalence of animal imagery in the chapter these sayings suggest a wry or humorous tone to the whole. In short, these verses satirize pride and greed while simultaneously commending humble contentment, exhibiting coherence in terms of tone and theme.

In chapter 6, "Agur in His Own Words," the conclusion, I synthesize my reading from chapters 3–5 and develop some of its broader implications. Having presented my interpretation of Agur's words, I reflect on the genre of the chapter as a whole and on the role of genre in interpretation. This discussion naturally leads me to engage Fox's contention that Agur's words do not qualify as wisdom literature and his theology is out of step with Proverbs more broadly. This, I will argue, is not the case and Agur's theology rather deepens the presentation of wisdom in Proverbs by subverting its misappropriation and orienting it toward a proper relationship with God. Fox's approach to the chapter is a good example of how scholarly opinion, in this case concerning wisdom literature as a genre classification, can determine how we read texts. In closing, I offer a brief hermeneutical reflection on philological reading, that is, the value of reading texts on their own terms.

Throughout this book I will usually assume my own translation of Prov 30, which is included as an appendix. Argumentation supporting my translation is found throughout chapters 3–5 and in the philological notes, which are also included as an appendix. These notes offer a wide-ranging, verse-by-verse commentary on philological issues in the chapter. Although this material stands outside the main argument of the book, it is nevertheless integral to it. In terms of research these philological notes were the first material I wrote, and they laid the foundation for everything that comes before them in the finished version of this monograph. Including them as an appendix serves two purposes. First, it supports my hermeneutical conviction that robust philological work is indispensable to constructive readings of ancient texts. If my close reading of Agur is compelling, I credit that to diligent work in laying this foundation. Second, it allows me to focus on close reading and exegetical discussions in the main text without continually getting lost in a lexicon, turning off to explore the versions, or weighing down the argument with lengthy footnotes on syntactical difficulties. It is not always easy, however, to decide on the division of labor between this appendix and the main body of the book. In some places the philological issues are so bound up with the exegetical questions that I feel compelled to include them in the main text. In other places, I am able to proceed with my interpretation while the philological issues remain in the background. In these cases, I refer the reader to the appendix for more extensive discussions grounding my decisions about text-critical issues, the meaning and usage of words, obscure syntax, and the like.

2
Agur and His Interpreters: Wisdom Literature, Form Criticism, and the Hermeneutical Potential of Proverbs 30

2.1. How Has Agur Been Read?

In the first chapter, I introduced Prov 30 with its many puzzles and curiosities, not least its intriguing attribution to an unknown sage, Agur Bin-Yakeh. Although scholars have generally found little to no coherence in this text, its attribution, along with the anthological nature of ancient compositions more generally, encourages us to attempt to read it as a coherent collection animated by the voice of Agur as a literary persona. Before I develop my own reading of Prov 30, however, it is instructive to think about how these verses have been read in modern scholarship. Particularly, we might consider how broad scholarly trends concerning genre have influenced readings of the chapter. For Agur's words such questions will focus on ideas about wisdom literature that emerged in the nineteenth century as well as ideas about form criticism that arose in the early twentieth century. First, although Agur's words have been construed in many and varied ways over the last two hundred years, I will argue that wisdom literature, as a genre classification, and form criticism, as a critical method, have largely precluded unified interpretations. Second, I will suggest that the history of reading Agur's words nevertheless presents some interpretive opportunities. For example, commentaries adopting thematic and theological approaches suggest that we might find more coherence in the text by paying sustained attention to issues like voice and tone. To this end, growing skepticism surrounding established ideas about wisdom literature could facilitate a fresh reading by removing its principal impediments.

To be clear, this will not be a comprehensive survey. The purpose of this chapter is not to provide an accurate genealogy of interpretations, where I identify the first or most influential scholar to propose a certain view of Prov 30. Rather, I intend to investigate how and why Agur's words have been read in such a wide variety of ways and how we might read his words more constructively. I chose my examples because they seemed particularly illustrative of broad trends in reading the chapter, and they help us to get behind the most recent commentaries and examine the assumptions of the guild.

2.1.1. Agur and the Birth of Wisdom Literature

2.1.1.1. The Wisdom Literature Category

In his monograph *An Obituary for "Wisdom Literature,"* Will Kynes (2019) offers a prescient account of the birth of the genre known as wisdom literature in nineteenth-century German scholarship. Kynes identifies Johann Friedrich Bruch's *Weisheits-Lehre der Hebräer: Ein Beitrag zur Geschichte der Philosophie* [The wisdom teaching of the hebrews: a contribution to the history of philosophy] (1851) as the decisive work:

> In Bruch's repeated affirmation that Wisdom is never in conflict with Hebrew religion, he repeats an idea Umbreit and Ewald had emphasized. Bruch's work is therefore not without its precedents, but he appears to be the first to draw these earlier views together into a compelling systematic and comprehensive examination of the issue. If not its father, we could at least call Bruch the Wellhausen of Wisdom. (Kynes 2019, 98, see also 82–85)[1]

"Like ... Wellhausen after him," Kynes elaborates, "Bruch solves the problem of the continuity between Judaism and Christianity by arguing that the Jewish emphasis on theocracy, cult, and law are a distortion of the original religion. His distinct contribution is to make the wise the conduit of those essential beliefs" (97). In the work that feeds into and flows from Bruch's work, Proverbs, Job, and Ecclesiastes (as well as Ben Sira and Wisdom of Solomon) come to be treated as a distinctively philosophical tradition within ancient Israelite religion. This tradition spoke of God using different methods and in a different register from the Law

---

1. Unless otherwise indicated, all translations of modern and ancient languages are my own.

and the Prophets. The Hebrew wise men "transcended every feature of the theocracy of their religion," thus their wisdom literature presents the essence of the biblical religion independent from "the particularism of Israel's theocracy" (98). For these nineteenth-century scholars there was a strong analogy to their own day. Many of these scholars—under the sway of intellectual titans like Immanuel Kant—hoped to find within the Hebrew Bible speech about God that was as enlightened and enlightening as their contemporary philosophers.

In the introduction to his commentary on Proverbs, Crawford H. Toy (1899) embraces the category of wisdom literature as it existed in the 1890s. In contrast to the prophet or the priest, Toy explains, "The sage speaks in his own name, without reference to divine inspiration or to any book as authority. The 'law' of which he speaks is the law of his own conscience and reason; he does not name Moses or the prophets" (xxiii).

> In Proverbs and the other Wisdom books they ["wisdom" and the "wise"] relate to a definite class of sages whose function is the pursuit of universal moral and religious wisdom—men who, unlike the prophets, lay no claim to supernatural inspiration, but make their appeal simply to human reason. In at least one passage of the later preexilian time (Jer 9:23–24) there is the suggestion that the ethical prophets looked with suspicion on the contemporary "wise men" whose wisdom appears to be contrasted with the true ethical knowledge of Yahweh: but in Proverbs the sages present themselves as legitimate and competent teachers of this knowledge. (xxiii)

Although he is more circumspect, the wisdom literature category is also operative for Franz Delitzsch two and a half decades earlier.

> And how was this *Chokma* conditioned—to what was it directed? To denote its condition and aim in one word, it was universalistic, or humanistic. Emanating from the fear or the religion of Jahve (דֶּרֶךְ ה', the way of the Lord, x. 29), but seeking to comprehend the spirit in the letter, the essence in the forms of the national life, its effort was directed towards the general truth affecting mankind as such. (Delitzsch 1874, 41)

As Kynes (2019, 85) points out, Delitzsch (1874, 46) credits Bruch with first noting "*Chokma* or humanism as a peculiar intellectual tendency in Israel," although he disagrees with the way Bruch then opposes this tendency to the national law and cult.

Much scholarly attention given to wisdom literature in the last two centuries, then, focused on the relationship of Israelite wisdom traditions to prophetic and covenantal traditions. Such questions reflect scholarly interests in the study of ancient Israelite religion and biblical theology more broadly. Eventually, a consensus developed that wisdom literature represented an alternative religious worldview to the one espoused by the priestly and prophetic literature (e.g., Gunkel 1906, 69–72). Hartmut Gese (1958, 2; cited in Schipper 2019, 2) penned a famous line that encapsulates this consensus: "The teaching of wisdom is a foreign body in the world of the Old Testament."[2] Wisdom literature appeared uninterested in revelation and uninterested in priestly concerns or in Israelite history. Instead wisdom texts favored an internationally resonant eudaemonistic ethic of retributive justice based on empirical observation of the natural world. Thus the paradigmatic statement of Walther Zimmerli (1964, 147), "Wisdom has no relation to the history between God and Israel."[3]

If we want to understand how construals of wisdom literature have influenced the interpretation of Agur's words, it behooves us to trace how Prov 30 was interpreted throughout the nineteenth century, from before wisdom literature came to be understood as a genre reflecting an alternate worldview till after this idea became entrenched. To do this, I will consider three scholars that have just been mentioned: Heinrich Ewald, Franz Delitzsch, and Crawford Toy.

2.1.1.2. Georg Heinrich August Ewald

Ewald's work on Prov 30 offers an excellent starting point because he preceded and influenced the modern genre category of wisdom literature (Kynes 2019, 98), and he participated in the debates on poetry and orality that would eventually flower into form criticism.[4] In his *Die poetischen*

---

2. Although Schipper quotes Gese, he attributes the term *Fremdkörper* to Horst Dietrich Preuss.

3. Smend credits Zimmerli's 1933 German version of this essay with initiating the modern discussion of the traditions and literatures associated with wisdom (1995, 267; cf. Zimmerli 1933). Although there is often significant disagreement in the details, eminent scholars such as von Rad (1972, 314), Whybray (1974, 69–70), Crenshaw (2010, 11), and Blenkinsopp (1995, 52) propagated variations on this view.

4. Ewald (1803–1875), the son of a linen-weaver from Göttingen, started his academic career in 1824 having been influenced by J. G. Eichhorn. Later dismissed, he taught at Tübingen until 1867/1868 when he was again dismissed—both times for

Bücher des Alten Bundes [The Poetic Books of the Old Covenant], originally published in four volumes between 1836 and 1839, Ewald positioned the poetic books of the Hebrew Bible on a historical trajectory related to the development both of poetic literature and of religious thought. In terms of the development of religion, Ewald posits a rise of wisdom schools from the time of Solomon onward in Israel (Kynes 2019, 93). However, unlike later interpreters, he does not yet position these wisdom schools in opposition to the covenantal priestly and prophetic traditions. Rather, Ewald sees a philosophical threat to established religion coming from a "group of 'mockers' (לצים) and 'fools' (נבלים), who are mentioned in Proverbs and several prophetic texts" (Kynes 2019, 93; expounding Ewald 1848, 100). These were "theoretical atheists" and their voice is preserved in the words of Agur (Prov 30:1–14). In a fascinating analysis, Ewald (1848, 102) suggests that what we find in Prov 30:1–14 represents a proof for the nonexistence of God that is worthy of "our godless philosophers," invoking the likes of Ludwig Feuerbach, Friedrich Theodor Vischer, and David Friedrich Strauss.

Ewald's actual exposition of Prov 30 is contained in the fourth volume of his work on the poetic books of the Old Testament: *Sprüche Salomo's: Kohélet; Zusätze zu den früheren Theilen und Schluss* [The Proverbs of Solomon: Qohelet, Supplements to the Earlier Parts and Conclusion]. Although not late by current standards, Ewald (1837, 44) dates the material in Prov 30–31 to the late-seventh or early sixth centuries BCE. By his reckoning, then, these chapters postdate the Pentateuch and are part of the latest layer of Proverbs. Their content is completely external to the rest of the book and, moreover, it is unoriginal: "The poetry of the saying has here already completely disintegrated into small, neat descriptions of individual moral truths" (43). Ewald (44) sees the term *oracle* (משא) in 30:1 and 31:1, which he notes is a "most solemn prophetic flourish," as evidence of this lack of originality. Likewise, he sees the saying concerning the ant in 30:25 as dependent on Prov 6. Proverbs 30 seems not to rise above pastiche of other biblical passages. When he moves to address interpretive issues within the chapter proper, he frames his discussion in terms of the development of the doctrine of revelation. Ewald writes, "If … there is hardly

---

political reasons. "As a scholar he was non-conformist and disputatious" (Smend 2014, 360). His students included August Dillmann, Theodor Nöldeke, and Julius Wellhausen. For further discussion of Ewald in the history of biblical interpretation see Rogerson (1984, 91–103), Kynes (2019, 92–93), and Vayntrub (2019, 54–55).

any mention of revelation in the earlier sayings, then this proportion had to change gradually yet noticeably, since the written law became firmly established in the seventh century" (166). He makes the deft move—rarely made later—of positing a poetic author behind the chapter who experiences for himself "the peace and bliss of faithfulness" through his access to revelation but finds himself surrounded by many who are alienated from the same through their luxuriant and unjust life, their pride, and generally confused, haughty, and desperate lifestyle. In order to make us feel this horror, our faithful poet brings the voice of one such character to life in 30:2-4 before responding with Scripture in verses 5-6 and prayer in verses 7-9—a juxtaposition that commends faithful belief in God's word over the stubborn and prideful ignorance of atheistic arguments.

For Ewald (1837, 166), Agur is the name of this libertine interlocutor that is voiced by the poet, who designates himself according to the cypher איתיאל ואכל, which Ewald glosses as, "God-with-me and I-am-Strong." As for the coherence of the chapter, Ewald sees within it two distinct collections: verses 1-14 and 15-33. Proverbs 30:1-14 have an internal unity as a discourse about revelation and pride, but verses 15-33 find their unity in their common form and ethic (169). Ewald takes these numerical sayings as moral warnings. The crucial image is always set in either the first or the last place and the other images serve as comparisons to frame it. Ewald sees these numerical sayings as witticisms, "a synthetic form," which he connects back to Prov 6:16-19 where the moral is more clearly drawn out and developed (169). In Prov 30, by contrast, we are left with the bare artistry of the form and must fend for ourselves as to the moral. For Ewald, this exhibits a composition in a less refined and developed state.

The hermeneutical issues Ewald raises are the key issues that will be raised by nearly every interpreter down to today: (1) the identity of Agur and the designation משא, (2) the theology expressed in 30:2-4 and its relationship to both the immediate context and the wider context both of Proverbs and the canon, (3) the form and function of the numerical sayings, and (4) the internal structure and unity of the chapter as a whole. In addressing these issues Ewald is invested in teasing out the historical development of Israelite thought and its concomitant literary forms. His commentary gives a nod to the poetic voice behind the chapter that is invested in revelation and faith, but even this view, although he considers it to be correct, is rather passé. Proverbs 30 has fallen from the heights of Israelite thought.

2.1.1.3. Franz Julius Delitzsch

A generation after Ewald, Delitzsch devotes over fifty pages to the exposition of Prov 30 in his two-volume 1872 commentary (the English translation appeared in 1874–1875). An evangelical Lutheran, Delitzsch brought a rare and thorough engagement with rabbinic commentators while allowing the questions of Germany's burgeoning historical-critical industry to steer his exegetical analysis.[5] Breaking with Ewald, Delitzsch (1875, 262–63) cannot accept that משא indicates Agur's words are prophetic speech, because the chapter does not contain "an utterance of the prophetic spirit" but rather a "confession of human weakness and shortsightedness" and "proverbs not of a divine but altogether of a human and even of a decaying spiritual stamp." Instead, Delitzsch critiques and develops the theories of Ferdinand Hitzig and Ferdinande Mühlau that משא is a tribal designation that makes Agur (and Lemuel in 31:1) a descendant of Ishmael through his son, Massa (Gen 25:14; 1 Chr 1:30). For Delitzsch, then, Agur is not an Israelite but an adherent of Abrahamic religion who "recognized the religion of Israel as its completion" (266). He makes this argument through painstaking engagement with the philological particulars of all texts in question and the most careful geographic, ethnographic, and religious reconstructions available to him.

Delitzsch (1875, 268) rejects Ewald's idea that verses 1b–14 contain a dialogue with a "haughty mocker" on philological grounds because he cannot accept איתיאל ואכל as any kind of name—whether "actual or symbolic." Instead, he favors repointing these words as a corrupted declarative sentence. Delitzsch takes Agur to be "a man earnestly devoted to God" offering a sincere confession (270). Ultimately, he reads 30:2–3 as a failed quest for spiritual knowledge through the methods of human wisdom (272–73). In a poignant exposition, Delitzsch interprets the rhetorical questions of verse 4 as a profound longing to know the personal being behind creation, "the all-wise omnipotent Worker" (275). Pulling on

---

5. Delitzsch (1813–1890) was born in Leipzig where a conversion experience as a philosophy student led him to devote the rest of his life to scholarship in service of the Christian faith. He held posts in Leipzig, Rostock, and Erlangen and is best known for his commentaries in partnership with C. F. Keil. "An original and creative thinker within the confessional orthodoxy of his time," his commentaries are "marked by enormous learning and profound argument" and an increasing "willingness to accept some of the results of historical criticism" (Rogerson 2013, 497).

threads from the Rigveda and connecting them through Jewish interpreters like Gersonides to Prov 8 and even Heb 1:4, Delitzsch argues the son of Prov 30:4 is Wisdom, God's beloved Son, the idea of the Logos, the mediator in the creation of the world.[6] He concludes by lamenting that answers to these rhetorical questions must remain hidden because "the nature of the Godhead is hidden.... On this side of eternity it is beyond the reach of human knowledge" (277). While such comments might seem confessionally motivated to contemporary scholarship, Delitzsch presents them in good faith as a thoroughly historical and descriptive argument.

In coming to put the whole chapter together, Delitzsch attributes the composition to Agur as an anthology, a compilation of "Mashals" (i.e., "proverbs," משלים). The "utterance of the man" (נאם הגבר) that opens the collection in 30:1b–4 is a set piece—reported speech that may be Agur's own but speaks the proper humble confession of every man (Delitzsch 1875, 270). To this set piece Agur appended independent proverbs (30:5–6, 10), a prayer in the form of a "Mashal-ode" (30:7–9) and numerical proverbs that continue and develop the ideas (30:15–31). However, the relative lack of attention that Delitzsch pays to how these sayings link together and develop suggests he does not see a strong through-line of thought or argumentation. Rather, he refers to catch words and the form of the numerical proverb, which he defines as "a brief discourse, having a didactic end complete in itself, which by means of numerals gives prominence to that which it seeks to bring forward" (281). These sayings have moral and ethical goals, but drawing them out is of secondary importance to Delitzsch.

His commentary on the leech passage in 30:15–16 showcases his approach. Delitzsch devotes seven pages of close argumentation to teasing out the original form and meaning of these verses. He disentangles and reconstructs two original sayings and argues that the leech and its daughters are surely symbolic, "the leech is not meant here in the natural history sense of the word, but as embodied greediness, and is made a person, one individual being" (Delitzsch 1875, 292). Although the symbolism is somewhat hidden, the reconstruction reveals that the leech is not a reference to some type of demon, as ancient and medieval commentators suggested,

---

6. Although Delitzsch's appeal to the Rigveda may seem inappropriate to modern scholars, he is working in the classic philological mold, which was fundamentally *comparative*. Such comparison included not only etymologies and forms of literature but patterns of thought, narratives, and myths (Turner 2014, 382–83).

but rather refers to a type that is represented by the other items in the list, namely, the person characterized by the grave, the barren woman (293). This observation, however, does not compel him to reflect on what this symbol might import for people today (301). His primary concern is the resolution of philological challenges.

Delitzsch is far less interested in the kind of historical reconstruction of the prehistory of the text and the ancient religious context that may have produced it than is Ewald (the world behind the text) but neither does he explore contemporary religious meaning (the world in front of the text).[7] His job, rather, is the task of parsing out the language, explicating grammar and semantics, drawing lines from signifiers to historical species and perhaps making some comments on environment, behavior, or ancient conceptions as available (the world within the text). He does not feel the need to reflect on the implications of this or that proverb for the modern person or to integrate his readings of the numerical sayings with the lofty theological reflection that he so eloquently exposited in 30:4. The fact that Delitzsch's commentary steadily trails off in attempting to integrate the parts of the whole within the chapter and in offering theological and ethical reflections, demonstrates both that he does not see the chapter as exhibiting any particular unity nor as having much theological to say after verses 1–6. Although he never denies the chapter has ethical or thematic coherence neither does he discover any.

2.1.1.4. Crawford H. Toy

If Delitzsch's commentary is perhaps the most thorough, Toy's 1899 volume in T&T Clark's prestigious International Critical Commentary is surely a contender for the most influential English treatment.[8] Writing at the end of the nineteenth century, Toy's work represents the full flowering

---

7. The distinction between the world behind/within/in front of the text originates with Paul Ricoeur. See, e.g., Ricoeur 1976, 80–88. For helpful appropriations of Ricoeur's thought for biblical studies, consider Schneiders 1999, esp. 97–179; and, much more briefly, Moberly 2013, 17–18.

8. Toy (1836–1919), born to a devout pharmacist in Norfolk, Virginia, studied at the University of Virginia (AM, 1856) and the nascent Southern Baptist Theological Seminary (1859–1860). Ordained in 1860, he fought for the Confederacy as infantryman and chaplain. Following two years studying in Berlin (1867–1869), Toy taught at the Southern Baptist Theological Seminary (1869–1879) before controversial views on evolution and the "inspiration and accuracy" of scripture led him to resign (Lyon

of what has gone before. It is not necessarily the most original or creative work done on the chapter, but Toy synthesizes the approach of the preceding century and takes many ideas to their logical conclusions. Concerning the unity and authorship of Prov 30, Toy (1899, 517) pronounces, "Since the paragraphs are in thought independent, and must be treated separately, the question of unity of authorship is not important." As such, Toy does not clearly argue a position on how far the "words of Agur" extend, although, he assigns 30:1–4 to Agur's hand in his introduction (1899, vi). He rejects משא as a term for prophecy, calling it "inapposite … a form of utterance quite out of keeping with the individual and reflective tone of what follows" (517). Then, after examining other proposals for משא, such as reading it as the geographic proper name or emending to משל ("gnomic saying"), he rejects the word entirely as "a gloss or as unintelligible"—it can be omitted "without detriment to the sense" (518). Divorced from the content of the chapter and without genre or geography to tie him down, Agur becomes "a sage, Jewish or non-Jewish, not of the time of Solomon, but of the later reflective period, or else as a man (like Job) famous in tradition, and taken by some later writer as his mouthpiece for the expression of philosophic thought" (519). Because of its sarcastic and rhetorical tone, Toy reads the confessions and questions of 30:2–4 alongside of Job 38–41. This passage is not irreverent, nor does it deny the existence of God or of revealed religion; rather, it is aimed at "the pretend wisdom of the schools" (521–22). The attitude "is one of reverent agnosticism" (522). Agur—if indeed that is who is speaking in any meaningful sense—"belongs to the school of the last reviser of the Book of Job and Koheleth" (522).

Toy considers the later half of the chapter to be disorganized and corrupted, displaying deleterious scribal activity. For example, he imagines 30:14c–d is a scribal gloss on 14a–b because it provides a moral for the preceding images. "But the addition of an interpretation is not the manner of the numerical groups of this chapter"; he writes, "the aphorism is supposed to carry its own interpretation" (Toy 1899, 527). His analysis of 30:15–16 is more skeptical than Ewald or Delitzsch, both of whom he cites only to conclude, "These reconstructions, all arbitrary, are called forth by the desire to bring v. 15a into logical connection with the following lines" (528). For Toy, a reading that finds coherence in Prov 30 amounts

---

1920, 8). He then took up the post of Hancock Professor of Hebrew and Other Oriental Languages at Harvard University (1880–1909).

to wish-fulfillment. As he moves into the numerical sayings, he is clear in his assessment that the material is often incomplete and largely inconsequential. The quatrain in verse 17 is "out of place" and verse 20 is a scribal annotation on verses 18–19 that "misses the point of the aphorism" (530–31). When it comes to interpreting these numerical sayings, Toy cannot find any religious or moral value in them. Concerning the four consumers in verses 15b–16, he concludes, "Our proverb has no ethical meaning or application; it is simply a record of observation, which may broaden the pupil's knowledge of the world" (529). Likewise, although verses 18–19 are filled with wonder, "Apparently no religious sentiment is involved; the stanza is rather a lesson in natural history and physics" (531). Proverbs 30:24–28 are "a bit of natural history, without expressed reference to human life;" and verses 29–31 are "an admiring remark, without moral or religious suggestion" (534–35).

2.1.1.5. Summary

By the end of the nineteenth century, the key hermeneutical issues in the modern interpretation of Prov 30 have taken shape and been approached in various ways. Agur can be construed as an Israelite sage or a foreign wise man, as a faithful voice or a heterodox skeptic. His words can be read as both claiming inspired revelation and as a proof against the existence of God. It is not even clear whether the chapter itself presents a dialogue, a monologue, or an anthology of voices. The numerical sayings can be attributed to Agur from verse 1 or treated as scribal accretions. They can be interpreted as potent illustrations of moral lessons or as curious ruminations on the natural world. However, a few constants emerge. All scholars consider Prov 30 somehow distinctive within Proverbs such that its peculiar character warrants special comment. On the grounds of its theological and philosophical tone and sentiments, most scholars further consider the collection late relative to the rest of Proverbs. Finally, no interpreter attempts to treat the chapter as a whole in any meaningful sense. Agur's voice and message, his particular genius—assuming he has one—go largely unheeded and unappreciated at the end of the nineteenth century.

So how did the wisdom literature category influence the interpretation of Agur's words? Or to ask this question differently, What similarities do we see between Delitzsch and Toy that present a contrast with Ewald who wrote a few decades earlier, before Bruch's *Weisheits-Lehre der Hebräer*? For Ewald, Agur is still an Israelite and the term משא ("oracle") can still denote revelation, but for Delitzsch and Toy neither of these things are true. Importantly, Delitzsch and Toy make their arguments on philological grounds by examining the tone of the passage, the meaning of משא, and the possible geographical and/or ethnographical contexts of a place named Massa. Nevertheless, the wisdom literature category—which did not exist in the same way for Ewald—has a finger firmly on the scale when they are weighing the meanings of words and interpretations. It seems far less plausible to the later interpreters that Agur (interlocutor or otherwise) could claim any connection with divine revelation or prophetic speech. We also see a tendency to separate the material in the back half of the chapter from ethical or religious significance. Although Delitzsch maintains that the numerical sayings have connections to human life and symbolic significance (as in his analysis of the leech passage), he is reluctant to spell out these connections. Toy is abundantly clear that these sayings are the product of reason, perhaps even a form of protoscience, and they have no religious or ethical sense. The numerical and animal sayings bubble up rather from humanity's observation of the world in which they find themselves. Perhaps the failure of Delitzsch and Toy to draw any compelling morals out of this collection suggests that, like Ewald, they find the numerical sayings to be something of a fall from the heights of what wisdom literature is capable. They are the remainder from the universal and humanistic method of the sages that starts from creation and has no recourse to revelation and the cult.

2.1.2. The Form and Content of Agur's Words

2.1.2.1. Form Criticism and Wisdom Literature

At the beginning of the twentieth century the most significant advance in scholarship on the Hebrew Bible more broadly and on wisdom literature in particular came from the treasure trove of linguistic and literary material discovered at Ugarit (Ras Shamra) in 1929 and the explosion of comparative work following on from Adolf Erman's (1924) identification of parallels between the Instruction of Amenemope and Prov 22–24. Indeed, during this period wisdom literature's international and universalistic character became the chief hallmark of scholarly descriptions of the genre.[9] This was a welcome extension of the nineteenth

---

9. For examples, see Oesterly 1927 and Thomas 1960.

century emphasis on the rational and philosophical nature of wisdom over against the Israelite cult. Displacing references to the Rigveda with better analogies nearer to hand only strengthened the thesis. But hand in glove with revitalized comparative approaches came a new method known as form criticism. As it was conceived by Hermann Gunkel and practiced in the early twentieth century, form criticism was fundamentally historical and diachronic in orientation.[10] Gunkel (1906) himself employed the method to attempt the first comprehensive history of the literature of Israel.[11] He wrote:

> Hence, almost all genres existed in the form of oral traditions [*mundliche Uberlieferung*] before being recorded. In fact, "literary" genres, in the sense of written compositions, are quite rare, especially if we wish to distinguish historiography from folkloric, oral legends [*Sage*]. The strong rift dividing those who were educated from those who were uneducated, which runs through the society of developed peoples, hardly existed in ancient Israel. Rather, literature was an integral part of the people's daily life, and must be understood in this context. Thus, in order to understand an ancient genre, one first has to inquire about its context in the people's life [*Sitz im Volksleben*]. (Gunkel 1906, 53; trans. Siedlecki 2003, 30)

For the form critic, the text is not explicable as literature but rather contains fossilized *Gattungen*, or oral forms, which have their origins in a certain performance context or a real-life setting, the famous *Sitz im Leben*. Thus every form found in a literary setting has a history that connects to an oral setting. Form critics, at least in the early days, saw their task as reconstructing the history of the literary genres within the text. Reading composite texts as coherent wholes was ruled out more or less by definition. Instead scholars hoped to isolate and extract the various

---

10. For the history and evaluation of form criticism see Buss 1999, as well as the essays in Sweeney and Ben Zvi (2003). Especially relevant therein to wisdom literature are Van Leeuwen (2003) and Longman (2003). For a robust critique of form criticism with reference to wisdom literature, consider Weeks (2013, 2015) and, more broadly, Judd (2021, 105–12).

11. For the context of this work see Smend 2007, 127. In his helpful biographical analysis of Gunkel's work, Smend (2007, 118) is at pains to emphasize that "Gunkel was a historian all his life, and set great store by the fact."

generic elements in a given text in order to comment on their sociohistorical contexts. In origins lay significance.

To think about how form criticism affected the interpretation of Prov 30, I will consider the work of three further scholars: Berend Gemser, Georg Sauer, and William McKane. Although these three are somewhat idiosyncratic they have been surprisingly influential. Their approach to Prov 30 will allow us to trace how joining the methods of form criticism with assumptions about wisdom literature influenced the interpretation of Prov 30.

2.1.2.2. Berend Gemser

In 1963, Gemser published the second edition of his commentary on Proverbs in the notable series Handbuch zum alten Testament. Gemser's slim commentary lives up to its title as a Handbuch with detailed philological notes and commentary that focuses broadly on framing the material in the chapter and providing copious references to both primary and secondary literature without typically engaging in line-by-line analysis of the text. It has often been quoted because Gemser's prescient comments engage technical issues with a rare combination of concision and thoroughness. Gemser (1963, 103) takes the division in the Greek between 30:1–14 and 30:15–33 as decisive without argument. The implication, however, is that the form of the numerical saying in 30:15–33 implicitly supports the Greek division (105). Gemser is agnostic on the issue of unity of authorship in 30:1–14, but does find literary links through "associations of thoughts and words" (103). Likewise, Agur's identity remains unknown although Gemser amasses a range of data to suggest strongly that Agur is not an Israelite. He points to the apparently non-Israelite origin of the names "Agur" and "Jakeh," the possibility that הטריפני ("provide me," 30:8) reflects an Arabic meaning, and the use of different names for God (103). He concludes, "The formal correspondence with the sayings of Balaam and the material correspondence with the book of Job is tangible, and these two persons are also marked as non-Israelites, namely, as coming from Edomite-Arab regions" (103). The remainder of Gemser's comments on 30:1–14 analyze the form of verses 1–3 as "an oracle" (*eines Orakels*) with strong similarities to Ps 73. He glosses משא as "pronouncement" (*Ausspruch*) but attaches little significance to the word, since he acknowledges it may rather be המשאי, "then [Agur] would be from Massa like Lemuel" (103). Gemser finds the text's move from praising God's greatness and unfathomability to humble obeisance characteristic of later wisdom literature (e.g., Isa 40:12–14; Job 28:38; Sir 1:2-8; Bar 3:29–4:4; 1963, 105).

When Gemser turns to comment on Prov 30:15–33, he devotes nearly his entire discussion to describing the form of the numerical saying. It consists of two numbers in sequence followed by a list of items—usually pleasing or disgusting—that corresponds to the second number. At home in wisdom literature, this form probably originated from the riddle and has been subsequently adapted to religious poetry. Although the form is broadly Semitic, "there is hardly anything specifically Israelite in 15-33" (Gemser 1963, 105). Moreover, numerical sayings do not contain any moral admonitions, although there may be some moral sentiment. On the whole, "sharp observation of nature" characterizes this section and reminds Gemser (107) of Solomon in 1 Kgs 5:13. Throughout his commentary, Gemser's approach is descriptive and comparative. He is not wrestling with meaning; he is working to classify and label his subject matter. Particularly when he comes to the numerical sayings, the form is described thoroughly without being analyzed at all. Gemser (105) has little insight into what "one of the most interesting types of sayings" might mean or how it might be operating on a literary level. In sum, Gemser finds the voice of Agur operative in so far as it is a foreign voice but on formal grounds he finds no need to seek any broader coherence in the collection.

2.1.2.3. Georg Sauer

The same year that Gemser's handbook appeared, Sauer published a monograph entitled *Die Spruche Agurs* (1963). Sauer's book appears to be the only monograph dedicated to the chapter, but *Die Spruche Agurs* is a misleading title. Sauer's focus is not actually the study of Prov 30, but rather the influence of Ugaritic literature on the Old Testament. In a brief introduction, Sauer demonstrates how the discovery and decoding of the literature of Ugarit might shed light on the Old Testament:

> One stylistic feature is used to show the universal relationship between the two literatures. For this purpose, the use of numbers was chosen, which is present in the Ugaritic texts with a conspicuous frequency and finds its counterpart in formulaic phrases in the Old Testament. It may be expected that such a comparison will illuminate a part of the far-flung history of the Hebrew mind and a piece of its expressive power that strives after form. (Sauer 1963, 23)

Sauer's treatment of Prov 30 is incidental to his broader aims. The majority of his monograph is taken up with research to date on Ugarit and the Old Testament and the use of numbers, number series, and number sayings in Ugarit and Israel. As his climactic example, Sauer (1963, 92–112) undertakes a detailed study of Prov 30 because of its preponderance of numerical sayings. Given his focus on Ugarit and his extensive work on numerical sayings, Sauer's comments on Prov 30 make a distinctive contribution. Ultimately, he argues, "It is not only the external form of the numerical aphorisms of Prov 30 that are suitable to be compared to Ugaritic literature, but also the content and theme of this chapter" (92).

Sauer believes comparison with Ugaritic literature can solve long-standing problems in the Hebrew text. He notes that the name "Agur," although unknown in Hebrew, appears as a name in Ugaritic where it is derived from Akkadian and designates the messenger deity (Sauer 1963, 94–96). Likewise, Sauer finds a suitable Ugaritic explanation for בן־יקה in the root WQH (96). Sauer is less confident about the identity of משא ("oracle" or "Massa") than he is about the Ugaritic origin of Agur's name. He believes that the word names a north Arabian tribe, but in truth he is ambivalent about its authenticity, suggesting משא emerged here only after Prov 30 was collected alongside Prov 31 (97). The important thing for Sauer is that משא corroborates the non-Israelite origins of the passage. As to the theology of 30:2–4, Sauer treats them as a discrete unit and discusses their theology in comparison to Ps 73 and Job 38–41. Quoting Otto Eissfeldt's introduction, he concludes that Agur is a sage who captures in this short composition the solution and attitude that Job struggles toward throughout that massive poem. Before the majesty of God, man must be silent. But Sauer (1963, 100) is not surprised, because Job is non-Israelite in origin and, "In the form in which it is presented to us, its oldest parts contain Canaanite properties." Proverbs 30:2–4 likewise exhibits affinities in lexicon and grammar to Canaanite texts.

For Sauer (1963, 101), the numerical saying is a hallmark of Ugaritic literature—a concrete feature linking Agur to Ugarit that can "be grasped with the hands." Sauer classes both the prayer in 30:7–9 and the list of generations in verses 11–14 as numerical sayings despite their lack of headings with numbers. Their enumeration of items suffices for the form and proper introductions can be reconstructed on analogy with passages like Prov 6:16 (103). He does not analyze the rhetorical or literary effect of the numerical sayings, suggesting the collocations of images have more-or-less obvious significance. Instead his comments focus on identifying formal elements, attempting relative dating of these forms, and reconstructing them as necessary—he identifies words and images that have counterparts in Ugaritic texts for nearly every line. He argues the picture of slapping hand over mouth in 30:32 circles back to the theological stance of verses 1–4, namely, proper human humility before an omnipotent God. "This gesture is Job's reaction to the divine intervention" (Job 40:4; Sauer 1963, 111). This linkage between the beginning and the end of the chapter on thematic grounds holds together the rest of the content which is united on formal grounds. The presence of the numerical sayings as a distinctive feature uniting Prov 30:7–33, especially when combined with the Canaanite/Ugaritic features he already identified in verses 1–4, overrides the Greek division of the chapter at verse 15 and is indeed its defining characteristic (104, 112). Thus Sauer finds warrant for positing the unity of the chapter in the form of the numerical saying and its consistently Canaanite content.

2.1.2.4. William McKane

A few years after the work of Gemser and Sauer, McKane (1970) produced a commentary in the Old Testament Library that effectively synthesized previous research on Prov 30. On McKane's reading of the chapter, form-critical conclusions and the reconstructed trajectory of wisdom literature collide. As to Agur's identity, McKane opts to read the gentilic המשאי ("the Massaite") instead of the common noun המשא ("the oracle"). McKane argues that Agur's sentiments in 30:2–3 cannot be taken at face value but must instead be read as "ironical," with "a mock ruefulness" (646). The indecipherable verse 1 then becomes "a cry of despair … the cry of one who has searched to the furthest limits of his powers and has found nothing" (647). In 30:4, Agur is thus claiming that the knowledge of God, which constitutes wisdom, has no real basis in human experience. McKane compares this emphasis on the "hiddenness and unknowability of God" to Ecclesiastes. The scholar who responds to Agur's speech in verses 5–9 is "a scholar of sacred learning entrusted with the preservation and transmission of the Jewish scriptures" (648). He writes in such a way as to defend biblical learning by quoting scripture in his response. McKane, then, reads Agur as a non-Israelite voice from within the international wisdom tradition that has been included in Proverbs as a foil for a late, Yahwistic viewpoint. The wise man behind Prov 30 has become more the pious scholar, taking "the whole of the scriptures as his province" and perhaps peppering his compositions with prophetic vocabulary (e.g., נאם in 30:1).

When it comes to the material following verse 6, McKane leans heavily on the research of Wolfgang M. W. Roth (1965), among others, concerning the form of the numerical saying. In a way similar to Ben Sira, the scholar behind Prov 30:5–17 is using "*Gattungen* and themes which lie outside the strict province of wisdom literature and belong to psalmody and prophecy." This adapting of forms provides further corroboration that these verses hail from a late stage in the process of the development of wisdom literature. McKane (1970, 648) is not precise about what "a late stage" might mean, but seems to suggest a postexilic context. McKane also appeals to form when he considers the unity of 30:15–16. Although scholars like Gemser hold these verses together, McKane says this reading "is to be rejected on formal grounds" because it results in a unit that has no structural parallel in Roth's study of numerical sayings (652). As to the function of the numerical saying, McKane is keen to reject the view, expressed by Roth and Toy above, that they merely encapsulate "observations of nature" or "formulate a kind of natural science" (653). Rather, he argues they are directed toward human behavior and employ nature in a search for "'parables' which will serve as effective comments on human traits" (654).

Finally, McKane gives no real attention to the structure and unity of the chapter as a whole. His lack of engagement with the question suggests he thinks it insignificant. In his opening discussion on the extent of the Words of Agur, he makes clear that he finds no real continuity past 30:6. Beyond this the "arrangement is editorial" and dependent on superficial links such as "the catchword principle" and "affinity of theme" (McKane 1970, 643). He makes only a few comments in passing on the relationship of one saying to the next and these are merely to note there is *no* unity beyond loose associations (see comments on 30:10 [650] and 20 [658]). McKane seems to consider the lack of unity obvious—the burden of proof would surely lie on anyone suggesting otherwise.

2.1.2.5. Summary

Under the influence of broad scholarly conclusions about wisdom literature, approaches to Prov 30 solidified and historical concerns stemming from form criticism came to dominate interpretations of the chapter. Gemser and Sauer both seem to take it for granted that *describing* the formal features of the chapter and reflecting on their origins *explains* the meaning of the chapter. Gemser reflects this approach when he muses that the numerical saying was at home in wisdom literature and originated from the riddle. With this prehistory it is a fundamentally nontheological genre that was adapted later to various uses in prophetic texts and religious poetry. As such it is non-Israelite in both form and content. Sauer's study endeavors to trace this form and content as far back toward the source as he can go. He laments the lack of poetic wisdom texts at Ugarit, but nevertheless concludes that the numerical saying captures "a didactic moment," and muses toward a *Sitz im Leben*: "A numerical saying may well have had its place in the mouth of a wise man" (Sauer 1963, 64). But perhaps most significantly, Gemser and Sauer both see the form(s) present within the chapter as the essential component of the chapter's composition, although they construe this in different ways. For Gemser the Greek division of the material at 30:15 is decisive—the chapter was originally two smaller collections, the internal coherence of which is uncertain and immaterial. Sauer, however, argues on form-critical grounds that the chapter is coherent. Form unifies the entire discourse because he finds modified examples of the numerical saying from 30:7–31. But Sauer's interest in the numerical saying ultimately focuses on its historical origin in Ugaritic traditions. So, although he makes the prescient observation that 30:32–33 link thematically back to 30:1–4, he does not explore a unified reading at the level of theology or message. For decades following Gemser and Sauer's work, the form of the numerical saying was considered both necessary and sufficient explanation for the composition of Prov 30. Likewise, for McKane this fascinating chapter can only be mused at atomistically because the cryptic text and formal similarities preclude any search for real coherence. Most telling at this point in the story is what McKane does not feel he has to argue for. The idea that Agur is an interloper in Israel's wisdom traditions, that the chapter witnesses late, skeptical wisdom theology, and that there is no meaningful coherence can all now be assumed. Arguably, scholarly concerns around wisdom literature and literary forms are now determining what Agur can and cannot be saying. They are certainly determining what is worth listening for in the text. Proverbs 30, as a collection within Proverbs, is more of a literary illusion or a compositional accident than anything else. As such, we should not attempt to interpret it as a whole— doing so would be a historical distortion.

2.2. How Might We Read Agur?

Many more interpreters could be mentioned and the fine points of their readings teased out in tedious detail. Indeed there is so much variety in the specifics of how Agur's words have been construed that it would be most unhelpful to survey all of it.[12] But the diversity of interpretations is itself instructive in so far as it points to the challenging, evocative, and underdetermined nature of the text. Proverbs 30 defies our scholarly categories. In the remainder of this chapter, I will turn to fresh possibilities for reading Agur's words. First, I will consider how scholarly assumptions about wisdom literature are changing; second, I will explore how theological and literary approaches to the text have found thematic unity in the material.

2.2.1. Wisdom Literature in Contemporary Research

Over the last two to three decades, however, the scholarly consensus about wisdom literature that I described earlier has come under heavy criticism and the discipline stands in a state of flux (Kynes 2021b, 11).[13] In his revised doctoral dissertation, *Early Israelite Wisdom*, Weeks (1994, 158–60) challenged many sacred cows of the consensus view, including the idea that the earliest wisdom literature was secular, that it was composed by and associated with a particular class of "wise men," and that it was a school curriculum designed for educating an administrative class. Weeks (2007, 96–127) has gone on to argue that the instruction Proverbs seeks to commend is none other than the Jewish torah, particularly as it is described in Deuteronomy. Mark Sneed's (2011) seminal essay, "Was

---

12. E.g., I have not mentioned the landmark commentaries by Fox (2009) and Waltke (2005). These are easily the two most substantial treatments of the chapter in the last fifty years. However, hermeneutically, their approach does not differ substantially from their nineteenth-century forerunners, although their work shows significant advances in philological and literary sophistication. Fox (2009, 956), e.g., attributes 30:1–9 to Agur and calls the passage a reaction against the book of Proverbs. Proverbs 30:10–33 are a miscellaneous collection (849). This approach has much in common with Ewald and McKane, although Fox construes the dissonance of Agur's voice differently. Waltke (2005, 464), on the other hand, attributes the whole chapter to Agur and finds its coherence in structural elements and general themes. His approach combines evangelical piety with Delitzsch's robust philology and Sauer's eye for form (see also Steinmann 2001, 2009). In chs. 3–5, I engage Fox and Waltke at every turn as pertains to a close reading of the text.

13. For authoritative collections of essays that offer a window on the current state of the discipline see Sneed 2015; Jarick 2016b; Najman, Rey, and Tigchelaar 2017; Adams and Goff 2020; and Kynes 2021a. For an instructive counterpoint to these collections that shows how far the consensus has shifted from the state of the discipline some thirty years ago, compare the essays in Day, Gordon, and Williamson 1995.

There a Wisdom Tradition?," complicated the rigid view of genre inherited from form criticism and used recent research on scribalism, such as the monumental work of David M. Carr (2005) and Karel van der Toorn (2007), to argue that wisdom was not a distinct tradition or worldview in ancient Israel. In short, Sneed's thesis was that "literary sages," that is, elite scribes trained broadly in the literary traditions of Israel, bore the responsibility for copying, transmitting, and composing *all* of Israel's literature. "The wisdom literature, then," writes Sneed (2011, 54), "needs to be viewed as complementary, not inimical to the other types of literature found in the Hebrew Bible." The shifting consensuses on wisdom literature are on display differently in the most recent major critical commentary on Proverbs, Bernd Schipper's 2019 volume, *Proverbs 1–15*, in the prestigious Hermeneia series. On Schipper's (2019, 2) view, the close comparison of Proverbs to ancient Near Eastern texts, particularly the Instruction of Amenemope, eventually led scholars to emphasize similarities with international literature while downplaying associations with biblical texts.[14] Schipper considers one of the key contributions of his commentary to be the reintegration of the book of Proverbs into a discussion that includes Deuteronomy's discourse on torah (5).

Kynes (2019), however, has articulated the single most potent challenge to the general scholarly consensus surrounding wisdom literature. Kynes argues that wisdom literature did not exist as a genre for the ancient tradents of this material but was rather a scholarly construct developed in the German academy of the mid-nineteenth century.[15] The genre category itself drives a certain construal of the theology of these three books. While reading Proverbs, Job, and Ecclesiastes together as a set of texts has yielded various interpretive insights, it has shut down others. If Proverbs were read alongside Deuteronomy, Psalms, or Isaiah instead of Job and Ecclesiastes what facets of its theology might emerge? Kynes (2021b, 2)

---

14. Schipper helpfully contrasts this cosmopolitan view on Proverbs, dominant throughout the twentieth century, with the views of commentators from the late nineteenth century, particularly Wilhelm Frankenberg and Franz Delitzsch.

15. Kynes's work in tracing the wisdom literature category fills a desideratum in the field that Smend (1995, 258) noted over twenty-five years ago by anticipating and affirming the main thrust of Kynes's argument. Namely, Bruch was "the first to call attention to *Chokma* or humanism as a distinctive intellectual tendency in Israel," and this impulse was driven by the search for philosophy in the Hebrew Bible (Smend 1995, 265, quoting Franz Delitzsch).

has gone on to suggest that the study of wisdom literature is undergoing a Kuhnian revolution, "in which old paradigms and long-held assumptions may be questioned and new methods and theories proposed and debated."

One consequence of the breakdown of the scholarly consensus around wisdom literature, is a loss of historical knowledge. As the consensus crumbles, we know less about the historical context of wisdom books, who wrote them, for what purpose, and in what manner than we claimed to know fifty years ago. But what we have lost in terms of historical background we stand to gain in "theological and literary potential" (Kynes 2019, 254; see also Vayntrub 2019, 4). Without certain historical baggage, scholars have an opportunity to explore new hypotheses and reimagine old ones. Vayntrub's (2019) reanalysis of biblical משל (*māšāl*, i.e., "proverb") offers one example of the kind of illuminating study that might cut across the discipline in the wake of wisdom literature's demise.[16] Vayntrub's subject is not the משל per se, but rather the evolutionary model of biblical poetry that posits a progression from orality to literacy and eventually to "rational" prose. The native term משל has often been a lightning rod for such scholarly theories since it seems to represent the smallest literary unit of poetic expression, the proverb, the parallel line, even poetry itself (Vayntrub 2019, 89–90). But, Vayntrub argues, when we seek primarily to look "behind the text in its present form" for the sake of historical reconstruction, we stand to miss the literary claims of the text "on its own terms" (3–4).[17] Earlier analysis of משל focused on the idea that at its core משל signified *proverb*, that essentially oral unit at the root of the genre known as wisdom literature (Vayntrub 2019, 71–75).[18] In contrast, Vayntrub's study abandoned a hypothesized chronological progression of forms and broadened the category by attending to the term as presented in its biblical literary context. Her approach led her to offer this working definition of משל: "a type of assertive statement that sorts the world and its actors into categories, articulates relationships between these categories, and par-

---

16. Kynes himself points out that Vayntrub's work is notable in this regard in the last footnote of his monograph (2019, 254 n. 5).

17. My use of the phrase *on its own terms* at various points in this study is influenced by Vayntrub's approach.

18. Although he does not refer to the משל as such, Gunkel (1906, 69–70) articulates the classic form of this view. His idea has been pervasive and is often repeated in recent scholarship (e.g., McKane 1970, 3; Westermann 1995, 105). Vayntrub (2019, 72–76) cites these examples and others in her discussion.

ticularizes these general statements in their performance context" (13). Whether or not one agrees with all of the conclusions Vayntrub reaches or what one makes of their interpretive payoff, her study offers a compelling model for how biblical studies might move forward on particular questions. If we are less concerned to reconstruct the history of the world behind wisdom literature, what new insights might be gained from the way these texts present themselves?

2.2.2. Literary and Theological Approaches to Proverbs 30

In terms of reading for coherence, the most pertinent developments as we move further into the twenty-first century focus on constructive readings and go under various umbrella titles such as literary and canonical approaches. According to Christopher Seitz (2005, 100), historical-critical methods developed over the last two hundred years seek meaning and theology in "authorial intent at the level of the text's prehistory, in an alleged source or form, or tied to an historical audience." This process will inevitably mean giving priority to a particular historical voice or context—either to the earlier voice (as more pure or authentic) or to the later voice (as more mature or developed) or to no voice (as a cacophony of competing claims). In contrast, the canonical approach "reckons that the final form is itself a statement, fully competent to judge and constrain the prehistory" (101). "The final form—because it is not simply the most recent level of tradition, but is the aggregation of the entire history of the text's development, now in a given form—has a claim to our greatest attention" (102).[19] As a consequence of such approaches, fresh possibilities for considering coherence in Agur's words begin to emerge. Here I will engage the work of Leo G. Perdue and Ellen F. Davis, both of whom wrote commentaries targeted in the first instance toward the pastor or lay reader rather than the scholar. Because of the concerns of their audience, Perdue and Davis are both attuned to theological and literary aspects of coherence in the text that historical critics either minimize or overlook.[20] Still, as we will see,

---

19. Childs (1979, 556–57) briefly gives Prov 30:5–6 pride of place in his own comments on the canonical shaping of the book of Proverbs.

20. Earlier commentaries with mandates similar to Perdue and Davis's exhibit the same qualities (e.g., Fritsch and Schloerb 1955; or Kidner 2008 [1964]). For an analogous commentary from the nineteenth century, before the rise of the wisdom genre, consider Bridges 1847.

there are significant differences in how Perdue and Davis develop their readings, particularly when it comes to their engagement with historical questions. My principal concern, however, is to consider what possibilities Perdue and Davis open up for us in terms of reading Agur's words as a coherent collection.

2.2.2.1. Leo G. Perdue

Like McKane's, Perdue's reading depends on a particular construal of the relationship of Agur's words to historical reconstructions of wisdom traditions and prophetic schools in distinction from one another. Perdue opens his comments with a discussion of date and provenance. He is circumspect, but ultimately willing to triangulate the chapter geographically, temporally, and theologically. Everything hinges on משא: "either a term for 'oracle' or 'word' or the name of an Arabian tribe of Massa located to the east" (Perdue 2000, 251). Perdue feels that the content of the first four verses negates the possibility that משא "refers to prophetic, ecstatic speech" because these verses appear to deny the possibility of "special, revealed knowledge of God" (252). And so Agur becomes the Massaite. For Perdue, this designation is enough to locate Agur in the Transjordan as a member of a seminomadic Arabian tribe mentioned in Assyrian sources (251). He then reasons that the earliest date of composition is the eighth century BCE and the latest date of inclusion in the book of Proverbs is the early Persian period (252). This sociocultural background unmoors the theology of Agur's words from the theology of Israel's traditions in the Hebrew Bible because its origins lie elsewhere. The question, then, of how far Agur's words extend is basically answered, because in 30:5–6 "a pious sage, probably a later redactor," speaks to rebuke the "cynical sage," Agur (259).

Although Perdue (2000, 262) is clear that Agur's words extend only to verse 4, he is nevertheless satisfied to call the whole chapter "the collection of Agur" when he turns to discuss the numerical sayings. Again, the sayings seem to be united by their form rather than by their content (261). Material that does not gel in terms of form indicates the work of a redactor. Perdue does not see this as something he needs to argue for; variance in form sufficiently establishes redaction. Perdue briefly describes the numerical sayings, calling them a "traditional wisdom form" (261), but he does not discuss the form's development or hypothetical oral prehistory. Rather, the numerical sayings seem to be indirect redactional comments on Agur's theology similar to the way that 30:5–6 are a direct response to it (265). In a short reflection on the theology of the third numerical saying (30:22–23), Perdue suggests that in "this redactional setting" the saying does *not* "reinterpret" Agur as a radical skeptic who denies God or any possibility of knowing him (265). It merely shows Agur to be a humble man, untrained by the wisdom schools, who has nevertheless arrived at the conclusion that hubris drives the human quest for divine mastery and wreaks havoc on the social order.

In his final analysis, Perdue combines insights on the composition of the chapter with reflections on its theological message. He believes the "collection was built up over several centuries, beginning with the assertion of an Eastern man who, while not schooled in wisdom, claimed to possess a limited knowledge based on his own observations and conclusions" (267). For Agur, God is not directly accessible to humans either through prophetic speech or through the overconfident observations of the sages (267). Several layers were added to Agur's assertion by accretion: a pious response in verses 5–6, a prayer in verses 7–9, four sayings illustrating categories of wickedness (30:11–14) and five numerical sayings (30:15–16, 18–19, 22–23, 24–28, 29–31). Other redactional material framing the whole was added in verses 10, 17, 20. Proverbs 30:32–33 is also the work of a redactor who provides "a summarizing teaching" that functions to draw the whole chapter together (253). "Thus the sages would have agreed with Agur about the danger of pride and its associated vices, but they disagreed that they could not come to a divine revelation" (267). Although there is no clear timeline here and no way to determine how long this process took or how many hands were involved, Perdue recognizes a redactional strategy in the chapter that makes sense of dubbing it a collection. The proper response of the wise person is to stand silent before the majesty of the Creator and to reject arrogance and pride. For Perdue, Agur's voice is incorporated critically, but appreciatively, into the Israelite wisdom tradition. Later redactional material notwithstanding, the intended message for the reader is the appropriation of that critique.

2.2.2.2. Ellen F. Davis

For Davis, by contrast, historical-critical reconstructions of the date and provenance of the chapter play a small role. At the top of her interpretation, she acknowledges that Agur and Jakeh (30:1) are not Hebrew names, that the name YHWH is used just once in the chapter (30:9), and that calling Agur's speech "an oracle" (נאם), which connects him to Balaam, may all suggest that Agur is not an Israelite (Davis 2000, 138). But even if he is a foreign sage, Davis argues, "the chapter has been given an Israelite cast" being "full of echoes from other parts of the Bible" (138). Davis pivots then to address the issue of the chapter's unity as a literary whole. In making her case she focuses not on formal features but on tone, theme, and theology. She points out the numerical sayings not so much for their form as for the way they summarize "careful reflection" on the natural and social worlds in "sweeping statements" (138). The tone of the whole is "pervaded by a sense of wonder" and "a sly sense of humor." Moreover, she considers the location of Prov 30 *within* the book of Proverbs more broadly. Perhaps, she muses, "The collection seems to have been placed here at the end to lend humility to the whole enterprise of gaining wisdom" (138).

Davis's approach offers a positive spin on Agur's theology in 30:2–4. Like Perdue, she aligns Agur's perspective with Job and Ecclesiastes but situates it *within* the wisdom tradition of the Hebrew Bible as a self-correction rather than a debate *between* irreconcilable approaches. The contrast she establishes is between the broader Mesopotamian literature (such as the Dialogue of Pessimism), on the one hand, and the perspective of the Hebrew Bible on the other. According to Davis, in the Mesopotamian tradition rhetorical questions like those in Prov 30:4 lead to despair, while for Agur, within a context that includes the Psalms and Job, these questions must lead to God. Unsurprisingly, Davis does not read 30:5–6 as a rebuttal of verses 2–4 but rather "the traditional language of Israel's faith provides the substance of Agur's affirmation" (140). On a theological level, then, Davis sees the prayer in verses 7–9 as intimately connected to what precedes it because it drives toward an ethic that rejects false speech and pride. Such vices lead away from God.

When she examines the material in verses 11–33, Davis sees two broad units. The first unit (30:11–17) is again united by tone and framed by the topic of children who scorn their parents in verses 11 and 17 (142). The second unit (30:18–33) is characterized by numerical sayings and a stance of wonder toward the natural world, although it is admittedly less integrated than the rest of the chapter (145). Davis includes no discussion of the numerical saying as a form. In approaching both sections, Davis frames questions that hold together the various themes in driving at the theological substance. "In order to understand the unit as a whole," she writes concerning 30:11–17, "it is necessary to ask if there is any relation between the two main sins treated here: contempt of parents and insatiable greed?" (143). By drawing on other texts within Israel's scriptures, she suggests these sins are indeed linked. Showing contempt for parents is a way of despising our past, "taking ourselves as the beginning of history." This inflated view of oneself leads to an extreme form of arrogance that cannot even see the needy but grabs all goods in sight (see 30:13; Davis 2000, 143). Davis concludes, "Forming a living, respectful connection with the past—this is one avenue of healing from greed" (144). For Davis, Agur's chapter is perhaps structurally loose but formulated tightly around a set of theological concerns that are articulated in the first six verses. She does not find these concerns to be irreconcilable with broader wisdom traditions or with the rest of the Hebrew Bible. Agur speaks with a distinctive if somewhat elusive voice.

2.2.2.3. Summary

Although Davis and Perdue pursue their readings in different ways, one notable feature sets them apart from what has gone before: both scholars find a coherent message in Prov 30. For Perdue the chapter's message is bound up with the redactional layers of the text, which can be helpfully delineated on the basis of theological expression and formal considerations. The voices in the text create a dialogue on the nature of wisdom and revelation, humility and hubris. Generally speaking, Davis finds the same themes at work in the text but she associates the text with one voice, which she is happy to attribute to Agur. Still, much continuity with readings from the nineteenth and twentieth centuries remain—Agur is a foreigner and his words, to a greater or lesser extent, challenge traditional wisdom ideas. And yet, Perdue and Davis show a renewed interest in describing the theology, ethics, and themes of the text because historical questions no longer dominate their interpretations of the chapter as in Ewald, Delitzsch, Toy, Gemser, Sauer, and McKane. This shift offers new potential for finding coherence in Agur's words.

2.2.3. Interpretive Possibilities: Voice, Tone, and Themes

In view of the various ways Agur's words have been read, certain interpretive possibilities remain to be explored more fully. These possibilities largely concern the interplay of voice, tone, and themes in the text. With reference to written poetry, tone has come to refer "to those aspects of written lang. that are neither lexical nor syntactical, but that appear, at least at first, somewhat intangibly, as a quality of the text as a whole, or of a significant part of it" (Marno 2012, 1441).[21] This can be associated with "the mood or general atmosphere of the written text," but drawing on its origins in classical rhetoric tone often reflects personal attitudes—whether of the author or the implied speaker—including an awareness of how audiences might respond to a discourse (1441). Accordingly, tone tends to correlate with genre. So, for example, a lament psalm, such as Ps 88, might be said to have an anguished or despairing tone; whereas psalms of praise, such as Pss 145–150, might be seen as joyous or exuberant. Tone in prophetic discourses shuttles between blessings and curses: Ezekiel 16 is vulgar and scathing, but Isa 40 is famously consoling and confident. Indeed, the tone of the priestly creation account in Gen 1:1–2:3, which could easily be construed as grand, majestic, composed, or even liturgical, is one of the features that sets it apart from Gen 2:4–25. The tone of Gen 2–3, by contrast, might rather be described as earthy, mythological, or perhaps nostalgic. While these examples are clear enough, tone can be highly contested. Because biblical texts are recorded in writing and we cannot see or hear how they might have been performed, determining tone is a subjective judgment that can only be based on close reading and comparative analysis.[22] Such evaluations depend, as in David Marno's definition above, on an intangible "quality of the text as a whole." Because tone adheres in texts rather than words or syntax, determining tone is a process of delicate exegetical work that must necessarily start with words and grammar as it builds up to a reading that takes account of everything from diction and pragmatics to context. The interpreter builds a cumulative case for tone by attending to such features of the text as subject matter, word choice, paronomasia, pacing, voice, repetition, and imagery, among others.

Nearly every commentator on Prov 30 touches on tone and voice, but most do so in passing rather than paying the issues sustained attention. So for Ewald, the chapter contains a debate between a skeptical voice and a

---

21. The concept of tone in poetry is a metaphor since the literal sense in classical rhetoric was derived from music and referred to the actual pitch, intensity, loudness, or inflection of the voice in oral delivery. This usage connects back to the Greek τόνος, i.e., "stretching" (Marno 2012, 1441). For Aristotle tone was wrapped up with how the human voice could embody the proper emotions (see *Rhet.* 3.1, 7).

22. One can imagine an actor reading out the book of Qohelet or Job 38 to dramatically different effects. See further my discussion of tone in Job 38 at §4.2.2.2.

pious interlocutor both penned by the poet. For McKane, however, Agur's voice is isolated in 30:1-4. He finds these verses exhibit "a mock ruefulness" and ought to be read as a "cry of despair," while the sentiments of 30:5-9 are pious and sincere (McKane 1970, 646). Davis, however, sees no reason to posit a change of speaker at all, because she senses a consistent tone throughout. The question of voice, then, is largely bound up with the question of tone, since, for many scholars, shifts in tone represent dividing lines between speakers. By increasing and decreasing the sarcasm or the sincerity of one verse or another—like radio operators tuning for a signal—interpreters can hear this text as everything from a unified discourse to a sharp debate, or from piety to skepticism (Franklyn 1983). In short, tone colors content.

Moreover, how scholars understand the coherence of the chapter tends to be bound up with how they construe Agur's voice. For those scholars who find no meaningful coherence, Agur's voice is characterized as dissonant. Though it may unify the first half of the chapter, if only as a debate between conflicting viewpoints, it does not extend beyond verse 14 on any account. This approach was seen in the work of Ewald, Toy, Gemser, and McKane. For those scholars who do find coherence in the chapter, Agur's voice suggests a unified collection. The nature of this unity, however, is often somewhat superficial. Thus, for Delitzsch, the whole chapter ought to be attributed to Agur, but this does not bear on his interpretation substantially—Agur's collection is a miscellany. Far from being a secondary concern in the interpretation of the chapter, the relationship of tone and voice might ascend to the level of a hermeneutical key.

One noteworthy aspect of Agur's tone that many scholars have mentioned but none addresses in a direct or sustained way is humor. Many commentators explain 30:1-4 with recourse to sarcasm. Ewald (1837, 169) understands the numerical sayings to be witticisms. Toy (1899, 530) is happy to refer to them as "satirical and descriptive;" he calls 30:21-23 in particular "humorous or whimsical" (532). McKane (1970, 659) notes this comment with approval. Davis (2000, 138) goes so far as to say the whole chapter "is pervaded by ... a sly sense of humor." Picking up these threads, I will pursue the idea that humorous elements characterize Agur's tone throughout.

When it comes to themes, a number of scholars find unity in the material that encourages attempts to read the whole in a coherent manner. For example, Sauer (1963, 111) connects 30:32-33 with verses 1-4 and summarizes the theme of the whole according to the experience of Agur, "who has come to realize the frailty of man, measured against God's omnipotence." Likewise, Perdue locates the chapter's agenda in rejecting arrogance. Davis (2000, 138), however, gives the thematic unity of the chapter its most robust articulation when she identifies "a keen awareness of the limits of human understanding" operating "to lend humility to the whole enterprise of gaining wisdom."[23]

Such thematic approaches, however, have not convinced the guild, and they raise significant questions. Sauer's reading is underdeveloped and dubiously grounded in a form-critical approach to Ugaritic material that has not won any followers. Perdue's reading is heavily informed by critical approaches but remains fundamentally thematic and does not develop its philological moves in any detail. As such, it is grounded in assumptions about wisdom literature that are becoming more and more problematic. Davis's short reading, likewise, is pitched for the nonspecialist and is fundamentally theological in its approach. She does not work out the philology in support of her reading. In sum, thematic approaches have been underdeveloped by scholars. The general sense, which has been largely assumed rather than stated, is that seriously undertaking the philology would inevitably lead one to see incoherence in the text.[24]

Against the backdrop of the eroding consensus about wisdom literature, issues surrounding voice, tone, and themes encourage us to give Agur a fresh hearing. These aspects of the text have been unevenly addressed by scholars, but attending to them closely might offer an approach to the central hermeneutical questions from within, as it were. One of my goals in

---

23. Davis's approach to the chapter holds, in my view, the most promise, and, in the chapters that follow, my reading will take a line similar to hers on many points. It is important to note that, alongside Davis, there are other interpreters who have given the chapter a compelling literary and theological account. In place of Davis, I might have included the work of Yoder (2009a, 2009b) or O'Dowd (2017), among others. Their audience and approach, however, are similar to Davis's and, although they have many theological and literary insights, their readings also lack critical and philological development. Still, they have been constructive conversation partners throughout this study.

24. Waltke (2005) and Steinmann (2001, 2009) are notable exceptions. Their readings, however, rely on intricate structural patterning in the chapter, which I find to be a less-compelling basis for the coherence of Agur's words than voice, tone, and themes (see the comments in Fox 2009, 846). Nevertheless, Waltke's reading in particular was a generative starting point for my investigation and shares many points in common with my own.

this study is to show that theological and philological approaches need not be at odds, but that a reading that finds coherence in the collection can be firmly grounded in robust philological work. Indeed, given the philological puzzles, verbal dissonance, and general eccentricities of the text, these issues demand a thorough treatment. Over the next three chapters, I will attempt to set aside certain scholarly assumptions about wisdom literature and form criticism, while still dealing with philological challenges posed by the text in a rigorous manner. In doing so, I have endeavored to give Prov 30 a fresh hearing on its own terms as a coherent collection voiced by Agur. Part of my contention is that reading Agur's words as a coherent text is not simply a canonical or a final-form reading, but that by setting aside certain scholarly presuppositions and engaging the philological questions anew, we might arrive at a fresh reading that is more historically faithful rather than less.

3
Reframing Agur's Words: Reading Proverbs 30:1 as the Superscript of a Collection

3.1. Burdened with Many Problems

Over the next three chapters, I will develop a reading of Prov 30 as a coherent, anthological collection. In chapter 1, I argued that, because Proverbs is carefully structured by a series of seven headings, the superscript preserved in 30:1 plays an important role in marking out the chapter as a collection within the book. I also proposed that we might helpfully imagine Agur as an eccentric sage, the voice animating the collection, and it is in the superscript that we meet Agur. The superscript of any text carries crucial interpretive information that frames the way it is read, such as genre, authorship, speaking voice, tone, audience or addressee, historical provenance, and setting. A philological reading that endeavors to take the text seriously on its own terms as an artifact must wrestle with these considerations. Attempting to read Prov 30, then, as a coherent text and a discrete collection amounts to taking the superscript in verse 1 with full imaginative seriousness as an editorial frame.

In Prov 30, however, reading, much less interpreting, the superscript is no simple task. As Richard Clifford (1999, 256) puts it, "Verse 1 is textually damaged beyond sure recovery and its uncertainty taints the whole passage." Truly, the textual problems in the second half of the verse are nearly inscrutable, leading McKane (1970, 644) to despair: "Where there is hardly a glimmer of light, one feels powerless to make even the first move towards its elucidation." But the obscurities are exegetical as well as textual. Even where the text is secure, as in Agur's name or the phrases המשא ("an oracle," NRSV) and נאם הגבר ("thus says the man," NRSV), its translation and connotations remain matters of dispute. In Otto Plöger's (1984, 358) laconic formulation, verse 1 is "burdened with many problems."

How we make sense of the challenges inherent in this verse will frame how we approach the whole collection. There are at least three major philological questions facing us. The first question is about the name Agur Bin-Yakeh itself. What does this name suggest? Does it tell us anything about who Agur is or where he comes from? How might it color our reading of the collection attributed to him? The second question deals with the word *maśśā'* (משא) and its relationship to genre. There is general disagreement in the scholarly literature as to whether this word introduces the text as a prophetic discourse ("oracle" or "utterance"), or whether it introduces Agur as a sage from *Maśśā'*. Is the discourse term at all appropriate in this context and, if so, what does it connote? The third challenge, a nearly unreadable string of letters, is perhaps the most obscure of all: לאיתיאל לאיתיאל ואכל ("to Ithiel, to Ithiel and Ucal," NJPS). While this text has come to be treated as a series of proper names suggesting the addressees of the collection, it has almost certainly become corrupt. In all likelihood it contains the beginning of Agur's words, but what is the nature of this opening? Can we discern a meaningful start to his discourse in these letters?

The hermeneutical capital that 30:1 holds and the philological challenges with which it is burdened encourage us to spend significant energies here. In what follows, I offer a series of three essays working through each of these philological issues in turn with an eye toward their significance for understanding Prov 30 as a collection. I will argue that Agur's name encourages us to read him as the persona of a sage, that משא ought to be read as a discourse term whose primary connotations relate to tone and purpose and that 30:1b may open the collection on a note of intense exasperation.

3.2. Invoking Agur

The first philological challenge we face is the name Agur Ben-Yakeh itself and what associations, if any, it is meant to evoke. This is indeed a philological problem because this mysterious sage is completely unknown to us apart from this passage. Broadly speaking, there are two approaches to his name in the history of interpretation. The first approach sees Agur Bin-Yakeh as a straightforward proper name, usually attributed to a non-Israelite, while the second approach sees Agur Bin-Yakeh as an allegorical cypher for Solomon. There are variations and twists on both approaches, and I will attempt to chart a way through each in turn.

3.2.1. The Philology of a Name

The first approach is characterized by attention to the Hebrew etymology of the name within its ancient Semitic context. The root of the name appears to be אגר ("to gather," BDB, s.v. "אגר"), a verb that occurs just three times in the Hebrew Bible and nowhere else in ancient Hebrew literature. All of these examples refer to gathering during harvest and two of them feature in Proverbs, positively associated with wise behavior (Prov 6:8; 10:5; Deut 28:39). Since the root is more widely attested in Ugaritic and Aramaic dialects and clearly related to day-labor, wages, and farming, it is probably better to think less of "gathering" generally and more narrowly of something like "harvesting."[1] If we relate אָגוּר in the present verse to this root, then it is either a *qal* passive participle or a nominal formed on the *qatūl* pattern.[2] "Yaqeh," on the other hand, appears to come from √יקה. Another rare root, it shows up only twice in the word יְקָהָה ("obedience," Gen 49:10; Prov 30:17, see appendix at v. 17: לִיקֲהַת). As pointed here, יָקֶה could theoretically be a third-person mascular single *qal qatal*, but more likely it is a *qatal* pattern substantive.[3] Delitzsch (1875, 261) compares the sense of יקה to שמר ("to keep, guard"). Significantly, neither אגור nor יקה feature as a name in any other ancient Hebrew text.

To fill this lacuna, scholars turn to Israel's Northwest Semitic neighbors. The idea that Agur is a foreign wise man has been appealing to many scholars (e.g., Crenshaw 1995, 372; Weis 1986, 375; Franklyn 1983, 239; Sauer 1963, 94–95; Montgomery 1934; 171–72). Boldly, William Albright (1956, 7) claims, "Disregarding the vowels, 'GR and YQH are both well documented in North and South-Arabian inscriptions of the first millennium B.C." Indeed, G. Lankester Harding's (1971, 22, 648, 681) concordance of pre-Islamic Arabian names does list numerous attestations of nominals built from roots that could be cognate (e.g., 'JR, WQH, YQHMLK). Likewise, the name appears to be present in multiple Ugaritic texts, perhaps connected to the meaning "hireling, labourer" (see *DULAT*, s.v. "'-g-r"; Watson 1990, 114; 2003, 244). While these data establish clearly that Agur *could* be a foreign name, it falls far short of proving that Agur *is* a foreign name. And, with

---

1. See *HALOT*, s.v. "אגר," "to gather, pile up;" and cf. Jastrow 1903, s.v. "אגר"; *DNWSI*, s.v. "אגר," 1:10–12; *DULAT*, s.v. "'-g-r."

2. Joüon §88 E.c.; e.g., יָקוּשׁ "fowler," שָׁבוּר "breaking," חָרוּץ "mutilation," i.e., rare cases, action nouns.

3. Joüon §88 D.a. and 96 B.f.; e.g., יָפֶה "beautiful," שָׂדֶה "field," קָנֶה "reed," מָנֶה "weight."

possible origins in Ugaritic or Old South Arabian, we have not narrowed down an interpretive context or supplied anything really helpful by way of background information (see Toy 1899, 518–19). The important thing may simply be that *Agur* sounds foreign, perhaps Eastern to boot (1 Kgs 4:30).

The second approach is characterized by attention to the Hebrew etymology of the name as mediated by the versions and rabbinic exegesis. In his commentary on Prov 30:1, Rashi interprets the names according to their roots in a midrashic manner, which he applies to Solomon as a relative clause: "The words of Solomon who gathered understanding and vomited it" (דברי שלמה שאגר את הבינה והקיאה). In Rashi's exegesis, each element of the name Agur Bin-Yakeh takes on a symbolic meaning rooted in the letters and applied to Solomon. In keeping with the Biblical Hebrew usage and clear Aramaic cognates discussed above, אגור is connected to the idea of gathering, but יקה is connected to √קיא ("to vomit") rather than obedience. Interestingly, even בן ("son") is connected to √בין ("understanding"). Perhaps this is due to the rare pointing the word exhibits here with *hireq* (בִּן) rather than the expected *tsere* (בֵּן). In commenting on Deut 25:2, Ibn Ezra notes this spelling and relates it to יהושע בִּן־נון ("Joshua son of Nun," twenty-five times), as well as the present verse and a few other rare examples that use בן to classify a type (1 Sam 25:17; Jonah 4:10).

Rashi's exegesis does not come to us out of the blue, but is clearly connected to an established interpretive tradition. Thus Midr. Tanh. (Vaera 5:2), "Why was he named Agur? Because he stored up [אגר] knowledge of the Torah and wisdom. And the son of Yakeh? Because he vomited it up [קיא]." Exodus Rabbah (6:1) is similar, "the words of him who assembled the words of the Law and vomited them forth" (quoted in Gordon 1930, 411; see also Song Rab. 1.1.10; Eccl. Rab. 1.1.2; b. Sanh. 70b). Whether the idea of vomiting up words of wisdom carries a positive or a negative sense seems ambiguous. The positive sense would be regurgitating this teaching, that is, writing it down in a book for the instruction of others (see Ibn Ezra on Prov 30:1 and Rashi on Eccl 1:1). The negative sense, in contrast, would be rejecting the teaching with a high hand of hubris (as in Midrash Tanhuna, and Rashi on Eccl 1:17). Ecclesiastes Rabbah (1.1.2) illustrates the tension here nicely, "He was called 'Jakeh' because he discharged (*meki'*) words [of wisdom] like a bowl that is filled at one time and emptied at another time; similarly did Solomon learn Torah at one time and forget it at another time" (Cohen 1951, 3–4). Midrash Mishle presents a variation on this theme by connecting all the names in Prov 30:1 to Solomon, but giving each one a positive allegorical meaning: "*Agur*—he who girded (*'agur*) his loins for wisdom; *son of Jake* (*yaqeh*)—a son who is free (*naqi*) from all sin and transgressions" (Visotzky 1992, 117; emphasis original). Finally, in the masora parva, the Masoretes draw lines between אגור and √גור ("to fear") via Deut 32:27, as well as יקה and √קיה ("to vomit") via Jonah 2:11. The Masoretes thus illustrate the kinds of connections that lie behind this method of interpretation.[4]

While this midrashic approach is likely a later interpretive tradition that has developed, either to make sense of foreign, unknown names, or to bring the whole book under Solomonic hegemony, it is nevertheless very ancient in its own right. We know this because the Vulgate (V), and to a lesser extent G, witness to it. In place of אגור בן־יקה, V reads "*verba Congregantis filii Vomentis*" ("the words of Gatherer the son of Vomiter"), reflecting the same etymological exegesis as Midrash Tanhuma, Rashi, and the rest. By comparison to the citations above, Jerome is clearly aware of this rabbinic approach to our verse, perhaps even our earliest witness to it (Barthélemy 2015, 774–775; Gordon 1930, 411). In many ways, the Greek reflects a departure from this tradition:

Τοὺς ἐμοὺς λόγους, υἱέ, φοβήθητι
καὶ δεξάμενος αὐτοὺς μετανόει·
τάδε λέγει ὁ ἀνὴρ τοῖς πιστεύουσιν θεῷ, καὶ παύομαι·
My son, fear my words,
and repent when you receive them;
this is what the man says to those who believe in God: Now I stop.
(NETS)

At first glance this appears to have practically no connection to the Hebrew; however, most scholars find correspondences for all the major elements based on etymological exegesis:[5]

---

4. In an idiosyncratic modern extension of this type of reading, Skehan (1971, 42–43) finds √גור ("to sojourn") behind אגור, connecting this name to the idea of mortality. Via Prov 30:4, Agur, the son, is then connected to Jacob/Israel (Prov 30:4; Gen 28:12–13; Exod 4:22; Deut 32:19; Wis 10:10). If Agur is Israel then Yakeh, the father, must refer in some way to God. Skehan (43) suggests that יקה is an acronym for "*YHWH qādôš hû*'." This ingenious idea never caught on, although Murphy (1998, 229) cites it approvingly and O'Dowd (2018, 112–14) develops a similar line of thought.

5. This may be an extreme instance of the overall translation character of G Proverbs, which Fox (2014a, 16–17) has described as "flexible" for the sake of "control;" and Forti (2017, 254) has described as "free and even periphrastic." It remains a matter

דברי	Τοὺς ἐμοὺς λόγους (with a different vocalization, e.g., דְּבָרַי)
אגור	φοβήθητι (reading as √גור, "to fear")
בן	υἱέ
יקה	δεξάμενος (reading as √לקח, "to take")
המשא	μετανόει (possibly associating via √נשא with the idea of repentance, e.g., Isa 33:24; Ps 32:1; Fox 2015, 379)
נאם הגבר	τάδε λέγει ὁ ἀνὴρ (taking נאם verbally, cf. Jastrow 1903, s.v. "נאם")
לאיתיאל (1x)	τοῖς πιστεύουσιν θεῷ (periphrastic, reading ל + את + י + אל = "to me is God," cf. Neh 11:7)
ואכל	καὶ παύομαι (reading as √כלה, "to complete, finish")

While these connections are compelling enough, I am skeptical that they give us any real insight into G's thought process. We do not know to what extent G's *Vorlage* matched what we have in MT. Nevertheless, given what we can see, G's approach seems cousin to the rabbinic impulse to connect all the names in the text to Solomon. But rather than interpreting the names as cyphers for Solomon, G seems to have enterprisingly read the verse as a sentence thereby removing any reference to an author at all. Again, either G has here adopted a free hand in rendering the text, or G has a *Vorlage* differing in significant details from MT. The Vulgate therefore serves as a valuable spotting flag, marking an underground line that connects the tradition witnessed to by G's obscurantist approach to the names of 30:1 and the later rabbinic exegetical tradition that interprets those names as appellatives for Solomon. If the impulse of this tradition stretches back all the way to the Greek, which some scholars believe represents a different and probably older recension of the book than we have in MT (Tov 1990; Aitken and Cuppi 2015, 342), then it could suggest that Agur Ben-Yakeh was originally a composite sage, a literary figure to serve as the source of a strange collection of wise sayings. Thus "Agur Ben-

---

of debate, however, to what extent G is working from a different *Vorlage* (Tov 1990; Cuppi 2011, 92), or carrying out a quasi-authorial agenda (Cook 1997; Waltke 2005, 454 n. 1). In either case, G represents a different recension of the book of Proverbs. On the relationship of G Proverbs to MT consider the works above, as well as those mentioned in §1.2.4. n. 21.

Yakeh" would essentially function as Qoheleth—a Solomon-evoking pen name (cf. Rashi on Eccl 1:1). At first, the Aramaic targum (T) and Syriac Peshitta (S) might appear to depart from this fairly uniform tradition by leaving אגור בן־יקה untouched. But we should be careful because this does not mean that T and S rule out the rabbinic interpretation—indeed, they may assume it—they simply do not see the need to alter or embellish MT in order to draw it out.

It is easy enough to imagine how the interpretive tradition could have transformed the name of an unknown, possibly foreign sage into the renowned King Solomon—particularly as later recensions of the book and the canonical process consolidated around his divine wisdom (Cuppi 2011, 92–93). It is less easy, although not entirely implausible, to imagine that the figure of Agur was originally intended as a coded reference to Solomon. In that case we ought to ask why Solomon, who is already named in three other passages of the book (1:1; 10:1; 25:1), would go under a pen name? On the whole, therefore, I am drawn to think that Agur is best imagined as a foreign sage espousing faith in the God of Israel. I base this on the Northwest Semitic links to his name, the parallel with Lemuel in Prov 31, the content of Prov 30 generally, and the greater plausibility that Agur became associated with Solomon than that Solomon is here writing under a pseudonym. However, we should not rule out the distinct possibility that this foreign sage is a literary creation. Toy's (1899, 519) comparison to Job is apt: "a man ... famous in tradition, and taken by some later writer as his mouthpiece for the expression of philosophic thought." Etymologically, both "hireling" and "harvester" are possible but difficult to choose between, not least because the senses are probably related and overlapping. For "Yaqeh," I think the strongest etymology is found in a connection to obedience. However, we must bear in mind that *if* this is truly the name of a foreign sage, then it is likely that no particular meaning is intended—any more than most modern parents intend in Alexander the meaning "defender of man."[6] If this is the name of a literary construct of a foreign sage, however, then an ancient Israelite poet may well have intended something like "Harvester born of obedience." The harvesting involved could be the collection of wise sayings (Prov 25:1; 1 Kgs 4:29–34). This appellation bears some analogy to קהלת (Qoheleth),

---

6. Greek: Ἀλέξανδρος, from ἀλέξω, "to defend," and ἀνδρός, genitive of ἀνήρ, "man" (Montanari 2015, s.v. "ἀλέξανδρος" 84).

and the door would have been left standing open for the rabbinic tradition to associate such a name with Solomon.

3.2.2. Agur Bin-Yakeh as Persona

In light of the enigmatic philology and opaque historicity of Agur Bin-Yakeh, I propose that we can make the best sense of this name by applying the concept of a literary persona. The term *persona* was "originally used to denote the mask worn by an actor in Roman drama" (Izenberg 2012, 1024), but when applied to literature, especially poetry, it is a metaphor that denotes the speaking voice within a poem and distances that voice from the author or poet who created the work (Maxwell 2007, 260).[7] The category of persona is beneficial for thinking about Agur's role in Prov 30 precisely because it is nearly impossible—philologically or otherwise—to provide any surefooted historical data about him. He remains a name in a superscript and we know him only through his words as contained in these thirty-three verses. As Nathan Dean Maxwell (2007, 93) explains, this is precisely where the concept of persona can be helpful: "The idea of drawing a line of separation or distinction between historical author and literary voice is significant because it means that a poem's speaker is hermeneutically bound to the text, in the sense that it relies on the world of the poem rather than the reader's knowledge of or access to the historical author. In short, a persona is predicated by the world of the poem, not by its author."

Reading Agur as a persona is not then an ahistorical reading nor even a final-form reading. As Richard Briggs (2021, 42–43) remarks, the category of persona enables the scholar "to take the best of the historical specificity of an author focus and to reconstrue it in terms of the text in front of us." Treating Agur as a persona means that we take him seriously as the voice animating the text and that we locate him within the world of the text with its language, symbols, and beliefs, without necessarily making historical claims about how the text was authored or redacted. Again, Qoheleth is a helpful analogy. The quest for the historical Qoheleth and the question of

---

7. In biblical studies, the idea of persona has been constructively applied to Jeremiah by Polk (1984) and to Qoheleth and Song of Songs by Fox (1977 and 1985). More recently, Maxwell's (2007) unpublished dissertation on the Psalms provides the most helpful and fully developed approach to persona in biblical studies, while Briggs (2021, 35–48) presents a helpful application of the concept to a reading of Ps 23.

whether that figure ought to be associated with Solomon—whether historically or by legend—can serve to distract from and distort the literary portrait of Qoheleth within the book (Weeks 2012, 42–43). At any rate, we have no access to Qoheleth apart from Ecclesiastes. Indeed, recent scholarship has increasingly drawn attention to the fact that Qoheleth, not to mention the narrator who frames his words in 1:1–2 and 12:9–14, may well be literary personas of the author (Fox 1977; Weeks 2012, 13–19). In the same way, we cannot know whether Agur was a historic individual, whether he uttered or wrote down all or any of what we find in Prov 30, who the author or editor of the collection as we have it was, and whether that author or editor created Agur out of whole cloth to voice this collection.[8] Given that he is located in the superscript of the chapter we can imagine him as the animating voice behind the collection in the way that we imagine Solomon animating Prov 10–22 or Qoheleth animating the monologue from Eccl 1:3–12:8. Although it must remain mysterious, the evocation of this name and the associations it creates may be something of a genre tag in and of itself. If Agur's name suggests associations of teaching or gathering, if it sounds foreign, perhaps eastern, and if it is somewhat enigmatic, then we might expect to find an eccentric collection of wise sayings to which we might give heed.[9] Agur Ben-Yakeh would seem to be that kind of name and his collection is that kind of thing.

3.3. What Might משא Mean?

The only thing we can relate to Agur beyond the philology of his name is this collection of sayings. The name Agur Bin-Yakeh is inseparable from the discourse term "words of" (דברי) to which it is bound. Although *words* is practically the most general term for speech that we have in ancient Hebrew, it is set in apposition to two more apparent discourse terms that

---

8. Again, we should not forget that G Proverbs has the same material as MT Proverbs but without mention of Agur. If G Proverbs represents an earlier redaction of the book, as some scholars hold, then Agur would appear to be a creation of the redactors of MT Proverbs. If, however, MT represents the earlier redaction, then later editors, or the translator of G, saw fit to erase his voice thereby assimilating his collection to Solomon's voice. It is possible that no actual obfuscation was intended since these tradents may have already viewed Agur as a cipher for Solomon.

9. Proverbs 30:1, of course, could hardly have been intended to mean anything apart from the other superscripts of the book (1:1; 10:1; 22:17; 24:23; 25:1; 31:1). For a helpful analogous discussion see Weeks (2020, 236–37) on Eccl 1:1.

we must think about at some length: *maśśā'* (משׂא), possibly meaning "burden" or "oracle," and "utterance" (נאם). As we will see, משׂא is the far more complicated term and נאם will ultimately help us to understand it. So, it is to משׂא and its elucidation I must now turn.

3.3.1. The Meaning of משׂא and the Question of Genre

The letters מ-שׂ-א occur sixty-nine times within the Hebrew Bible; there are nearly thirty more occurrences from Qumran, Ben Sira, and Northwest Semitic inscriptions. Most scholars divide these examples among three distinct lexemes. The entries from BDB (s.v. "מַשָּׂא") are representative:

> I-מַשָּׂא "n. pr. gent. et terr. 1. 'son' of Ishmael ... 2. realm of King Lemuel."
> II-מַשָּׂא "n. m. ... load, burden, lifting, bearing, tribute."
> III-מַשָּׂא "n. m. ... utterance, oracle."[10]

There are two clear examples of I-משׂא (Gen 25:14; 1 Chr 1:30). The rest of the biblical examples are split more-or-less evenly between II-משׂא and III-משׂא, with a handful of examples that are difficult to classify.[11] This schema, however, still raises several persistent questions. One question, which we will consider in a moment, is whether or not there is an historic relationship between the senses in II-משׂא and III-משׂא. In other words, should III-משׂא be understood as descended from or related to II-משׂא so that there may be some connotation of burden present in the name of the discourse, or are the terms unrelated so that their meanings have no hint of each other? Another related question is how we ought to understand the connotation of III-משׂא. Is there a particular form and/or content it entailed for ancient speakers? What expectations might this term raise for readers? In other words, Does משׂא denote a genre?

When it comes to Prov 30:1, scholars are not agreed even on which lexeme is present, and the question of genre is at the heart of the debates.

---

10. For the sake of clarity and space, in this section I will make reference as needed to different uses with the shorthand I-משׂא (i.e., proper name), II-משׂא (i.e., "burden, load"), and III-משׂא (i.e., "utterance, oracle"). This will help partially to avoid constantly providing glosses that preempt my analysis.

11. In my opinion, these are: Hos 8:10; Prov 30:1; 31:1; 1 Chr 15:22, 27; 2 Chr 17:11; and 19:7.

Without emendation, הַמַּשָּׂא cannot be read as I-משא (a proper name). The alternative is to read III-משא (a discourse term), however, a number of modern scholars find this reading impossible on the basis that III-משא denotes a prophetic genre. The sentiment of Delitzsch's (1875, 262) commentary from nearly a century-and-a-half ago has held sway, "This משא of prophetic utterance does not at all harmonize with the following string of proverbs." He relates משא etymologically to the idea of raising one's voice (√נשא) and asserts that by definition it entails "divine utterance," that is, "an utterance of the prophetic spirit" (261). What follows in Prov 30, however, "begins with a confession of human weakness and short-sightedness," and the proverbs therein are of human origin and "a decaying spiritual stamp" (262). Case in point of his observation is that the "authorial 'I'" emerges from the background into the foreground in this chapter. Delitzsch further argues that to call something a משא in the singular suggests a driving theme or a unifying message throughout the composition, which he cannot find in Prov 30. Finally, Delitzsch notes that משא, in the sense of a divine utterance never occurs alone but is always further specified in context. More recent commentators betray a similar thought process by giving the issue no real discussion (Toy 1899, 217; Murphy 1998 226 n. 1.a.; Clifford 1999, 260). For these scholars III-משא simply does not suit the context.

Scholars who cannot accept the discourse term often prefer to emend the text by swapping the article (-ה) for the preposition "from" (-מ) or by adding the gentilic suffix (-י) in order to read המשא as the proper name of a tribe or region (Gen 25:14; 1 Chr 1:30). After all, an old hallmark of wisdom literature is its association with foreign figures and cosmopolitan influences (1 Kgs 5:10; Job 1:1; 2:11; Whybray 1974, 57), thus many scholars find emending to I-משא more palatable than reading III-משא. Proverbs famously reworks the Sayings of Amenemope, an Egyptian text from the New Kingdom (Prov 22:17–24:22), so why not posit another foreign collection?[12] In this context, Richard Weis (1986, 377) draws our attention to a noteworthy text in Baruch:

22 οὐδὲ ἠκούσθη ἐν Χανααν οὐδὲ ὤφθη ἐν Θαιμαν, 23 οὔτε υἱοὶ Αγαρ οἱ ἐκζητοῦντες τὴν σύνεσιν ἐπὶ τῆς γῆς, οἱ ἔμποροι τῆς Μερραν καὶ Θαιμαν οἱ μυθολόγοι καὶ οἱ ἐκζητηταὶ τῆς συνέσεως ὁδὸν τῆς σοφίας

---

12. Sometimes leveraged in support of this reading is the idea that the name Agur Bin-Yakeh is not an Israelite name (Albright 1956, 6; Weis 1986, 375 n. 8; and see discussion at §3.2.1).

22 She [Wisdom] has neither been heard of in Chanaan nor been seen in Thaiman—23 nor the sons of Hagar who seek out intelligence upon the earth, the merchants of Merran and Thaiman and the story-tellers and the seekers for intelligence. (Bar 3:22–23a, NETS)

This verse is significant because it represents the only hint of a wisdom tradition associated with "the sons of Hagar," that is, Ishmael and his offspring (Gen 25:14), thus further opening the door for reading משא as a proper name.[13]

For many scholars the use of משא in Prov 31:1, where the case for reading a proper name is stronger, also strengthens the case for reading l-משא in 30:1. Transparent Aramaic words such as "my son" (ברי) and "kings" (מלכין) color the speech of Lemuel's mother giving Prov 31:1–9 an indisputably foreign flavor (31:2–3). Moreover, while it is possible to read משא as a discourse term in 31:1 in apposition to the "words of Lemuel," the syntax of the verse leans toward reading משא as a proper name.

דברי למואל מלך משא אשר־יסרתו אמו:
The words of Lemuel, king of Massa, whom his mother instructed.

Because מלך is indefinite, one would naturally read מלך משא as a bound phrase in apposition to למואל, meaning "Lemuel, King of Massa" (Fox 2009, 884). This is a standard way of applying a royal title in Biblical Hebrew. On this interpretation the relative clause that follows modifies למואל, which comports well with the semantics of "to instruct" (יסר). Elsewhere, that verb always takes the recipient of instruction as its object rather than the instruction itself. Moreover, as Weis (1986, 371) notes, would a king named nowhere else in the Hebrew Bible not be identified in some way? The versions, however, come out against this interpretation, unanimously

---

13. There are two ways to understand Bar 3:23. Either it suggests independent corroboration of a foreign wisdom tradition (cf. 1 Kgs 5:10; Jer 49:7; and Job 2:11) or it is evidence of an exegetical tradition that associated משא in Prov 30:1 (and 31:1!) with Gen 25:14 and "the sons of Hagar." Weis (1986, 377–78) favors the second option and notes that the supposedly failed hunt for wisdom in Prov 30:2–3 matches the idea expressed in Bar 3. If Weis is correct, it would not be impossible that the author of Baruch had a different text from MT, but this is conjectural and there is no clear link between the texts.

reading משא in 31:1 as a reference to prophetic speech or revelation. The Masoretes likewise accented the verse with the *atnach* on מלך, suggesting they separated מלך from משא, making the sense, "The words of Lemuel, a king, the *maśśāʾ* that his mother taught him." The picture is not crystal clear, but the proper name analysis seems more robust in 31:1 than in 30:1. For one thing, it requires no textual emendation. For many scholars, then, a proper name in Prov 31 weighs like a gravitational pull on their reading of משא in chapter 30 (Crenshaw 1995, 373).

But must we treat 31:1 and 30:1 identically? If the textual tradition has *any* integrity, the syntax of the two verses suggests we ought to read them differently. We can read *maśśāʾ* in 31:1 and "the burden" or "the oracle" in 30:1 (Fox 2009, 852; Alter 2019, 3:445 and 450). The issue, then, comes down to whether III-משא suits the genre of Prov 30. After all, this text contains some of the most distinctive and theological material in the book. If one wanted broadly to associate anything in Proverbs with prophecy, these verses would be contenders (Saur 2014; Sneed 2021).[14] But more to the point, the sense of what משא entails is nowhere near as clear as Delitzsch implies. In the remainder of this section, I will argue that if we broaden our understanding of what משא entailed for an ancient Hebrew author, Delitzsch's objection can be largely dealt with and the term may even help to illuminate the collection in terms of tone and purpose.

3.3.2. Resurveying משא

Lexicography can be likened to fence building—we cordon off pastures so that we can manage them easily.[15] Generally, such sound land management makes essential distinctions, identifies the edges of connotation and denotation and puts each to its proper use. But sometimes these fences create anachronistic conceptual barriers, leaving allotments that once

---

14. Indeed, Sneed (2018, 42; 2021, 30) calls Prov 30 and 31 "sapiential oracles" and argues for a "confluence of wisdom and prophecy" in these texts. And Kynes (2019, 171, 238) draws attention to various ways that Prov 30, or portions thereof, have been read as prophecy.

15. Lexicography lies at the root of philology—the study of words and their meanings in texts. Yet even the way that we approach this most fundamental of scholarly tasks reveals interpretive assumptions in the way that we establish comparisons. This reflects on our age and its conception of scholarship no less than on past ages. See Turner 2014, e.g., 132 and 231–35.

encompassed a diverse landscape artificially divided into tracts too small to yield a real interpretive harvest. This, I believe, is what has happened to משא. Nearly all published studies of משא as a genre fail to include examples of משא from Proverbs, Ben Sira, Qumran, or ancient inscriptions as they attempted to define a prophetic genre.¹⁶ Nonprophetic texts were ruled out a priori and then a genre called משא was constructed in such a way that they were excluded by definition. This is a classic example of circular reasoning, constraining the way the ancients use their own terms with modern ideas about genre.¹⁷ But if Prov 30:1 and other overlooked משא texts were considered examples of III-משא then this would necessarily affect the way the discourse term was conceived. What I propose, then, is a sort of philological thought experiment. What happens if we tear down the lexical fences that criss-cross משא and resurvey the terrain? What could tracing the contours of משא over hill and dale teach us about how the ancients thought about the texts they were composing? To this end, I will reassess III-משא as a discourse term with particular attention to narrative, traditional wisdom texts, and noncanonical texts. I hope especially to make it clear that the way the ancients employ this term is dynamic and versatile, cutting across modern genre divisions so that we should be reticent both about using our definitions of משא to categorize texts and our selective reading of texts to delimit משא.

3.3.2.1. Getting the Lay of the Land: The Concrete Sense and Prophetic Genre?

The concrete sense of the word משא is "burden" or "load" (II-משא), nicely illustrated by Naaman the Syrian who asks for earth from Israel equal to "the load of a pair of mules" (משא צמד־פרדים; 2 Kgs 5:17).¹⁸ This straightforward and unproblematic sense is figuratively extended to tasks and responsibilities of carrying loads or burdens (e.g., Num 4:15, 19, 24, 27, 31–32, 47, 49). Here the sense of bearing a burden approaches the idea of

---

16. Müller 1998 is the sole and partial exception.
17. More and more compelling work is rethinking genre in relationship to biblical texts; see, e.g., Newsom 2005; Weeks 2016; Najman 2017b; Kynes 2019; Vayntrub 2019; and Judd 2024.
18. Morphologically, this *maqtal* noun is derived from √נשא ("to lift, carry"), related etymologically to that which is lifted or carried (Müller 1998, 20; Joüon §88 L.e., where it is glossed "weight, burden, debt").

responsibility. It is no surprise, then, to find that משא is indeed used figuratively with just such a connotation when Moses complains to YHWH in Num 11:11 that he has done Moses evil "by setting the burden of all this people on me" (לשום את־משא כל־העם הזה עלי; see also Num 11:17; Deut 1:12; 2 Sam 15:33; 19:36).

Alongside of this concrete sense and its figurative extensions, are twenty-seven examples that apply to prophecy and are generally translated "utterance" or "oracle" (III-משא).[19] Sixteen examples appear in superscripts within prophetic books, eleven of which introduce the oracles against the nations in Isa 13–30. In these superscripts משא is nearly always the first element and is usually in construct with a place name that is the object or recipient of the prophecy. Because these sixteen superscripts form such a clear pattern they have become more-or-less definitional for III-משא and the content of the compositions they introduce has come to be understood as a prophetic genre. Indeed, much of the most intensive work that has gone into defining משא has been taken up with form-critical studies of these prophetic passages (Weis 1986; Floyd 2002, 2018; Boda 2006).

Scholars who believe III-משא denotes a prophetic genre tend, particularly in more recent scholarship, not to find any connection between II-משא and III-משא. Instead, they frequently hypothesize a distinct etymology in the idiom "to raise the voice" (נשא קול) and treat the two words as homonyms.[20] I am personally dubious about this etymology of III-משא, but we need an altogether different approach to illumine the connotations of the word.[21] For that I now turn to little-discussed examples of משא that expand our understanding of the word by blurring the lines between the concrete sense and the prophetic discourse term.

---

19. Second Kings 9:25; Isa 13:1; 14:28; 15:1; 17:1; 19:1; 21:1, 11, 13; 22:1, 23:1; 30:6; Jer 23:33–34, 36, 38; Ezek 12:10; Nah 1:1; Hab 1:1; Zech 9:1; 12:1; Mal 1:1; Lam 2:14; 2 Chr 24:27.

20. Müller (1998, 21) traces this etymology to Karl Heinrich Graf's 1862 commentary on Jeremiah. See further discussion in Stolz (1997, 271–72) and Vayntrub (2016, 631–35). For arguments supporting a relationship between II-משא and III-משא, see Gehman 1940; de Boer 1948; and Naudé 1969. For arguments that the words are entirely unrelated see McKane 1980; and Müller 1998.

21. Ultimately, this etymological approach resulted in a scholarly stalemate (cf. Stolz 1997, 773; with Müller 1998, 21) because it is rooted in conjecture and risks interpreting the actual uses of משא in their literary contexts in light of their purported histories (Boda 2006, 340).

3.3.2.2. משא in 2 Kings 9

The only example of משא within a narrative context is instructive. In 2 Kgs 9:25b–26, after Jehu has killed Ahab's son Joram, he recalls to his aide, Bidkar, Elijah's prophecy from 1 Kgs 21:19–21:

25b כי־זכר אני ואתה את רכבים צמדים אחרי אחאב אביו ויהוה נשׂא עליו את־המשא הזה: 26 אם־לא את־דמי נבות ואת־דמי בניו ראיתי אמש נאם־יהוה ושלמתי לך בחלקה הזאת נאם־יהוה ועתה שא השלכהו בחלקה כדבר יהוה:

25 Remember when you and I were riding side by side behind Ahab his father? Then YHWH lifted up this *maśśā'* against him: 26 "As surely as I saw the blood of Naboth and the blood of his sons yesterday—an oracle of YHWH—I will repay you on this plot—an oracle of YHWH." So now, carry and throw him on the plot in accordance with the word of YHWH. (2 Kgs 9:25b–26)

Jehu remembers Elijah's prophetic death sentence pronounced over Ahab and uses it to justify what could easily be construed as the murder of Joram. For Jehu, this prophetic death sentence that encodes symbolic justice is a משא. Only here in all of ancient Hebrew is a spoken משא "lifted on" someone (√נשא + על; cf. Num 11:11 above).[22] In Jer 17:21 and 27 √נשא is used with משא as its object complement to describe bearing physical burdens: "Do not bear a burden on the Sabbath day" (ואל־תשאו משא ביום השבת). In 2 Sam 15:33 and Job 7:20, משא is used of figurative burdens with על indicating the bearer of the burden (cf. Num 11:11 above). The idiom of 2 Kgs 9:25 with the verb נשא and the preposition על strongly suggests there is some conceptual overlap between II-משא and III-משא. Even though it is sometimes contested (e.g., Naudé 1969, 95), the same idiom probably pertains in 2 Chr 24:27 regarding Joash in the phrase "the *maśśā'* upon him" (המשא עליו).[23] The identical use of the preposition is the tell. Of course, it feels more natural to translate על as "against" or "concerning" in 2 Kgs 9:25,

---

22. There are, in fact, surprisingly few verses where משא is the object complement of the verb נשא: Num 11:17; Deut 1:12; 2 Kgs 9:25; and Jer 17:21, 27.

23. There are no exact parallels to 2 Kgs 9:25, but it must be remembered the majority of examples of III-משא are in superscripts where the addressee is usually indicated with a bound phrase rather than a preposition. The exceptions are Zech 9:1 (ב); 12:1 (על); and Mal 1:1 (אל).

but in light of the biblical idiom it may well picture the prophetic word laid "on" someone becoming a metaphorical burden they carry until—like Joram—it catches up to them.²⁴ In these contexts, משא comes close to how we conceptualize the word *curse*.²⁵

3.3.2.3. משא in Ben Sira

The five uses of משא in Ben Sira draw together the concepts of weight and speech in ways that do not quite match the lexica. In 6:21 wisdom is a משא that a fool refuses to carry (cf. 33:25).

כאבן משא תהיה עליו / ולא יאחר להשליכה:
Like a stone, she will be a *maśśāʾ* upon him, / and he will not hesitate to cast her away. (Sir 6:21)

It is worth meditating on this image—in what sense might wisdom prove a burden? Ben Sira develops his idea as an extended metaphor in 6:18–37. Plowing and sowing and then waiting for harvest is likened to bearing the heavy burden of wisdom (6:19, 21). If the youth seeks out and willingly bends his back to this burden its weight will transform to rest and joy (6:28–29) and its yoke (עלי) will adorn him as riches (6:30–31). Toward the end of the poem, images of labor, farming, and constraining burdens fall away and reveal themselves as thinly veiled metaphors for learning and seeking out "the fear of the Most High and his commandments" (6:37). Conceptually, then, the משא of 6:21 is connected closely with the content of wisdom, namely, every "meditation" and "proverb of understanding" (6:35).

In the final autobiographical poem, Sir 51:26 again uses משא in parallel to עלה "her yoke," that is, Wisdom's.²⁶

---

24. Something conceptually similar is probably lying behind Jer 23:31–40, which treats משא as a similarly weighty term. This highly complex passage seems to be punning on the different senses of משא. While Jeremiah could be punning on homonyms—two unrelated words that sound the same and serve the poet's purposes—could it not rather suggest that there is conceptual overlap at work? See McKane 1980 for a detailed discussion.

25. Thanks to Stuart Weeks for this acute suggestion.

26. Skehan and Di Lella (1987, 193–95) draw a line from this verse and Ben Sira's final autobiographical poem back to the poem about wisdom's yoke in Sir 6:22–31.

וצואריכם בעלה הביאו / ומשאה תשא נפשכם:
And your necks bring under her [wisdom's] yoke, / and her *maśśāʾ*
your soul will bear. (Sir 51:26)

Here the Greek text of Ben Sira has ζυγόν ("yoke") in place of על—a fairly literal equivalent. But in place of משא the Greek reads παιδείαν ("teaching, instruction").[27] The juxtaposition of these two verses from Ben Sira suggests to me that the grandfather is using II-משא figuratively but that his grandson has resolved the metaphor in Greek, understanding the burden in question to be teaching that carries a responsibility.[28]

The most obscure example of משא in Sirach is 38:2:

מאת אל יחכם רופא / ומאת מלך ישא משאות:
The physician has his wisdom from God, / but he bears his *maśśāʾ*
from the king.[29]

In this difficult verse, Tadeusz Penar (1975, 63) argues, based on the parallelism, that ישא משאות ("he bears his *maśśāʾ*") should be broadly synonymous to יחכם רופא ("the physician has his wisdom"). Noting that משא is often translated "utterance," he takes it to refer to a type of communication and translates "directions."[30] This "refers to directions about curing, which the physician receives from God" since Penar also considers God and "the king" coreferential in the verse (64). Admittedly, this verse is obscure but within the context of Ben Sira we may simply note another text where משא is not a term for prophecy but stands in parallel with terms suggesting knowledge or the content of wisdom. Indeed, it seems to me

---

27. Concerning the translation style of Ben Sira's grandson, Benjamin Wright (1989, 115) concludes, "The grandson's approach to the Hebrew seems to reflect more of a concern for the message than the medium. This is especially true of lexical representation in that *the grandson seems primarily concerned with what is communicated rather than consistency of representation*" (emphasis added; see also Wright 2011, 77).

28. In fact, the semantics of משא itself may have suggested the extended metaphor that Ben Sira expounds. This presentation is perhaps not worlds away from the prophet's extended punning on different senses of משא in Jer 23.

29. My translation is informed by Penar 1975, 63.

30. Skehan and de Lella (1987, 441) render משאות as "rewards" or "sustenance." Similar glosses have been commonly proposed for 2 Chr 17:11 and 19:7. In Phoenician, admittedly, *mšʾ* appears to mean "due" or "payment" (*DNWSI*, s.v. "mšʾ") and this meaning is not out of the question here as another metaphorical extension of II-משא.

just plausible that here again משא could connote the idea of a burden as task or responsibility, so that this verse suggests the physician's knowledge comes from God and his commission comes from the king.[31]

The final example of משא in Ben Sira perhaps most clearly denotes nonprophetic verbal material.

ביטה נורא בעד איש לשון/ ומשא על פיהו ישונא:

A gossip is feared because he is a man of the tongue, / and a *maśśāʾ* on his mouth will be hated. (Sir 9:18)

This verse is situated in a collection of proverbial advice about relationships in society—whom to interact with and how to do so. A gossip, or "a man of the tongue," who is feared and hated is contrasted with the ruler who is proved right by wisdom and judges between his people. But what might a משא on his mouth mean? It is possible to understand משא as a burden that the *gossip* hates because it restrains his speech, but I do not know of another place where the term highlights restraint. Rather, I think the parallelism suggests a type of speech, the result of a wagging tongue. The gossip is hated because he mishandles harsh words and damages his community.[32] Fox (2009, 852) admits that in this one case משא cannot refer to "a type of prophetic utterance."[33] I would argue, however, that Ben Sira usually relates משא to teaching, instruction, and speech and in none of these examples is there a prophetic connotation in view. Instead, the idea is generally of a weighty message that conveys a responsibility or burden.[34]

---

31. In rabbinic usage the phrase משא ומתן (lit. "carrying and giving") can denote "business dealings; worldly affairs" (Jastrow 1903, s.v. "משא"). My guess is that this idiom descended from the use of משא in some of the exilic and postexilic literature that refers to bearing burdens on the Sabbath (Jer 17:21–22; Neh 13:15, 19).

32. Again, cf. Jer 23:31–40.

33. At the very least Fox seems to have overlooked Sir 51:26. Sirach 6:21, it can be argued, is a literal burden used metaphorically (II-משא) while Sir 38:2 is debatable.

34. For some readers, no doubt, the appeal to Ben Sira (not to mention the Dead Sea Scrolls) will raise methodological questions about the dating of Prov 30 and the validity of these examples for understanding משא therein. There could, of course, be a diachronic shift in the semantics of משא from a certain kind of prophetic vision in Isaiah to something more generic in Ben Sira. However, the fact that the metaphorical usage of משא in Sir 6:21 and 51:26 seems to be closely connected to the concrete sense of משא in Numbers suggests to me that the senses are connected. In short, Ben Sira, although late, provides evidence that the senses of משא in Isaiah and Numbers

3.3.2.4. משא in the Dead Sea Scrolls

In the Dead Sea Scrolls, משא inhabits a different landscape, a genre-bending environment where the texts are not easy to classify. Here משא operates in a more explicitly revelatory sphere.[35] The enigmatic text known as 1Q/4QMysteries (1Q27, 4Q299–300[301?]) offers a telling example.[36] The first fragment, 1Q27, uses משא to refer to a prophetic message (1Q27 1 I, 8). A few lines before this 1Q27 describes the elimination of wickedness from the world in the way that light drives out darkness (1Q27 1 I, 5–6). This eschatological vision is described in sapiential terms: "knowledge will fill the world and foolishness will be there no longer" (1Q27 1 I, 7). The genre of this text is greatly debated. Most commentators have classified it as a wisdom text but other suggestions include apocalyptic and eschatological/prophetic (Goff 2007, 93). The reality is that 1Q/4QMysteries presents a constellation of features that are typically thought to belong to different genres. Goff identifies "practical advice," "pedagogy" and "instruction," and "rhetorical questions" (94–97). Although he wants to class 1Q/4QMysteries as a wisdom text, he admits that it "contains elements that are foreign to traditional wisdom." A parade example of such a feature is the use of משא in the passage above (94). Goff calls this "a form that is well attested in the biblical prophets" but hints that here it may be used in a slightly different manner (98).[37] Menahem Kister (2004, 47) has this evaluation: "On the whole Mysteries is a fusion of concepts

---

are connected. This is subtly strengthened by the use of משא + על in 2 Kgs 9, which plausibly falls between Isaiah and Numbers, on the one hand, and Ben Sira, on the other. I am somewhat agnostic on the dating of Prov 30, but it is not a stretch to place it between Numbers and Ben Sira.

35. There are some twenty attestations of משא in the scrolls. By my count eight of these suggest the concrete sense of II-משא. A further five occur in contexts so fragmentary we should not venture a guess as to their meaning. The remaining seven examples probably refer to some type of speech in a prophetic context (cf. Abegg, Bowley, and Cook 2003, who construe the examples slightly differently).

36. For *editio princeps* see Barthélemy and Milik 1955, 102–7; Elgvin et al. 1997, 31–123.

37. In contrast to the prophetic examples of משא, where an audience or addressee is clearly delineated, 1Q/4QMysteries seems to be proclaiming a general judgment that will come against all wickedness—those who "did not know the secret of the way things are nor did they understand the things of old" (1Q27 1 I, 3; trans. Wise, Abegg, and Cook 2005).

3. Reframing Agur's Words

and genres: biblical and postbiblical wisdom, biblical and pseudepigraphic prophecy, astrology, and sectarian ideas." At Qumran, משא roams to the very edges of the territory staked out for it within the Hebrew Bible.

Another noteworthy example comes from 4Q160 (4QVision of Samuel), a fragmentary text that includes a prayer, bits of 1 Sam 3:14–17, and an intriguing variant.

[--]להגיד את המשא לעלי ויען עלי ו[--]
[--] הו[ ]דיעני את מראה האלוהים אל[ ]ο[--]
[--] to declare the *maśśā'* to Eli. And Eli answered and [--]
[-- ma]ke known to me the vision of the gods to [--] (4Q160 1 4–5)

ושמואל ירא מהגיד את־המראה אל־עלי: ויקרא עלי את־שמואל ויאמר...
But Samuel feared declaring the vision to Eli. And Eli called Samuel and he said... (1 Sam 3:15b–16a)

Where MT has "the vision" (המראה), 4Q160 has המשא. In addition to 2 Kgs 9, this Qumran text provides another narrative context in which it made sense to an ancient scribe to use the word משא. Moreover, this word was understood to be a close enough synonym to מראה to describe the same revelatory event. In 4Q160 1 4 // 1 Sam 3:15 the narrator is speaking, but in the next verse Eli calls Samuel's experience a מראה (4Q160 1 5).[38] Could this observation suggest that משא refers more to the content of the vision than to the vision itself? This distinction subtly strengthens the argument that משא connotes something weighty or heavy, a conceptual burden. In other words, having seen the vision (מראה) Samuel now bears a responsibility to deliver its weighty message (משא), which will lie on Eli like a burden. There is not enough context here to make any conclusive judgments, but suffice it to say that within a narrative text, the content—the message—of Samuel's vision is deemed a משא for Eli. Although both 1Q/4QMysteries and 4Q160 use משא in a revelatory or prophetic sense, they open new vistas by doing so in a manner that does not clearly conform to the pattern of usage in the canonical prophetic books. Rather than suggesting a genre of prophecy, משא suggests the revelatory message itself.

---

38. Although, to my knowledge, משא is not associated elsewhere with מראה, there seems to be a fairly strong association between משא and √חזה: Isa 13:1; Hab 1:1; Nah 1:1; Lam 2:14.

3.3.2.5 משא in the Balaam Text from Deir ʿAlla

As we conclude our survey, we should take a brief detour to Deir ʿAlla in the Transjordan. Parallels between the Deir ʿAlla plaster inscription and Num 22–24 demonstrate a common tradition, but unlike 4Q160 and 1 Sam 3 these are fundamentally different compositions. Each of Balaam's seven prophetic speeches pronounced over Israel in Num 22–24 begins with the phrase "and he lifted up his *māšāl*" (וישא משלו). Fascinatingly, when we turn to the account of Balaam in the plaster text from Deir ʿAlla we find a unique epigraphic use of משא but no examples of משל.[39] Consider the opening of the text:

1 [...] ֯ס֯פ֯ר [.] בלעם·ברבע[ר·]אש·חזֹה·אלהן [.] הא [.] ויאתו·אלוה
אלהן·בלילה·ו֯יחז·מחזה 2 כמשא·אל·

1 ... The book of [Balaam, son of Beo]r, a man who saw gods. The gods came to him in the night, and he saw a vision, 2 <u>as a *maśśāʾ*</u> from El. (*KAI* 312 1.1–2)

The text is badly damaged and translations vary wildly, so I will merely make simple observations. The narrative opens with a scene similar to the account in Num 22:19–29. The משא is something that is revealed to Balaam through observation of the divine council in a vision at night (אלהן, שדין; 1.5–6).[40] What Balaam observes pains him, causing him to weep and fast (1.3–4). This foreboding vision is contained in an "account" (ספר) and it is called both a "vision" (מחזה) and a *maśśāʾ*. Similarities to

---

39. The *editio princeps* is Hoftijzer and van der Kooij 1976. I ought to register here my awareness that the Deir ʿAlla text is not Hebrew, however, it is not entirely clear just *what* language it is. Clearly written in a NW Semitic dialect, the composition exhibits a blend of diagnostic linguistic features. The consensus seems to be that it is closest to Old Aramaic, but it is a mixed dialect—another boundary-crossing text. Against that cultural-linguistic backdrop and for the purposes of this study it is fascinating to note that *KAI* 312 is probably the only example of משא in Aramaic. For discussion of the dialect of Deir ʿAlla, see Hackett 1984; Hoftijzer and van der Kooij 1991; Lipiński 1994.

40. Lipiński (1994, 119), for one, however, does not associate this word with a prophetic form as in Isaiah, but rather with wisdom forms. In fact, he calls this text "not a simple 'utterance,' but an 'instruction' imposed on the addressee like a burden" (cf. Dijkstra 1995, 47). Lipiński (119) goes on to draw a direct connection to Prov 31:1 and hints at some kind of common milieu by noting the Aramaizing dialect of that passage in Proverbs, "which reveals a not-Israelite or Judahite origin."

prophetic occurrences of משא in the Hebrew Bible are clear. Three times in the Hebrew Bible a משא is described as something that a prophet *sees* (חזה; Isa 13:1; Hab 1:1; Lam 2:14, cf. Nah 1:1), and Nah 1:1 begins with the phrase "the book of the vision of Nahum" (ספר חזון נחום), which is highly suggestive of the opening of Deir ʿAlla. Additionally, as we just saw, 4Q160 also describes a divine night vision that must be relayed by the recipient to those it concerns.

3.3.2.6. Topographic Report on משא

The tract of land portioned out for משא runs across rocky hills, high plateaus, and down to fertile lowlands. From this survey of the terrain, I draw several preliminary conclusions. First, in both 2 Kgs 9 and Ben Sira there seems to be conceptual overlap between the concrete sense of משא and its metaphorical extension to name a message or a type of speech. A משא is something that can be set on someone and *carried*, with a sense that comes close to *curse* or *burden*. Second, building on this conceptual overlap is the idea that משא often seems to connote something ominous or foreboding—a portent. We see this in 2 Kgs 9, 1Q/4QMysteries, Deir ʿAlla, and perhaps in 4Q160. Third, while the משא is commonly a message revealed by or received from the gods, it seems to function broadly so that it is not confined to any one context. So, while it is correlate to "vision" in Deir ʿAlla and 4Q160 and "declaration of YHWH" in 2 Kgs 9, it also refers to the instruction of wisdom in Ben Sira, and in 1Q/4QMysteries it sums up an eschatological wisdom prophecy. In all of these texts, משא seems to capture the message or the substance of the vision or the instruction. To be clear, I am not arguing that משא is a prophetic term that is sometimes used in wisdom literature, nor yet that משא is associated as much with wisdom texts as it is with prophetic ones.[41] Rather, I wonder if משא is not more of a neutral term that is at home in different contexts. Perhaps the thing that matters is not prophecy or wisdom as genres but rather the purpose of the message: to place a burden (i.e., responsibility) or a curse on someone. In fact, I do not see sufficient evidence to warrant treating

---

41. This is where my approach differs from Sneed (2021). Sneed treats משא as a fundamentally prophetic idea whose presence in a wisdom text shows the "confluence" of prophetic and sapiential traditions in ancient Israelite scribal culture. My philological work on משא suggests that the term is the property of neither tradition, if, indeed, tradition is the best way of thinking about them (Sneed 2011).

II-משא and III-משא as separate lexemes. Rather, I believe III-משא is a figurative extension of the concrete meaning, *burden*, so it makes sense to gloss the term this way even when a message is in view. The term משא probably designates a tone and a purpose more than a genre. We ought not to move the ancient boundary stones, but rather seek to discern where they lay through close attention to all משא texts.

3.3.3. משא and the Ancient Boundary Stones

Returning to Prov 30, then, ancient readers do not seem concerned about the prophetic connotation of משא. On the contrary, ancient versions and the early exegetical tradition unanimously treat משא in Prov 30:1 with discourse terms that suggest prophetic revelation. Jerome has "vision" (*visio*). Both S and T have "who received prophecy" (ܕܩܒܠ ܢܒܝܘܬܐ and דקביל נביותא respectively). The notable outlier here is G. The G translator is either working from a different *Vorlage* (Tov 1990; Cuppi 2011, 92), or carrying out a quasi-authorial agenda (Cook 1997; Waltke 2005, 454 n. 1). In neither case does G Prov 30:1 offer the interpreter a clear indication of what the translator took משא to mean.[42]

There remains here, however, the specter that an exegetical tradition conveniently misread the proper name משא for the discourse term משא at an early stage, either in service or as a consequence of the move to read the names Agur and Lemuel as cyphers for Solomon (see §3.2.1). Still, it is worth pointing out that on this analysis the scribes who initially misread משא in this manner—either intentionally or unintentionally—saw no significant difficulties with discovering the discourse term in the context of

---

42. Despite the ingenuity of text critics in connecting these dots between G and MT (see the chart at §3.2.1), no compelling explanation for משא has emerged (Cuppi 2011, 89). By process of elimination, משא must correspond to G's μετανόει because every other component of MT has a conceivable counterpart in G. Fox (2015, 379) has attempted an explanation arguing, "G probably thought that the idea of repentance was implicit in המשא, which he associated with נשא." The verb √נשא can occasionally mean "forgive" and in the passive "to be forgiven" (Fox cites Isa 33:24 and Ps 32:1). If the precondition to forgiveness is repentance, Fox reasons, then perhaps G made that connection and changed "'be forgiven' to 'repent,' to make the human role in the process explicit" (379). It is impossible to rule out Fox's reconstruction, which is plausible enough given how G handles the rest of the verse; however, it is equally impossible to verify it and it remains a conjecture. Moreover, μετανόει appears as an equivalent to משא in no other text.

Proverbs more broadly or the material in Prov 30 more narrowly. Their approach to transforming Agur into Solomon might have failed if they had traded gentilic משא for an infelicitous discourse term.

At this point, Genesis Rabbah offers a moment of clarifying philological reflection:

> [Prophecy] is expressed by ten designations: prophecy [נבואה], vision [חזון], preaching [הטפה], speech [דבור], saying [אמירה], command [צווי], burden [משא], parable [משל], metaphor [מליצה], and enigma [חידה]. And which is the severest [קשה] form? R. Leazar said: Vision, as it says, *A grievous vision is declared unto me* (Isa. xxi, 2). R. Johanan said: Speech (*dibbur*), as it says, *The man, the lord of the land, spoke* (dibber) *roughly with us*, etc. (Gen. xlii, 30). The Rabbis said: Burden, as it says, *As a heavy burden* (Ps. xxxviii, 5). Great then was the power of Abraham that [Divine] converse was held with him in vision and in speech. (Gen. Rab. 44:6; Freedman 1951, 364; emphasis original)

According to this passage, the type of prophecy designated by משא is considered by a critical mass of rabbis to be the harshest kind. From this list of ten names it is clear these words are not understood *only* to designate prophecy (e.g., צווי, אמירה), but rather these words *may* designate prophecy. Moreover, some of the terms in the list we might readily perceive to be synonyms (e.g., אמירה and דבור), while others we might think of as being mutually exclusive (e.g., משל and חזון). This passage ought to suggest to us that, though the ancients did indeed make distinctions between these terms, the way these distinctions operated for them is often difficult for us to intuit.

In a similar vein to Genesis Rabbah, Dominique Barthélemy (2015, 775) draws our attention to Sa'adya's reading, "Now, the first exegete who had the audacity to recognize the names of authors here was Saadya. Although he was familiar with onomastic exegesis, he opted for the peshat." Likewise, Sa'adya understands משא according to the phrases "and he lifted up his *māšāl*" (וישא משלו; Num 23:7, 18; 24:3, 15, 20, 21, 23) and "to take up his *māšāl*" (שאת משלו; Job 27:1; 29:1) as a designation for a collection of *sayings* or *proverbs* (משלים), although Sa'adya is happy to roll together Balaam's oracles, Job's discourses, and Agur's words (Barthélemy 2015, 775). Thus, at least one premodern commentator read משא as designating a type of speech and connected that term to proverbs. Most modern interpreters would look at the word *proverb* (משל) and think *wisdom literature*, although, as we just saw, the rabbis consider משל another possible name for prophecy. It seems that ancient authors simply had very different ideas from us about what words belonged in what pastures and where the fences ought to go.

3.3.4. נאם and the Meaning of משא

The very next word in Prov 30:1, "oracle" (נאם), is a case in point. Scholars who emend משא to read a proper name must immediately explain another prophetic term, and for those who read "utterance," נאם is another indication that traditional genre boundaries are inadequate. The noun נאם is "an almost completely fixed technical expression introducing prophetic oracles" (*HALOT*, s.v. "נְאֻם"). Though it appears 376 times, its uses are so overwhelmingly formulaic that scholars cannot even shade in a meaningful semantic profile.[43] Usually, these formulas open or close rhetorical units containing prophetic speech in order to emphasize that "the message of the prophets comes from God through whom their words are true and effectual" (Eising 1997, 112; e.g., Ezek 37:14). There are, however, only three passages that contain the collocation of נאם with הגבר: Num 24:2–3, 15–6; 2 Sam 23:1; and Prov 30:1.

וישא משלו ויאמר
נאם בלעם בנו בער / ונאם הגבר שתם העין:
נאם שמע אמרי־אל / וידע דעת עליון
מחזה שדי יחזה / נפל וגלוי עינים:

Then he lifted up his speech and he said:
"An oracle of Balaam son of Beor, / the oracle of the man with the open eye,
an oracle of the one hearing words of El, / knowing knowledge of Elyon,

---

43. Of these occurrences, 307 (82 percent) are found in just four prophetic books (Jeremiah, Ezekiel, Isaiah, and Amos), and 267 times (71 percent) נאם is in construct with the divine name (יהוה). The raw fact that the literary distribution of נאם is heavily skewed makes it a distinctly prophetic and possibly archaic term. It occurs just twice in the Psalms, once each in Proverbs and Chronicles, and is completely absent from Daniel, Job, Lamentations, Esther, Song of Songs, Jonah, Ecclesiastes, Ben Sira, and the Dead Sea Scrolls (apart from biblical citations, e.g., CD XIX, 8 simply rephrases Zech 13:7).

visions of Shaddai he will see, / falling with eyes unveiled." (Num 24:15–16)

ואלה דברי דוד האחרנים
נאם דוד בן־ישי / ונאם הגבר הקם על
משיח אלהי יעקב/ ונעים זמרות ישראל:
רוח יהוה דבר־בי / ומלתו על־לשוני:

Now these are the last words of David,
"An oracle of David son of Jesse, / the oracle of the man who was raised on high,
the anointed of the God of Jacob / the soothing singer of Israel
the spirit of YHWH spoke through me, / his word is on my tongue." (2 Sam 23:1–2)

Two features of these verses are worth noting. First, in Num 24 and 2 Sam 23 the phrase נאם הגבר is part of an extended poetic escalation that develops the speakers' credentials, particularly their connection to the divine. Both passages feature repetitions of נאם and these repetitions are modified by epithets extolling the speakers' exploits and attributes. Second, in Num 24 and 2 Sam 23, נאם is combined with other terms designating the speech to follow, namely, משל in Num 24:15 and דבר in 2 Sam 23:1.[44] Zechariah 12:1 is the only other superscription in the Hebrew Bible to combine נאם and משא in the introduction of a rhetorical unit. Like Prov 30:1; Num 24:15–16; and 2 Sam 23:1, Zech 12:1 also stacks up terms for prophetic speech in parallel lines: נאם // דבר // משא. The only other biblical text that holds משא and נאם together is 2 Kgs 9:25–26. As Jehu recounts the משא to Bidkar, he punctuates it with a parenthetical נאם־יהוה ("an oracle of YHWH"). Rhetorically, this gives YHWH'S blessing to Joram's murder. For our purpose, Jehu has also shown that משא and נאם, if not synonyms, are at least applicable to the same prophecy.

If it is unclear precisely what calling Agur's words a נאם portends, it certainly creates a strong intertextual link to Num 24 and 2 Sam 23 with heavy prophetic overtones, thereby connecting Agur's words with

---

44. Based on the poetic lineation of these verses and use of "and he said" (ויאמר) in Num 24:15, I believe that נאם occurs within Balaam and David's speeches rather than being part of the narrator's frame (Toy 1899, 517). If Balaam and David introduce their speech by declaring it an "oracle" (נאם), this concurs broadly with the peppering of נאם in prophetic speeches for emphasis.

Balaam's words and David's words—all poetry but three very different discourses. As we saw above, multiple texts from Qumran show this kind of genre blending, particularly with regard to wisdom, prophetic, and apocalyptic elements (e.g., 4Q418 [4QInstruction[d]] or 4Q416 [4QInstruction[b]]). If ancient texts often cross generic boundaries, why couldn't Prov 30 combine features we associate with wisdom traditions and features we associate with prophecy?

3.3.5. The Tone and Purpose of a משא in Isaiah 13–14

To this point, I have argued משא is a discourse term that names a type of speech, but it is not a modern genre term, because it does not line up with any particular type of prophetic oracle or wisdom composition. Although the majority of extant משא texts are prophetic, prophecy itself does not seem to be the essence of the term. Instead, I have suggested its essence might lie in the tone or purpose of the message. Before we bring our study of משא to a close, then, we ought to think about what tone and purpose the term entails. We have already begun to do this in the texts we have surveyed above, but it remains to take a sustained look at one of the definitional משא texts. With eleven distinct משא compositions, Isaiah's oracles against the nations are the most concentrated cache of משא texts (Isa 13:1; 14:28; 15:1; 17:1; 19:1; 21:1, 11, 13; 22:1, 23:1; 30:6). Given First Isaiah's antiquity and prominence, Isa 13:1–14:27—the first משא—holds pride of place in any attempt to describe the term.[45] In what follows, I will undertake to describe its contents in terms of tone and voice.

משא בבל אשר חזה ישעיהו בן־אמוץ:
The *maśśāʾ* of Babylon that Isaiah Ben-Amoz saw. (Isa 13:1)

---

45. This text may have been composed when two distinct compositions, 13:2–22 and 14:4b–21, were combined with the addition of editorial framing elements: 13:1; 14:1–4a, 22–23 (Williamson 1994, 158; Childs 2001, 122–24; Vayntrub 2019, 146). Williamson (1994, 158) notes that editorial material in 14:22–23 moves beyond the death of a single king back to the crimes of the whole city of Babylon, thus linking the fate of the city (13:2–22) and the fate of the unnamed king (14:4b–21) and summarizing the oracle against Babylon into a whole. In a different manner, Erlandsson (1970, 109–27, 166) also argues for the unity of 13:2–14:27. For a powerful discussion of the purpose behind the editorial shaping of Isa 13–14, see Seitz 1993, 127–37.

Isaiah 13 is delivered in the first-person, and the speaker appears to be YHWH as channeled by the prophet. As for tone, it is a striding rebuke, an ominous text gathering to a greatness like an army on the edge of a battle (13:4) until the inbreaking "day of YHWH" is announced in 13:6 and 9. After this, the cosmos begins to unravel:

על־כן שמים ארגיז / ותרעש הארץ ממקומה
בעברת יהוה צבאות / וביום חרון אפו:

Therefore I will rock the heavens / and the earth will totter from her place
with the wrath of YHWH of Hosts, / in the day of his furious anger. (Isa 13:13)

Brutal, retributive justice reigns (13:14–16). YHWH will wield the merciless Medes against Babylon to bring her low (13:17–19). Interestingly, YHWH does not detail Babylon's infractions, but pledges generally to visit "on the wicked their own iniquity" (13:11a). The only sin that is singled out is pride (Seitz 1993, 122, 133):

והשבתי גאון זדים / וגאות עריצים אשפיל:

I will ruin the pride of the pompous, / and the pridefulness of the ruthless I will bring low. (Isa 13:11b)

Not only does the couplet in 13:11b underscore this particular corruption, the oracle circles back to the theme in 13:19, calling Babylon "the splendor of kingdoms, the beautiful pride of the Chaldeans."[46] The declaration of judgment ends with an evocative description of Babylon abandoned. The animals have switched places with people in 13:20–22, which parallels the unraveling of creation and world upside down motif from 13:10–13. Like Sodom and Gomorrah, Babylon will be a wasteland, abandoned even by nomadic "Arabians" and "shepherds." Instead "desert animals" (ציים), "screechers" (אחים), and "owls" (בנות יענה) will take up residence; and

---

46. Kim (2021, 70) notes that the oracles against the nations in Isa 13–23 single out hubris for censure as a major theme (16:6, 14; 17:4; 23:9; and cf. 10:12; 37:23–29). In terms of denotation, the word גאון seems to shuttle between the object of pride (e.g., wealth, splendor, strength) and the feeling or vice itself. Thus the thing that is brought low may be imagined here as the real material stuff that induces pride or as the emotion induced (Bordjadze 2017, 22; *DCH* 3, s.v. "גָּאוֹן"; e.g., Isa 24:14; Prov 16:8).

the voices of "hyenas" (אִיִּים) and "jackals" (וְתַנִּים) will echo in abandoned towers and palaces.[47] When the proud and beautiful Babylon has been abandoned by people and haunted by animals from the margins, then her humbling is complete (cf. 14:23).

Although there is no formal transition to a new unit within the text, 14:1–3 turns a corner in terms of tone and voice. The frame is now third-person speech emphasizing YHWH's love and attention toward Israel. This laying low of Babylon facilitates a grand reversal. Where Babylon is driven out, Israel will be settled in homes (14:1). Even their servants and maidservants will become "captors to their captors" (14:2). It is in this context, then, that the text introduces a speech within a speech (Vayntrub 2019, 146):

והיה ביום הניח יהוה לך ...
ונשאת המשל הזה על־מלך בבל ואמרת

And so it will be in the day when YHWH gives you[48] rest … that you will raise this *māšāl* against the king of Babylon, and you will say. (Isa 14:3a, 4a)

Now, this passage has been the subject of extensive commentary and research, not least because of its designation as a *māšāl* (משל).[49] The challenge is how to capture the essence of the word—the thing that might somehow hold together the diverse texts preserved under its label. Scholars have suggested various translations, including "proverb," "parable," "saying," "byword," "similitude," "song," "poem," and even "parallelism" itself (BDB, s.v. "משל"; and *HALOT*, s.v. "מָשָׁל"; see also Vayntrub 2019, 59–60).[50] This challenge is ancient. The traditional rendering of the

---

47. For philological discussion of the identities of these animals and their significance as part of this oracle see Williamson 2020. He summarizes, "These are all animals which are known to haunt deserted territory, including ruins, thus bringing the description of the anticipated destruction of Babylon to a fitting climax, in line with other biblical as well as wider ancient Near Eastern rhetoric" (234).

48. The true addressee of the text emerges as Israel in the "you" of 14:3. And so this משל is projected into the mouth of a people at rest, freshly vindicated by their God, who have endured a long injustice (Vayntrub 2019, 148).

49. Indeed, the proverbial ink has been spilled in discussing משל. For helpful entry points with reference to Isa 13–14, see Bordjadze (2017, 39–49) and Vayntrub (2019, 146–65).

50. Etymologically, √משל means "represent, be like" (BDB, s.v. "משל"). This meaning is not only present in Classical Hebrew (typically in the *niphal*, e.g., Isa 14:10;

word is "parable," a translation we owe to G's preferred gloss, παραβολή.[51] But at Isa 14:4, G has "lamentation" (LEH, s.v. "θρῆνον"). This idea, that somehow Isa 14 contains a lament or a dirge, has gained ground with interpreters in the last few decades. Gale Yee (1988, 582) argued compellingly that Isa 14 intentionally reworks the dirge form, exemplified by David's lament over Saul and Jonathan in 2 Sam 1:19–27, in order to craft a parody "ridiculing a nameless tyrant." The poet achieves "irony, humor, and satire" by copying the form of a dirge but inverting the content so that rather than praising a dead hero the poem critiques a living despot (581). Thus Karlo Bordjadze (2017, 46) asks, "Might one anticipate finding in this poem an ancient analog to Voltaire, Jonathan Swift or George Orwell?" Perhaps, but without our being quite aware of it, this discussion of genre has now taken us far away from the meaning of the word משל. To say Isa 14:4–23 is a satirical parody of a dirge is *not* to say anything about the meaning of משל, even if it does justify the impulse to gloss the word with "taunt" in this passage (Budde 1882; Eissfeldt 1913, 25; 1965, 93; Jahnow 1923, 242; Sweeney 1996, 228–29).[52] However, when we consider the rhetorical purpose of the משל within the broader משא then perhaps we can come full circle.[53] Bordjadze (2017, 46) argues that the term משל captures the parody mode and invites "a sardonic mood" by suggesting the incongruity between the dirge form and the mocking content. Vayntrub (2019, 163) captures it: "The mashal is like a formalized speech parallel to a gasp in horror or a deriding remark, whose point is to generalize the causes and effects of the behavior that

---

Ps 28:1; 49:13, 21) but across ancient Semitic languages (*HALOT*, s.v. "מָשָׁל"; McKane 1970, 25–26).

51. BDAG has the following definition for παραβολή: "2. a narrative or saying of varying length, designed to illustrate a truth especially through comparison or simile, *comparison, illustration, parable, proverb, maxim*" (emphasis original). In addition to the New Testament, it cites classical authorities such as Diogenes Laertius, Aristotle (*Rhetorica*), and the Life of Aesop.

52. "The line going from Budde to Eissfeldt to Yee represents a major scholarly tradition regarding the function of משל in Isaiah 14.3–23" (Bordjadze 2017, 45). Bordjadze provides extensive bibliography at this point.

53. Schipper (2009, 2) argues, "Nearly 30 years ago, the general scholarly consensus shifted to suggest that we should not define a *mashal* by its type or form, be it a proverb, a parable (i.e., short story), or a song. Rather, we should concentrate on its content and function." Polk 1983 is a helpful study and an excellent illustration of the shift Schipper describes.

led the humiliated person or group to this point" (see also Alter 1985, 146–47).

Turning to examine the speech in this light, it begins with the oppressed exulting that YHWH has disarmed the wicked and brought rest to the whole earth.⁵⁴ Exultation shades into *schadenfreude* and mockery in 14:8.

גַּם־בְּרוֹשִׁים שָׂמְחוּ לְךָ / אַרְזֵי לְבָנוֹן
מֵאָז שָׁכַבְתָּ לֹא־יַעֲלֶה / הַכֹּרֵת עָלֵינוּ:

Even the cypresses rejoice over you, / the cedars of Lebanon:
"Ever since you lay down, the woodcutters / stopped rising against us!" (Isa 14:8)

I think we might entertain reading this verse as a joke.⁵⁵ David Marcus (1995, 10 n. 10), for one, considers it an example of biblical satire. The oppression of the king of Babylon was so severe, even the trees felt it. The woodcutters came constantly against them, felling logs for siege works or as part of their infamous slash-and-burn tactics (Roberts 2015, 209).⁵⁶ The incongruity is twofold. First, you have the anthropopathic application of rejoicing to trees, who obviously cannot sustain such emotions. Second, you have those trees reflecting on their lot and speaking within the מָשָׁל. Peter Machinist (1983, 734) notes this verse may invert Assyria's mockery of YHWH in Isa 37:24, where the king brags he sent expeditions to the west to fell the most valuable trees. The humbling of the king of Babylon brings peace where it was least expected; even the plants were oppressed.

This מָשָׁל seems to revel in these kinds of reversals.⁵⁷ In 14:9–20, a *katabasis* takes the king of Babylon down to Sheol, where even the kings of the nations get the chance to gloat (14:10–11, 16–17). As with the speech

---

54. The wordplay in 14:4–5 underscores this truth (Yee 1988, 575; Alter 1985, 147). The root מָשָׁל is used both in the sense of "parable" and "ruler" in the space of two verses, and the sounds of שׁ, ט/תּ, and מ skate across the lines, emphasizing that rest is the result of shattering the staffs of rubbish rulers.

55. Yee (1988, 576) almost gets here, but not quite. By suggesting this verse is a joke, I do not mean to suggest for a moment that its scathing critique of pride is mitigated in any way. On the contrary, I think the joke may intensify the critique. For a thorough discussion of interpretations of this verse, see Bordjadze 2017, 57–64.

56. E.g., see Essarhaddon's accounts of his Syro-Palestinian campaigns (*ANET*, 291) or Nebuchadnezzar II's expedition to Syria (*ANET*, 307).

57. The reversal from the heights of pride to depths of humiliation is matched by

against the city, wrongs are defined in the broadest terms as "oppression" and "wickedness" (14:4–5). Again, the only sin that the prophet singles out is pride (גאון), which expands to cosmic, mythological proportions in the *katabasis* scene. The famous appellative "Shining one, Son of Dawn" (14:12) is soaked in sarcasm against the backdrop of the horrific, skin-crawling description of sleeping on maggots with worms for covers (14:11; Alter 2019, 2:668; Childs 2001, 126). Here the poet gives voice to the king of Babylon, who condemns himself with staggering arrogance:

השמים אעלה ממעל / לכוכבי־אל ארים כסאי
ואשב בהר־מועד / בירכתי צפון:
... אך אל־שאול תורד / אל־ירכתי־בור:

I will ascend the heavens above, / to the stars of El, I will ascend my throne.
And I will sit on the mount of assembly / on the extremities of Zaphon.
… But surely to Sheol you will descend / to the extremities of a pit.
(Isa 14:13, 15)

The arrogance that seeks to ascend to the heavens is instead brought down to the grave. Not only is this reversal pictured by the tight contrast of ascent and descent (עלה/ירד), but a scathing irony underscores it with the repetition of "extremities" (ירכתי). Because he is set on a seat in the assembly of the gods at the summit of Mount Zaphon, the king will instead see the deepest part of the pit that is Sheol. The משל poem ends on a note of vicious retributive justice. We are meant to *feel* the irony and repulsion of pride.

This complex text is structured by several frames with the voices of the prophet and YHWH intermingling to address Babylon indirectly through Israel, and then to address Babylon's king by means of a speech (משל) within a speech (משא).[58] In terms of tone, it is a blistering prophetic takedown that mocks and reviles its target as it promises judgment.

---

the reversal of form and content and therefore of the reader's expectations through parody (Yee 1988, 574).

58. Within the משל itself, the voice of the prophet is spliced with that of the kings of the nations, the king of Babylon himself, and even the aggrieved forests of the Levant. Distinguishing where voices shift is not always obvious or, perhaps, necessary. E.g., it is not clear to me precisely where the kings of the nations leave off

3.3.6. Proverbs 30 as a משא

In closing, let me draw an analogy between these "genre" terms: משל ("proverb") and משא. Vayntrub (2019) has argued that the way משל is employed—on its own terms—simply does not match the scholarly construals of what משל means. Instead, משל ought to be understood to denote something like "speech performance." In fact, משל offers us something of a mirror image for משא. Whereas משל takes its primary definition from wisdom literature but then appears conspicuously in prophetic texts (e.g., Isa 13–14; Num 23–24), משא takes its primary definition from prophecy but then appears conspicuously in several wisdom texts (e.g., Prov 30:1; 31:1; 1Q/4QMysteries; Sir 6:21; 51:26). Proverbs 30 is a משא within a collection of משלים, but Isa 13–14 is introduced as a משא although it contains within it a משל (Isa 14:4–21). Perhaps whatever a משא is lies in the common ground between, say, Prov 30, Isa 13–14, and Deir 'Alla. If our definition of משל must be broad enough to encompass both Balaam's prophetic speeches in Numbers and Solomon's couplets in Proverbs, then is it so hard to imagine that an ancient reader could somehow draw together Balaam's vision of doom from Deir 'Alla, Isaiah's oracle against Babylon, and Agur's words?

To sum up this argument, I see little warrant for Delitzsch's dismissal of reading משא as a discourse term. Such a reflex seems to reflect modern scholarly genre boundaries more than the ways משא is used in ancient texts. There is nothing about the usage of משא in other texts that prohibits reading a discourse term, that is, "burden" or "message" in Prov 30. In fact, given the Hebrew text of verse 1, this is the most judicious reading. What is more, the uses of משא elsewhere in ancient literature cast Prov 30 in an intriguing light. Although the discourse term משא does not necessarily entail prophetic inspiration or divine speech, it does have overtones heading strongly in that direction. The collocation of המשא with נאם הגבר and the association with Balaam's speeches and David's last words further this impression. If this passage is being drawn into the orbit of prophetic discourse, then what might that suggest? The greatest implication of the

---

their first taunt. Does the prophet pick back up as narrator of the poem in 14:11, 12, or 13? Because their speech focuses on explicating the phrase "you will be like us" (10b), it most likely ends with verse 11. Isaiah 14:12 seems to return to the register of the narrator who reinforces the sentiment of the kings with his own perspective (Yee 1988, 575).

term משא may not be, as it might seem at first blush, to denote divine imprimatur. Instead it may have more to do with tone and purpose. In this regard it seems to connote a warning or a burden, a weight of teaching that must be responded to. In Isa 13–14 this takes the form of a satirical taunt and dressing down with implications for the observers as much as the addressees. I propose that the use of משא to describe Agur's words in Prov 30:1 encourages us to look for something similar in the collection.

3.4. Toward a Reading of Proverbs 30:1b

If משא moves us toward considerations of tone in Prov 30, this discussion finds ample grist for the mill in the nearly indecipherable string of letters at the end of verse 1: לאיתיאל לאיתיאל ואכל. Perhaps one of the most confounding text-critical dilemmas in the Hebrew Bible, this dizzying double palindrome defies reading. As pointed in MT, these letters appear to be three personal names indicating the addressee of this composition, "to Ithiel, to Ithiel, and Ukal" (NJPS). Whether or not one adopts this reading, nearly all scholars admit the text is corrupt (Toy 1899, 520; Plöger 1984, 358; Sæbø 2012, 359 n. 5). Although the name Ithiel is attested (Neh 11:7), the name Ukal is unheard of, and a double addressee with just one name repeated feels unusually awkward. Furthermore, no other addressee is named within the book of Proverbs, which, like instructional material generally, does not identify addressees by name but rather as son(s) of the teaching voice (Fox 2015, 378). Finally, 30:2 opens with a כי clause, leaving scholars with the distinct impression that Agur's discourse began in 30:1, since כי generally depends on what precedes it. Lacking useful manuscript evidence and compelling variants, there is little hope for a breakthrough, and yet there may still be a story to tell. In this section, I will examine the evidence of the versions then survey some recent text-critical approaches to Prov 30:1b. Emerging from this process, I argue that Prov 30:1b may have once read לאיתי ולא* אוכל, "I am weary and powerless."

This challenging text appears to have been understood to contain a name by at least one tradition. This interpretation was then preserved within a manuscript as a double reading. Eventually, scribes harmonized this double reading, which then calcified in MT. I will support this proposal by appealing to documented scribal practice concerning the preservation of doublets, the cognitive process of reading, and the creation of ghost names in manuscripts. In conclusion, I will consider what this opening line might suggest about Agur's discourse, particularly in terms of tone.

3.4.1. Narrating the Versions

The readings of the versions do not allow us to establish an original text with any confidence but rather to explore the backstories of the text, that is, available interpretations of our verse as it developed.

MT:	לאיתיאל לאיתיאל ואכל	to Ithiel, to Ithiel and Ukal
G:	τοῖς πιστεύουσιν θεῷ, καὶ παύομαι	to those believing in God, and I stop
α':	τῷ 'Εθιὴλ, καὶ τέλεσον	to Ithiel, now stop
θ':	τῷ 'Εθιὴλ, καὶ δυνήσομαι	to Ithiel, and I will be powerful
S:	ܐܝܬܝܐܠ ܘܐܡܪ. ܘܐܫܟܚ ܒܚܝܠܐ.	and was able with strength, and he spoke to Ithiel
T:	לאיתיאל לאיתיאל ואוכל	to Ithiel, to Ithiel and Ukal
V:	cum quo est Deus et qui Deo secum morante confortatus ait	with whom God is, and who being strengthened by God, abiding with him said (Douay-Rheims)

Two broad approaches to 30:1b emerge from this line-up. The first approach, represented by MT, α' (Aquila), θ' (Theodotion), T, and S, recognizes לאיתיאל as a proper name and the addressee of this composition. Within this approach only MT and T contain two occurrences of לאיתיאל and also allow for recognizing ואכל as a proper name, although nothing requires one to interpret it that way.[59] Aquila, θ', and S register only one

---

59. The masorah parva at ואכל has the annotation ל וחס indicating that the Masoretes believed this form only occurs here written defectively. This notation suggests they associate ואכל with the plene form וְאוּכָל (1cs qal yiqtol √יכל) that occurs in Jer 20:9; Ps 101:5; and Job 31:23 and is always qualified by the negator לא. In other words, the Masoretes appear to be reading with θ'. Kennicott (1780, 474) records sixty-four out of two hundred manuscripts with the reading ואוכל and an additional three originally contained that reading. While this evidence cannot be used to suggest anything about the original text, it does suggest there is a strong minority tradition within MT that read ואכל as a verb.

occurrence of לאיתיאל and treat ואכל as a verb. The second approach, represented by G and V, interprets all of the words understood to be proper names in other witnesses as verbal phrases. I will first look more closely at the Greek versions, followed by S and V in turn.

Nearly all the major interpretive options are already available in the Greek versions. G's τοῖς πιστεύουσιν θεῷ could represent a periphrastic rendering of לאיתיאל.[60] Fox (2015, 379) suggests that G read ל+איתי+אל ("to whom there is God"), with איתי construed as the Aramaic particle of existence ("there is," e.g., Ezra 4:16; 5:17, cf. Biblical Hebrew יש). This could plausibly amount to etymological exegesis of the postexilic name איתיאל, which appears in Neh 11:7, perhaps meaning "God is with me" (אתי אל for איתי אל; Delitzsch 1875, 268; cf. Franklyn 1983, 241–42 n. 14). The Greek plural is universalizing: "to those whom God is with" = "to anyone whom God is with." The second element in G, καὶ παύομαι, suggests G read a first-person common singular *qal wayyiqtol*/jussive from √כלה ("to be complete, finished") for ואכל (Cuppi 2012, 35; Fox 2015, 378).

The Hexaplaric recensions, α' and θ', break from G by reflecting לאיתיאל as a proper name + ל. Aquila's reading, καὶ τέλεσον ("now [you] stop"), agrees with G in finding √כלה ("to be complete, finished") in ואכל, although it transposes the form from the first to the second person.[61] On the other hand, θ"s καὶ δυνήσομαι interprets ואכל as deriving from √יכל ("to be able, prevail"). Theodotion thus supports the vocalization represented in M^L and even more so the masora parva and the manuscripts that read ואוכל.[62] Interestingly, both α' and θ' use the future tense.[63] This strongly suggests the translators read *yiqtol*s in their *Vorlage(n)*, but does not require a different consonantal text from MT.

---

60. G Prov 30:1 does not give a clear indication of what the translator understood לאיתיאל to mean. See the chart in §3.2.1.

61. This possibly echoes G's apparent תגור for אגור in 30:1a (Cuppi 2011, 89–90 and n. 25).

62. On spelling conventions in ancient Hebrew texts and especially MT, see Barr 1989. Barr (93–94) makes the salient point that while most variable spellings were inconsequential semantically, occasionally, especially with I-י verbs, a vowel letter could distinguish one root from another. So, while ואכל could represent either √כלה or √יכל, ואוכל could *only* represent √יכל. Thus it would seem that α' was reading a manuscript that had ואכל, while θ' could have been reading *either* ואכל or ואוכל, although it seems most likely his *Vorlage* had the plene spelling.

63. For G, R-H; Swete 1891; and Holmes and Parsons 1823 all record a variant with the future: παύσομαι.

Like the Greek versions, S registers just one occurrence of לאיתיאל, which it treats as a proper name. Moreover, like θ′, S treats ואכל as a verb from √יכל. However, S differs from θ′, and from G, by apparently conflating the sense of ואכל with גבר earlier in the verse and altering the word order to produce ܘܐܫܟܚ ܒܓܒܪܐ ("and was able with strength"; cf. Cuppi 2011, 90). We can deduce this because S has no other element synonymous with "man" that might correspond to גבר, and נאם is rendered verbally by ܘܐܡܪ. The reading in S tacks most closely to θ′, the vocalization of MT, and the Kennicott manuscripts with ואוכל (Fox 2013, 53).

Although it might appear that V departs drastically from MT, Jerome's interpretation reflects early rabbinic exegesis (Gordon 1930, 411). Consider V alongside the treatment of our verse in Midr. Tanh., Vaera 5:2, "The man saith unto Ithiel is written because he [Solomon] would say: 'God is with me' (iti-el), and I will be able (ukhal) to withstand temptation.'… The names Ithiel and Ucal were written in that verse because he said: 'I will multiply wives, but I still will not turn my heart away (Ithiel) from God; and I will multiply the number of my horses; but I will not cause the people to return.'"[64] This midrashic approach to the names in the verse is reflected in Jerome's translation; he may even be our earliest witness to it (Barthélemy 2015, 774–75). The etymological exegesis Jerome engages in to translate the names as phrases is not far from the impulse reflected in G's reading. However, G registers only one occurrence of לאיתיאל while V exhibits two equivalent elements: (1) לאיתיאל = *cum quo est Deus*; (2) לאיתיאל=*et qui Deo secum morante*. V appears to witness clearly, albeit at low resolution, to MT.

3.4.2. Evaluating Contemporary Readings

Having thus oriented ourselves to the versions, we can now consider stories modern scholars have told about them. Nearly seventy years ago, Charles C. Torrey (1954, 94) hypothesized that in order for our text to become as

---

64. Trans. Samuel A. Berman via Sefaria.org. Note Midrash Mishle employs the same strategy as Tanhuma when handling the names but arrives at a different interpretation: "to *Ithiel* (*iti'el*)—[so named] because he understood the letters of God (*otiyyotaw shel el*); or because he understood the signs (*otiyyotehen*) of the ministering angels; and *Ucal* (*ukal*)—[so named] because he could (*yakol*) stand by them" (Visotzky 1992, 117; emphasis original). Both Tanhuma and Mishle derive Ukal from √יכל, suggesting their Hebrew manuscripts contained ואוכל.

corrupted as it appears to be, a scribe must have intentionally moved to blot out a statement he found theologically reprehensible by translating it into Aramaic. The original Hebrew text, on Torrey's (95) reading, was לֹא אָנֹכִי אֵל לֹא אֲנִי אֵל וְאוּכָל ("I am not a god, I am not a god, that I should have power"). By translating into Aramaic, Torrey's scribe obfuscated this scandalous phrase and produced לְאִיתַי אֵל לְאִיתִי אֵל, which merely needs to be run together, repointed, and the names of MT materialize.[65] Inspired by Torrey's approach, Timothy Sandoval (2020b, 162) claims, "the line represents an unsuccessful rendering of an original Aramaic text into Hebrew." Based on suggested theological and thematic parallels, he proposes לאית אלה לאיתיני אלה ואוכל for the original Aramaic ("I am weary, O God; I am not divine but I will prevail," 164). Sandoval imagines this Aramaic was poorly translated into Hebrew through a series of scribal errors resulting in a confused text. There is simply no evidence, however, that Prov 30:1b was originally composed in Aramaic, unless one counts the general disarray of the text as evidence. These approaches have produced an ingenious solution to the problem without recourse to the textual evidence we actually possess. For example, Sandoval (2020b, 165) interacts with G and V in passing by citing their readings in footnotes, largely to claim, "the textual traditions had difficulty understanding" their Hebrew *Vorlage* (see 161 n. 16 and 165 n. 31). The complexity and diversity of the evidence from the versions, however, suggests a more interesting and complex process is underway than mere misunderstanding.

Based on his attribution of haplography to G and S, Jan de Waard (2008, 54, 55–56*) thinks the longer text represented in MT, T, and V is the earlier one (also Cuppi 2012, 34–35). However, I find this unlikely. Why would the older witnesses—G, α′, θ′, and S—all exhibit an element corresponding to only one occurrence of לאיתיאל? Surely the slavish α′ and θ′, which render לאיתיאל as a proper name, would have repeated that name again had it appeared twice in their respective *Vorlagen* (Meade 2017, 268; see also Fox 2015, 380). This observation is strengthened by the fact that S, α′, and θ′ all read לאיתיאל as a proper name, whereas G reads it as a verbal phrase—the only thing they all agree on is that לאיתיאל appears once. Dittography in the tradition behind MT seems more likely than haplography

---

65. It is not clear to me how translating to Aramaic—the lingua franca of Palestine and international language of trade and diplomacy—would effectively obfuscate anything. Nevertheless, the core of Torrey's proposal was adopted with modifications by Scott (1965) and Murphy (1998).

behind G and S (Fox 2015, 380).⁶⁶ However, a more complex process is at work than a simple scribal slip.

Cuppi (2012, 35) and Fox (2015, 378) redivide and repoint the consonants of MT to arrive at the same suggestion: לָאִיתִי אֵל לָאִיתִי אֵל וָאֵכֶל, "I became tired, God, I became tired, God, and I may fade away." Barthélemy (2015, 775) has a slightly different take: לָאִיתִי אֵל לָאִיתִי אֵל וְאֻכָל, "I have exhausted myself, O God, I have exhausted myself, O God, to succeed." All three scholars agree on redividing לאיתיאל and identifying it as first-person common singular *qal qatal* from √לאה ("to be weary, impatient") with אל as a vocative. The vocative of אל tends to be signaled by the article ה, but there are exceptions (Num 12:13; Ps 83:2). More significantly, however, none of the versions or ancient manuscripts suggest this vocative was ever part of the reading tradition. It appears to be the invention of modern scholars.

Where scholars differ is their handling of ואכל. Following the vocalization implied by G and α′, Cuppi and Fox repoint ואכל as a first-person common singular *qal wayyiqtol*/jussive from √כלה. This form does not occur in the Hebrew Bible but is plausible (see Job 33:21; Exod 39:32). Fox (2015, 378) argues √כלה fits the context well since it "reverberates in the clause 'before I die' in 30:7b." Drawing connections to Ps 73:22 (כלה) and 2 Sam 23:1 (נאם), Fox construes Prov 30 as Agur's last words. Cuppi (2011, 91) speculates לאיתיאל was understood as a proper name first and this interpretation eventually contributed to ואכל being taken the same way. But why this text was misread in the first place remains a question. Cuppi (91–92) tentatively suggests that without vowels an Aramaic speaker might have scanned the consonantal text of MT as לָא יָתִי אֵל לָא יָתִי אֵל וְאֻכָל, meaning, "God is not with me, God is not with me, and I will succeed." The translations of G and V, along with the Midrash Tanhuma, support the plausibility of this. Barthélemy, however, opts to retain MT's pointing of ואכל as a first-person common singular *qal yiqtol* from √יכל. He is supported by θ′, S, and, indirectly, by V. Moreover, Barthélemy's suggestion has the strength that it does not require altering MT at all and is even supported by the Kennicott manuscripts reading ואוכל.⁶⁷ Barthélemy's most significant insight—the scale-swaying piece of evidence—is his observation that לאה is followed by יכל in Isa 16:12; Jer 20:9; and Job 4:2. No verse, however, brings together לאה and כלה.

---

66. But cf. Barthélemy (2015, 775): "It is not possible to conclude with certainty whether it was dittography or haplography."

67. See nn. 59 and 62 above.

3.4.3. Weary and Powerless: A Proposal for Reading Proverbs 30:1b

Taking all this evidence and scholarly ingenuity under advice, what can we say with any confidence? Lines of correspondence connect elements of G, V, and MT despite the meaning being changed systematically. This indicates the periphrastic interpretation in G and V is intentional and exegetical. The midrashic tradition latched on to these words. Because interpretive traditions are in play, and G's translation style is flexible overall, retroversion is challenging. Still, first and foremost, it is probable that only one instance of לאיתיאל is original and that ואכל began life as a verb. This is the majority opinion of the ancient versions, including all of the oldest witnesses. I cannot see how ואכל could have originated either as a second addressee or hanging off the end of the title line as a lonely verb, stranded from the body of the poetic composition as in G. If ואכל was originally a verb then לאיתיאל probably represented a verbal phrase as well. We already have two early interpretations represented in Greek. First, G takes לאיתיאל as a verbal phrase ("to those believing in God") while α' and θ' take it as a proper name ("to Ithiel"). But these traditions both interpret this phrase as indicating the addressee through the use of the preposition ל. Perhaps this was the inciting incident. If לאיתיאל originally contained a verbal phrase, then it is easy to imagine how a ל on a strange lexeme in the superscript of a discrete collection could have triggered a scribe to think in terms of an addressee. Perhaps eventually both the verbal phrase and the tradition representing an addressee were included in one manuscript as a double reading by a scribe who did not know which was correct. This scribe may have inserted a double reading that differed by as little as a word division or the transposition of two letters. Over time, MT's baffling reading calcified as the distinctions between these two interpretive options were lost.

But how might this have occurred and what could the original text have been? Building on Barthélemy's approach, I will suggest a reading for Prov 30:1b that produces a plausible history of the transformation of the text grounded in both the evidence of the versions and emerging text-critical methodology. Recall that Barthélemy connects ואכל to √יכל and observes that לאה is collocated with יכל in Isa 16:12; Jer 20:9; Job 4:2. The verb יכל occurs just thirty-four times in the *qal*. Twenty-seven of these are negated. Two of the three examples where לאה is followed by יכל fall into this category:

ונלאיתי כלכל ולא אוכל
I am weary from containing [it] and I am no longer able. (Jer 20:9)

והיה כי־נראה כי־נלאה / מואב על־הבמה
ובא אל־מקדשו להתפלל / ולא יוכל:
So it will be when he appears that Moab / has wearied himself on the high place,
and he will enter his sanctuary to pray / but he will not be able. (Isa 16:12)

Might Prov 30:1 be reflecting this collocation of לאה + negator + יכל that we find in Jer 20:9 and Isa 16:12? Perhaps in place of אל—the proposed vocative—the text had the adverb לא negating the verb?[68] The proposed earlier text would have been:

לאיתי ולא א(ו)כל*

I am weary and not able (i.e., powerless).

Apart from the optional ו, this phrase contains identical consonants to MT, differing only in word division and the transposition of letters.[69] In contrast to other text-critical proposals, such an ancestral text may plausibly have produced the readings in the versions.

First, note that √לאה is a relatively rare verb with just nineteen occurrences and of those only three are in the *qal*. This form would be unique in the Hebrew Bible although it is quite plausible. Second, remember that אכל potentially derives from several different roots when written defectively. Third, consider the density of לs (thrice), אs (thrice), and יs and וs (thrice) in the proposed text. These four graphemes account for nine out

---

68. In 1891, Gustav Bickell proposed something similar: לא]לא / לאתי אל [לא]לא אכל (1891, 293). He translates, "Saying of the man who struggled for God: I struggled for God and failed." Unfortunately, Bickell's project concerns justifying a theory of prosody and he provides little explanation for his proposal, but he anticipated two important aspects of mine. He discerned that the repetitions of לאיתיאל originally preserved different readings and that אכל was likely negated.

69. I represent the ו in א(ו)כל in parentheses to indicate it may or may not have been present in different manuscripts and stages of the transmission process. If one considers plene and defective spellings, various orthographic options emerge. My argument is not married to one spelling, but is aided by the fact that orthography was not standardized in ancient texts. See Barr 1989, 7–11.

3. Reframing Agur's Words

of eleven letters. Considering the semantic and graphic difficulty in this clause, there are many things that could go wrong in transcription. All it would take to trigger a process of transformation is one of several common scribal errors. This is the first stage in the process. By simply misdividing the words and running them together, the scribe may have produced *לאיתיולא. Graphic confusion between ו and י would yield *לאיתו ולא or *לאיתי ילא. These readings are primed for elision, producing *לאיתילא or *לאיתולא. Likewise, the back-to-back אs could easily have been elided. Finally, metathesis of the ל and the א would produce *לאיתי ואל. Once one of these shifts occurred a second would be even more likely if only to make sense of the first. For example, the elision of an א could have produced *לאיתי ולא וכל. Searching for a meaning for וכל, a scribe may have vocalized it as the imperative (כְּלֵה) and then overcorrected by adding a ה. Once וכלה is read as an imperative there is no meaningful role for לא, which could have been absorbed into לאיתי to create *וכלה לאיתיאל—and a reliable retroversion of α' is born. It is easier to arrive at a retroversion of θ'. The letters of ולא simply have to be reversed and redivided and *לאיתי ולא אוכל becomes לאיתיאל ואוכל*.

In my opinion, such errors need not represent stages in manuscript transmission. Rather, they probably occurred as simultaneous elements of the translator-scribe's natural mental process of reading. As John Screnock (2017, 178–79) argues in *Traductor Scriptor*, scribes and translators both construct mental versions of texts based on but not identical to the physical *Vorlagen* in front of them. By using resources from translation studies, particularly *intra*lingual translation, Screnock argues that translation and transmission of manuscripts involve fundamentally similar cognitive processes (92). He explains, "the translation process does not involve one single move from the physical *Vorlage* directly to the physical text of the translation; rather, there are additional intermediary stages in the translator's mind, appropriately conceived of as texts, through which this move is channeled" (177). Through a process of working memory and phonological loops, the translator-scribes produce physical copies of their *Vorlage* from their mental text (86–88). One of the implications of Screnock's study is that many variants in the textual tradition stem from the decoding (i.e., reading) process within the translator's mind rather than errors of the eye and ear or the *Vorlagen* (see 2017, 35 and 179). To recall Emanuel Tov's (2015, 178) dictum, "One simply has to accept the fact that some reliable retroversions never existed in writing."

I propose that a reading glitch triggered a scribe to decode לאיתי ולא as a proper name. While it is possible that one of the classic errors of textual criticism was at work (e.g., dittography, haplography, or metathesis as described above), it is equally likely the scribe simply misread a difficult string of letters in a fraught context. For example, in the Antiochene recension of G, Natalio Fernández Marcos (2003, 598) has identified a phenomenon he dubbed *ghost names*.[70] Ghost names appear when a challenging string of letters in a Hebrew *Vorlage* is interpreted as a proper name and then translated as such. This device creates a meaning in the target language that did not exist in Hebrew (Fernández Marcos 2001, 20). For example, in 1 Kgs 15:22 the Hebrew phrase אין נקי ("without exception") emerges in the Antiochene recension as Ἐναχείμ (cf. G: Αιναχιμ; Fernández Marcos 2001, 16). Or, in a different kind of example, 1 Sam 14:33 has the verb בְּגַדְתֶּם ("you acted treacherously") represented in the G as a place name Γεθθεμ. The Antiochene recension, however, represents it as a place name *twice*; once as in G and again as Ἡμάρτετε—still a proper name but translated "*ad sensum* with recourse to the verb ἁμαρτάνειν" (Fernández Marcos 2001, 16). Fernández Marcos emphasizes that the vast majority of ghost names are "attested in sequences of double readings" (2001, 19) and "occur especially in the genealogical material at the start of 1 Chronicles where the absence of a meaningful context cause [*sic*] major confusion of similar letters in Hebrew and throughout the Greek tradition" (2003, 600). He cautions scholars to attend to proper names because they often convey semantic information: "they have been incorporated by the scribes to the narrative, circulated for centuries as part of the official biblical text for a community, and gave rise to new meanings, exegesis and commentaries. And in a few cases they preserve very ancient, alternative variants that may go back to a Hebrew text different from the Masoretic one" (2001, 21).

The phenomena analyzed by Screnock and Fernández Marcos help explain the process I believe took place in the transmission of Prov 30:1b. While transcribing the superscript of a new collection within Proverbs,

---

70. The term *ghost names* is derived on analogy with the phenomenon of *ghost words* famous in classical philology from Greek lexicography. Ghost words are "created in the minds of the editors of texts (especially papyri and inscriptions) as a set of conjectures which eventually, in the light of new studies or new witnesses, have proved to be false readings" (Fernández Marcos 2001, 14). The lexicons typically record these words in brackets.

3. Reframing Agur's Words

a scribe sees a ל followed by a string of letters (לאיתי). In context, he processes this relatively rare set of letters as the name Ithiel (Neh 11:7). Once לאיתי ולא* was transcribed into a physical manuscript as a name, the traditions diverge—the earlier verbal phrase was preserved in one tradition and the newly fashioned addressee in another. At stage two the novel text may have read:

לאיתיאל א(ו)כל*

To Ithiel: I am able.

At this point—if they had not already done so—the traditions represented by the Greek and Syriac versions diverge from MT. Orthography—the optional ו in אכל—could have been the factor differentiating α' and θ''s readings. In my opinion, G probably also witnesses to this second stage, although it interpreted the name by translating its constitutive elements (Fernández Marcos 2003, 592).[71] A conjunction on אכל may have been inserted at any stage in the process after לאיתיאל was interpreted as a proper name in order to make sense of the verb and smooth out the reading. Alternatively, if אוכל was in the *Vorlage*, the scribe could have engaged in exegetical metathesis of the ו and the א, whether intentionally or unintentionally, in order to make sense of his text (de Waard 1993).

Years pass. Faced with alternative readings in competing *Vorlagen*, a scribe is unable to adjudicate between them and represents both side by side in a fresh manuscript, presenting them as complementary options for the interpreter.[72] This is stage three, and the text may have looked like this:

לאיתיאל לאיתי ולא א(ו)כל*[73]

To Ithiel, I am weary and powerless.

---

71. There is no way to rule out the possibility that G is working from a Hebrew *Vorlage* similar to example 1. In which case, G represents a rendering of the translator's mental text.

72. Talmon (1960) details the process whereby this happened relatively frequently in many different manuscripts. He emphasizes that identifying instances where doublets entered the text is devilishly hard.

73. There would have been a consonantal difference between the two options at this point for the scribe to preserve both.

Despite the lack of direct evidence for this stage, a double reading seems the most plausible explanation for how לאיתיאל came to be duplicated in MT.[74] First, the versions testify that there was a time before the double reading entered the manuscript tradition. Second, לאיתיאל has not always been a name but has sometimes been understood as a verbal phrase, and the midrashic approach of G and V suggests it was originally a verbal phrase different from those that have been preserved. Third, the phenomenon of incorporating alternative textual traditions into one manuscript as a double reading is a known practice whereby texts grew and preserved "alternative wordings of the same texts" (Talmon 1960, 150).

In the fourth and final stage of transmission, the traditions preserved in the double reading—still graphically and semantically challenging—were harmonized toward one another. This could have been accomplished through a similar set of scribal errors described above or through a simpler process of homeoarchy resulting in dittography of לאיתיאל triggered by the reduplication of no less than five consonants in the postulated *Vorlage* (לאיתי). Once both readings were harmonized as this double addressee, we arrive at the text of MT and at T and V, which witness to it. The move to interpret ואכל as a name only comes at this stage. Strictly speaking, "Ukal" is not part of the textual tradition, since MT can still be read as a verb, especially if one adopts the minority reading of the Kennicott manuscripts. The same is true of T (cf. Dan 2:10; 5:16). Only V, in reflecting the midrashic tradition, demands to be read as a name.

3.4.4. Agur's Opening Words

If my reading of Prov 30:1b is persuasive, then Agur's words open on a line that confesses his weakness and ineptitude in a striking manner (Sæbø 2012, 363). Both "to be weary" (לאה) and "to be able" (יכל) pertain

---

74. Indirectly supporting this conclusion, both Plöger and Waltke prefer emendations that handle the occurrences of לאיתיאל differently. Building on Bickell's proposal, Plöger (1984, 353–54, 358) takes the first לאיתיאל as part of the superscript, a further description of הגבר: לָאָה אֶת־הָאֵל, "the one who struggled for God." This third-person description is immediately echoed in the first person in the opening of Agur's discourse: לָאִיתִי אֵל. I believe Plöger is correct in offering two readings that are similar consonantally but distinct semantically. Similarly, Waltke (2005, 455) deduces the purpose for which I believe the doublet was originally preserved by transliterating the first instance as "Ithiel" and translating the second instance, "I am weary, O God" (לָאִיתִי אֵל).

to physical exhaustion and the ability to take action (e.g., Gen 19:11; Isa 16:12; Jer 12:5). Particularly in the prophets, however, these words have uses where the emphasis is clearly on an acute psychological weariness, mental exhaustion, and emotional exasperation over sin (Exod 7:18; Isa 1:14; 7:13; 47:13). In Job 4:2 and 5, Eliphaz uses לאה twice to describe Job as edgy, impatient, easily offended. Similarly, in certain distinctive phrases יכל means "to endure" within the spiritual/psychological realm (Ps 101:5; Job 31:23). In Ps 139:6, לא + יכל describes the psalmist's inability to attain to the knowledge of God. Notably, when לאה and יכל are used in close quarters they focus on spiritual exasperation. In Isa 1:13–14, YHWH denounces Israel, saying he "cannot endure" (לא־אוכל) their iniquity and assemblies; and he "grows weary of bearing" (נלאיתי נשׂא) their feasts. Jeremiah 20:9 pictures the prophet in dire straits—unable to restrain the word of YHWH even to protect his own life. When Agur says he is "weary and powerless," we should not imagine he is elderly or sleepy. The combination of these two lexemes in a context where he goes on to confess his intellectual limits suggests his weariness is not necessarily physical but acutely psychological and even spiritual. For now it suffices to note that these words set a distinctive tone as the opening of Agur's discourse. Most of the parallel uses hail from prophetic contexts, and/or, like Job 4, from contexts where the addressee is being rebuffed. Such diction is in keeping with the tone suggested by the discourse terms *burden* (משׂא) and *oracle* (נאם) in 30:1a. If Agur's speech begins with the confession, "I am weary and powerless," it opens on a note of profound exasperation.

3.5. Proverbs 30:1 as the Superscript of a Collection

In this chapter, I have attempted to plumb the significance of 30:1 as both the superscript of a discrete collection and as Agur's opening words. Doing this required three philological deep-dives into particularly inhospitable waters. The nature of the philological challenges here means they will always be—to some extent—unfathomable. And yet, whatever decisions we make as readers in 30:1 affect our perception of the whole collection, so dive we must. In regard to the name, Agur Bin-Yakeh, I conclude that it could plausibly evoke foreign airs, and "harvester born of obedience" is the best guess if a meaning is intended. As such, the name conjures up the likes of Job or the wise men of the East (1 Kgs 5:10 [ET 4:30]), shadowy figures associated with great wisdom. Early in its exegetical history, however, Agur's name was drawn into Solomon's orbit, much like Qoheleth.

Likewise, we should not imagine this philological profile gives us a real historical description. We have to reckon with the possibility that Agur is a literary creation designed by an unknown author to give voice to a distinctive collection. It seems most judicious and faithful to the text to treat Agur as the persona animating the collection, the voice of an eccentric sage. After all, if Agur *were* a historical individual, we have no knowledge of or access to him beyond this text. Next, I considered משא—the key term that the text uses to characterize Agur's words. Although many would emend this word to discover a national origin for Agur, this move is largely motivated by a misunderstanding of what משא denotes in terms of genre. The word משא is an ancient discourse term that is strongly associated with prophecy, but not one that conforms to modern understandings of a prophetic genre. Instead, I argue that משא deals more with the tone or purpose of a composition. Conceptually, a משא is like a burden the addressee bears. It conveys a responsibility in the form of a teaching, message, or portent. Characterizing Agur's words as a משא might suggest that they are in some manner a warning or a rebuke, perhaps with weighty themes and shades of dark humor. Finally, I considered the fraught textual state of 30:1b. While we must remain duly circumspect about our conclusions, I argued that reconstructing "I am weary and powerless" (לָאִיתִי וְלֹא אוּכָל) makes the best sense of the text as we have it in light of the versions. Moreover, this line makes a suitable and intriguing beginning to Agur's words as he opens on a note of exasperation and personal confession.

In sum, 30:1 encourages us to read the collection in Prov 30 as something of a sardonic warning, animated by the voice of an eccentric sage, and opening on a note of emotional and spiritual exasperation. In chapters 4 and 5, I will develop such an approach to the chapter as a coherent collection.

4
Agur's Wisdom:
Voice, Tone, and Theology in Proverbs 30:2–10

4.1. Will the Real Agur Please Stand Up?

Thus far I have suggested Agur might be read as an eccentric sage, a literary persona who gives voice to this collection, perhaps lending it a foreign and archaic air. I have also argued Agur's words are framed as a "burden" (משא), an ancient discourse term that may connote a sardonic tone of chastisement meant to warn the audience to amend their ways. Finally, I have considered the intriguing possibility that Agur's speech begins on a note of deep existential exasperation. What I have not yet attempted, however, is an actual description of *what* Agur says in terms of wisdom, theology, and ethics. This is by no means a straightforward task. As I argued in chapter 2, few voices in the Hebrew Bible have come in for such radically different construals. Is Agur a theoretical atheist as Ewald (1848, 102; 1837, 166) would have it, a struggling yet sincere convert as Delitzsch (1875, 266) believes, or a sarcastic drop-out from the wisdom schools as Toy (1899, 522) describes him? Who is the real Agur Bin-Yakeh? *What* Agur is saying depends on *how* we construe his voice and tone. So how might we better adjudicate tone so that we can describe Agur's theology and delineate voice with greater precision? As I attempted to show in chapter 2, theological and diachronic theories about wisdom literature have often influenced readings of Prov 30. I propose, therefore, that we set aside larger theological constructs and attempt to work on the issue of tone from within, as it were. Here, I find it helpful to turn to another feature of the text that many commentators have noted, namely, its highly allusive and intertextual nature.[1]

---

1. The issue of intertextuality may again raise questions about dating. With the exception of the quotation of Ps 18:31 [30 ET] // 2 Sam 22:31b in Prov 30:5 and the

Again, this intertextuality has been variously construed. I propose to pursue intertextual connections less in terms of the influence of one text on another and more in terms of tone and theological context. To preempt my own analysis, I will suggest that when we set Agur's statements alongside similar biblical passages we don't actually find a cacophony of "clanging symbols," nor yet anything approaching Feuerbach or Voltaire.[2] Instead we find a collocation of ideas with ample precedent in the Hebrew Bible. Agur is not an atheist, nor yet a skeptic, but is rather styled as a faithful if unconventional sage, offering a distinctive perspective within the book of Proverbs. Agur serves to warn his readers off of pride and greed while commending a stance of humility and contentment in relationship to God.

4.2. Reading Proverbs 30:2–10

For the purpose of describing Agur's theology and construing his voice, I will confine myself in this chapter to 30:2–10. My focus, however, is the coherence of the whole chapter, so this division is more heuristic than descriptive. Proverbs 30:2–10 make an appropriate unit for analysis precisely because of the dynamics of voice in the text. The interplay of voice(s) that I described in chapter 1, decreases abruptly after 30:10, and verses 11–33 are largely a collection of aphoristic material presented in the third person. Moreover, as we saw in chapter 2, debates about how far Agur's words extend and how to construe his theology are largely focused on the first nine verses.[3] I include 30:10 with this material because together with verse 6 it forms a frame in the second person around the prayer in verses 7–9. Since I treated 30:1 exhaustively in the last chapter, I will touch on it only in passing here.

---

probable allusion to Deut 4:2 in Prov 30:6, I do not believe the intertextuality in the chapter requires historical dependence of one text on another. Instead, my interest in employing intertextuality is broadly thematic, theological, and comparative. I am not positing dependence of Prov 30 on the other texts I discuss, nor am I suggesting that they were aware of Prov 30. Instead, I am using these texts to help triangulate Agur's tone and theology, i.e., to establish precedents and analogies for what he might be saying and in what way. Still, if Prov 30 is dependent on Ps 18:31 [30 ET] // 2 Sam 22:31b and aware of developing traditions around Deuteronomy (see appendix at 30:5 and 6: כל אמרת and אל־תוסף), this does not make it a particularly late text.

2. The phrase "clanging symbols" was used to describe Prov 30:1–14 by Crenshaw in an oft-cited 1995 article.

3. For studies dedicated to Prov 30:1–9, see Franklyn 1983; Gunneweg 1992; Moore 1994; Saur 2014; Passaro 2014; and O'Dowd 2018.

4.2.1. An Ignorant Beast: Proverbs 30:2–3

כי בער אנכי מאיש / ולא־בינת אדם לי:
ולא־למדתי חכמה / ודעת קדשים אדע:

2 Though I am more of a beast than a man,
and I do not have the understanding of humankind,
3 and I have not learned wisdom,
yet knowledge of the Holy I know. (Prov 30:2–3)[4]

The first truly intelligible thing Agur says debases his own wisdom by comparing himself to an animal. In the next line, Agur further distances himself from humanity by denying that he has the mental capacity attendant to his species. In 30:3a, then, he appears to make a blanket denial of wisdom and knowledge. While many scholars read verses 2–3 as a strong and surprising repudiation of understanding, wisdom, and knowledge (Schipper 2021, 270; Perdue 2000, 255; McKane 1970, 647), this is not the only, nor perhaps the best, way of understanding these verses.

Because of the tenuous philological state of 30:1, the כי clause in verse 2 raises a problem for interpreters. While most commentators treat כי as causal (i.e., "because"), I suggest we might better read it as a concessive (i.e., "even though").[5] Because concessive כי precedes the clause to which it is subordinated (Aejmelaeus 1986, 205–7), it avoids the exegetical trap of subordinating the thought in verse 2 to the unintelligible line in verse 1b (*pace* Franklyn 1983, 244; McKane 1970, 646). On this reading, the final line of verse 3 is the main clause and the three preceding lines are dependent on it, thus all four lines develop one idea: "Though I am more of a beast than a man, / and I do not have the understanding of humankind, / And I have not learned wisdom, / yet knowledge of the Holy I know."[6] In effect, then, Agur's confession moves conceptually from 30:2a to 3b: despite the fact that I am beastly, *I know* the Holy. Here I am read-

---

4. For convenience, in this chapter and the next I put the text under discussion at the beginning of each section. For the whole text of Prov 30 as well as in-depth discussion of various philological issues, see the appendix.
5. E.g., Ps 23:4; Jer 14:12; Bekins and Kirk 2017, 367–68; *BHRG* §40.29.1.(1); Joüon §171b.
6. Syntactically this reading is similar to that of Richter (2001, 420–21), who proposes reading כי as a conditional so that the lines run, "Suppose I were more clumsy than anyone / and did not possess the acumen of [other] people / and I had not learned any skill, / could I attain knowledge of the holy?"

ing 30:3b as a positive statement rather than carrying the force of the negative from 3a into the second line (Delitzsch 1875, 273; Waltke 2005, 456).⁷ Both the structure of the quatrain and the poetic diction of verse 3 support this decision. In the outer frame, the first and last lines make positive statements, while in the inner frame the second and third lines make negative statements. In 30:3, the word order places verbs of knowing in the outer frame and objects of knowledge in the inner frame so that the noun "knowledge" (דעת) is fronted in 3b. This chiasm suggests a contrast between the lines (*BHRG* §47.1). The use of the forward-looking *yiqtol* verb, אדע ("I [will] know"), departs from the backward-looking *qatal*, למדתי ("I have not learned"), furthering the sense of contrast.⁸ Syntax and poetry thus conspire to delay the verb "I know" (אדע) till the last slot in the verse so that it functions almost like a punch line, revealing the surprising turn at the end. Rhetorically, all this shifts the emphasis of Agur's opening statements onto the final line in which he claims that he *does* have knowledge.⁹

While these two verses contain several words commonly associated with wisdom ("understanding" בינה, "wisdom" חכמה, "knowledge" דעת; Schipper 2013, 56), reflecting on Agur's most distinctive term helps to clarify his ideas. Consider the adjective "brutish" or "beastly" (בער).

---

7. Although this puts me decidedly in the minority of interpreters, the syntax is open-ended. Most scholars think the negative in 3a applies to the verb in 3b as well, e.g., Rashi; Ibn Ezra (see commentary at Deut 32:31 or Lev 10:6); Toy 1899, 526; Murphy 1998, 226 n. 3a; and Fox 2009, 855. Both T and S support the majority position by making the negative particle explicit in 30:3b. However, in a thorough article, Miller (2005, 52) established basic criteria for identifying the ellipsis of negative particles across poetic lines in Biblical Hebrew. Even when all the criteria are met, it is still possible that the "syntax is not determinative and the polarity of the second line can be ascertained only through semantics. That is, an interpreter must decide which syntactic structure to assign on the basis of exegesis" (51). In a footnote, Miller (51 n. 35) specifically draws attention to Prov 30:3, "most translations understand the negative to be gapped (e.g., NJPS, NRSV), but it is not necessarily the case (e.g., JPSV)" (cf. Ps 50:8). Fox (2009, 855; cf. 2000, 112, 309), who changed his position on this issue between volumes of his Anchor Bible Proverbs, acknowledges, "In the Hebrew the extension of the force of the negative is more strained than in English, because nonsequential Hebrew verbs normally require their own negations."

8. See Cook 2005 on the use of *qatal* and *yiqtol* in Proverbs.

9. In G, 30:3 has no negative at all (see appendix at v. 3: אדע ... ולא). This is not determinative for reading the syntax of the Hebrew because there may be a text-critical issue, but it shows that reading 30:3 as a positive statement has ancient roots.

Because it is quite rare, it is probably not incidental (Saur 2014, 576).[10] If the author had wanted to indicate generic foolishness, more obvious terms like כסיל or אויל come to mind. However, unlike these more common words that are translated "fool," בער emphasizes animal-like simplicity vis-a-vis God and/or humanity rather than moral cupidity (Donald 1963, 292).[11] In the Torah, the collective noun בעיר appears five times denoting herds of cattle (Gen 45:17; Exod 22:4; Num 20:4–11; cf. Ps 78:48). Although the word בער is usually rendered "foolish" or "stupid" (e.g., Franklyn 1983, 244), this approach erases any animalistic connection for English readers, whereas the Hebrew Bible itself highlights the beastly connotations of the word (Ps 73:22; Ps 49:11, 13 also make the connection but less clearly). Translating as "beast/beastly" or "brute/brutish" better captures this distinctive color.[12] In commenting on Agur's self-application of this descriptor, many scholars invoke tropes whereby the speaker is hyperbolically self-effacing (e.g., Ps 22:7 [6 ET]; Job 25:4–6; Clifford 1999, 261). Perhaps Agur applies the term sarcastically (Toy 1899, 521; Gunneweg 1992, 255; Van Leeuwen 1997b, 252). But when we examine the tone and context of other passages that use the word בער, they suggest Agur is not so much playing dense as he is introducing a metaphor by which he compares himself to an animal (McKane 1970, 646). In what sense then does Agur assert this comparison?

To reflect on this question we must turn to the Psalms, where בער occurs most often. Psalms 49:11, 92:7 [6 ET], and 94:8 use the word to connote human finitude, particularly in terms of knowledge and lifespan. In each of these psalms, בער is certainly not a positive designation, but neither is the בער singled out for particular hostility. Rather, the term appears in the context of circumscribing human finitude in relationship to God. Psalm 73:22, however, offers the closest parallel to Prov 30 and draws out the beastly connotations of the lexeme explicitly.[13] Other

---

10. As an adjective בער occurs just five times (Pss 49:11; 73:22; 92:7; Prov 12:1; 30:2).

11. In Arabic, Aramaic, Old South Arabian, Akkadian, and Ethiopic √בער means either camel or ox/beast of burden (see *HALOT*, s.v. "בער"; and Ringgren 1977, 204–5).

12. In British English, however, these terms may have certain connotations of unfeeling cruelty that go beyond what Hebrew בער connotes.

13. Clifford (1999, 258) observes "verses 1–6 are a dramatic narrative like Psalm 73," and Fox (2009, 861) finds Prov 30's "closest affinities are with certain psalms, in particular Ps 73." I am not suggesting that either of these texts is alluding to the other. Instead, I am trying to show how another biblical text employs the word בער in a

than Prov 30:2, this is the only passage where a speaker self-applies בער as the predicate in a verbless clause; but unlike Prov 30, Ps 73 uses בער within a more developed theological discourse. The psalmist opens with a statement of confidence in the goodness of God (73:1), but immediately pivots to recount his existential crisis (73:2–3). His perception that the wicked grow rich in their wickedness while he labors "to clean his heart" and "bathe his hands" yet is daily stricken anew threatens to overwhelm and undercut his confidence in God (73:12–13). The only way he is able to think his way clear of this existential crisis is by reorienting to God. The transition takes place in verse 17, where he says, "When I entered the sanctuary of God, I understood their end." The psalm then reflects this reorientation by switching to second-person speech addressing God directly (73:18–28).[14] Here we come to 73:22–26, the stanza where he likens himself to a beast.

> 22 I am like a beast [בער] and I do not know;
> a herd animal I am with you [עמך].
> 23 But I am always with you [עמך];
> you grasp my right hand.
> 24 In your counsel you lead me
> and after glory you take me.
> 25 Who is for me in heaven unless I am with you [עמך]?
> I do not rejoice on the earth.
> 26 My flesh is finished; and my heart—my heart is a rock.
> But my portion is God forever. (Ps 73:22–26)

In 73:21, the psalmist recalls the psychological anguish of watching the wicked prosper with which he opened the poem. The insolubility of this existential dilemma prompts solace in the ignorance of a beast. Specifically, this ignorance directs him toward the protection of God. Having adopted a beastly posture, he is in a position to be led (73:24). This posi-

---

context that has many thematic similarities with Prov 30. Moreover, because Ps 73 offers a more fully articulated context it helps us to see the theological logic that holds these themes together and sheds light on how בער might be operating as a descriptor in Prov 30.

14. Language addressed to God is commonplace in the Psalms, but it is significant that Prov 30:7–9 reflects this reorientation by including the only prayer in the book of Proverbs. On Prov 30:7–9 as a prayer, see Kline 2021.

tion gives him access to God's counsel (v. 24), but perhaps more than this it gives him access to God (vv. 23, 26). Despite his lack of knowledge, he is with God (עִמָּךְ; a phrase repeated three times in four verses, vv. 22, 23, 25). He does not pontificate across the expanse of heaven and earth but clings to God as his portion when strength fails (vv. 25–26). This intimate relationship with God allows him to operate according to God's counsel, and this relationship becomes the resolution to the existential challenge of 73:2–3: "For look—those who are far from you will perish.… but as for me, it is good to be near God" (vv. 27–28). "Here, as in Proverbs," reflects Paul Franklyn (1983, 245), "the weary and embittered person confesses ignorance of God and, in the same breath, he seizes the outstretched hand of the divine presence." The posture of the beast who does not know seems to have enabled this relational knowledge, whereas the more the poet struggled on his own to understand the prosperity of the wicked, the more psychological anguish he experienced (Saur 2014, 576). Knowledge of God and a certain confession of ignorance seem to go hand in hand in Ps 73.

While it may have shades of irony, Agur's use of the word בַעַר need not be self-effacing hyperbole nor yet sarcasm, but rather suggests an image of sincere, humble dependence—like that of a dumb beast toward its master. The epistemological stance evoked by the use of the word בַעַר is a metaphor for relationship with God (cf. Ps 23). When existential problems and intellectual dilemmas become overwhelming, one strategy is adopting the ignorance of faith that leans into God, perhaps less for answers than for the reassuring presence that changes one's perspective. This profile of Agur's language opens the door to the possibility that a subtle contrast is being drawn across Prov 30:2–3.

Agur does not claim to have knowledge generally but specifically "knowledge of the Holy" (דַעַת קְדֹשִׁים). However, precisely what קְדֹשִׁים is meant to entail is vague (see appendix at v. 3: קְדֹשִׁים). As an adjective, "qdš is a term for the deity's status or quality (i.e., God is holy), and for what belongs to or is in the realm of the deity, whether persons or objects (e.g., holy priests, holy temple)" (Clines 2021, 16). As a substantive, then, it can stand for holy people, "saints" in anachronistic parlance, divine beings generally, or God himself (Hos 12:1). As Simon Parker (1999, 719) puts it, "It is not always easy to distinguish when 'holy ones' refers to divine beings and when it refers to Yahweh himself (as a 'plural of majesty') or to human 'saints.'" If we look, then, for analogs to קְדֹשִׁים within the immediate context of Prov 30:1–10, the best parallels are the designations for God (אֱלוֹהַּ,

vv. 5, 9; יהוה, v. 9). God's inalienable holiness suggests the connection but strong support comes from Prov 9:10, the only other verse in the Hebrew Bible with the phrase דעת קדשים (cf. Prov 1:2; Isa 11:2):

תחלת חכמה יראת יהוה / ודעת קדשים בינה:

The beginning of wisdom is the fear of YHWH, / and knowledge of the Holy is understanding. (Prov 9:10)

This verse aligns "the fear of YHWH" with "knowledge of the Holy," strongly suggesting that קדשים is synonymous with or related to YHWH.[15] This case is only strengthened when we consider Prov 2:5–6:

אז תבין יראת יהוה / ודעת אלהים תמצא:
כי־יהוה יתן חכמה / מפיו דעת ותבונה:

Then you will understand the fear of YHWH / and you will find the knowledge of God,
for YHWH gives wisdom, / from his mouth knowledge and understanding.

Perhaps surprisingly, this is the only verse with the phrase "knowledge of God" in all of Proverbs. Proverbs 2:5 places "knowledge of God" in parallel with "the fear of YHWH" in the same way that Prov 9:10 does with "knowledge of the Holy" thus strengthening the equation between "God" (אלהים) and "the Holy One" (קדשים). The context of Prov 2:1–4 makes clear that by seeking after wisdom the faithful person will in fact discover God, because God is himself the source of wisdom.[16]

In sum, Agur appears initially to be downplaying his knowledge in a profound way only to make the unexpected claim that he nevertheless possesses knowledge of God. If a certain human wisdom is lacking, a remarkable knowledge of the divine seems to take its place. While it may

---

15. Thus the NJPS, NIV, and ESV render "the Holy One" in both Prov 30:3 and 9:10. The majority of interpreters also find this connection determinative: *DCH* 7, s.v. "קָדוֹשׁ"; Toy 1899, 521; McKane 1970, 368; Plöger 1984, 354 b; Crenshaw 1995, 375; Clifford 1999, 107; Fox 2000, 308; O'Dowd 2018, 109.

16. One ancient Jewish interpreter, the Malbim, understood דעת קדשים as "sacred knowledge, which transmits the secrets of creation and the celestial spheres" (Ginsberg and Weinberger 2007, 618). He considered such wisdom the most advanced, requiring total integration of more basic learning.

not be clear what to make of it at this point, I think it is fair to say there is something ironic and subversive about the way Agur has structured these verses and self-applied the term בער. As in Ps 73, Agur seems to have made a godly virtue of his beastly qualities.

4.2.2. Toward the Knowledge of God: Proverbs 30:4

מי עלה־שמים וירד / מי אסף־רוח בחפניו
מי צרר־מים בשמלה / מי הקים כל־אפסי־ארץ
מה־שמו ומה־שם־בנו / כי תדע:

Who ascended to heaven and then descended?
Who gathered wind in his palms?
Who bound waters in a robe?
Who established all the ends of the earth?
What is his name and what is the name of his son?
Surely you know! (Prov 30:4)

Following Agur's self-abasing yet epistemologically positive stance in 30:2–3, the reader meets a series of pointed rhetorical questions in verse 4. On my reading of verses 2–3, the most natural question to ask is how Agur attains such knowledge, not to mention what such knowledge might entail, particularly since he contrasts it to human understanding and wisdom. A gesture toward an answer has already been suggested by the use of בער in Ps 73. A certain posture toward God allows God to lead the psalmist in his counsel. Proverbs 30:4 may provide further answers, but it does so by posing questions. One way into the text is through a question the commentaries generally take up: What figure are these rhetorical questions meant to evoke? Is it YHWH, a human figure, or someone else? Framing the discussion this way has its shortcomings, but it nevertheless suggests a way into the material that helps us think about the imagery. We will first consider ascending and descending in 30:4a, then the cosmic imagery of 4b–d, and finally the name of his son in 4e. In short, I will argue that the tone and imagery of verse 4 do not at all demand a theological break from what precedes it but rather suggest significant connections: in an evocative but somewhat oblique way the imagery of 30:4 relegates human wisdom and power to divine wisdom and power, but holds out the possibility that humans can access wisdom through relationship and revelation. To be sure, verse 4 does not engage the questions of verses 2–3 directly but rather extends their themes through juxtaposition of evocative imagery.

4.2.2.1. Ascending and Descending

No text describes YHWH as ascending to heaven, although there are a handful of texts where he descends (e.g., Exod 19:11, 18, 20; 2 Sam 22:10 // Ps 18:9; Ps 144:5). What is more, the starting point for the verbs here is the earth from whence the figure journeys to heaven and then returns (Toy 1899, 521).[17] Even if it is not decisive on its own, this observation implies a mortal figure is in view. Conversely, a few human figures ascend though they never descend (e.g., Elijah in 2 Kgs 2:1, 11; Enoch in Gen 5:24; see Fox 2009, 857), but these figures are exceptions that prove the rule. Their ascent to heaven takes place through divine initiative and highlights their special relationship to YHWH. These positive ascents of the righteous find their foil in the more common hubristic attempts to take heaven by force. In Isa 14:13, the king of Babylon aspires to ascend to heaven and establish his throne among the stars of El, sitting in the divine assembly. This description is parodied by the prophet as the very height of hubris—a goal whose arrogance guarantees its own failure and a one-way ticket to *She'ol* (Greenspahn 1994, 37; cf. Jer 51:53; Job 20:4–7; Gen 11:4–5).

This so-called ascent-descent topos occurs in many manifestations in ancient Near Eastern texts. One variation appears as a proverb at the climax of the Dialogue of Pessimism:

> 83 Who is so tall as to ascend to the heavens?
> 84 Who is so broad as to compass the underworld? (Lambert 1996, 149)

This proverb "is utilized to express not only the general distinction between human and divine, but more specifically, the notion of the remoteness of divine *wisdom*, the key for understanding the secrets of the universe, from human kind" (Samet 2011, 6, emphasis original).[18] In the Sumerian fragments known as Gilgamesh and the Land of the Living, for example,

---

17. The rare use of a *wayyiqtol* verb form in poetry suggests the order of events here is intended to be sequential rather than merely presentational, i.e., "ascends *and then* descends," rather than "ascends *and also* descends."

18. For examples of the theme in Akkadian wisdom literature, see Ludlul Bel Nemeqi, or the Poem of the Righteous Sufferer, 2.36–37 (Lambert 1996, 41) and the Babylonian Theodicy 24.256–257 (Lambert 1996, 87). For instances of this proverb in Sumerian literature, see Alster 1975b, 88; and Samet 2011, 3–6; with comments in

Gilgamesh utters the proverb to capture the human condition and justify his quest for immortality (lines 28–29; Kramer 1947, 11). In biblical texts as in their ancient Near Eastern analogs, those who attempt to ascend to heaven are met with failure and judgment.

So the image of ascending and descending evokes ideas of human mortality and finitude, a theme that surfaced both in Agur's apparent expression of exasperation (Prov 30:1b) and in his confession that he is more beast than man (v. 2). This imagery also connects to another acute aspect of human finitude that has been squarely in focus, namely, *knowledge*. Consider Deut 30:12 where Moses assures the people that the command he is delivering to them is attainable:

לא בשמים הוא לאמר מי יעלה־לנו השמימה ויקחה לנו וישמענו אתה ונעשנה:

It is not in heaven, so as to say, "Who will ascend for us to heaven and take it for us and make us hear it so that we might do it." (Deut 30:12)

Thus one reason to ascend to heaven would be to secure the words of God. Indeed, revelation is often in view in the few places where YHWH descends. The key text, of course, is Exod 19, where YHWH descends on Mount Sinai to declare the law to Israel (Exod 19:11, 18, 20; 20:1–17; Neh 9:13; cf. Exod 34:5; Num 11:25; 12:5). Moses's exhortation in Deut 30 has this tradition as its background. YHWH has graciously revealed his law, thus empowering Israel to keep it. Moses's point, in part, is that the law is not an esoteric thing but something they know because it has been revealed. They do not have to ascend to get the word because it is written in "this Book of the Law" (Deut 30:10); "it is very near you; it is in your mouth and in your heart" (30:14).

But the text in the Hebrew Bible with the most verbal parallels to Prov 30:4a is Gen 28:12. Only here do beings ascend and descend—in that order—between heaven and earth:

ויחלם והנה סלם מצב ארצה וראשו מגיע השמימה והנה מלאכי אלהים עלים וירדים בו:

Lambert 1996, 327. For further background and analysis of this proverb, with many examples, see also Greenspahn 1994; Van Leeuwen 1997a; and Greenstein 2003.

And then he dreamed—and look!—there was a staircase standing on the earth with its top touching the heavens. And look!—divine messengers were ascending and descending on it. (Gen 28:12)

Again, this description relates to revelation. YHWH speaks to Jacob in a dream (Gen 28:13–15) and, on waking, Jacob realizes he has slept in a place where the veil between heaven and earth is thin. His dream, it seems, enabled him to perceive this reality in the form of a staircase to heaven. The beings that are ascending and descending are not human figures but divine messengers. Genesis 28 suggests again that the ascent-descent topos is related to revelation, but the figures capable of ascending and descending are divine beings and the means of their ascent and descent is supernatural. Jacob is not invited to ascend the staircase.

The motif of ascent and descent to heaven is vast and many more texts could fill in the picture, but in short, in biblical texts as in ancient Near Eastern texts more broadly, ascent and descent imagery focuses on human limitations as contrasted with the divine. Although it might go without saying that YHWH *could* ascend and descend between heaven and earth, the question rather places the spotlight on humanity and evokes a broad tradition of failed attempts to grasp after divinity from Gilgamesh to the tower of Babel. Nevertheless, the trope does not preclude communication between human and divine realms. On his prerogative, God descends to enlighten humanity.

4.2.2.2. Cosmic Knowledge

If the imagery of Prov 30:4a suggests human limitation, 4b–d rather uses anthropomorphic language to describe YHWH's total power over the whole scope of creation. Elsewhere in the Hebrew Bible "palms" (חפנים) are associated with literal acts of holding a substance in human hands (Exod 9:8; Lev 16:12; Ezek 10:2, 7), but the image can be extended figuratively (Eccl 4:6). "Binding" (צרר) evokes the idea of restriction, most often in the sense of being trapped or distressed, however, a telling set of passages describe wrapping up physical objects so they remain fast (e.g., Prov 26:8). In Exod 12:34 the Israelites bind up kneading bowls in their cloaks as they flee from Egypt (צררת בשמלתם); and in Job 26:8 God holds back the cosmic waters by binding them with clouds (צרר־מים בעביו). Texts focused on YHWH's freedom and power in creation often employ such language of limiting or circumscribing the cosmos (Isa 40:12; Ps 104:2–6; Job 38:4–

11). Likewise, the "the ends of the earth" (אפסי־ארץ) is most often used as a metonym for the populations at the farthest reaches of geographic dispersion (1 Sam 2:10; Isa 45:22; 52:10; Ps 2:8; Sir 36:22), but it can also be used for the physical edges of the inhabitable universe (Mic 5:3; Zech 9:10; Jer 16:19; Ps 72:8; Sir 44:21). The sheer scope of this imagery, if we imagine it seriously, evokes a cosmic body—one large enough to handle the forces of nature as a man might scoop soot or coals into his hands or wrap up household goods in a cloak (Exod 9:8; 12:34). Establishing the ends of the earth, gathering winds, and binding up waters all suggest the Creator's sovereign power over a limited creation.

While this might seem unrelated to the ascent and descent imagery in Prov 30:4a, the frame of the scope and limits of creation holds together power and knowledge in many biblical texts. The closest parallels to Prov 30:4 in terms of both tone and rhetoric on the one hand and imagery on the other are in Isa 40 and Job 38.[19] In both those contexts—although to different purposes—rhetorical questions similar to Prov 30:4 are used to emphasize God's freedom and omnipotence in creation and underscore the same contrast between divine knowledge and human ignorance that 4a evokes. These two passages help us to frame our reading of Prov 30:4 in terms of both tone and content.

Isaiah 40:12–14 uses a barrage of rhetorical questions to highlight the gap between YHWH and humanity.

12 Who measured the waters in the hollow of his hand [בשעלו],[20]
or gauged the heavens with a span,
or contained the dust of the earth in a measure,
or weighed mountains in the balance,
or the heights on scales?
13 Who gauged the spirit of YHWH?

---

19. Nearly all of the secondary literature points out these parallels, but I have not seen them meaningfully developed as part of a reading of Prov 30.

20. The conceptual parallel to Prov 30:4b–c at Isa 40:12 is quite close although the wording is not identical. Isaiah 40:12a uses not "in his palms" (בחפניו) but a close synonym "in the hollow of his hand" (בשעלו; BDB, s.v. "שעל"; DCH 8, s.v. "שֹׁעַל"). Isaiah 40 has water measured whereas Prov 30 has winds gathered and waters being bound up. Despite these differences in the nuance of expression, both passages clearly depict a cosmic deity handling the stuff of creation.

What man informed him [יודיענו] of his counsel [עצתו]?²¹
14 With whom did he consult that he might
make him understand [ויבינהו],
or teach him the path of justice [וילמדהו בארח משפט],
or teach him knowledge [וילמדהו דעת],
or inform him of the way of understanding [ודרך תבונות יודיענו]?
(Isa 40:12–14)

These rhetorical questions are focused squarely on humanity to press home the weight of their limits. Humanity's inability to gauge the stuff of creation in Prov 30:12 gives way in verses 13–14 to wisdom language and humanity's inability to instruct YHWH. If we reverse these questions, as it were, they imply a set of affirmations about God. He *can* measure the waters in his hands, he *does* possess knowledge. Significantly, the whole chapter is framed in terms of divine speech. Isaiah 40:1–9 contain a complex interplay of voices introducing the commissioning of a prophet who will deliver words of comfort from God to his people. Although we read the voice of the prophet, the text reminds us at key points that it relays the words of God. Indeed, 40:8 contains one of the great theological assertions on behalf of the word of God in Scripture: "Grass withers, flowers fade / but the word of our God will stand forever." For the tradents behind Isa 40, the unfathomable wisdom of God and the untraceable scope of his creation converge in divine speech that breaks through to reframe human knowledge.

While the tone of Isa 40:12–14 could be construed in isolation as scathing or dismissive, it is probably better characterized as grand and triumphant. The rhetoric of the chapter overall is not to tear down the addressee or to debunk human knowledge, but rather to declare the triumphant return of YHWH and in so doing encourage the nation (Isa 40:1–4). The primary means of doing this is by exalting YHWH (40:9–11), and in this context we encounter the first barrage of rhetorical questions (40:12–14). But from these questions focused on creation and knowledge, the text

---

21. The wisdom language in Isa 40:13b–14 ("understand" √בנה, "teach" √למד, and "knowledge" דעת), all have counterparts in Prov 30:2–3; while several more terms, "counsel" (עצה, Prov 1:25; 8:14; 12:15; 19:20–21; 27:9), "inform" (√ידע, Prov 1:23; 9:9; 22:19, 21), as well as the language related to the path metaphor (ארח, Prov 2:8, 13, 15, 19–20; 17:23; דרך, Prov 2:13, 20; 3:6; 4:19; 10:9; 14:12; 28:18; 29:27) have resonance in the broader context of Proverbs.

4. Agur's Wisdom

moves straight to a critique of the nations and their idols. The theme of the text is not any one attribute, but YHWH's overall incomparability (40:18, 25). Throughout the whole discourse, rhetorical questions elevate the tone by presenting YHWH's majesty as incontrovertible (40:21, 25, 28). The chapter ends with a strong affirmation of God's creative power and comprehensive knowledge on behalf of a frail people (40:28–31). Creating a bookend with 40:1, these verses surely intend to comfort and encourage: "The Lord is God from of old, / Creator of the earth from end to end, / he never grows faint or weary, / His wisdom cannot be fathomed. ... they who trust in the Lord shall renew their strength.... They shall run and not grow weary, / they shall march and not grow faint" (40:28, 31, NJPS).

Perhaps no text, however, develops themes of creation, divine knowledge, and human finitude at greater length and with more remarkable power of expression than YHWH's speeches in Job 38–41. Here God also speaks in rhetorical questions, but this time for 129 verses, extending the device to its limits. Particularly in the imagery of Job 38, the scope and breadth of the material cosmos is in view in a manner analogous to Prov 30. However, the clearest connection in terms of tone, is the identical expression "for you know!" (כי תדע) in both Prov 30:4 and Job 38:5. Because YHWH uses forceful rhetoric and does not appear to answer Job's questions or account for his suffering, many commentators have described the tone of Job 38 in largely harsh and negative terms.[22] As Whybray (1998, 159) puts it, "The posing of questions to which the speaker knows the answer is a particular rhetorical device ... their function is to put the person addressed at a disadvantage—here by the use of heavy irony." Indeed, one function of the rhetorical questions in Job 38 is to highlight Job's lack of wisdom and knowledge. However, Fox (1981, 58) makes the keen observation that this need not be construed as malicious or hostile—even if there *is* an element of irony—but can in fact be a genuine, relational, didactic strategy. While it is certainly plausible to read the emphatic כי תדע ("Surely you know!")

---

22. Thus von Rad's evaluation, "All commentators find the divine speech highly scandalous, in so far as it bypasses completely Job's particular concerns, and because in it Yahweh in no way condescends to any kind of self-interpretation" (1972, 225). Although Clines acknowledges a range of interpretations and cautions against importing our own standards of politeness to the ancient dialogue he concludes, "there is little denying that the tone of Yahweh's speech tends more toward the severe, if not the savage, than toward the gracious" (2011, 1088). For further surveys of viewpoints on the tone of YHWH's speeches, see Clines 2004, 242–45; and Ham 2013, 527–28.

as sarcasm or even a mocking put-down, the phrase can also be seen as sincerely underscoring the rhetorical nature of the questions (Fox 1981, 60).[23] As if YHWH is saying, in effect, "Come on, you know this!" As a literary thought experiment, Fox suggests rephrasing the rhetorical statements in Job 38 as indicatives. Doing this, he argues, would change the tone dramatically.

> God's remarks receive a harsh, bragging, bullying tone that they do not have in the original, mainly because in the indicative version God is not drawing Job in, not making him participate in the knowledge, but merely rubbing Job's face in his own feebleness. Through these rhetorical questions God does speak of his own wisdom and power and Job's relative weakness and ignorance, but he does so with compassion and gentleness, albeit a stern gentleness.... God demands humility, not humiliation. (Fox 1981, 59)

The tone of the questions, concludes Fox (2018, 12), "is not ridicule but persuasion, though, as is typical in pedagogy, they are not devoid of rebuke."[24]

---

23. In Prov 30:4 as in Job 38:5, it seems best to read כי as a modal adverb, i.e., "indeed," "surely," "truly" (*BHRG* §40.29.2.(4); Franklyn 1983, 248; Clines 2011, 1053 n. 5.c). As a modal adverb, כי emphasizes confirmation, similar to its use in oaths (e.g., Gen 42:16). I ought to emphasize, however, that this analysis of כי is deictic since the word fits neatly into no one grammatical category (Aejmelaeus 1986, 194). Moreover, English glosses tend to import semantic values that כי does not properly carry. Nevertheless, I base my analysis on the discourse in Job 38:4–5. In Job 38:4, YHWH asks where Job was when he laid the foundation of the earth (איפה היית ביסדי־ארץ) and then demands Job respond (הגד) to him "if you know understanding" (אם־ידעת בינה). In the next verse, YHWH fires off another rhetorical question followed by כי תדע. After YHWH's question in verse 4 ("I was founding earth") it would be nonsensical if Job was unable to answer the question of verse 5 ("Who set its measurements?"). The expression כי תדע is no command for Job to respond but rather an emphatic statement. The clause כי תדע underlines the rhetorical questions that precede it. As Fox (1981, 58) writes, "The parenthetical 'for you know' is not sarcastic but emphatic: God is reminding Job that he knows quite well who the architect and builder of the universe is." In my opinion, this understanding of the tone of כי תדע also applies in Prov 30.

24. Or as Habel (1985, 548–49) puts it, "The tone of his [YHWH's] response is ironic but not vitriolic." Irony is indeed central to Job 38–41. It explains how the speeches can seem simultaneously both aggressive and consoling. A deep sense of irony that even approaches humor is part and parcel of these speeches as they push toward the absurd in the scope and level of detail. Cf. Ham (2013), who makes a notable but ultimately unconvincing case that YHWH's tone is gentle and comforting.

But what does YHWH teach Job? A series of rhetorical questions is a poor vehicle for communicating information but they serve powerfully to reveal how little Job knows about the universe—how poorly he understands its inner workings and remote places. On my reading, God levels three types of questions at Job in chapter 38. The most common type of question simply demands a negative response. These tend to be questions that point out Job's finitude in terms of mortality, power, or knowledge: "Have you commanded the morning since your days began?" (38:18, NRSV); or, "Do you know the ordinances of the heavens?" (38:33, NRSV). The second most frequent are questions to which the only plausible answer is God/YHWH. Generally, these are questions of the "who did X" variety followed by a cosmic task such as shutting the doors of the sea (38:8) or numbering the clouds by wisdom (38:37). Finally, there are a few questions that confront Job with his lack of knowledge and to which he must respond, "I do not know:" "On what were earth's foundations sunk?" (38:6); or, "Where is the way to the dwelling of light?" (38:19, NRSV). The total effect of all these questions is continually to relegate Job and his knowledge while simultaneously holding up God alone as the one who possesses comprehensive knowledge and power. The first question established this point and all the others develop it: "Where were you when I established the earth? Declare understanding if you know" (38:4).

In terms of the content of knowledge, then, Job learns practically nothing. The only information that Job could be construed as learning is the kind of information that serves to deepen his understanding of his own ignorance. One gets the impression at times that God is asking Job to weigh in on things that he did not realize existed and events that he did not know took place—as if you asked a person in the street who was defenestrated in Prague or what language the Deir 'Alla plaster inscription was written in. By virtue of the question one might learn such an event took place or the inscription exists, but this is not the point. Job himself seems to acknowledge this in his response to YHWH's first speech: "What can I respond to you? My hand I have placed over my mouth" (ידי שמתי למו פי, Job 40:4; see §5.3.3). But in terms of wisdom and relational knowledge, everything is reframed. Job has encountered God. He has heard God speak and he has glimpsed the world from God's perspective. This reality is reflected in Job's response to YHWH's second speech when he says, "I have uttered what I did not understand, / things too wonderful for me, which I did not know.... I had heard of you by the hearing of the ear, / but now my eye sees you" (Job 42:3, 5; NRSV). God hasn't taught Job anything, per se, but he has revealed himself and his glory shines a light on Job's finitude. Thus Job is educated.

To sum up this discussion of Isa 40, Job 38, and Prov 30:4, the vivid imagery of 30:4b–d pictures actions that are the domain of YHWH alone. In both Isa 40 and Job 38, such cosmic language is used to underscore the distance between God and humanity in terms both of power and wisdom. These rhetorical questions, then, are surely double-sided because in as much as they comment on God, they comment on humanity in contrast with God. The questions in Prov 30:4 evoke a response of "Not I, but only you."[25] While the tone ranges from encouragement and awe in Isa 40 to rebuke and even friendly mockery in Job 38, I would suggest the main point of these questions in this location is to relegate human wisdom to the experience of God. In the course of commenting on Job, Samuel Balentine (2006, 634) says this about Isa 40:

> The objective of such questions is not to condemn persons for their failures. It is to encourage them to believe that the Creator of the world can construct new possibilities where none seem to exist. The objective is not to silence those whose doubts threaten to eclipse faith. It is to summon forth new affirmations that transform brokenness and loss by embracing the unfathomable certainty of God's promise to redeem.

As Fox (1981, 60) says concerning Job 38, "the limitation of Job's wisdom is not the main point. The main point is something that man can see quite clearly if he only broadens his perspective: God's wisdom and power in creating and ruling the cosmos." In a similar manner, perhaps Prov 30:4 captures both the appropriate awe for and exaltation of the one who has accomplished the ordering of the cosmos and carries with it an implicit rebuke directed at those who are foolish enough to hem him in with words. By the juxtaposition of 30:4 with verses 2–3, Agur expresses a conclusion that is quite similar to Job in 42:1–6. In light of the divine speeches, Job diminishes his own knowledge and wisdom but he holds onto the knowledge of God that he has received through the encounter. Agur likewise demurs from human wisdom and understanding and yet maintains he

---

25. My handling of these issues contrasts with others who compare Job 38 to Prov 30:4 on this point. Schipper, e.g., writes "This answer cannot be 'YHWH.' On the contrary, the nature of the questions,… emphasizes the very inadequacy of human knowledge" (2021, 271).

4.2.2.3 The Name of His Son

It remains to say something about the intriguing reference to "the name of his son" (שם־בנו) in Prov 30:4e. While many Christian interpreters have found this line bursting with theological potential, it is somewhat enigmatic from the perspective of the Hebrew Bible.[26] It might help us to think through these questions if we reflect further on their significance. Why ask for a name at this juncture at all? What does it mean to ask for a name? And what might the father-son relationship entail?

Names in the Hebrew Bible capture something of a person's significance and essence.[27] If this is true of names generally, surely it is true of God's name. The revelation of God's name is often at issue in moments of intense encounter with the divine when the relationship between God and his people is at stake (Gen 32:28–30, Exod 3:13; 33:18–19; 34:6–7).[28] God's name is a metonym for his character and his reputation as based on his mighty acts and faithfulness toward his people (Exod 20:24; Deut 28:58; Josh 9:9; 1 Kgs 8:41–43; Ps 18:50; Isa 30:27; Imes 2018, 48–49). In light of the cosmic language discussed above, the question, "What is his name?" (מה שמו), should evoke an obvious answer, "YHWH is his name" (Franklyn 1983, 247; cf. יהוה שמו in Amos 5:8; 9:6).[29] But going on to ask for the name of his son raises the question of whether, not to mention in what sense, YHWH might have a son. If the answer to this question

---

26. See Keefer (2016, 38–39) for the use of this verse in Christian systematic theologies. Novenson (2019) gives a sense of the complexity of the issue in ancient Jewish sources.

27. Names are not always meaningful, but narratives often draw attention to their origins and significance (Gen 25:25–26; 27:36; Ruth 1:20; 1 Sam 25:25). On the symbolism of names in the Hebrew Bible generally, see Barr 1969. For a review of the significance of God's name in relationship to Israel see Imes 2018, 46–87.

28. Surprisingly, these passages, along with Judg 13:17–18, are the only close parallels to the phrasing of the question in Prov 30:4. All these texts have to do with asking God for his name in moments of divine encounter or revelation and the answer to all these questions is YHWH, in one manifestation or another.

29. To those scholars who think the answer to the questions in 4a–d is "no one," the request for a name is emphatic (Clifford 1999, 262; Fox 2009, 856). This reading would work best if the tone of 30:4 was sardonic, "Go on then, what's his name?"

was obvious to ancient readers, it has not been so to modern ones. This might be part and parcel of the rhetoric at work in this passage. Agur seems to speak elliptically and by association of images and ideas rather than through declarative, sequential logic.[30] This could cause the reader to slow down, reflect, and puzzle over these things.

The father-son dynamic in the Hebrew Bible reflects a relationship in which one's identity and legacy is established and handed down (Gen 48:5–6, 16; Num 11:28; Deut 25:6; Ruth 4:10). By extension, "son" in Biblical Hebrew can apply to any member of a group or class who shares a defining feature or characteristic (Num 17:25; 1 Sam 14:52), especially to a student, protege, apprentice, or even a vassal (1 Kgs 20:35; 1 Chr 9:30; 2 Kgs 16:7). Only a few entities in the Hebrew Bible bear this designation with reference to God. Most famous, perhaps, is the messianic king in Ps 2:7, but a number of texts name the nation of Israel as God's son (e.g., Exod 4:22; Jer 31:20; Hos 11:1; Wis 18:13).[31] This list expands dramatically if we include verses that evoke the metaphor of God as father and Israelites as children more generally.[32] In commenting on Hos 11:1, Hans Walter Wolff (1974, 198) says YHWH's delivering Israel and calling him as his son lays the foundations for "an intimate relationship of care, guidance, and obedience." To be God's son, then—whether David or Israel—suggests a relationship within which something of God's character is displayed and passed on (Deut 32:6; Jer 3:19; Ps 103:13).

---

30. God has been alluded to as "the Holy One" (קדושים) in Prov 30:3, and he will be called Eloah (אלוה) in verse 5, but he is not named as YHWH until verse 9 when the blasphemous utterance "Who is YHWH?" (מי יהוה) is set in parallel to "the name of my God" (שם אלהי). Agur seems to be building slowly and deliberately to the unveiling of God's name toward the end of his opening discourse (Moore 1994, 100 n. 12; Ansberry 2011, 168 n. 24).

31. At least one ancient Jewish tradition seems to have understood Adam as a "son" of God (Luke 3:38), perhaps based on reading Gen 5:1–2. Some scholars have argued that Jacob is in view in Prov 30:4 based on an ingenious network of word-play and allusions (Skehan 1971, 43; O'Dowd 2018, 114), but, in my opinion, these allusions lack interpretive capital and are too clever to be convincing. Ansberry (2011, 167) suggests the king is intended because Proverbs has a royal orientation and "son" always has an individual referent. However, the royal context is not in the foreground here and the individual referent/addressee in Proverbs, i.e., "my son" (בני), is the idealized audience of the book—not an imagined individual but rather any and every Israelite/reader.

32. E.g., Deut 14:1; 32:5–6, 18–19; Isa 1:2–4; 43:6; 45:11; 63:16; 64:8 [7 ET]; Jer 3:4, 19; Hos 2:1; Mal 2:10.

If we bring the question to the book of Proverbs as our interpretive horizon, then the mention of a son resonates with the book's implied audience, that is, the student of wisdom (e.g., 1:10; 2:1; 3:1; 6:20; 23:19; 24:21; 27:11). Particularly noteworthy here is Prov 3:12 with its emphasis on God as instructing parent, "For the one whom he loves YHWH will rebuke, / as a father a son he is pleased with" (cf. Deut 8:5; Weeks 2007, 103).[33] Within the book of Proverbs, then, "What is the name of his son?" might be rephrased as "To whom has YHWH taught wisdom?"[34] YHWH has taught wisdom to those who know his name—to those who are in relationship to him as sons to a father, as students to a teacher (Prov 3:11–12; Yoder 2009a, 261).[35] To the extent that YHWH is being presented as the source of wisdom, the addressee/reader is being invited to posture themselves as the son/Israel.

In conclusion, it is by no means obvious what "the name of his son" is meant to evoke, but the image suggests a relationship within which YHWH's character and wisdom is passed on. This relates both to the father-son relationship within the literary imagination of the book of Proverbs *and* to the depiction of Israel as God's son in the Hebrew Bible more broadly. The fact that God's name *is* known while the name of his son is less clearly determined both holds out the possibility of divine knowledge and provokes self-reflection—who is called YHWH's son?

---

33. "The father's instruction, then, is not crudely identified as the Law, any more than the father is identified as God, but the language and imagery forge a close relationship between them. Something similar has already been implied in the complicated, summarizing poem of chapter 2, where receiving the father's commandments leads to a relationship with God that, in its turn, provides an understanding of God and everything that he values, along with protection on the right paths" (Weeks 2007, 126).

34. Fox (2009, 856) cannot see why asking for the name of Israel would be relevant here, but this may be because he rules out the possibility of revelation/divine instruction in wisdom texts. If we think in terms of Israel as God's son and the student of wisdom, then it makes perfect sense rhetorically (Waltke 2005, 474).

35. This is how Baruch reads these traditions: "He found the whole way to knowledge, / and gave her to his servant Jacob / and to Israel, whom he loved.... You forgot the everlasting God, who brought you up, / and you grieved Jerusalem, who reared you." (3:36 and 4:8, NRSV; O'Dowd 2018, 113). And Wisdom of Solomon, in a slightly different mode, presents the reasoning of the wicked who characterize the righteous man as one who "professes to have divine knowledge / and calls himself a child of the Lord" (2:13, cf. 18). Continuing along this trajectory, Midrash Mishle says that the name of his son in Prov 30:4 is Israel and cites Exod 4:22 (Visotzky 1992, 118).

4.2.3. Invoking Scripture: Proverbs 30:5

כל־אמרת אלוה צרופה / מגן הוא לחסים בו:
All the speech of Eloah is refined;
he is a shield for those taking refuge in him. (Prov 30:5)

As we observed the details of voice that are part and parcel of the text itself, one verse surfaced as distinctive. Proverbs 30:5 is a propositional statement in the third person. What is more, verse 5 appears to be a quotation from 2 Sam 22:31 // Ps 18:30 [31 ET] (see appendix at 30:5: כל אמרת).[36] That the only propositional statement in the chapter appears to be a quote from another biblical text raises intriguing possibilities.[37]

At first glance, Ps 18:30 is a stock piece of theological affirmation. The confession that God's words are "refined" (צרופה) is a metaphor from metallurgy (Isa 1:25; Prov 25:4). To be refined is to have the dross burned off, to be purified and fit to purpose. When used of people it suggests purity of heart (Mal 3:3; Ps 26:2); when used of speech it suggests words purified of falsehood and therefore trustworthy (Ps 12:6; 119:140). The image of God as a shield (מגן) is a ubiquitous metaphor for his protective presence with his people.[38] Those who seek his protection find it. To delve deeper we might ask what these images have to do with the larger context of Ps 18 and Prov 30. To do this well we must first consider the relationship of the two lines to each other. What is the connection between God's trustworthy speech and his protective qualities? The connection emerges if we consider *how* one might take refuge in God. In Ps 18 there are two answers to this question. The first is prayer. In his distress, the psalmist calls upon YHWH (אקרא יהוה; Ps 18:3, 6) and cries for deliverance (אשוע; Ps 18:6). The second is obedience or law-keeping, as when the psalmist maintains that God has rewarded him according to his righteousness because he has

---

36. In English translations of Ps 18, verses are numbered one higher than in Hebrew. In the discussion that follows, I will only give references to the Hebrew.

37. Given the clear overlap with Ps 18:30 or a very similar tradition, nearly all commentators agree that Prov 30:5 reflects a so-called orthodox Israelite perspective. But the question, then, persists as to whether this differs markedly from the theology and tone of what has gone before and whether it implies a change of speaker (Toy 1899, 523; McKane 1970, 645–46; Gunneweg 1992, 257; Murphy 1998, 229; Perdue 2000, 259).

38. E.g., Gen 15:1; Deut 33:29; Pss 3:3; 7:10; 33:20; 59:11; 84:9; 115:9–11; 119:114; 144:2.

4. Agur's Wisdom

kept to the ways of YHWH and all his rules and statutes (Ps 18:20–22). This context resonates strongly with Prov 2:7, the only other use of the shield metaphor in the book: "He will hide deliverance for the upright / a shield [מָגֵן] for those walking in purity." In the broader context of Prov 2's instruction, the one who receives the father's words, calls out for insight, and seeks after wisdom will find the fear of YHWH and the knowledge of God: "YHWH gives wisdom, / from his mouth knowledge and understanding" (Prov 2:6). YHWH's wisdom has a protective quality because it watches over and saves people from bad paths and perverted, that is, untrustworthy, speech (Prov 2:10–12). In Proverbs as in Ps 18, the one who seeks YHWH and obeys his words trusts him and finds protection.

The context of this couplet in Ps 18 has multiple illuminating points of contact with Prov 30. As I argued in chapter 3, Agur begins his discourse with a confession of weakness and finitude that he then extends to his intelligence and knowledge (30:1b–3). Similarly, Ps 18 finds the psalmist on the brink of death and without recourse other than to cry out to God (Ps 18:4–6; Clifford 1999, 262). In response to the psalmist's prayer, YHWH descends from heaven in a swirl of cosmic language that shares imagery with Prov 30:4 (Ps 18:7–15). In the immediate context of Ps 18:30, the psalmist declares what is perhaps the central idea of the psalm: "For you will save a humble people, but the eyes of the exalted [וְעֵינַיִם רָמוֹת] you will cast down" (Ps 18:27; cf. Prov 30:13 and 17). Agur's words likewise commend a stance of rhetorical humility before God. Finally, as Van Leeuwen pointed out, the very next line of Ps 18 effectively answers the question of Prov 30:4 when it asks: "For who is God except YHWH?" (כִּי מִי אֱלוֹהַּ מִבַּלְעֲדֵי יְהוָה, Ps 18:31; Van Leeuwen 1997b, 252; cf. appendix at 30:5: אֱלוֹהַּ). I am not arguing that Agur necessarily intends to drag all this background from Ps 18 into Prov 30. I merely intend to point out that the theological context of the statement in Prov 30:5 and Ps 18:30 is broadly similar, and in both places the line is bent toward a similar goal: to commend humble dependence on God through his word as an antidote to human weakness.

In sum, Prov 30:5 reinforces themes Agur has been developing: a dependence on God for wisdom/revelation (5a) and an acute awareness of human finitude (5b). But verse 5 goes beyond the intimations of 30:2–4 to explicitly identify God's word, even if the source of divine speech is not specifically identified (Yoder 2009b, 282).[39] In contrast to Agur's wisdom, God's word

---

39. Many scholars have found in 30:5 a clear reference to written Scripture (Gun-

is pure; in contrast to professed weakness, God is a shield. It seems natural that an ancient Israelite author dwelling on these themes would have gravitated to Ps 18:30, which brings the two ideas together. Again, as we saw with Prov 30:4, verse 5 develops the thought of verses 1b–4 not through logical argumentation but through juxtaposition and imagery.

4.2.4. Enacting Humility in Prayer: Proverbs 30:6–10

6 אל־תוסף על־דבריו / פן־יוכיח בך ונכזבת:
7 שתים שאלתי מאתך / אל־תמנע ממני בטרם אמות:
8 שוא ודבר־כזב הרחק ממני / ראש ועשר אל־תתן־לי
הטריפני לחם חקי:
9 פן אשבע וכחשתי / ואמרתי מי יהוה
ופן־אורש וגנבתי / ותפשתי שם אלהי:
10 אל־תלשן עבד אל־אדנו / [Q: אדניו] פן־יקללך ואשמת:

6 Do not add to his words,
lest he rebuke you and you are shown to be false.
7 Two things I ask from you;
do not withhold them from me before I die:
8 Emptiness and falsehood remove from me,
poverty and riches do not give me,
tear me off my portion of food.
9 Lest I am sated and deny,
and I say, "Who is YHWH?"
Or lest I am destitute and steal,
and I grasp the name of my God.

---

neweg 1992, 257; Toy 1899, 523). McKane (1970, 647–48) suggests verses 5–6 reflect a time when "an authoritative text of the written scriptures was taking shape." Childs (1979, 556) asserts, "reference to an authoritative body of scripture is clearly implied. As an answer to the inquirer's despair at finding wisdom and the knowledge of God, the answer offered is that God has already made himself known truthfully in his written word." To my mind, Childs is a bit too confident here. Without making any claims about the shape of the canon or the canonical status of Ps 18 at the point when Prov 30:5 was first penned, I maintain that by making his point through a formulation found in another sacred text, Agur is building toward a concept of Scripture, even if that concept remains somewhat anachronistic. His use of traditions found in Ps 18:30 suggests he has a sense that some texts mediate divine words and these texts carry more authority than others. If Agur is quoting from Ps 18:30, then his use of a sacred text subtly reinforces the point the text itself is making.

10 Speak not against a servant to his lord,
lest he curse you and you are punished. (Prov 30:6–10)

In 30:6–10, Agur exhorts and models the stance he adopted in verses 1b–5 with his personal reflection on human finitude that embraces the knowledge of God for protection. While most commentators hold verses 5–6 together because both have God's word as their topic and both contain scriptural allusions, I suggest the shift in voice from third-person speech in 30:5 to second-person prohibition in verse 6 is significant. In terms of tone and voice, verse 6 is a close match for verse 10. Clifford (1999, 263) noted that verses 6 and 10 are highly similar in syntactic structure.[40] Not only do these couplets mirror one another in terms of syntax, they are the only candidates for "sentence literature" in the chapter. This has often been noted regarding 30:10, but it is no less true of verse 6 although it is obscured by the thematic connection shared by verses 5 and 6 and the allusion to Deuteronomy (see below). If Prov 30:5 is the theological substance of Agur's confession in 1b–5, verses 6–10 shift to the second person, to application as it were, to work out the practical consequences of his confession. In between the two bookends of verses 6 and 10, the prayer in 7–9 focuses on ethics, speech, and relational dynamics.

Internally, verses 6–10 are one of the most finely tuned stanzas in all of chapter 30. This strategy of balancing lines that share grammar and themes not only applies to 30:6 and 10 but continues in the prayer itself. The couplet that introduces the prayer in 30:7 uses consonance of M-sounds (seven times) and T-sounds (five times) across the lines: *shetayim sha'alti me'ittak / 'al timna' mimmeni beterem 'āmut*. Proverbs 30:8a–b has a lilting poetic euphony that unites word pairs with consonance. Droning V- and Z-sounds link *shaw' udbar-kazab*, while sawing R- and Sh-sounds tie together *re'sh wa'osher*. Assonance and rhythm at the end of the lines plays on the I-sound of the first-person common singular object suffixes to create an effect not unlike rhyme: *mimmenni // titten-li*. Balanced and bound by sound, these two lines capture the conditions Agur prays to be spared from. Jumping to verse 9, grammatical parallelism and euphony are still at work. Following the subordinating conjunction (פֶּן), the lines have an identical grammatical sequence of verbs (1cs *yiqtol* +

---

40. To describe this structure schematically: אַל + 2ms jussive + prepositional phrase (object complement) + 3ms clitic pronoun (possessive) / פֶּן + 3ms *yiqtol* + 2ms clitic pronoun (object complement) + 2ms *weqatal* (result).

weqatal + weqatal). The mirrored syntax shares vowel patterns and stress, and the divine names, as vocalized, rhyme at the end of the line: *we'amarti mi 'adonay // wetapasti shem 'elohay*. The four lines of verse 9, then, also form a tight pair that balances the four lines in 7–8b. However, verse 8c has no pair in terms of sound, syntax, and sense, but stands dead center of the broader structure of 30:6–10 with six lines preceding it and following it. Most significantly, this is the only line that begins with a nonnegated second-person verb and makes a positive request. The poetic structure of verses 6–10 emphasizes the content of 8c within a double frame that could be schematized thus:[41]

Verse 6 (two lines)	Prohibition with reason
Verse 7–8b (four lines)	Petitions (stated negatively)
Verse 8c (one line)	Central petition (stated positively)
Verse 9 (four lines)	Reasoning behind petitions
Verse 10 (two lines)	Prohibition with reason

Having considered how the poetics of 30:6–10 focus on Agur's central request, I turn now to the content of his prayer. The first line of verse 7 casts the discourse in an I-Thou mode: Two things *I* ask from *you*. Although verses 4 and 6 both feature speech in the second person, the shift from rhetorical questions and instruction to petition would seem to carry with it a change in addressee. Although God is not explicitly invoked, imagining him as the Thou seems appropriate. The diction of 30:7 matches Ps 27:4 more closely than anything else in the Hebrew Bible: "One thing I asked of YHWH" (אחת שאלתי מאת־יהוה). And in terms of tone, "before I die" (בטרם אמות) recalls the gulf of mortality and finitude that contrasts humanity to God.[42] But ultimately, identifying the addressee as God and

---

41. Proverbs 30:6 and 10 can be read into other structures that include what precedes and follows them. However, verses 6 and 10 are Janus verses and it is entirely within the power of a capable poet to accomplish multiple interlocking structural devices simultaneously.

42. Some commentators have read "before I die" (בטרם אמות) as a reference to Agur's imminent expiration, as if his is a deathbed speech (Fox 2009, 853; Waltke 2005; 479; Franklyn 1983, 249). I think, however, that a more general sense of mortality is intended. The phrase occurs in Gen 27:4 where Esau employs it sarcastically to chide Jacob into giving him some soup. In Gen 45:28 Jacob uses the phrase as he resolves to travel to Egypt to see Joseph one more time, because he knows he is nearing the end of his days. Neither text, however, amounts to a last will and testament.

4. Agur's Wisdom

the poem as a prayer hinges on the nature of the requests in Prov 30:8. Although two requests are mentioned in verse 8, three lines state petitions. I believe 8a–b make one negative request in two parallel lines and 8c makes a second positive request that breaks from the preceding parallelism. Negatively, Agur prays to be spared the temptations that could lead him to damage his relationship with God; positively he asks for God's provision.

In Prov 30:8a, Agur prays against a kind of hollowness and falsehood that the Hebrew Bible most readily associates with idolatry, false prophecy, and the misuse or denial of God's name. The combination of "emptiness and falsehood" is a hendiadys (Waltke 2005, 458 and n. 31). The word "emptiness" (שוא) is a highly evocative word in biblical literature. It occurs first and at its most theologically resonant in the Ten Commandments: "You will not raise up the name of YHWH your God to emptiness" (Exod 20:7 // Deut 5:11; cf. Ps 24:4; 139:20). The core meaning of שוא is "to be empty, hollow, worthless" (BDB, s.v. "שוא I"), hence the traditional rendering of the third commandment: "Thou shalt not take the name of the LORD thy God in vain" (לשוא, KJV). But this core meaning is applied in a diversity of contextual and metaphorical ways, particularly in contexts relating to idolatry.[43] Hollow speech is a lie (Ezek 13:8; Ps 12:2; Lam 2:14), and hollow gods are idols (Isa 1:13; Jer 18:15; Jonah 2:9). Although the expression "emptiness and falsehood" (שוא ודבר־כזב) is unique to this text, several passages bring together שוא and כזב in significant ways. Most of these are in Ezekiel (13:6–9, 23; 21:28 [29 ET]; 22:28):

> והיתה ידי אל־הנביאים החזים שוא והקסמים כזב ... וידעתם כי אני אדני יהוה:
> And my hand will be against the prophets who are seeing empty visions and divining falsehood.... And you will know that I am the Lord YHWH. (Ezek 13:9)

> ונביאיה טחו להם תפל חזים שוא וקסמים להם כזב אמרים כה אמר אדני יהוה ויהוה לא דבר:
> And her prophets spread for them whitewash, seeing empty visions and divining for them falsehood, saying "Thus said the Lord YHWH," but YHWH did not speak. (Ezek 22:28)

"Before I die" means "for the rest of my life," however long that may be (Toy 1899, 524; Murphy 1998, 229).

43. See the proliferation of contextual glosses in *DCH* 8, s.v. "שוא."

With heavy overtones of blasphemy, Ezekiel pairs שוא and כזב to condemn false prophecy, which obscures God's true wishes and leads the people of Israel astray. Ben Sira also pairs the terms but now it is knowledge of Lady Wisdom rather than YHWH that eludes people: "Worthless people [מתי שוא] will not catch up to her and proud men will not see her … false men [ואנשי כזב] will not remember her" (Sir 15:7–8). The terms שוא and כזב are not referring to two different states, but rather the terms operate together to denote what is hollow, deceptive, unreliable—the opposite of the words of God (Prov 30:5). Such emptiness and falsehood obscures divine knowledge.

Unlike "emptiness and falsehood," which are best understood as a unit, "poverty and riches" in 30:8b represent opposite extremes. All seven examples of "poverty" (ראש) in the Hebrew Bible are in Proverbs and all are grim. Poverty overtakes one like a bandit (6:11; 24:34); shame and misery travel with it (13:18; 31:7). It is a ruin (10:15) and the recompense for vain pursuits and ignoring instruction (28:19; 13:18). Unlike poverty, "riches" (עשר) travel with wisdom and honor (Prov 3:16; 8:18), they are a crown for the wise (Prov 14:24), the reward for humility and the fear of YHWH (Prov 22:4; Ps 112:3; cf. 1 Kgs 3:13). But riches are not an unqualified good in Proverbs. A good reputation is worth more (Prov 22:1) and trusting in riches is fraught (Prov 11:28; Pss 49:7 [6 ET]; 52:9 [7 ET]). In Ecclesiastes riches are ambiguous; a gift from God that not everyone can enjoy (4:8; 6:2) and no one can take with them (5:14). Despite this mixed profile for riches, there is no other text where a character pushes them away as forcefully as Agur does. In terms of tone this might be part and parcel of Agur's communicative strategy that revels in paradox, surprise, and subverted expectations.[44] To understand why Agur feels these things pose a particular danger, we must consider the reason clauses in Prov 30:9.

The two couplets in 30:9 each begin with פן and present the reasoning behind the request of 8b in terms of the request of 8a. The first couplet in verse 9 explains the dangers associated with riches and the second with poverty. In 9a, it is easy to see how riches would lead to being "sated" (שבע). This overwhelmingly positive image of satisfaction pictures having plenty to eat and some left over (Ruth 2:14). It can be applied broadly to the blessings of the covenant whether concrete or figurative (Deut 6:11;

---

44. Indeed, for Solomon the unasked-for gifts were the seeds of his destruction (1 Kgs 3:12–13). Such a narrative could plausibly inform the startling request not to be granted riches.

8:10, 12; 11:15; 14:29; 26:12; 31:20), and extended metaphorically to the results of life in general (Eccl 1:8; 4:8; 5:9; 6:3). But, as we noted, riches are fraught and such a state of satisfaction can lead to ease and overconfidence that fosters denial. Although "deny" (כחש) has a wide range of contextual nuances, it finds shape here in the question "Who is YHWH?" (מי יהוה).⁴⁵ This is precisely the question pharaoh uses as a retort to Moses in Exod 5:2—it is dismissive in the extreme. In Prov 30:9b it is equally easy to see how poverty leads to destitution, which motivates theft. The expression "I grasp the name of my God" (ותפשתי שם אלהי) is clearly a metaphor or idiom, but we find it nowhere else in ancient Hebrew and there is no clear parallel. The sense of "to grasp" seems to be "mishandle" or "handle in an unworthy manner."⁴⁶ Elsewhere תפש overwhelmingly occurs in contexts of intense action or violence, including rape, destruction, and capture (Gen 39:12; Deut 9:17; 22:28; 1 Kgs 11:8; 18:40; 2 Kgs 14:7).⁴⁷ Applying the term to the name of God creates an alarming image. Perhaps the connotation of theft as a "hands-on" crime and destitution as a desperate state motivated the use of a concrete image for the dishonoring of God's name,

---

45. There may well be a pun in the use of כחש. In Aramaic and Rabbinic Hebrew כחש often means "to become lean, weak" (Jastrow 1903, s.vv. "כְּחַשׁ," "כְּחַשׁ") or "to become lean, infertile, deteriorate, weak, decrease in value, contradict" (Sokoloff 2002, s.v. "כחש"). It is difficult to say whether this usage is connected to the most common biblical meaning, which is "to deny, deceive" (see *DCH* 4, s.v. "כחש"; *HALOT*, s.v. "כחש"), but in Ps 109:24 the verb conforms to the later usage meaning "to grow lean" (cf. Hos 9:2; Hab 3:17; Job 16:8). If this meaning is attested in biblical texts, then there may be a bit of irony or even black humor to the line. Being "sated" (שבע), i.e., overeating, can lead you to "deny" (כחש), i.e., become gaunt, weak, emaciated. This pun works if the two senses of the words are homophones, but it is even more potent if there is a metaphorical link between "being thin" and being deceptive. The *niphal* means "to submit," "be compliant," which could suggest the sense "to make oneself thin" (see *DCH* 4, s.v. "כחש"; and Deut 33:29; 2 Sam 22:45 // Ps 18:44 [45 ET]; Ps 66:3). In the rest of Agur's collection devouring/greed is a recurring theme and the pun suits the tone of the chapter (see Prov 30:14–17, 20, 22).

46. The gloss in T is √חלל ("to defile, profane"), but G, followed by S, glosses תפש with ὄμνυμι ("to swear"). Swearing on God's name is one way of mishandling it. The versions did not translate the metaphor directly, but they understood it to mean dishonoring or mishandling.

47. The verb תפש may have metaphorical uses in Ezek 14:5 ("to seize the house of Israel by their hearts"; תפש את־בית־ישראל בלבם) and Jer 2:8 ("those who grasp the law do not know me"; ותפשי התורה לא ידעוני). In each of these cases the sense seems to be to handle roughly.

whereas the ease of wealth leads to denial, a crime of the tongue. Although the dangers take different paths, the extremes of wealth and poverty lead to the same place: sins against God's name. Significantly, Prov 30:9a is the only use of the divine name in the chapter. Within the discourse of this collection, then, verse 9 seems to state implicitly the answers to the questions of verse 4; and these sins against God's name in verse 9 are meant as expressions of the idolatry and rebellion evoked by שוא ודבר־כזב in verse 8a. When Agur prays that he be given neither poverty nor riches, he is in effect praying that emptiness and false speech be kept far from him. In this way 8a–b ought to be understood as one request, the first of the two mentioned in 30:7a. Agur wants to be spared the conditions that could lead to the breakdown of his relationship with the God whom he knows (v. 3b).

The negative requests in 30:8a–b and the reason clauses of verse 9 frame the one positive request in 8c. Nearly every modern interpreter renders 8c something like, "feed me with the food that I need" (NRSV; Fox 2009, 850; Waltke 2005, 458). But the verb glossed "feed me" (הטריפני) is distinctive. Similar to the beastly connotations of בער in 30:2, this verb carries animalistic, predatory overtones. It occurs twenty-four more times in the Hebrew Bible. Twenty examples are in the *qal* and mean "to tear" normally with a predatory animal as subject (e.g., Ezek 19:3, 6; 22:27; cf. 4Q174 [4QFlor] 9 X, 3 in Allegro 1968; *HALOT*, s.v. "טרף"). The further four examples are divided between the *niphal* and the *pual* meaning "to be torn, savaged," as when Jacob laments that Joseph has been "torn to pieces" by wild beasts (Gen 37:33; 44:28). Moreover nominal forms טֶרֶף and טְרֵפָה mean "prey" and "carrion" or "torn animal" respectively.[48] In fact, √טרף is

---

48. From this root we get the rabbinic designation *terefah* (טרפה), i.e., an animal that is not kosher because it died unnaturally or improperly (Gen 31:39; Lev 7:24; Ezek 4:14). Of the twenty-two examples of טרף, three might be rendered "food" rather than "prey": Mal 3:10; Ps 111:5; and Prov 31:15. The Malachi text, however, is talking about the temple and so טרף likely refers to slaughtered animals. The same could go for Ps 111:5, but the sense would certainly not be lost if translated "prey." But nearest and most similar to Prov 30:8 is Prov 31:15: "She rises while it is still night and gives meat [טרף] to her house and a portion [חק] to her servant girls." Given that the woman is pictured in her strength as a capable and even lavish provider, טרף may suggest something closer to "meat" (בשר) than generic "bread" (לחם). Concerning 31:15, Fox (2009, 894) writes, "Still the word's predominate meaning, 'prey'… gives it overtones of aggression and pugnacity, as if to hint that the Woman of Strength is something of a lioness in providing for her young" (see also Waltke 2005, 511 n. 71). Although Fox does not make the same connection in 30:8, I think it apt.

occasionally part of metaphorical descriptions coloring humans as predators: "I broke the fangs of the unjust and made prey fall from his teeth" (ואשברה מתלעות עול ומשניו אשליך טרף; Job 29:17); "Her nobles are in her midst as wolves tearing prey [כזאבים טרפי טרף], to shed blood, to take lives, for the sake of profiting by violence" (Ezek 22:27). I contend that there is something violent and animalistic in the connotation of this word and we bleach it of its nuance by simply glossing "to feed." I wonder if it does not subtly characterize the petitioner as a sort of dependent animal while coloring God as the provisioning hunter.[49] This nuance is admittedly subtle, but it maintains the animal metaphor and humble posture of receiving from God that Agur initiated in Prov 30:2 with בער. Indeed, the object "my portion of food" (לחם חקי) suggests a chunk appropriate to Agur's needs being "torn off" for him such that he falls neither into satiety nor destitution. Agur's positive request, the center of his prayer, pictures humble dependence on God in animalistic terms, a posture inimical to the emptiness and falsehood, denial, and theft that he prays to be spared.

Having considered the prayer now in some detail, we can return to consider how 30:6 and 10 frame it. Again, many commentators have seen these verses as sentiments floating free from their context (Fox 2009, 864). As I already argued, there is a tight formal connection between verses 6 and 10, but is there also any substantive or thematic connection that goes deeper than these formal similarities? We might begin by noting that just as verbal sins were a primary concern of Agur's prayer (vv. 8a, 9a), 30:6 and 10 are likewise preoccupied with sins of the lips: adding to God's words in verse 6 and "speaking against" (תלשן) a servant in verse 10. But to dig deeper into the substance of these sayings it will again help to ask what motivations might lie behind these actions.

In Prov 30:10 the key word, תַּלְשֵׁן (*hiphil* jussive), is unique as pointed and the root only occurs as a verb in one other text, where it is sandwiched between condemnations of "the perverse of heart" (לבב עקש) and "high eyes and a proud heart" (גבה עינים ורחב לבב, Ps 101:4–5). The root is common as a nominal, meaning either tongue as the organ of

---

49. This verse is the only example of the *hiphil* of √טרף in Biblical Hebrew, but it occurs once at Qumran in a similar context (4Q417 [4QInstruction^c] 2 I, 20–21 in Strugnell, Harrington, and Elgvin 1999; Goff 2013, 203). There is no clear reason why the *hiphil* would entirely lose the predatory connotations the word carries elsewhere but might better suggest "to tear for" or "cause to eat prey." Delitzsch (1875, 282) has, "to give anything as טֶרֶף."

speech or tongue as the medium of speech, that is, language. On a quite literal approach, תלשן is a denominative meaning "to use the tongue" (BDB, s.v. "לָשׁוֹן"; *IBHS* §27.4.a), but most often תלשן has been glossed "slander" (see *HALOT*, s.v. "לשׁן"; *DCH* 4, s.v. "לשׁן").⁵⁰ While, it is not clear to me from the evidence that תלשן must refer to *false* speech, it clearly represents malicious speech (cf. b. Pesaḥ. 87b; Song Rab. 1.6.1; cf. Fox 2009, 864). Better, I think, to say that תלשן means something like "snitch" or "malign," that is, "speak against."⁵¹ What might motivate a person with "perverse heart" and "high eyes" to malign a servant to his master? Perhaps revenge or pure malice, but the most likely motives might be a blend of jealousy and self-promotion. Keeping in mind that עבד can refer to any subordinate in the Hebrew Bible, the stories of Mephibosheth, Daniel, and Mordecai offer concrete scenarios of character assassination in the service of self-promotion (2 Sam 16:1–4; 19:26–28; Dan 6; Esth 7:3–8:2).⁵² The arrogant qualities and duplicitous actions of Ziba, Darius's satraps, and Haman may be precisely the kind of thing this proverb envisions. Indeed, the proverb warns against a reversal whereby the master curses you and you are punished (ואשמת), which is precisely what befalls the satraps and Haman (Dan 6:24; Esth 7:9–10). If this motivational structure is near the mark, then Prov 30:10 speaks against the kind of arrogance, deception, and greed that are central to Agur's concerns.

---

50. Support for this comes from Ugaritic and Aramaic cognates (Dahood 1963, 57; *DULAT*, s.v. "l-š-n"; Jastrow 1903, s.v. "לִישָׁן"; Sokoloff 1990, s.v. "לשׁן"; 2002, s.v. "לשׁן").

51. The way the versions handle תלשן suggests they understand the word to denote speech that aims to bring someone down or harm them: The Greek has παραδῷς ("to deliver, hand over"). Perhaps because this verb is extremely rare, G simply rendered the sense as he understood it; Fox (2015, 382) suggests the scribe is influenced by G Deut 23:16, which has παραδώσεις corresponding to סגר ("to give up, hand over") in a similar construction. The Syriac's reading is similar to G with ܬܫܠܡ ("to hand over, betray"). De Waard (1993, 257–58) argues that this reading could be reached through exegetical metathesis of תלשן—but would also require graphic confusion of ן for ם. If de Waard is correct, then S may be an attempt to harmonize the sense of G with the letters of MT (Fox 2013, 53). Cf. T: תלשין "slander" (CAL, Tg. Neof. Gen 47:21).

52. In the story of Mephibosheth, Ziba promotes himself through a clear case of slander (note that b. Shabb. 56a calls Ziba's sin "slander" [√לשׁן]). Although the charges brought forward are truthful in the cases of Daniel and Mordecai, they demonstrate that bringing forward a damaging report about an official can result in his demotion and your own promotion.

4. Agur's Wisdom

Returning then to 30:6, What might motivate someone to add to God's word? Like verse 5, verse 6 also raises the question of Agur's relationship to the Hebrew Bible and its theology more broadly, because most commentators have been happy to read Prov 30:6a as a quotation of or allusion to the first half of the so-called canon formula from Deut 4:2 (cf. 13:1 [12:32 ET]).[53] It is difficult to establish with certainty that there is textual dependence here, but it seems legitimate—at the very least—to treat Prov 30:6 as a periphrastic allusion to the prohibition in Deuteronomy (see appendix at 30:6: אל־תוסף).[54] We might note that Deut 4:1–8 is the most significant passage in the Torah for reflecting on the relationship of the concepts of wisdom and law (Weeks 2007, 110). Within Deut 4, the purpose of the canon formula is to protect (שמר, 4:2, 6) the statutes and ordinances (חקים ומשפטים, 4:5, cf. 4:1, 8) that Moses has taught the Israelites (למד, 4:1, 5) so they can do them. Protecting the statutes and ordinances and doing them *is* Israel's wisdom and understanding before the nations (Deut 4:5–6; Franklyn 1983, 249).[55] It seems that adding to God's words could lead the people into idolatry, robbing them of their unique wisdom vis-à-vis the nations. The threat of idolatry is ever near. In 4:3–4 Moses reminds them that they saw what happened to all the men who went after the Baal of Peor. This is also in keeping with the context in Deut 13:1 (12:32 ET) where false prophecy that encourages the people to go after other gods is the principal concern. Adding to God's word suggests lies that lead to idolatry and obscure God's true purposes. Rather than suggesting a tight connection, this background to the canon formula in Deuteronomy is meant to fill in

---

53. One question is why our text doesn't go on to quote the other half of the formula: "and do not subtract from them" (ולא תגרעו ממנו; Deut 4:2). Some scholars have argued that the omission reflects Agur's view that the wisdom tradition is a dangerous addition to Torah (Schipper 2021, 272). Another possibility is that his focus is on falsehood and idolatry and in such a context *subtracting* from God's word simply does not seem as pressing a concern.

54. Indeed, this allusion, being that it evokes the canon formula, is an even stronger affirmation of the existence of a body of written Scripture than 30:5. Fox's (2009, 858) comment is apropos, "Agur [like Deuteronomy] must have in mind a defined corpus of revealed instruction, though he does not identify it further. It could be the Pentateuch or an earlier stage in its growth, such as Deuteronomy or the code it contains."

55. Note the shift from the plural objects in Deut 4:5a (חקים ומשפטים) to the 3fs pronoun (הוא) in the כי clause in Deut 4:6a. It is not the laws but the act of guarding and doing them that is Israel's wisdom and understanding.

the context of the prohibition against adding to God's word. Even those skeptical of an intentional allusion can see how Prov 30:6 and its concern with lying connects to the petitions of Agur's prayer, particularly the language of idolatry in 30:8a and the potential for denying and defiling God's name in verse 9. In terms of a motivational structure, again greed and self-promotion might come into play.[56]

To sum up, Agur's prayer takes the themes and ideas that were developed in Prov 30:1–5 and casts them in terms of a personal spiritual ethic within verses 6–10. At the center of this ethic is animal-like dependence on God for provision (30:8c). Agur intimates that real wisdom, that is, knowledge of the divine, is found in this humble, beast-like posture. Foundational to his prayer are requests to be spared from "emptiness and false words" on the one hand and "poverty and riches" on the other (30:8a–b). Lying behind these requests are the lurking specters of pride and greed, that could threaten Agur's relationship with God. Plenty and pride could lead him to deny God (30:9a), while emptiness and poverty could lead him to steal, tarnishing God's name (30:9b). Likewise, adding to God's word and speaking against a servant are verbal sins that suggest self-promotion (vv. 6, 10). In all cases, Agur would be taking things into his own hands and risks being branded a liar, cursed, and punished (vv. 6, 9–10). The prayer is framed within these warning texts that are spoken in the second person and addressed to the addressee of the chapter—the same "you" to whom Agur poses the rhetorical questions in 30:4. It is as if Agur is saying, if you hope to avoid the pitfalls of pride and greed and the chastisement of God, then pray like this.[57] The prohibitions and prayer work together to preserve beast-like dependence on God and faithfulness to his word. Key words and expressions in Agur's prayer, not to mention the allusion

---

56. In this context, recall the collocations of שוא and כזב in Ezekiel where those who add to God's words with false prophecy "whitewash" (Ezek 22:28) the deeds of Israel's nobles who practice extortion and oppress the poor, acting "in her midst as wolves tearing prey [כזאבים טרפי טרף] to shed blood, to take lives, for the sake of profiting by violence" (Ezek 22:27; cf. 22:23–29; 13:1–23). Other prophetic invectives could no doubt be invoked.

57. The Lord's Prayer presents an analogy where a model prayer is given as part of an instruction (Matt 6:9–13). Byargeon (1998) has argued that there are intentional links between Matt 6:9–13 and Prov 30:7–9. Byargeon makes many interesting observations, although I do not ultimately find his argument convincing. I think the link between the prayers is better found in how they function within their respective theological discourses.

to Deut 4:2 in Prov 30:6a, evoke the context of Torah and law-keeping. As Deut 4:1–8 describes, Israel was supposed to guard and do all God's statutes because doing so was their wisdom and understanding. While we cannot insist that Agur has this whole context in mind, the substance of Prov 30:6–10 is similar. We might say he grounds knowledge of God in humble dependence and obedience—although he does not use the term, he embodies the fear of YHWH in his prayer (Deut 4:1–2; 6:1–2; Prov 1:7; 9:10).

4.3. Finding Agur's Voice

I have been attempting to make an argument for the cohesion of Prov 30:2–10. I am certainly not the first to argue for the unity of these verses, but what I hope I have added is a thicker description of Agur's theology over against the rest of the Hebrew Bible in relationship to his voice. To conclude this chapter, I will summarize Agur's theology as I understand it, reflect on the interplay of tone and voice in the text, and offer a brief hermeneutical reflection.

In short, Agur holds that attaining knowledge of God is possible through God's words and that human beings achieve access to this knowledge through a relationship with God maintained by humility, contentment, and torah-piety. Proverbs 30:2–3 open with Agur using a potent metaphor in which he compares himself to a beast and downplays his human understanding. Thus, he subverts our expectations for a sage in Proverbs, but by means of this metaphor he adopts a posture of epistemological humility before God. In terms of tone, this metaphor is crucial. Agur is not making totalizing claims about wisdom and human epistemology any more than he literally claims to be a beast. He may be ironic without being insincere. Indeed, the image is pregnant with faith and Agur transitions startlingly to a statement of theological knowledge. Proverbs 30:4, is best read not as a contradictory statement, and certainly not as a denial of the possibility of wisdom or human knowledge, but rather as deepening the sentiments of verses 2–3 by emphasizing human finitude and circumscribing human knowledge. Human beings cannot ascend to God or encompass creation in order to gain divine wisdom. But the flip side of this language reminds us that there is one who can—there is one who descends and speaks. The final rhetorical questions point to God's unique identity and prompt reflection on how one might learn from God. The general tenor of this interpretation is confirmed when verse 5 explicitly surfaces the issue of divine speech and does it with a scriptural citation no less. This statement effectively answers the question raised by Agur's claim to divine knowledge in 30:3b. That the commendation of God's word comes from a protocanonical text implicitly suggests divine knowledge can be found in a growing body of inspired texts containing divine revelation. Staying on the issue of God's words, verse 6 turns to the ethical implications of verses 2–5. While verses 2–5 modeled a stance of epistemological humility and dependence, verses 6 and 10 present a warning against pride, greed, and self-promotion because such things leave one guilty before God. But the center of Agur's ethics is a prayer for radical contentment that uses Torah-laced language to elevate piety above all else. On my reading, then, Agur comes off a surprisingly orthodox, if eccentric sage. The kinds of things he says have been said in Ps 18 and 73, Isa 40, Job 38, and Deut 4.[58] While the juxtaposition of his ideas and his provocative expressions seem to revel in irony and evoke a sense of astonishment, he is no skeptic, much less an atheistic philosopher.

So, are there multiple voices present? The theory that these words are a dialogue seems to be prompted by the scandalous things Agur says. Competing voices are a strategy to deal with his shocking and unorthodox theology.[59] If Agur's theology, however, is perhaps not so unorthodox, then there is nothing in the text itself that demands a shift in speaker. Rather, common themes unite the verses, so that Fox (2009, 850) describes Prov 30:1–9 as "a cohesive first-person meditation … with its own shape and message."[60] Agur's opening confession in the first person seems meant to be arresting and slightly puzzling. His rhetorical questions in verse 4 are reflective, drawing the reader in by extending and deepening the themes of verses 2–3. The quotation from Ps 18 is appropriately maintained in the third person to ground his claim; the theological means by which Agur can—rhetorically—diminish his own intelligence and lay claim to divine

---

58. Within Proverbs they have resonance in chs. 2, 3, 9, 28 and elsewhere. I will further consider the role of Agur's words within Proverbs in ch. 6.

59. The most vivid examples of this are the interpretation of Dillon (1895), which I excerpted for an epigraph to this volume, and the more recent article by Crenshaw (1995). Much like Dillion's comparison, Crenshaw's formulations are often so extreme they nearly self-destruct. Agur's speech, which he characterizes as "radical skepticism" spans 30:1–4, while in verse 5 "a new speaker takes a sacred scroll and beats Agur over the head with it" (Crenshaw 1995, 375, 377).

60. However, Fox (2009, 850) insists there is no "significant connection" to 30:10–14 and including those verses "makes Agur's words into a miscellaneous collection." Chapters 5 and 6 will address such concerns.

knowledge. In Prov 30:6, the discourse shifts back to the second person and takes on an ethical rather than a reflective tone. Proverbs 30:6 and 10 share the same grammatical structure and are phrased as commands ostensibly addressed to the reader. Between these commands, however, there is a prayer also phrased in the second person. But here the "you" of the prohibitions in verses 6 and 10 cannot be the "Thou" of the prayer in verses 7–9. Perhaps this does not need an explanation. The material is simply loosely and thematically framed so that the reader is meant to navigate such a transition of addressee without getting hung up on it.[61] No change of speaker is required. The prayer itself may be presented as instruction for the reader—a model or set piece rather than a live prayer in situ, as it were. Van Leeuwen's (1997b, 251) description of these verses as "an anthological poem" is apt. If Agur's words are somewhat anthological and allusive—not to mention distinctive in terms of tone—they stop far short of being so disjointed or contradictory that diatribe or rejoinder is the only explanation.

Finally, let me offer a few sentences of reflection on how such readings came to be. First, Agur's expressions are compelling, his imagery evocative, and his words marvelously underdetermined. This combination of elements yields a text as deeply intriguing as it is perplexing. His meaning—in so much as this can be summarized—is not found in logical argumentation but in the juxtaposition of images and the extension of metaphors. This quality gives the text power, but it also gives interpreters the bandwidth for highly creative argumentation. Second, the text poses a serious challenge in 30:1 where there seems to be a nearly total breakdown in meaningful content. This bit of "white noise" has been reconstructed in highly creative ways to produce the most extreme construals of Agur. But third—and I think here lies the nub of the issue—scholarship always tends to bring contemporary issues and questions to the text. Going back to Ewald and beyond, scholars naturally brought the intellectual trends of the eighteenth and nineteenth century to the study of the Hebrew Bible. Wisdom literature as a genre was in part born out of a desire to find voices such as Dillon's "Hebrew Voltaire" and Ewald's "godless philosophers" reflected in the text (Kynes 2019, 95). For nineteenth-century interpreters, Agur's challenging and fascinating words could convincingly channel

---

61. In the Psalms, for example, the reader frequently encounters shifts in voice that must be inferred from changes in pronouns or subject matter.

such voices. The same interpretive openness, however, that has invited and indeed allowed scholars to read Agur as everything from the Hebrew Voltaire to a pious sage might also caution humility. Surely if Agur's words are so open-ended, so underdetermined, then a little interpretive restraint might yield the better part of wisdom.

5
Agur's Beastly Ethics:
The Numerical Saying, Animal Imagery, Humor, and Coherence in Proverbs 30:11–33

5.1. Coherence, Form, and Content in Proverbs 30:11–33

In the previous two chapters, I argued that Agur's voice and ironic tone unify Prov 30:1–10 around themes of divine knowledge, torah-piety, and a humble relationship with God. Nearly all scholars, however, find that Agur's voice and these themes fade out, if they do not cease abruptly, in the later part of the collection. In this chapter, I will present a close reading of 30:11–33 to argue that they ought to be considered a coherent collection in terms of tone and theme. What is more, verses 11–33 extend the tone and themes from verses 1–10, opening the door for reading the whole chapter as a coherent collection voiced by Agur. Whereas 30:1–10 was often explicitly theological in its outlook and exhibited something akin to a progression of thought, verses 11–33 have a fundamentally ethical perspective and present individual vignettes side-by-side to build up a collage. These vignettes do not exhibit logical progression, per se, but rather thematic development that is matched by a development of tone. Agur's voice can still helpfully be imagined to animate the whole. In short, these verses satirize pride and greed while simultaneously commending humble contentment.

In terms of coherence, the most striking formal feature of 30:11–33 is the distinctive and intriguing numerical saying. More of these sayings appear together in close proximity here than anywhere else in ancient literature. Scholars who do find coherence in this material have usually done so with recourse to this curious construction. For some scholars, the use of numbers is an elaborate compositional technique that suggests authorial intent and a unifying message (Waltke 2005, 481–82; Steinmann 2001).

For other scholars, this formal feature is itself the occasion for the collection because these verses have little else in common (Whybray 1994b, 153). In fact, the emergence of this feature—often noted at 30:7, 11, or 15—is usually taken to mark the end of Agur's words. As Whybray tells it, verses 15–33 are "clearly not an original unit. No attempt has been made to maintain a unity of style or a logical sequence of content" (150). Formal unity, then, provides a fragile basis for a reading that posits real coherence because it may only run skin deep. But the form of the numerical saying is not the only striking feature of 30:11–33. The next thing that nearly any reader would notice is the preponderance of animals in these verses. There are, in fact, eleven animals mentioned in just twenty-three verses. Agur's veritable zoo begs for an explanation as strongly as the numerical sayings. At least one aspect of that explanation, as I will argue, has to do with tone. In verses 11–33, Agur's ironic undercurrent takes on a humorous cast and this is facilitated both by the animal imagery and by the rhetorical device of the numerical saying. Attending to the way animal imagery and tone work in tandem helps to ascertain the themes Agur is concerned with and proves a better guide to reading for coherence than formal features alone.

Before I proceed to the close reading that will occupy the bulk of this chapter, numerical sayings, animal imagery, and humor all warrant further consideration.

5.2. The Numerical Saying, Animal Imagery, and Humor: Hermeneutical Perspectives

5.2.1. The Numerical Saying

In the past, scholars have been most interested in the numerical saying (*Zahlenspruche*) for what it might reveal about the historical development of wisdom genres and the oral forms behind them.[1] According to Hans-

---

1. Scholarly discussions tend to connect the numerical saying to the phenomenon of numerical parallelism more broadly, e.g., Amos's famous refrain in 1:3, 6, etc. (Roth 1962, 1965; Sauer 1963; Watson 1984, 144–49). The numerical saying proper, sometimes called the "graded numerical list saying" (Haran 1972), uses a couplet employing numerical parallelism to introduce a number of items that share a certain feature followed by a list that specifies the set. Although scholarly counts differ slightly, there are some eighteen of these numerical sayings extant in ancient Semitic literature (*KTU* 1.4 iii.17–21; Ahiqar 187–88; Ps 62:12–13; Prov 6:16–19; 30:15b–16, 18–19, 21–23, 24–28,

5. Agur's Beastly Ethics 149

Peter Müller (1970, 486), Johann Gottfried Herder was the first to propose a connection between the numerical saying and the riddle in his 1787 work *Vom Geist der Ebräischen Poesie* [Concerning the spirit of Hebrew poetry]. When form criticism came into its own in the early twentieth century, this connection was ripe for appropriation.[2] Two scholars in particular seem to have popularized the connection. Eissfeldt (1964 [ET: 1965]) developed it briefly in his *Einleitung in Das Alte Testament* [Introduction to the Old Testament] and Gerhard von Rad (1970 [ET: 1972]) followed him in like manner in his *Weisheit in Israel* [Wisdom in Israel]. Both scholars were searching for an oral *Gattung* and a historical context behind the present numerical sayings. Because we find the numerical saying almost exclusively in proverb collections or in wisdom books, these scholars naturally looked for its *Sitz im Leben* in this context.

Eissfeldt develops his argument by moving from the Hebrew word חידה, usually translated *riddle*, to the narrative contexts in which such riddles are preserved within the Hebrew Bible. Samson's riddle in Judg 14:14 is the parade example:

מהאכל יצא מאכל / ומעז יצא מתוק:
From the eater came something to eat / and from the strong something sweet.

The answer to this riddle—"What is sweeter than honey? What is stronger than a lion?" (Judg 14:18)—is not altogether satisfying, because the connection between lions and honey presents a non sequitur rather than an aha moment. Because the answer is phrased as a question, Eissfeldt (1965, 86) speculated that perhaps *it* is the riddle and the answer is "love." He also noted that the queen of Sheba arrives at Solomon's court "to test him with riddles" (לנסתו בחידות, 1 Kgs 10:1). Eissfeldt (85) connects this text to scenes in Second Temple literature, concluding "such a contest with riddles as is here described did in fact have its place at court."[3] Finally, he points out the tight connection between "proverb" (משל) and "riddle" (חידה) in Prov 1:6. Eissfeldt (85–86) concludes his discussion: "So we may assume

---

29–31; Job 5:19–22; 33:14–29; Sir 23:16–17; 25:1, 2, 7–11; 26:5–6, 28; 50:25–26). See further Rüger 1981; Steinmann 1995; and Bodi 2013.

2. On the riddle in the Old Testament, see Torczyner 1924 and Müller 1970, in addition to the works discussed above.

3. See Josephus, *A.J.* 8.5, 3; 1 Esd 3–4; and Let. Aris. §§187–300.

that a type which is a favourite in the later wisdom literature, namely the numerical saying—like the one which begins: Three things are never satisfied: four never say 'Enough,' ... developed out of a riddle which asked: 'Which are the three which are never satisfied?"

Although von Rad does not cite Eissfeldt, his logic in developing the connection between the numerical saying and the riddle is similar. However, he muses at greater length on the conceptual link:

> The aim of this form of proverb [the numerical saying] is always the same, the collection of things which are similar where the assertion of similarity is the real surprise element, for, regarded in isolation, the cases listed are quite dissimilar. Probably these proverbs also served in the schools for teaching and learning purposes. But in saying this we have still not answered the question concerning the stylistic peculiarity of this type of proverb. This form possesses, as one can assert with a great degree of probability, something of the nature of a riddle. The question: What is the highest? what is the worst? the quickest? etc. is found all over the world. Once raised, it contains an element of stimulation, since everyone—"I'll give you three guesses"—wants to get to the answer first. Thus the introduction to numerical sayings has, for all practical purposes, the character of a challenging question, for the giving of numbers alone and the silence about what is meant stimulates the listener and keeps his curiosity in suspense. (von Rad 1972, 35–36)

Von Rad (35) ultimately connects the numerical saying and the riddle embedded within it to the universal human need for order that is "planted deep within man."

While the line of thought developed by Eissfeldt and von Rad feels compelling, it is based on no evidence beyond the circumstantial association of משל and חידה. No numerical saying is ever actually called a חידה and riddle-game scenarios, whether in Judg 14 or in Second Temple texts, do not actually feature numerical sayings, numerical parallelism, or a list of answers.[4] What is more, von Rad's assertion that the aim of the proverb is

---

4. First Esdras 3–5 certainly comes closest with the challenge "to state what one thing is strongest" (1 Esd 3:5) followed by three answers (wine, the king, and women; 3:10–12) that are ultimately trumped by a fourth: truth (1 Esd 3:12; 4:35–41). The text frames the challenge as a sort of debate or contest of wits where each of the bodyguards speaks in turn to defend his answer. It would have been easy enough to conclude by recasting the whole thing as a numerical saying, but it does not. The question, after

"always the same" and that it deals with a surprising assertion of similarity cannot be maintained. Rather, the numerical sayings function differently in different rhetorical contexts and not all of them have the paradoxical aura of the riddle (Müller 1970, 487). The structure serves different rhetorical goals in different settings and cannot be sourced to any one historical social setting. Even if it were possible to connect the form to riddle games in the school or the court, the present literary context of the sayings has largely obliterated this so that it is not clear what interpretive capital its origins would still carry.

Although space does not permit a survey of all the extant numerical sayings, I will look briefly at three that illustrate well the adaptability and diversity of the device. The oldest numerical saying we know of is in Ugaritic and comes from the Baal epics. It bears the further distinction of being set in dialogue rather than a collection of sayings like most examples.[5]

> 14–16 I drank disgrace at my table, / dishonor from my cup I drank.
> 17–18 For two feasts Baal hates, / three, the Cloud-Rider:
> 18–21 A feast of shame, a feast of strife, / and a feast of the whispering of servant-girls.
> 21–22 For in it shame indeed was seen, / for in it the whispering of servant girls. (*KTU* 1.4 iii.14–22)[6]

These lines seem to be delivered by Baal himself (Smith and Pitard 2009, 470–71). The context is somewhat mysterious because the end of column II and the first ten lines of column III are too badly broken to reconstruct (Smith and Pitard 2009, 469). Still, Baal appears to stand in the assembly of the gods and speak about a time when he was grossly disrespected at a feast. He was "abased" and "spat on" (*KTU* 1.4 iii.12–14). The public affront he experienced set the servant girls twittering, which only magnified his shame. The numerical saying and the couplet that follow it set up and denounce this feast with punishing composure. Rhetorically, Baal speaks in the third person, which projects a sense of intensity. The form

---

all, seeks one correct answer rather than a set cleverly held together by an observation (Müller 1970, 486).

5. In this respect, it resembles the numerical sayings in Job 5 and 33. Incidentally, these sayings are the only examples that suggest a *Sitz im Leben*, and it is persuasive rhetoric rather than a riddle game.

6. I lightly modified the translation in Smith and Pitard (2009, 462–63).

of the numerical saying seems to be a stall tactic allowing the force of his denunciation to build. Baal is not listing out three different types of feast as if a feast where the servants talk among themselves in the corners is one type of bad party and a feast where fights break out is another. This can be clearly seen from the way the numerical saying plays in context. Baal has been describing one feast where he was disgraced (12–16). Then he delivers his numerical saying to build up the description of a bad feast in the abstract. Finally, he connects his description with his experience in lines 21–22. The device allows Baal to underscore his condemnation by drawing out all the feast's disgraceful features.

Two other numerical sayings also feature a list of things a deity likes or dislikes: Ahiqar 187–188a and Prov 6:16–19. Consider Ahiqar first.

תרתין מלן שפירה / וזי תלתא רחימה לשמש
ש[תה] חמרא ויניקנהי / כבש חכמה] [.......]
וישמע מלה ולא יהחוה :

There are two things that are good, / and a third that is pleasing to Shamash: / one who drinks wine and shares it, / one who masters wisdom [*and observes it*]
and one who hears a word but tells it not. (Ahiqar 187–188a)[7]

Unlike *KTU* 1.4, the numerical saying in Ahiqar is found relatively decontextualized within a collection of proverbial material. Immediately preceding it we find a smattering of animal proverbs that approximate fables (180–186). Following on from the numerical saying we find another saying about what is "precious" (יקיר) before Shamash, which—although the line is badly damaged—appears to develop the same themes as the numerical saying, since wine and wisdom are again mentioned (188b–189). While the list in 187–188a may be relatively arbitrary, it is also possible an element of climax or intensification is intended. The title line suggests an escalation in moving from what is generally pleasing to what is favored by a god. But more notable, perhaps, is the rhetoric of the list. The first two items in the list are magnanimous and active—if you have wine, spread it around; if you have wisdom, practice it. Wine and wisdom are qualities

---

7. Translation is adapted from Lindenberger (1985, 499). Aramaic text and lineation follows the authoritative critical edition of Porten and Yardeni (1993, 49; C1.1 12:187–88). For a helpful discussion of the lineation of this text in differing editions see Bledsoe 2013.

5. Agur's Beastly Ethics

that benefit from use, from amplification. But the third is just the opposite—a word does *not* benefit from amplification. In fact, here the pleasing thing to do is counterintuitive, to suppress rather than to share. The saying structures this shift from action to inaction almost like a joke. The crucial words that signal the shift—"but tells it not" (ולא יחוה)—are delayed like a punch line so they are the final two words in the saying. As the rest of the cluster suggests, observing wisdom is central, allowing one to navigate the incongruity between spreading wine and suppressing words. On my reading, then, the crucial insight is not captured by the generalization of the heading but by the difference introduced in the third line.

Finally, let us consider the numerical saying in Prov 6:

שש־הנה שנא יהוה / ושבע תועבת נפשו:
עינים רמות לשון שקר / וידים שפכות דם־נקי:
לב חרש מחשבות און / רגלים ממהרות לרוץ לרעה:
יפיח כזבים עד שקר / ומשלח מדנים בין אחים:

16 There are six things YHWH hates / and seven are an abomination to his soul:
17 Elevated eyes, a lying tongue, / and hands that shed innocent blood,
18 A heart plotting wicked plans, / feet rushing to run toward evil,
19 A false witness testifying lies / and casting strife among brothers. (Prov 6:16–19)

Like *KTU* 1.4 we again find a list of things that *dis*please the deity. But like Ahiqar 187–188a we find this saying relatively decontextualized in the collection of Prov 6:1–19. In keeping with the heading, seven items are clearly listed, however, it is *not* clear that these seven items are in some way comprehensive or distinct. In fact, they appear to overlap and snowball. Several of the items in the list are more-or-less identical. For example, lies are invoked in 6:17a and 19a, and it is difficult to draw a meaningful distinction between "wicked plans" and "evil" in 6:18. In this latter verse, the only difference is the subject—the heart in the first instance and the feet in the second. This distinction suggests a movement from planning to implementation rather than different crimes altogether. Finally, body parts feature in the first five items: eyes, tongue, hands, heart, feet. This description moves from head to toe before describing the whole person in the final couplet. Casting strife among brothers is not a seventh sin, it rather glosses all that came before. The number seven is probably symbolic of total wickedness (Lee 1973, 205–6; Bodi 2013, 35).

While *KTU* 1.4, Ahiqar 187–188a, and Prov 6:16–19 share a surface-level similarity in that they enumerate things that a deity likes or dislikes, each saying functions in its own rhetorical context toward its own purpose. Baal's numerical saying emphasizes the way he was shamed. Ahiqar's numerical saying creates a clever spin on the different ways wisdom might handle wine and words. Proverbs 6 paints a total portrait of the "wicked man" (6:12). What, then, does a numerical saying do? I suggest it is simply a rhetorical structure that allows the speaker or poet to juxtapose a series of items under one rubric. Even if we deny a historical origin to the riddle, Eissfeldt and von Rad, among others, are certainly not wrong to detect a riddling quality at work, which Whybray (1994b, 152) goes so far as to call "a touch of humour." The numerical saying is an incubator for ambiguity, a forum for wit, and a rhetorical structure well-suited to fostering reflection. Unfortunately, in practice the form-critical approach often suggested that by describing structural features and pointing to historical origins the numerical saying was effectively interpreted. In reality, however, its significance, particularly in regard to its literary context, is left largely unaddressed. Close reading, then, remains the best way to analyze the trope—there is no one way it functions or one purpose to which it is put. In approaching Prov 30:11–33, I offer a close reading of each saying with an eye to both its internal playfulness and its rhetorical setting in the collection. In so doing, I hope my reading of Prov 30—the most concentrated extant collection of numerical sayings—will reinforce what I have briefly argued here.

5.2.2. Animal Imagery in the Hebrew Bible, Especially Wisdom Literature

The second most notable feature of Prov 30 is its parade of beasts, perhaps in turns puzzling and amusing if not mildly disgusting. There is some irony in the fact that commentators consistently devote words to the formal feature of the numerical saying, while little research has asked why so many animals are packed into so few verses. Older commentators suggested that the preponderance of animals in these numerical sayings was a primitive form of natural history—"science by list" as von Rad (1972, 123) memorably put it. Married to this idea is the notion that the sayings are collected here merely due to similarity of form, "the catchword principle and affinity of theme" (Toy 1899, 526; Whybray 1994a, 412; Fox 2009, 849). And born from the union of these two ideas is the conclusion that the chapter has no real ethical or theological message. It will be helpful for us to take a wider view on animal imagery in the Hebrew Bible—particularly in didactic, wisdom texts—in order to frame our close reading. The argument of this section is simple yet foundational: animals are a generative resource for theological and ethical reflection, particularly in Proverbs and other wisdom texts where animals frequently serve as analogues for humans.

Ancient life was in near constant contact with animals, and so, in narratives and law, animals are a pervasive presence, an integral part of the world in which the characters operate (e.g., Gen 22:3; 24:19; 37:33; Lev 11; 22:28; 25:2–7; Deut 22:6–7, 10; Sherman 2020, 41–42). In the Latter Prophets and the Writings, however, animals take on a different cast (Sherman 2020, 43). Here, they are most often used as vivid illustrations and object lessons (Isa 1:3; 11:6–9; Jonah 4:11; Pss 8:6–8; 104:17–20), potent symbolic portents (Ezek 1:10; Dan 7:2–12; 8:2–8), even metaphors for human beings (Isa 14:9; Ezek 32:2; 38:13; Amos 4:1; Nah 2:14). The symbolic value of animals is hardly surprising given their ubiquity in human life and the elaborate analogy between humans and animals. Like humans, animals eat and sleep, fight and have sex, bear and raise young, travel and make homes. From a theological perspective, as articulated in Gen 2; Pss 8; 104, and other texts, both humans and animals share a common creaturely ontology that they receive from God (Patton 2000, 428). Although biblical texts present humanity alone as made "in the image of God" (בצלם אלהים; Gen 1:27), there is something of the Creator's stamp on all his creatures. God creates both humans and animals out of his generative freedom. They stand below God in the created order and relate to God as creatures, thus they also relate to each other with reference to God. Humanity can look "up" the chain of being and see themselves in God, and they can look "down" the chain of being and see themselves in the animals (Lakoff and Turner 1989, 166–67; cf. Lovejoy 1936; Patton 2000, 407–8, 432). Because they are simple creatures who operate by instinct in place of what might be termed reason, animal imagery focuses and intensifies the human traits it pictures (Lakoff and Turner 1989, 168–71).[8] Thus animals have potent potential to figure aspects of human behavior.

But beyond animals' ability to instruct humanity by imaging aspects of ourselves back to us, animals are depicted as having something of spiritual consequence to teach (Riede 2002, 6). What animals know by instinct is a

---

8. E.g., Job 18:3; 25:6; 30:1, 29; Pss 22:7 [6 ET], 17 [16 ET]; 59:7; 73:22; 118:12.

pure and valuable knowledge of the world that is untroubled by rebellion and thus affords an access to the divine that may transcend that of humans (Beverly 2020, 150, 152). Lying behind this depiction of animals' special divine knowledge is the depiction of animals in close dependence on God (Riede 2002, 26–28). One recurring image pictures animals as dependent on God for food and sustenance (Pss 104:21; 147:9; Job 38:39–41). God, likewise, extends special care to his animals and maintains relational knowledge of them (Ps 50:10–11). Nowhere does this theme emerge more clearly than in YHWH's speeches to Job. In 38:39–39:30 YHWH considers ten creatures—the lion, raven, mountain goat, doe, wild donkey, aurochs, ostrich, horse, hawk, and vulture. In the foreground of picture after picture the animals live and move and have their being beyond Job's ken, while YHWH's provision, knowledge, and power over them is constantly in the background. Although Job—and by extension all of humanity—is absent from this drama, God is nevertheless fully engaged with his creation (Clines 2013, 2). Such a relationship allows animals to orient to God apart from humanity.

> גם־חסידה בשמים ידעה מועדיה / ותר וסיס ועגור
> שמרו את־עת באנה / ועמי לא ידעו את משפט יהוה:
>
> Even a heron in the sky knows her meeting places, / and a turtledove, a sparrow, and a crane—
> they keep their time of arrival, / but my people do not know the laws of YHWH. (Jer 8:7)

Birds know the fundamental behaviors that pertain to their natures. They act in keeping with the patterns that God has established for them and so they are a law unto themselves. In contrast to this, the people of God lack basic knowledge of his laws that ought to govern their flight. What the birds know, they know because they have not departed from their God-given nature.

> ידע שור קנהו / וחמור אבוס בעליו
> ישראל לא ידע / עמי לא התבונן:
>
> An ox knows its owner / and a donkey the crib of its master.
> Israel does not know. / My people do not understand. (Isa 1:3)

As Peter Riede (2002, 20) points out, the ox and donkey would have been integral members of the household economy, fundamental to the daily life of human beings. The *knowledge* of the ox and donkey represents their understanding of this benevolent and reciprocal relationship. Israel has lost this knowledge through rebellion (Isa 1:2). Implicit in this picture of animal knowledge is the idea that humanity might look to the animals to learn something. It is precisely this point that Job puts to Zophar when he patronizes him with basic lessons in wisdom.

> But if you ask the beasts, then they will teach you,
> or a bird in the sky, then it will declare to you,
> or a bush of the earth, then it will teach you,
> and the fish of the sea will recount for you.
> Who does not know all these things—
> that the hand of YHWH has done this,
> who holds in his hand the spirit of all living things
> and the breath of all man's flesh? (Job 12:7–10)

Job's concern in bringing up the knowledge of the beasts is to focus the issue on God's sovereignty. While Zophar gives a nod to divine freedom (Job 11:7–12), the beasts know that what has happened to Job is from God's hand as they know that God holds all life in the balance. Animals have knowledge that complements human knowledge.

The Psalms and wisdom books are a particularly fecund source of animal instructors.[9] Oftentimes, the message of such imagery is explicitly theological as it develops the relationship of humanity to God via comparison or contrast with the relationship of animals to God (Job 39; Pss 29:6; 78:52; 104:14, 27; 147:9; Dell 2000, 287). Within the book of Proverbs itself, figurative animal imagery abounds toward ethical ends.[10] Proverbs favors making comparisons between humans and animals through similes that illustrate the moral clearly within the context of the instruction or the saying.[11]

> ככלב שב על־קאו / כסיל שונה באולתו:
> Like a dog returning to its vomit, / a fool repeats his folly. (Prov 26:11)

---

9. See Dell 2000 for a survey; and Forti 2008 and 2018 for in-depth treatments of Proverbs and Psalms respectively.

10. The following verses use animal imagery: Prov 1:17; 5:19; 6:5, 6; 7:22, 23; 11:22; 12:10; 14:4; 15:7; 17:12; 19:12; 20:2; 22:13; 23:5, 32; 26:2, 3, 11, 13, 17; 27:8, 23, 26–27; 28:1, 15; 30:15, 17, 19, 25–28, 30–31.

11. See also Prov 6:5; 7:22, 23; 11:22; 19:12; 20:2; 28:1 and 15. Only 5:18–19a uses a formal metaphor.

כְּצִפּוֹר נוֹדֶדֶת מִן־קִנָּהּ / כֵּן־אִישׁ נוֹדֵד מִמְּקוֹמוֹ:
Like a bird straying from its nest— / thus is a man straying from his place. (Prov 27:8)

Other verses employ animal imagery to great effect without using formal structures of comparison, although one is implied by the logic of the poetry. In these types of examples the animals illustrate characteristics of wise and foolish people. Perhaps the most famous of these is Prov 6:6, where the ant is presented as a paradigm of industry that the sluggard ought to learn from. In 1:17 bloodthirsty hooligans are more foolish than birds who can easily spot a snare. In 17:12 a fool is more dangerous than a bereaved bear. And in 26:3 the fool is lined up for a beating alongside horse and donkey like a pack animal. Still other verses make no explicit comparison to human types or behaviors, but a symbolic or, better, proverbial interpretation is implied. The fattened ox is a synecdoche for a great feast in 15:17. The lion is a metonym for a perceived, life-threatening danger in 22:13 and 26:13. Finally, animals do occasionally feature in a nonfigurative sense. Proverbs 27:23–27 is a short, instruction-like passage that commends intimate maintenance of your flocks and herds. There is no clear symbolic meaning here, however, in light of the examples above and the context of Prov 27–28, it seems that the lambs and goats mentioned in 27:26–27 could stand for any valuable investment capable of providing clothing, nourishment, and income when other sources fail (cf. 15:17). They are not, then, unlike the human communities entrusted to your care. In sum, animals are often presented as types of humanity in a way that focuses certain attributes or behaviors with pedagogical clarity.

In this regard, Proverbs is typical of ancient Near Eastern didactic literature more broadly. A mere two examples must suffice. The oldest proverbial material in the world comes from Sumer and animals feature prominently as foils for humans in collection 5 (Alster 1997, 1:119–43 with commentary in 2:400–408). Some Sumerian proverbs make an explicit comparison: "The fettered oxen are stronger than the men who fettered them" (5.15); while others are structured as a simile: "Like an ox, you don't know how to turn back" (5.13); still others use animals as types by means of anthropomorphism: "If a lion has made a hot pot (of soup), who will say, 'It is not good?' as they say" (5.66). Since lions do not cook, it is clear that this is a symbol for any powerful and dangerous individual. Chronologically and linguistically closer to Proverbs, Ahiqar contains many animal sayings that are nearly fables. Their narratival structure suggests anthropological significance. Occasionally, the sayings make this explicit, as in lines 121–122, where a bear approaches lambs and promises to be content after he has devoured just one of their number. "The lambs replied to him, 'Take whichever of us you will.... For it is not in men's own power to lift their feet or set them down apart fro[m the gods]'" (Ahiqar 121–122 in Lindenberger 1985, 502; cf. Porten and Yarden 1993, 47; C1.1 11:168–171). Such explicit morals strongly imply that animals like this scorpion are themselves character types: "The scorpion [finds] bread and will not eat it; but (if he finds) something foul, he is more pleased than if he were (sumptuously) fed" (Ahiqar 86 in Lindenberger 1985, 499; cf. Porten and Yarden 1993, 49; C1.1 12:181). When animals appear in these texts, it is far less likely they are meant to teach or illustrate to the reader something about animals qua animals than about humans qua animals.

Given the pervasiveness of moral and theological animal imagery in the Hebrew Bible, especially in didactic and wisdom texts, and given the preponderance of animals in Prov 30, I will focus a good deal of attention on them in the close reading to follow. It would not just be surprising but almost unparalleled if the animals in Prov 30 were, as Toy (1899, 529) wrote long ago, "simply a record of observation, which may broaden the pupil's knowledge of the world" with "no ethical meaning or application." Rather, we ought to expect that animal imagery in Prov 30 is likely to have a moral or ethical application to humans and we ought not to rule out theological resonances either. Still, interpreting animal imagery requires that we place the images in a literary context within an ancient cultural milieu that may construe the value of the symbols in unexpected ways. No conceptual background can take the place of close reading.

5.2.3. Humor in the Hebrew Bible and Agur's Wry Tone

The final hermeneutical issue that we ought to consider has to do with humor in ancient texts. Both in discussing the numerical saying and now in thinking about animal imagery we have encountered elements of wit and amusement. It seems that on one level the numerical saying is contrived to showcase clever comparisons, startling juxtapositions, and amusing turns of phrase. Likewise when one reads through collections of animal sayings, types like "the dog" or "the ox" frequently appear as the butt of jokes. Agur's wry tone is like glue bonding his form and content. Thinking back to chapter 3, I argued that משא, as a discourse term, implies a mocking or satirizing tone. In chapter 4, I drew out elements of

Agur's discourse in 30:2–10 that were best described as ironic or even sardonic. Such observations bring us into the realm of humor.[12] The instincts of many commentators also detect a humorous strain in Agur's words. Nearly every scholar who has treated these verses notes at one point or another the possible presence of humor.[13] But no commentator I am aware of has developed humor as a persistent quality in the collection and no one saying is considered humorous by all. In the close reading that follows, I will argue that elements of humor unify the collection and suggest Agur's main theme: satirizing pride and greed. To support my reading, I will conclude this hermeneutical prolegomena by sketching my approach to humor in ancient texts.

Since the mid-twentieth century, incongruity theory has reigned as the leading theory of humor.[14] The key insight is simple yet powerful: humor arises from the perception of incongruity in the world. Noël Carroll (2014, 18), a leading philosopher of humor, explains, "Incongruity is a comparative notion. It presupposes that something is discordant with something

---

12. Defining humor is notoriously fraught, so I will be content with Carroll's (2014, 5) broad definition: "The general name for all those objects that give rise to comic amusement is humour." Several points of clarification are in order. First, humor need not elicit laughter or even a smile; amusement can be quite subtle. Second, humor may be present in an artifact without being the purpose of the artifact. In other words, amusement does not drive out other goals (e.g., persuasion, education, edification) but can augment them. Third, humor travels with many synonyms and in many guises, e.g., wit, irony, satire, mockery, puns, comedy, but these are all best subsumed under humor as the broader category. For approachable introductions to humor theory, see Carroll 2014; Morreall 2020; and, with an eye to religious contexts, Berger 2014.

13. So, e.g., Kidner (2008, 173) comments that the text moves suddenly from comic to tragic in the shift from 30:15a to 15b. Fox (2009, 872) muses, "the incongruity of the beautiful and bawdy" in verses 19–20 may have been intended to be funny. McKane (1970, 659) considers verses 21–23 "humorous or whimsical … a species of satire." Murphy (1998, 237) calls verse 28 "a humorous gibe" at social climbers. Sæbø (2012, 374) wonders about verses 29–31 whether "this numerical saying was made with much humor." Finally, Davis (2000, 138) suggests verses 32–33 exhibit "a sly sense of humor."

14. Incongruity theory has roots going back over two hundred years to James Beattie's 1764 work, "An Essay on Laughter and Ludicrous Composition" (Beattie 1778, 321–486; Morreall 2020; Carroll 2014, 17). However, scholars are increasingly acknowledging that the ancients—e.g., Plato, Aristotle, Quintilian, and Cicero—also reflect elements of incongruity theory in several key insights (Perks 2012).

else. With respect to comic amusement, that *something else* is how the world is or should be" (emphasis original). The crucial elements behind incongruity are therefore *perceptions* and *norms*. Incongruity occurs when we perceive something dissonant with our expectations, mental patterns, or the cultural standards (Morreall 2009, 248).

> Prototypical incongruities, then, include deviations, disturbances, or problematizations of our concepts, rules, laws of logic and reasoning, stereotypes, norms of morality, of prudence, and of etiquette, contradictory points of view presented in tandem, and, in general, subversions of our commonplace expectations, including our expectations concerning standard emotional scenarios and schemas, our norms of grace, taste, and even the very forms of comedy itself. (Carroll 2014, 27)

The best way to grab hold of the theory is simply to consider examples of humor.

In his classic study of humor in cuneiform literature, Benjamin Foster (1974, 69) acknowledges that the principle of incongruity is fundamental: "The sense of humor revels in the inevitable gap between what is and what is supposed to be."[15] "In Mesopotamia," he goes on, "cowardice, conceit, ambition, bad manners, deficient education, and inordinate desire provided the background for humorous remarks" (85). One common technique for leveraging incongruity employed animal fables or represented animals as men (Foster 1974, 80; Alster 1975a, 204). For example, Foster (1974, 80) cites what he calls "abuse texts" which dress down a target with a string of insults that were likely meant to amuse onlookers. Samples include such stinging jibes as "He is spawn of a dog ... / the stench of a mongoose ... / a fox with a turtle shell, an addlepated mountain monkey / whose advice is nonsense."[16] Here incongruity is pushed over the line into hyperbolic absurdity. As in modern roasts, it seems the idea was to top the last insult in wit or ridiculousness. For an Egyptian example we have a passage in the Myth of the Sun's Eye where Thoth humors the goddess Tefnut with animal fables (Lazaridis 2012; cf. Jasnow 2001, 65 n. 19). Such fables may be visualized in the Satirical Papyrus (ca. 1250–1150 BCE) where animals

---

15. On humor in the ancient Near East generally, with many more examples, see Foster 1974, 1992, 1995; Alster 1975a; Meltzer 1992; George 1993; Deist 1997; D'Agostino 1998; Houlihan 2001; Jasnow 2001; and Lazaridis 2012.

16. Fuller treatment of this text as well as other "abuse texts" can be found in Sjöberg 1972.

ape human behaviors (Bunson 2012). Other iconography suggests "the existence of popular stories about a war between cats and mice" (Foster 1995, 2464; Meltzer 1992, 326). These drawings have scenes where armies of mice lay siege to a fortress filled with cats, where cat leaders appear to surrender to mice officers, and where cats serve mice in domestic roles "serving food, fanning them, assisting a mouse grande dame at her toilette, and undertaking mouse child-care" (Foster 1995, 2464). If certain gods and the nobility of Egypt were sometimes associated with cats—who threaten and dominate mice easily—then the peasantry are the mice.[17] The incongruity here turns on the reversal of roles in the social order. While this may be, on some level, a serious and terrifying political prospect, the depiction of human social classes in terms of animals makes it absurd and undercuts any sense of real existential terror.

Instructional literature offers more fine examples of humor in the form of proverbs that probably doubled as jokes. One widely acknowledged example of humor is from the Instruction of Ankhsheshonq.

> If you are powerful throw your documents into the river; if you are weak throw them also. (18.6; Lichtheim 2006a, 173)

This proverb has a structure similar to a modern one-liner (Lazaridis 2012). The first line is the setup. It states what is probably an accepted truth about power—you don't need to worry about the details because you can afford to be reckless. The second line packs the punch. It leads us to expect a different conclusion by presenting a different subject in the same manner as the first line. But it delivers an abrupt, incongruous pivot with "throw them also." The incongruity is found in the fact that while we would expect the outcome to be different for the powerful and weak, it is actually the same but for different reasons. If you are powerful you have no need for paperwork, but paperwork is useless without power. Whether weak or strong, paperwork proves pointless.

Another example of humor in a proverb comes from Hellenistic wisdom literature.

> Ὀλίσθημα ἀπὸ ἐδάφους μᾶλλον ἢ ἀπὸ γλώσσης,
> οὕτως πτῶσις κακῶν κατὰ σπουδὴν ἥξει.

---

17. On this trope see Brunner-Traut 1977; and Vycichl 1983.

5. Agur's Beastly Ethics

A slip on the ground is better than on the tongue;
in this way the fall of the wicked will come with speed. (Sir 20:18)

Here the incongruity is loaded into a pun. Although the word *slip* (ὀλίσθημα) is not repeated in the Greek (the verse is not preserved in Hebrew), the repeated preposition *on* (ἀπό) facilitates the wordplay by linking "slip" to both "the ground" and "the tongue." Two different senses of slip are pictured and while the one can leave you in physical pain, if not actually injured, the other seems innocuous enough. The incongruity, however, comes from pointing out that the figurative slip of the tongue rather than the physical slip on the ground is the one that will fell the wicked. What is more, this will happen *fast*, like a literal slip and fall.

Sumerian sentence literature furnishes our final example:

When the ox has diarrhea, the trail of dung is a long one! (2.92; Foster 1974, 84 n. 53; cf. Alster 1997, 1:64; Gordon 1959, 242)

The incongruity here comes from using animal imagery with bawdy humor to make a serious point. When powerful people are sick, the effects are equally powerful (Foster 1974, 84 n. 53). Picturing this in terms of an ox with diarrhea debases whatever real-world scenario may be playing out and perhaps enables those within earshot of the quip to laugh (if only sardonically) at the misfortune unfolding outside their control.

Although scholars are sometimes skeptical, humor is similarly pervasive and incongruity-driven in biblical texts.[18] Many aphorisms in Proverbs make their point by bottling an incongruity and may well contain elements of humor in their striking wit and absurd images (Alter 1985, 176).

נזם זהב באף חזיר / אשה יפה וסרת טעם:
A gold ring in a pig's snout / [is] a beautiful woman abandoning taste. (Prov 11:22)

---

18. For studies of humor in the Hebrew Bible, see Good 1965; Radday and Brenner 1990; Greenstein 1992; Marcus 1995; Whedbee 1998; Brenner 2003; Jackson 2012; and Biddle 2013. For an excellent study of humor in Second Temple Jewish literature see Gruen 2002, 135–212. Many studies have offered humorous readings of particular texts or episodes, e.g., Yee 1988; Radday 1990; Kaminsky 2000; Johnson 2022; Southwood 2021 and 2022.

Suzanna Millar (2020, 94) calls the first line "an evocative, comical image of gross incongruity." The gold ring, a status symbol worn by the wealthy, is absurdly out of place with the pig—the very symbol of ceremonial uncleanness. By juxtaposition the first line becomes a striking visual satire of the woman in the second line.[19] Similarly, the string of proverbs in 26:13–16 read like a roast of "the sluggard" (עָצֵל).

הדלת תסוב על־צירה / ועצל על־מטתו:
The door turns on its hinge, / and the sluggard on his bed. (Prov 26:14)

Again, this image satirizes the sluggard with a clever incongruity (Waltke 2005, 356). In staying fixed to one place and rotating back and forth the door accomplishes its intended purpose, but in doing the same the sluggard fails spectacularly at his. Pertinent to Agur's wry and sardonic tone, scholars have even found humor in those most depressing of all biblical books, Job and Qohelet.[20] Concerning the latter, Weeks (2020, 13 n. 17) writes, "I am inclined ... to think that there probably is humour in the book, and at least a humorous use at times of the grotesque and unexpected, but suspect that Qohelet's own part is often as the straight man, who might make us laugh, but does not laugh with us." To this end, Weeks suggests it might help us hear Qohelet's voice more clearly if we think about him as a performer, akin to a sort of stand-up comedian who moves "through different topics with a mixture of anecdotes, one-liners, and maybe even poems" (13). In much the same way, I am arguing that by invoking humor as a category for listening to Agur we stand to hear his voice more clearly.

We will always struggle to hear the humor in what Nikolaos Lazaridis (2012) calls this "'silent' corpus of ancient material." In propounding these examples, I hope I have both illustrated how incongruity drives humor *and* that there is humor driven by incongruity in ancient Near Eastern and biblical texts. Rarely do ancient texts record the responses of audiences or the intentions of humorists. "Instead, their identification is wholly based upon their form, style, and manner: they might, for instance, have included

---

19. There is, however, a great deal of interpretive openness in this aphorism. For prescient analysis, see Millar 2020 and cf. Heim 2008.

20. For Job see Southwood 2021; Whedbee 1998, 221–62; cf. Good 1965, 196–240. For Qohelet see Levine 1990, 1997; des Rochettes 1996; Greenstein 2007; Jarick 2016a; cf. Good 1965, 168–95.

absurd elements, or they might have contrasted, in terms of tone and message, with their serious context" (Lazaridis 2012). Any particular example could be quibbled over, and indeed, may or may not have been intended to produce amusement, but incongruity remains our best heuristic for identifying and explaining the mechanisms of humor in ancient texts. The presence of more concrete rhetorical features in a text, such as wordplay, sarcasm, hyperbole, irony, or elements of suddenness and surprise, can serve as incongruity signals alerting us to the possibility of humor. With a preponderance of examples we can tune our ear to an ancient Near Eastern sense of incongruity and humor, which, after all, is a human universal.

In the close reading to follow, I will be alert to tonal features that might suggest elements of humor are in play. It is my assertion, moreover, that attending to Agur's wry tone will help reveal the coherence in the collection in so far as it is attuned to his themes and ethical purposes.

5.2.4. Summary of Hermeneutical Perspectives

In the preceding section my goal was to lay a hermeneutical foundation for the close reading of Prov 30:11–33 that follows. I focused on three key issues that the text itself raises: the numerical sayings, animal imagery, and humor. While the numerical saying has often been treated as the key to the unity of the chapter, it is merely a rhetorical structure that allows a poet to present a series of images in a clever arrangement that promotes reflection. Animal imagery, although no less striking or pervasive, has received less attention as a unifying feature but it gives the collection a decidedly ethical cast. Together the numerical sayings and the animal imagery contribute to the tone of the chapter and suggest an element of humor may be present. The close reading to follow will argue that a certain wry or satirical mode of expression characterizes Agur's tone throughout the second half of Prov 30 and facilitates his theme of satirizing pride and greed while commending humility and contentment. Noticing this wry humor helps us read for coherence because it holds together the numerical sayings, animal imagery, and the themes of the chapter.

5.3. Reading Proverbs 30:11–33

5.3.1. The Generation of the Leech: Proverbs 30:11–17

11 דור אביו יקלל / ואת־אמו לא יברך:

12 דור טהור בעיניו / ומצאתו לא רחץ:
13 דור מה־רמו עיניו / ועפעפיו ינשאו:
14 דור חרבות שניו / ומאכלות מתלעתיו
לאכל עניים מארץ / ואביונים מאדם:
15 לעלוקה שתי בנות הב הב
שלוש הנה לא תשבענה / ארבע לא־אמרו הון:
16 שאול ועצר רחם / ארץ לא־שבעה מים
ואש לא־אמרה הון:
17 עין תלעג לאב / ותבוז ליקהת־אם
יקרוה ערבי־נחל / ויאכלוה בני־נשר:

11 A generation curses its father
and does not bless its mother.
12 A generation is pure in its own eyes,
but it is not washed of its excrement.
13 A generation—how high are its eyes!—
and its eyelids are raised up.
14 A generation—its teeth are swords,
and its fangs are knives
for devouring the poor from the land
and the needy from humankind.
15 The leech has two daughters—give, give!
There are three things that will never be sated;
four that never say, "Too much!":
16 Sheol and a sealed womb,
land that is never sated with water,
and fire that never says, "Too much!"
17 An eye that derides a father
and despises obeying a mother—
ravens of the wadi will carve it out,
and fledgling vultures will devour it.

Starting in 30:11, issues of voice recede, and the material takes on a more distanced and impersonal tone as a series of illustrations and object lessons are presented to the reader. Three short stanzas, verses 11–14, 15–16, and 17, comprise a subunit. Proverbs 30:11–14 form a clear sequence built around the use of anaphora with the repetition of *generation* (דור) at the head of each couplet. The use of *curse* (√קלל) in verse 11 creates a loose link back to verse 10 (Plöger 1984, 361), and references to *eyes* (עין) and *eyelids* (עפעפים) create further links between verses 12 and 13. Proverbs 30:15a appears to be a one-line saying, but it links to 15b–c both thematically and through the use of ascending numbers in consecutive lines (two, three, four). Proverbs 30:15b–c is the heading of a numerical saying, the body of which spans verse 16. Although verses 15–16 have no verbal links to verses 11–14 or 17, verses 11–14 and 17 share strong links and envelop 15–16 (Sæbø 2012, 372). Disrespect for parents (אב and אם) resurfaces in verse 17a as in 11 (Sauer 1963, 106; Plöger 1984, 363). Moreover the eye (עין) is singled out for reproach in 30:17 as it was in 12–13. Finally, "devouring" (√אכל) features prominently in both verses 14 and 17. Thus every verse from 11–14 has a verbal link to 17, which brings the themes of the subunit to a fitting conclusion (Davis 2000, 142). As I have reflected before, such formal patterns and catchwords mean little on their own, but these are substantiated by a thematic arc that develops across 30:11–17: these verses utilize humor and animal imagery to paint a repulsive picture of pride and greed.

5.3.1.1. Sons of Pride: Proverbs 30:11–14

The move from second-person prohibition in verse 10 to third-person descriptions starting in 11 is like a poetic scene change. There is no obvious thematic or logical link. Instead, verse 11 introduces "a generation" that will be the subject of the next four verses (see appendix at 30:11: דור ... דור).[21] Contrastive parallelism marks out the kind of people who flagrantly violate the fifth commandment: both actively cursing and failing to bless their parents (Exod 20:12; Lev 19:3; Deut 5:16; cf. Prov 10:1; 19:26; 20:20; 23:25; Schipper 2021, 273; O'Dowd 2017, 399). Although Prov 30:11 offers no evaluation, verses 12–14 develop the portrait of such offspring.

Proverbs 30:12 sketches a highly ironic picture that lampoons such disrespect. Although their own self-evaluation deems them "pure" (טהור), this generation is in flagrant violation of the law, symbolized by their filth clinging to their backsides.[22] "Feces are the main elicitors of disgust"

---

21. Some commentators take 30:11–14 to describe four *different* kinds of people (Toy 1899, 527; Murphy 1998, 231). However, the use of anaphora and apposition suggests a layered description of one generation (Plöger 1984, 361; Waltke 2005, 484).

22. The vocabulary of 30:12 probably adds a flavor of ritual impurity to the flagrant law-breaking introduced in 30:11. Lexemes טהור ("pure") and רחץ ("to wash") occur far more often in ritual prescriptions of the Pentateuch than anywhere else in

cross-culturally, and, in the Hebrew Bible, "a rhetoric of shit" is often employed to associate sin and idolatry with disgust (Staubli 2019, 119, 121; cf. Isa 4:4; 28:8). The extreme, bawdy incongruity of this imagery could well be humorous.[23] The parallelism again lends the verse the structure of a one-liner. The phrase "in its own eyes" (בעיניו) leads the reader to suspect an ironic reversal, which is held briefly in tension till it is resolved at the end of the line by "not washed" (לא רחץ). A pun may well be in play here. The letters מִצֹּאָתוֹ, as pointed in the MT, can be rendered "of its excrement," but if the same letters are vocalized מִצֵּאָתוֹ the gloss becomes "from its exit/going out," which is a euphemism for the anus (Fox 2015, 383). Thus the Greek reads: τὴν δὲ ἔξοδον αὐτοῦ (literally, "and from its exit," but NETS, "its anus;" LSJ, s.v. "ἔξοδος [A]"). Such ambiguity, which allows for a more concrete physical image, deepens the bawdiness and strengthens the humorous reading. Once you reject your parents, who will wipe your bottom?[24]

The exclamation in 30:13 emphasizes the absurdity of the imagery in 12 (see appendix at 30:13: דור מה־רמו עיניו). But it also develops the portrait of the disrespectful generation by clarifying its underlying sin (Waltke 2005, 484). In 30:12–13 the eyes of the disrespectful generation symbolize pride by metonymy. The phrase "in one's own eyes" (בעיניו) is always a negative evaluation in Proverbs. It represents a distorted self-assessment that is overconfident and out of touch with reality (Prov 12:15; 16:2; 21:2; 26:16; 28:11; Van Leeuwen 1997b, 253). Likewise to have "high eyes" is elsewhere associated with arrogance, rebellion, and pride (2 Kgs 19:22; Pss 18:28 [27 ET]; 131:1; Prov 6:17; Fox 2009, 867). Though the sin of pride is not named, it is clearly pictured.

While the characterization of Prov 30:12–13 has been ironic, even laughable, verse 14 turns toward the deadly serious to describe the prideful generation in terms of their violent intentions (Davis 2000, 143).[25] The

---

the OT (e.g., Gen 7:2; Exod 29:4; Lev 10:10; 14:8). And צאה ("filth" or "excrement") occurs likewise in contexts where impurity and sin are in view (Deut 23:13–14 [12–13 ET]; Ezek 4:12; Zech 3:3). The metaphorical language of Prov 30:12 suggests that sin defiles this generation however oblivious it may be. Clifford (1999, 263) points out that Prov 20:9 adds, "Who can say ... I am cleansed [טהרתי] from my sin?"

23. As evidenced by several examples above, much ancient Near Eastern and even biblical humor deals with the vulgar or bawdy (Foster 1974, 85; Ullendorf 1979).

24. Thanks to Stuart Weeks for this formulation, I have rephrased it slightly.

25. On this passage, Gersonides observed that arrogance is not only objectionable

verse is one sentence stretched across a poetic quatrain in two couplets. The substance of the verse is conveyed by the first line of each couplet and, indeed, these could be linked to match the form of the other verses, for example, "A generation—its teeth are swords,... / for devouring the poor from the land." But instead the poet has crafted a double-long climax where each line of this potential couplet is echoed with euphonic grammatical parallelism as if for emphasis (Clifford 1999, 263). Here we see the real danger—the true nature—of such people. The disrespectful generation of 30:11 is ultimately characterized as "a ravening beast" whose mouth is weaponized (Toy 1899, 527; Fox 2009, 867; cf. Ps 57:5 [4 ET]).[26] Although שן is the standard word for tooth in Biblical Hebrew (e.g., Exod 21:27; Jer 31:29), the word מתלעות is a specialized term that I gloss "fangs." In its other three occurrences מתלעות is parallel to שן, belongs to a lion, and this lion (with its teeth!) is a metaphor for wicked humans (Joel 1:6; Ps 58:7). Job 29:17 captures it.

ואשברה מתלעות עול / ומשניו אשליך טרף:
I break the fangs of the unjust, / and I cast prey away from his jaws.

This word connotes predators' teeth—if not specifically lion's teeth—and would have likely triggered figurative overtones for ancient readers.[27] Some people are predators who prey on the weak and the vulnerable in society (Deut 15:11; 24:14; Hab 3:14; Ps 14:4). The kind of person that rejects parental authority, from above as it were, will unscrupulously devour those below them. In light of Prov 30:14's animalistic flavor, then, the filth-smeared rumps of verse 12 also suggest animalistic connotations (Hays 2007, 319–20).[28] The generation of 30:11 has undergone a metaphorical metamorphosis from disrespectful offspring to rapacious beast.

---

in itself but for the grievous sins it leads people to commit (Ginsburg and Weinberger 2007, 627).

26. The term "sword" (חרב) clearly evokes a weapon and, as Waltke (2005, 486 n. 166) points out, the word "knife" (מאכלת) is only used in three other places, all of which require a tool large and sturdy enough to butcher a human being (see Gen 22:6, 10; Judg 19:29).

27. The Aramaic corroborates this. The targum and S render all four occurrences of מתלעות with √ניב "sharp tooth" (Sokoloff 1990, s.v. "ניב"); "tusks, canine teeth" (Jastrow 1903, s.v. "נִיבָא"); "molar or canine tooth" (Sokoloff 2009, s.v. "ܢܝܒܐ").

28. Hays (2007) draws attention to the frequent use of animal characteristics to portray demons, the dead, and sufferers in the ancient Near East. One such charac-

In sum, the tone of the stanza from 30:11–14 is sardonic, employing elements of humor and disgust to mock such wicked progeny by characterizing them as rapacious animals. Pride that leads to dishonoring parents degrades you, turning you into an animal smeared with your own filth, thoughtlessly devouring the weak. Although the text does not condemn this generation outright, it repels the reader by painting such people as exceedingly unsavory (Fox 2009, 865).

5.3.2.2. Daughters of Consumption: Proverbs 30:15–16

The theme of greed embodied in the idea of devouring that was introduced in 30:14 takes over the discourse in verses 15–16. The one-liner in verse 15a begins by changing the topic from the generation of verses 11–14 to the figure of a leech and her two daughters. The leech is the first specific animal named in the chapter but it is operating as a symbol of "embodied greediness" (Delitzsch 1875, 292).[29] Again, there is no formal link but the thematic connection seems intuitive: just as the rapacious generation thoughtlessly devours, so the leech lives to drain the lifeblood from its victim (Whitekettle 2012, 95 n. 9). In terms of tone, the leech presumably triggers feelings of disgust, and elements of humor may again be at work. The way the line opens, "The leech has two daughters," suggests the beginning of a fable or the setup for a joke. This naturally leads us to expect the names of the two daughters or a further description. What we find immediately following, however, is syntactically and semantically incongruous: "Give! Give!" (הב הב). Morphologically the forms are imperatives, but syntactically they are in apposition to "two daughters" (שתי בנות), which suggests proper names (see appendix at 30:15: הב הב). This arresting poetic expression, then, names the daughters for what they say, forcing the reader to momentarily reprocess the line to arrive at the realization that, of course, such greedy clamoring is definitional for the leech (Fox 2009, 867; Yoder 2009b, 284). There may be a further humorous note in the irony that *both* the leech's daughters share the

---

teristic, perhaps associated with deprivations of the underworld, was familiarity with excrement (Hays 2007, 319). E.g., "I spend the night in my dung like an ox. / And wallow in my excrement like a sheep," Ludlul Bel Nemeqi, or the Poem of the Righteous Sufferer, 2.106–107 (Lambert 1996, 45).

29. Targum Ps 12:9 features a leech: "Around, around the wicked are walking like the leech [כעלוקא] that sucks its blood from humankind."

same name and characteristic.³⁰ The leech and her all-consuming attribute reproduce greed and conflict generation to generation (Whitekettle 2012). Fox (2009, 867) calls the line a "jibe." The humor here serves to underscore that leeches breed leeches and only care about one thing.

Thus the two daughters of the leech transition the reader from the rapacious generation to the first numerical saying proper in 30:15b–16 (Sæbø 2012, 371–72). Four consumers are personified under a heading as striking illustrations and their juxtaposition prompts reflection on their common trait. Like the leech that breeds greed, these four things are insatiable. As noted in chapter 4, to be sated (√שבע) is overwhelmingly positive. However, not to be sated or to be insatiable, either through greed or as a curse, is strongly negative (Isa 9:19; Joel 2:26; Amos 4:8; Mic 6:14). For properly calibrated people, "wealth" or "riches" (הון) ought to bring satisfaction (Ezek 27:33; cf. Eccl 1:8; 4:8; 5:9; 6:3). The first two consumers, Sheol and the barren womb, are joined by ו and bear no qualifying clause, while the second two, earth and fire, are also joined with ו and bear qualifying clauses that repeat the evaluations of the heading. Thus the numerical saying presents two pairs and the first—Sheol and a barren womb—is foregrounded. These consumers are chasms on either side of human life. Sheol is the great void that stands at the end of life while a barren womb is a void that nullifies the beginning of life (Van Leeuwen 1997, 253).³¹ Sheol is the archetypal devourer in the Hebrew Bible. Her throat can expand to swallow the grandeur of Jerusalem (Isa 5:14), and none escape death's maw (Hab 2:5). Notably, Proverbs compares Sheol elsewhere to human eyes and presents both as symbols for insatiable greed:

שאול ואבדו לא תשבענה / ועיני האדם לא תשבענה:
Sheol and Abaddon are not sated / and the eyes of humankind are not sated. (Prov 27:20; cf. 1:12)

---

30. Commentators have often asserted that the daughters are the leech's twin suckers (Schneider 1961; Waltke 2005, 487). While this seems plausible, I have not discovered any evidence for it. Given the broader context that emphasizes progeny in 30:11–14 and 17, I rather imagine the leech cloning greedy copies of herself (see the excellent analysis in Whitekettle 2012).

31. Consider Rachel's plea to Jacob, "Give [הבה] me children, for if there are not I will die!" (Gen 30:1). Ewald (1837, 170) also sees connections between the portraits of cosmic insatiability, birds forever pecking out organs, and mythological tropes. For a fascinating study of G Prov 30:15–16 in relation to Greek mythology, see Olivero 2021.

While this first pair consume life, the second pair—parched earth and fire—must consume to live. The arid land of Palestine must continually absorb water or it will become cracked and lifeless, and a fire will burn only as long as there is fuel (Prov 26:20; Perdue 2000, 263). These consumers work in concert offering concrete images of bottomless greed in four dimensions.[32]

Although 30:15b–16 offers no moral, in connection with the leech these striking figures suggest there are people whose appetite for consumption matches the grave. Such people are defined by their appetites, they cannot be satisfied, they live hollow lives.

5.3.1.3. Of Children and Vultures: Proverbs 30:17

Much like 30:14 offered a climactic quatrain describing the apogee of the wicked generation's sin, verse 17 offers a climactic quatrain describing their ultimate comeuppance (Bridges 1847, 513). As many commentators note, dishonoring parents is a capital offense in the Torah and here the offspring of 30:11–14 find their fitting end (Exod 21:17; Lev 20:9; Deut 21:18–21). The verse is a masterpiece of poetic justice. Whereas the eye in Prov 30:12–13 symbolized arrogance, here it is a synecdoche for the wicked generation itself (Plöger 1984, 363; Forti 2008, 81).[33] That this particular organ should stand for the whole poetically foregrounds the sin for which the generation is being punished. Just as they defiled themselves with sin and became like animals devouring the vulnerable (אכל, v. 14b), in their death they do not receive a proper burial and unclean animals feed on their exposed carcasses (אכל, v. 17b).[34] The verbs in 30:17b are not synonyms but rather picture a progression as the ravens "carve out" the

---

32. Scholars commonly assert that the final element in a numerical saying is climactic. While this sometimes seems to be the case (e.g., 30:18–19), Prov 30:15b–16 presents a strong argument to the contrary. Attempts to argue that fire is somehow a more potent devourer than Sheol feel like special pleading and the point of the saying as a whole is surely an overwhelming sense of greed.

33. The use of the singular "eye" in 30:17 vs. the plural in 30:12–13 signals the synecdoche (Delitzsch 1875, 293).

34. "Ravens" (ערב) and "vultures" (נשר) appear in both the Torah's lists of unclean birds (Lev 11:13, 15; Deut 14:12, 14). On the identification of the vulture, see appendix at 30:17: בני־נשר. For brief surveys of ravens and vultures in the Hebrew Bible and antiquity see Forti 2008, 79–81, 30–31; and Kronholm 1999. Leaving unburied bodies for scavengers was a form of humiliation (Deut 21:23; Jer 7:33; 2 Sam 21:10; 1 Kgs 21:24;

eye from its socket (√נקר, Num 16:14; Judg 16:21; 1 Sam 11:2) before vultures actually devour it.[35] This horrific end is affective (Yoder 2009b, 284). The irony is thick and the descriptions are cringeworthy so that we can imagine an audience hooting and howling with disgust.[36] In the Hebrew Bible, laughter frequently erupts when evildoers get what they deserve (Pss 37:13; 52:6; Prov 1:26). So, while I would not say that Prov 30:17 is a joke, it nevertheless smacks of dark humor and contributes to the pervasive sardonic tone of verses 11–17.[37] If the reader was not already sufficiently put off by the wicked generation and their leech-like insatiability, their horrific end should repel all but the most hardened fools.

5.3.1.4. Summary of Proverbs 30:11–17

Proverbs 30:11–17 presents a sustained portrait of pride and greed. In addition to the formal features noted in the introduction to this section, these verses are united by theme, tone, and their use of animal imagery. Proverbs 30:11–14 introduces the theme in terms of prideful and disrespectful offspring who morph into rapacious predators. In juxtaposition to verses 11–14, the images of the leech and the four insatiables further the portrait of the rapacious generation in verses 15–16, and verse 17 pictures their fate. Those driven by pride to dishonor parents and devour the poor are like leeches on society—they will never be satisfied. Not only do these verses further 30:11–14 conceptually, the tone is quite a close match. Their sardonic perspective, including elements of disgust, mockery, and humor, seeks to instruct through vivid, affective illustration rather than exposition.

McKane 1970, 656; Murphy 1998, 235). For discussions of proper burial in ancient Israel see Bordjadze 2017, 80–95; Johnston 2002, 128–42; and Bloch-Smith 1992.

35. Although ravens and vultures are unclean in the Hebrew Bible, both have positive associations as agents of divine purposes (Gen 8:6; 1 Kgs 17:6) or as images of God's deliverance (Exod 19:4). This may lend weight to the idea that Prov 30:17 pictures divine retribution.

36. The work of Quentin Tarantino offers a modern analogy. The ultraviolent climactic slaughter of slave-owners at the hands of slaves (*Django Unchained*, 2012) or Nazis at the hands of Jewish soldiers (*Inglourious Basterds*, 2009) typically garner roars of uncomfortable laughter.

37. Toy (1899, 530) calls this a "serious quatrain, out of place in a string of satirical and descriptive tetrads." I wonder, however, if satirical material surrounding it ought not to suggest a sardonic edge, and likewise whether 30:17 does not itself suggest serious ethical weight in these descriptive tetrads.

Finally, verses 12 and 14 subtly profile the rapacious generation as animalistic, verse 15 presents the leech as a symbol for greed, and verse 17 stars ravens and vultures as the agents of retributive justice. The four insatiables are inanimate—despite being personified their behavior is automated and unreflective. Thus the dehumanizing of the greedy generation progresses from ungrateful offspring, to ravening beasts, to blood-sucking parasite, to lifeless devourers.

5.3.2. Four Ways to Live: Proverbs 30:18–31

18 שלשה המה נפלאו ממני / וְאַרְבַּע [Q: וְאַרְבָּעָה] לא ידעתים:
19 דרך הנשר בשמים / דרך נחש עלי צור
דרך־אניה בלב־ים / ודרך גבר בעלמה:
20 כן דרך אשה מנאפת / אכלה ומחתה פיה
ואמרה לא־פעלתי און:
21 תחת שלוש רגזה ארץ / ותחת ארבע לא־תוכל שאת:
22 תחת־עבד כי ימלוך / ונבל כי ישבע־לחם:
23 תחת שנואה כי תבעל / ושפחה כי־תירש גברתה:
24 ארבעה הם קטני־ארץ / והמה חכמים מחכמים:
25 הנמלים עם לא־עז / ויכינו בקיץ לחמם:
26 שפנים עם לא־עצום / וישימו בסלע ביתם:
27 מלך אין לארבה / ויצא חצץ כלו:
28 שממית בידים תתפש / והיא בהיכלי מלך:
29 שלשה המה מיטיבי צעד / וארבעה מיטבי לכת:
30 ליש גבור בבהמה / ולא־ישוב מפני־כל:
31 זרזיר מתנים או־תיש / ומלך אלקום עמו:

18 There are three things that are too difficult for me,
and four that I do not know:
19 The way of the vulture in the sky,
the way of a snake on a rock,
the way of a ship in the heart of the sea,
and the way of a man in a girl.
20 Thus is the way of a woman who commits adultery.
She eats and wipes her mouth,
then she says, "I have not done wrong."
21 Under three things a land quakes,
and under four it cannot endure:
22 Under a servant if he becomes king,
or a destructive man if he is sated with food;

23 under a loathsome woman if she gets married,
or a maidservant if she disinherits her mistress.
24 There are four insignificant things in a land,
but they are inherently wise:
25 The ants are not a powerful people,
and yet they prepared their food in the summer.
26 Rock hyraxes are not a mighty people,
and yet they put their house in the cliff.
27 The locust swarm does not have a king,
and yet it went out—the whole thing by divisions.
28 A lizard you can grasp with the hands,
and yet she is in kingly palaces.
29 There are three things that march well,
and four that walk well:
30 A lion—champion among the beasts—
he will not turn back before anything,
31 a strapping rooster or a he-goat,
and a king—{let there be no rising against him.} (Prov 30:18–31)

At 30:18, we find another shift in voice and tone that marks a new phase of Agur's collection. First-person speech reappears in verse 18. This is the only time we find first-person speech in the chapter after 30:9 and, though it is not sustained, the return of "I" language recalls the opening of the chapter and serves to mark a seam in the collection. In verse 32, the numerical saying is abandoned and second-person speech reappears marking another seam. Formally, 30:18–31 consists of four numerical sayings, each of which contains a list of four items under a heading. The first two numerical sayings again make use of anaphora as 30:4 and 11–14 did. But unlike the numerical saying in 30:15b–16 the four sayings in 30:18–31 seem to stand alone as observational reflections. They do not typically share connections or terminology between the sayings. What key words we can find tend to connect from individual sayings to the collection more broadly: for example, "vulture" (נשר, vv. 19 and 17), "to eat" (אכל, vv. 20 and 17), "to be sated" (שבע, vv. 22 and 9, 15–16), and "destructive man/to be destructive" (נבל, vv. 22 and 32). Thus, some commentators suggest that there is no ethical purpose here and the quizzical form alone unites these sayings. But the tone also shifts notably at 30:18. Gone are the prophetic denouncements and the darker imagery. An almost playful cheekiness emerges in their place as the sayings become more cryptic and reflective.

Apart from the form of the numerical sayings, the most notable feature of verses 18–31 is the presence of nine different animals. No longer portents of doom, these animals are more like characters in a fable. The humorous undercurrent stays constant—the irony is thick and many types of expectations are subverted. Again, these four numerical sayings draw no explicit morals. In much the same way that 30:15b–16 presented a graphic illustration of bottomless greed, the four numerical sayings in 30:18–31 present various snapshots of the world and particularly how one might live in it. All four numerical sayings, with their curious headings and bold images, revel in irony, incongruity, and reversals, amounting to a subversive commendation of humility and contentment in place of pride and greed.

5.3.2.1. Four Incomprehensible Wonders: Proverbs 30:18–20

The first numerical saying of this four-part sequence immediately strikes a different tone with its heading. First-person speech resurfaces at precisely the point we return to themes that echo 30:2–3. Just as Agur's humble confession played down his own wisdom, the first-person language of verse 18 proclaims ignorance.[38] For many scholars, verse 18 amounts to a confession of awe-filled wonder at the mysteries of the natural world (Roth 1965, 22–23; Van Leeuwen 1997b, 254; Yoder 2009b, 284). Agur is in awe of the laws of lift that keep the vulture afloat and ignorant of the mechanism by which a snake can so rapidly traverse a rock face without limbs. The fourth item in the list is understood as climactic and it often receives a romantic treatment. What is even more mysterious than these natural wonders? The way a man loves a woman (Sutcliffe 1960, 131; Murphy 1998, 235; Forti 2008, 127). On this reading, 30:20 is sometimes treated as secondary so that we ought to interpret it separately from 30:18–19 and other times treated as an abrupt pivot to make a point that is more-or-less the opposite of verses 18–19. In what follows, I will argue that verses 18–19 amount to something more like a wry joke in which Agur both parodies sexual immorality and rhetorically distances himself from it. In its present context, then, 30:20 is closely connected to 30:18–19 so that it serves as a hermeneutical key for the numerical saying and vice-versa.

---

38. In keeping with my approach in this study, I will continue to refer to the "I" in 30:18 as Agur, since verse 18 connects thematically to verses 2–3 and no other speaker is invoked or signaled.

5. Agur's Beastly Ethics 177

The key phrase in verse 18 is "they are too difficult for me" (נפלאו ממני). Although √פלא is often translated using the word "wonder," contemporary connotations of that word in English probably do not capture the ancient Hebrew idea. The word פלא finds its primary reference in the exodus (Exod 3:20; 15:11; 34:10)—many occurrences of the root in the Prophets and the Psalms reflect back on these salvific events (Mic 7:15; Pss 78:12; 106:7). Where the sense expands beyond these concrete remembrances, emphasis lies on the incomprehensible character of God's purposes (Ps 139:14; Job 5:9; 9:10; Dan 12:6). In fact the precise idiom we have here—the *niphal* of √פלא + מן—appears in numerous verses and is rightly translated "to be too difficult for" (Gen 18:14; Deut 30:11; Ps 131:1). The closest parallel to our verse comes from Job's mouth after YHWH has appeared in the storm to render him speechless by matching him against Behemoth and Leviathan:

לכן הגדתי ולא אבין / נפלאות ממני ולא אדע:
Thus I declared, but I did not understand / matters that were too difficult for me, and I did not know. (Job 42:3, cf. Job 37:5)

The phrase נפלאו ממני seems to be less something you utter when gazing at a breath-taking sunset and more something you confess in the midst of inscrutable divine initiative. The emphasis seems to land on God's freedom and power to act in ways man cannot predict or comprehend (Isa 9:5 [6 ET]; 25:1; 28:29; 29:14).[39]

So how are the four ways depicted in Prov 30:19 "too difficult" for Agur? How do they exceed his knowledge and overwhelm his comprehension? Even without the heading, the fourfold anaphora of *way* (דרך) and the tight grammatical parallelism of each phrase push us to find a common denominator between the vulture, snake, ship, and man, or, perhaps, between the sky, rock, sea, and girl. The best analysis of this list is that these things leave no track or trace of their path when they are gone.[40]

---

39. *Pace* modern interpreters, all the ancient versions understand נפלאו ממני to suggest mystery and impenetrability, not the wonder, i.e., beauty, of nature. The Greek has "impossible for me to understand" (NETS; ἀδύνατά μοι νοῆσαι); T has "which are hidden from me" (CAL; דגניזן מיני); similarly S, "which are concealed from me" (ܕܟܣܝ ܡܢܝ); and V, "difficult to me" (*difficilia mihi*).

40. This interpretation has an ancient pedigree. Calling him the earliest interpreter of this passage, Fox (2009, 871) notes that the editor who added 30:20 to verses 18–19 seems to have understood tracelessness to be the common theme. The major-

This understanding is supported by Wis 5:9–11, which uses two of our four images in a different context:

> 9 All those things have vanished like a shadow,
> and like a rumor that passes by;
> 10 like a ship that sails through the billowy water,
> and when it has passed no trace can be found,
> no track of its keel in the waves;
> 11 or as, when a bird flies through the air,
> no evidence of its passage is found;
> the light air, lashed by the beat of its pinions
> and pierced by the force of its rushing flight,
> is traversed by the movement of its wings,
> and afterward no sign of its coming is found there. (NRSV)

Wisdom of Solomon goes on to add the image of an arrow cutting through the air to the ship and the bird. In that context these images are figures for the ephemeral existence of the wicked who are "like thistledown carried by the wind" (Wis 5:14, NRSV).[41] While the snake is lacking, it is easy to

---

ity of premodern Jewish interpreters shared this view, e.g., Rashi: "They are covered after they passed from my eyes, and I do not know where they went, because they hasten to hide from the eye" (trans. A. Cohen, https://tinyurl.com/SBL2653b; see also Ginsburg and Weinberger 2007, 633). Modern commentators who concur include Bridges (1847, 514), Delitzsch (1875, 297), Torczyner (1924, 136), Perdue (2000, 264), Forti (2008, 126), and Fox (2009, 871). Perhaps the most common modern approach, however, also has ancient roots, as in Midrash Mishle, where the mystifying element is the mode of locomotion across sky, rock, and sea (Visotzky 1992, 118; also Ibn Ezra). In my opinion, this interpretation has been popular in recent times because mysterious movement connects more readily than tracelessness to ideas of romantic love. Modern proponents of this interpretation include Ewald (1837, 171), Toy (1899, 531), Sutcliffe (1960, 130), Roth (1965, 22–23), McKane (1970, 658), Plöger (1984, 364), Van Leeuwen (1997b, 254), Clifford (1999, 266), Yoder (2009b, 284), and O'Dowd (2017, 408). There are also several more creative options: Böck (2009, 267), with reference to Mesopotamian literature, claims the vulture, snake, and ship are all metaphors of procreation realized concretely in the way of a man with a woman. Greenstein (2015, 266) thinks the man intuits his way toward the woman's genitalia in the same way vulture, snake, and ship navigate as if by instinct toward hidden destinations.

41. Scholars sometimes disregard this parallel on the basis that Wisdom of Solomon has a different tone or uses the images in a different context than Prov 30. No

see how its traceless glide across a smooth rock face suits this metaphor. Some commentators, however, feel this analysis fails spectacularly when it comes to the man and the woman because whether through pregnancy or other signs, intercourse *does* leave a trace (e.g., O'Dowd 2017, 408; Rico 2007, 276; McKane 1970, 655). But the saying is not concerned with pre-scientific virginity tests or with the possibility of procreation, but rather with undeniable reality that as we go about our daily lives you cannot tell just by looking who has had sex with whom.[42] It is a mystery. As Delitzsch (1875, 297–98) puts it, "Sins against the [seventh] commandment … are distinguished from others by this, that they shun human cognition … unchastity can mask itself, the marks of chastity are deceitful." The fact that Prov 30:20 develops this line of thought explicitly, in keeping with the parallel from Wis 5:9–11, should be considered strong evidence in favor of this reading.

The common lack of a trace may unite these images, but it is still not entirely clear how these things would be beyond Agur's comprehension. In biblical texts, as in the ancient Near East more broadly, wild animals haunt "the liminal space between the known world and the world beyond" (Jones 2011, 680). These descriptions represent the edges of the map, as it were, places beyond human civilization and beyond human ken (Newsom 1994, 22–23). The ability to fly gives the vulture access to the heavens so that it ascends and even nests in heights beyond human reach (Obad 4; Job 39:27–30; Prov 23:5). The snake haunts the deserted wilderness (Deut 8:15; Num 21:6; Jones 2011, 681; Forti 2008, 124), symbolized here by rock (צוּר), which could picture both inaccessible cliffs or rocky deserts without vegetation (Num 23:9; Isa 2:21; 48:21; Pss 78:15; 105:41).[43] The ship, although made by man, penetrates "the heart of the sea" (בְלֶב־יָם).[44] While this expression could indicate the trackless expanse of the open ocean, it

---

doubt this is the case, but it remains the only concrete parallel we possess. Surely the idea of tracelessness can be adapted to various literary purposes.

42. When I taught the book of Proverbs in Haiti, my students quickly intuited both the sexual reading of 30:18–19 and the lack of trace via a Haitian proverb. As I remember it, the proverb ran, "When a machete cuts the water, afterwards there is no scar." This was interpreted by my students to mean that you cannot tell if a woman has slept with someone just by looking at her.

43. In mythological contexts snakes are associated with chaos and the uninhabitable (Borowski 2002, 305; Forti 2008, 123–24).

44. Psalm 104:25–26 pairs ships with Leviathan since both are able to traverse "this great and wide sea" (KJV, הַיָּם גָּדוֹל וּרְחַב).

may equally well suggest sinking into the depths never to be seen again.⁴⁵ In sum, when Agur says these things are too difficult for him and he does not know them, it suggests he does not know the paths that traverse the sky, rock, and sea because these things are beyond common human knowledge. Once the vulture, snake, and ship have passed from sight there is no sign they were even there.⁴⁶

But how then does the picture of a man and a girl suggest the lack of trace and the edges of human knowledge? Indeed, this is precisely the point of reflection that the numerical saying is driving toward. The crucial thing is the relationship between the four pairs as expressed by the preposition. The wordplay and tension within the saying come from the fact that the most natural way to read the prepositions "in" (ב) and "on" (עלי) with sky, rock, and sea is locative, while this is the *least* natural way to read the preposition with "girl" (עלמה).⁴⁷ In the first three lines, דרך takes a concrete meaning such as such as "path" or "track," creating an expectation that "the way of a man" would be followed by a space to traverse parallel to the sky, rock, and sea. However, a girl is not a space across or within which one moves, unless, of course, this use of ב reflects an unusually literal description of sexual intercourse (Delitzsch 1875, 296–97; Waltke 2005, 491–92 n. 182; Fox 2009, 872). The very last word in the saying, then, is highly incongruous. It is a sort of punch line that unexpectedly debases a girl by treating her as a plain of movement that in turn evokes a sexual image.⁴⁸ On its own, then, the numerical saying in 30:18–19 seems to be a joke that unexpectedly compares a sexual encounter between a man and a girl to the way a vulture traverses the sky, a snake moves on a rock, and a ship navigates the oceans. In the same way that the vulture, snake, and ship leave no trace and soon pass out of common human knowledge, sexual encounters happen "behind closed doors" and leave no trace. This image,

---

45. The expression always appears in contexts of judgment or disaster and is not used with other geographic or topographic locations (Exod 15:8; Ezek 27:4, 25–27; 28:2, 8; Ps 46:3; Prov 23:34).

46. In my opinion, Rashi's pithy comment captures both the idea of tracelessness *and* the idea of a journey out beyond human knowledge. See n. 40 above.

47. This incongruity has prompted some interpreters to propose alternative glosses for עלמה. For further discussion of the philological issues at stake, see appendix at 30:19: בעלמה.

48. The Talmud understands "way" (דרך) as a euphemism for intercourse in this verse (b. Qidd. 2b).

then, prompts the reanalysis of דרך toward a more figurative understanding such as "manner" (see appendix at 30:19: דרך).

The final use of דרך in 30:19d, then, which can be read in multiple senses, links to verse 20, which introduces the דרך of an adulterous woman (Forti 2008, 129). The use of כן in verse 20 draws a tight connection back to verses 18–19 so that the numerical saying itself is understood as an illustration of this fifth way, the way of the adulterous woman (see appendix at 30:20: כן; also Rico 2007, 274; Forti 2008, 128). In light of the fact that she is identified as *adulterous*, it is no great leap to read "she eats and wipes her mouth" as a sexual metaphor (Veenker 1999–2000, 65; Avrahami 2012, 101–2). While other uses of the sex-is-eating metaphor suggest luxurious sensual delights (Song 4:16; 5:1; cf. Prov 5:3, 15; 9:17), here it is more prosaic and as a result more off-putting. The adulterous woman treats sex as a common meal (Plöger 1984, 364). The phrase "she wipes her mouth" (מחתה פיה) creates a graphic image that captures her blasé attitude.[49] Fox (2009, 873) calls the phrase "a deliberately crude jibe aimed at the adulteress." Because she finds it a simple matter to wipe away the evidence, she can treat her indiscretion as if it never happened. Thus she says, "I have not done wrong." Her cool denial suggests both that there is no trace of the deed and also that she does not evaluate her actions negatively (cf. 30:12). The common verbs predicated of the adulterous woman take on greater significance within the collection of Prov 30. The verb אכל characterizes her as a consumer (v. 14), which connects more broadly both to the idea of insatiable greed in verses 15–16 and the idea of smug satiation leading to lies and blasphemy (Davis 2000, 145). It is no surprise, then, that אמר has her speaking contrary to reality, more-or-less realizing Agur's fear that satiety would lead him to speak falsehoods and deny God (30:9).

Let me now attempt to draw the strands of this reading together. In the present literary context, 30:20 is bound closely to 18–19 by the adverb כן, the use of דרך, and sexual themes. While it is often argued that the picture of the adulteress is an explanatory gloss on verses 18–19, I want to suggest that we might also read 18–19 as the comment on verse 20.[50] Like the vulture,

---

49. Likewise, the Talmud is aware that "eating" can be a metaphor for sex (b. Ketub. 64b) and "mouth" a euphemism for female genitalia (b. Sanh. 100a; b. Menah. 98a).

50. Many scholars want to separate the interpretation of 30:18–19 from verse 20 altogether on the grounds that 30:20 is "secondary" (Oesterly 1929, 277; Scott 1965, 181; Murphy 1998, 235–36). But to what is verse 20 secondary? Murphy (1998, 236) asserts that 30:20 has entirely missed the point of 18–19 because it "seizes upon the

snake, and ship, the sexual encounter between a man and woman operates beyond human perception and leaves no trace. The adulteress capitalizes on these qualities to deny her wrongdoing. Perhaps the juxtaposition of these four ways with this fifth way is meant to suggest that the way of the adulteress is as incomprehensible as the ways of the vulture, snake, ship, and man (Perry 2008, 169). She is operating beyond the bounds of human civilization. Again, no application is drawn within the text, but the implication is that the attitude and actions of the adulterous are both brazen and prurient. All this suggests that the heading in 30:18 may be tongue-in-cheek. Given that פלא is usually reserved for the spectacular ways of YHWH, there may be a bit of hyperbole in applying it to the ways of the vulture, snake, and ship. Extending פלא to a sexual encounter starts to sound facetious (Fox 2009, 872). When by implication it is also applied to the portrait of the adulteress, the heading becomes downright sarcastic. The sense of נפלאו ממני shifts from "I find this amazing" to "I find this appalling"—two different ways to find something incomprehensible. The tone of this stanza is more playful than 30:11–17, but humor is still at work as the engine of meaning. The combination of the graphic metaphor in verse 20 and the audacity of the adulteress's denial approach the farcical. The adulteress herself may not feel the incongruity, but it cannot be lost on the reader so the joke is on her (Perry 2008, 169). Agur has once again made a virtue out of ignorance and restraint (cf. 30:2–3, 7–9). The adulteress's actions may be traceless but they are also tasteless. Agur wants the reader to refuse such eating, avoid such speech, and practice the contentment of ignorance (Ps 131:1).

5.3.2.2. Four Preposterous Travesties: Proverbs 30:21–23

In Prov 30:21–23 we come to a new vignette of four illustrations, again structured by anaphora, which also connects to the idea of contentment if only elliptically. The word תחת presents four things that cause the earth

---

misleading issue of no trace being left by the eagle in the air." But we have no evidence for a version of Prov 30 where verse 20 is not attached to 18–19. Whether or not verses 18–19 once existed independently of this context, verse 20 is our best guide to how the ancients understood it here. Is it not possible that Murphy has missed the point? Jettisoning verse 20, in effect, interprets a text that does not exist at the expense of one that does. The hermeneutical assumption that these sayings find their "real" meaning when extracted from their context will almost certainly result in a fragmented reading of Prov 30.

to "quake" (רגז) so that it "cannot endure" (לא־תוכל).[51] Such cataclysmic language is most reminiscent of passages in the prophets that picture the unmaking of creation in the face of gross sin and divine judgment or salvation (Joel 2:10; Amos 8:8; Ps 77:19). The verb רגז fundamentally denotes quaking or trembling and can picture both earthquakes and human beings wracked with emotion. So what four things could thus rock the earth? The use of תחת divides the four items into two well-balanced couplets, each with eight words and identical syntactic structures. The poetics of the stanza suggest various pairings. The pair in 30:22 gives male examples: a "servant" (עבד) becomes king and "a destructive man" (נבל) is sated with food. Proverbs 30:23 gives female examples: a "loathsome woman" (שנואה) gets married and a "maidservant" (שפחה) disinherits her mistress. In the outer frame, the servant and maidservant represent equivalent examples from the bottom of the social hierarchy. In the inner frame the destructive man and the loathsome woman are both social pariahs (see appendix at 30:22 and 23: נבל and שנואה כי תבעל). What all four images have in common is the frustration of social norms when people attain to positions not fitting to them (Clifford 1999, 267; Prov 19:10). The נבל is a shameless and destructive person whose antisocial behavior wreaks havoc in their communities (Job 30:8). But here the destructive man seems at his ease, eating till he is overfull (cf. Prov 12:11; 20:13; 28:19). For the loathsome woman to get married is likewise the opposite of what ought to happen—whether or not she is culpable it makes a poor match and a poor start to a domestic partnership (Gen 29:31, 33). Finally, like a servant becoming king, the dispossessing maidservant inverts the normal pattern of things where she ought to depend on and submit to her mistress (Gen 16:9; Ps 123:2). In short, these four things are totally inappropriate—the kinds of things that might make someone exclaim, "This is a travesty!"

Determining the tone of this saying, however, is not simple. The brevity of the stanza and the lack of a moral or application make it difficult confidently to determine how it is meant to be heard. On the one hand, the heading suggests that the things in this list are grave. On the other, the things listed may be distressing for an individual, family, or community but they are not earth-shattering. In other words, there is a perceived incongruity between the gravity of the heading and the items

---

51. The language here echoes my reconstruction of 30:1b and could conceivably represent the kind of thing that has so frustrated Agur.

in the list. For some scholars, this incongruity suggests humor, while for others it is evidence of how much more seriously ancient people took social hierarchies than we do.[52] Comparative texts often arbitrate these debates. The trope of *Chaosbeschreibungen* or "the world upside down" was common in ancient Near Eastern and Egyptian literature, but there was no one way the trope was employed (Van Leeuwen 1997b, 254).[53] In a text like the Prophecies of Neferti it is used hyperbolically for the sake of propaganda and entertainment (Lichtheim 2006c, 139–45, 149). However, a text like the Complaints of Khakheperre-Sonb might be read in a more somber light with touches of Ecclesiastes's or Ps 73's reflections on injustices in the world (Lichtheim 2006c, 145–49). On the other hand, in compositions like the Balaam text from Deir ʿAlla or Mic 7:1–6 the trope of the inverted world is clearly hyperbolic but put to serious use. So while these examples offer helpful analogies, they cannot on their own determine the tone of our saying. What these analogous texts *can* help us do—particularly since they are longer compositions—is notice certain literary similarities. Many of these *Chaosbeschreibungen* texts employ stock tropes and cannot be interpreted literally because various descriptions contradict each other (Lichtheim 2006c, 150). The point is not found in the individual examples, but the stylized and symbolic picture

---

52. Scholars who see the saying as humorous include Toy (1899, 532), Oesterley (1929, 278), McKane (1970, 659), Whybray (1994b, 152), and Clifford (1999, 266). While scholars who think the saying ought to be taken seriously include Bridges (1847, 516), Delitzsch (1875, 299), Roth (1965, 34–38), Plöger (1984, 364), Van Leeuwen (1986), Murphy (1998, 236), Davis (2000, 146), Perdue (2000, 264), Waltke (2005, 493), Fox (2009, 874), Sæbø (2012, 373), and O'Dowd (2017, 409). A few scholars make the point that the saying has "elements of humor" but still maintains a "sober social commentary" (Ansberry 2011, 172; cf. Van Leeuwen 1997b, 254; Yoder 2009b, 285).

53. The term *Chaosbeschreibungen* (literally, "descriptions of chaos") was coined by Assmann (1983, 346), who wrote, "With this view of things the conclusion is obvious that the extensive descriptions of chaos which the literature of the 'Middle Kingdom' and the shorter descriptions of disaster which certain royal inscriptions of the 'New Kingdom' have handed down to us are nothing else than particularly detailed formulations of the dogmatic fiction of the displaced disaster, ritual invocations of a happily banished and excluded counter-world, apocalyptic, fearful dreams of an exaggerated sense of order without any reference to real events or genuine experience of disaster." Other important treatments include Luria 1929, Weeks 2010b, Kruger 2012 (with copious bibliography), and, more generally, Babcock 1978. For a study of "the world upside down" with reference to Prov 30:21–23, see Van Leeuwen 1986.

that the composition evokes (Weeks 2010b, 41).[54] It may be worthwhile, then, to make a fairly pedantic grammatical point. The כי clauses in Prov 30:22–23 are conditional, thus these four situations are being imagined as possibilities rather than presented as realities (see appendix 30:22: כי ... כי). We ought to reckon with the possibility that, like the comparative texts, this numerical saying intends to provoke amusement and reflection by portraying a hypothetical vision of the world that is witty and absurd both in its expression and ideas. It amounts to a false dichotomy to suggest this saying is *either* humorous *or* serious.

The context in Prov 30 rather suggests this numerical saying has amusing features put to an ethical purpose. Yet, despite the fact that the heading identifies them as world-ending disasters, it is not easy to attach moral value to these four travesties. Certainly the "servant" (עבד) and "maidservant" (שפחה) are morally neutral designations and there is nothing inherently unethical about a servant ruling as king or a maidservant disinheriting a mistress. Surely "a destructive man" (נבל) denotes reprehensible antisocial behavior, but the "loathsome woman" (שנואה) may or may not be deserving of her reprobation—she may well be a victim.[55] Yet, the kind of social inversions pictured in these verses take on a negative cast in Prov 30 (Waltke 2005, 493). The strongest negative echoes are found in verse 22b and the picture of the נבל. Eating imagery has pictured consuming greed at nearly every turn in the chapter (vv. 9, 14, 15–16, 20) and the word שבע in particular has accrued negative associations (vv. 9, 15b–16). The נבל is not enjoying his "portion of food" (לחם חקי) as Agur prays for, but is rather "sated" (שבע), which poses spiritual risks (vv. 8–9). In connection with the נבל eating his fill, the שנואה getting married suggests another ill fit that Proverbs cautions against elsewhere (Prov 21:9, 19; 25:24; Yoder 2009b, 285). Although motivations of the עבד and שפחה are not spelled out, the collection thus far has been an indictment of pride and greed so it is not difficult to imagine them as

---

54. Perhaps the work of early Netherlandish/Renaissance painter Hieronymus Bosch (ca. 1450–1516), such as *The Garden of Earthly Delights* (ca. 1510–1515), could serve as an analogy. When translated to a visual medium we immediately recognize such descriptions are not literal although they are intended to evoke the way things actually are because deeper realities are hidden from plain view.

55. Midrash Mishle connects these verses to the story of Sarah and Hagar (Visotzky 1992, 119).

characters from 30:11–17 or 20.[56] Sa'adiah Gaon "explains these verses as warning a person not to seek a position beyond his social level, for even if he succeeds in attaining power, it will be not without resentment and opposition" (quoted in Ginsburg and Weinberger 2007, 635). But even if we allow that the context suggests we ought to frown on these four situations, the hyperbolic heading pushes us to imagine different ways such situations could be "earth-shattering." One possibility is to follow Sa'adiah in understanding ארץ as a metonymy for the *people* on the earth rather than a designation for the physical creation (see Fox 2009, 875; cf. Isa 14:9, 16; Jer 33:9; Joel 2:1; Ps 99:1; cf. Roth 1965, 34; McKane 1970, 659). On this reading the verbs in the heading no longer need be understood figuratively, but can instead be taken at face value: People fume and tremble with rage when they see the wicked or the undeserving prosper. Rather than picturing the dissolution of the cosmos, the heading pictures the kind of angst that can lead to existential crisis and even despair (Ps 73:2–3; Eccl 2:21; 7:15; 9:11). The point in context, then, might be quite close to what Qohelet cautions in Eccl 10:4–7: "If a spirit of leadership comes over you, do not forsake your place because composure forsakes great sins.... There is an evil I have seen under the sun, like an error that proceeds from the ruler: Folly is placed on many heights and the rich sit in a low place. I have seen slaves on horses and princes walking like slaves on the earth."[57] The point, then, is not so much that the four items in this list are *wrong*, but that they have disastrous effects.

In sum, the numerical saying in Prov 30:21–23 suggests that when social conventions are disordered it causes grave distress. The saying is not a joke and I would not call it tongue-in-cheek, but its wit and hyperbole suggest a certain amount of absurdity that may be intended to amuse.[58] Part of the point, then, might be to reveal that though these things happen "all the time," as it were, they are nevertheless highly destructive. In the context of Agur's collection this stanza illustrates the social consequences of the kind of pride and greed described in verses 11–17 and 20 and thus commends Agur's stance of humility as articulated in verses 6–10.

---

56. The verbs associated with the עבד and שפחה are active verbs, which could imply they are seeking to rise above their rank.

57. For commentary on this passage see Weeks 2021, 491–96. This translation is my own, but it follows Weeks's commentary and philological notes.

58. If the saying were entirely tongue-in-cheek it would suggest that the four situations of 30:22–23 were not actually problems at all.

5.3.2.3. Four Commendable Small Animals: Proverbs 30:24–28

The third numerical saying in this four-part sequence stands out for its title line, which differs from the others in not featuring the three-four pattern. This formal curiosity indicates a more significant rhetorical distinction: This is the only numerical saying in the chapter that presents positive images, that is, images the student of wisdom would do well to imitate. Despite their apparent insignificance and their inconsequential size these creatures are inherently wise, underscored by extreme alliteration: *wəhēmmāh ḥăkāmîm məḥukkāmîm*. The exceptional wisdom of these four beasts is built into their nature as if it were the flip side of their weaknesses (see appendix at 30:24: והמה חכמים מחכמים). Tova Forti (2008, 111) calls their wisdom an "inborn ability," and Riede (2002, 10), "intuitive *Weisheit*." Their wisdom presents a profound irony in comparison with humans: they are not capable of acting beneath their intelligence or training and they do not have to be formed in wisdom as people do. Thus they provide examples of wisdom that actually surpass humankind and in so doing offer a valuable model for reflection (Murphy 1998, 236; McKane 1970, 661). Proverbs 6:6—the only other text in the Hebrew Bible to feature the ant—highlights this pedagogical dynamic: "Go to the ant, sluggard! / Look to her ways and be wise."[59] The heading primes the reader for further irony in the examples to follow.

The first three animals are described along the same pattern. The a-line introduces the subject of the couplet and identifies its deficiency by means of a negation (לא in 30:25–26, אין in v. 27). The b-line begins with a *wayyiqtol* and identifies how these creatures effectively overcame their deficiencies to find success. The ant is described as lacking in "power" (עז), a word that usually indicates an intimidating and unyielding potency (Judg 14:18; Ps 18:18 [17 ET]; Prov 21:14), particularly when predicated of people (Num 13:28; Isa 25:3). But what ants lack in power they make up for by their famed industriousness that secures their provision (Prov 6:6–8).[60] The hyrax lacks "might" (עצום), which emphasizes strength in numbers

---

59. Both the ants and the hyraxes are called "a people" (עם) in 30:25–26, a rare anthropomorphism that implies analogy between humans and animals (Waltke 2005, 496; McKane 1970, 661; cf. Ps 74:14; Joel 2:2).

60. On the ant, see Forti 2008, 101–2; and the charmingly antiquated yet informative overview in Tristram 1867, 319–21. For the philology behind נמלה, see appendix at 30:25.

that renders a nation dangerous and unassailable (Exod 1:9; Num 22:6; Joel 1:6; 2:2). Although hyraxes are by no means solitary, they live in relatively small colonies in rocky cliffs that secure protection from predators by serving as a fortress (Ps 104:18; cf. Num 24:21; Ps 18:3; Job 39:28).[61] Unlike the ant and the hyrax, the locust is a potent biblical trope and nearly every mention of it in the Hebrew Bible is a picture of plague or judgment (e.g., 1 Kgs 8:37; Joel 2:25).[62] By invoking it, the tone of the saying shifts to show that even small creatures can wield devastating power. Individual locusts pose no threat (Ps 109:23), so the lack of a king, that is, organizing leadership, would seem a crippling weakness. Yet the swarm is a thing of dread that operates with military discipline, moving by divisions and ravaging all in its path (Joel 2:7–8; Judg 6:5; Jer 46:23; see appendix at 30:27: חצץ כלו).

The final saying, about the lizard, departs subtly from the pattern (Waltke 2005, 496).[63] In the a-line its deficiency is not identified in terms of a *lack* but rather through a concrete description of its size and its weakness. Notably, this is pictured vis-à-vis humanity: "A lizard you can grasp with the hands." The use of the second person encourages the comparison between humankind and the beasts (see appendix at 30:28: תתפש). In the b-line there is no *wayyiqtol* but rather a verbless clause that locates the lizard "in kingly palaces." By deviating from the pattern of syntax in the preceding three examples the poet subtly hints at an escalation of irony in this final illustration. Despite her vulnerability, this small creature, which a human being can easily grasp, achieves a feat of which few humans can boast: she inhabits the richest and most exclusive habitation in the land (Forti 2008, 117; Fox 2009, 879). Again, such irony carries the whiff of humor in the incongruity of the lizard's physical weakness vis-à-vis humanity when compared to her luxurious abode (Murphy 1998, 237).

The question we ought to ask, then, is: What lesson might humans draw from these creatures? What makes them wise and worthy of emulation?

---

61. For characteristics and behavior of the hyrax see Tristram 2013 [1884], 1–2; Firmage 1992, 1143; and Gilbert 2002, 21. Psalm 104:18 mentions the creature in a similar manner, "cliffs are a refuge for the hyrax" (סלעים מחסה לשפנים), suggesting such behavior was proverbial. For the philology behind שפן, see appendix at 30:26.

62. On the locust in the Hebrew Bible and ancient Near East, see Firmage 1992, 1150; Gilbert 2002, 40–41; and Forti 2008, 112–15.

63. The identification of this creature is tenuous (see appendix at 30:28: שממית). However, the particular identification of this animal does not seem to affect the interpretation of this saying.

One approach suggests people should be diligent like the ant, resourceful like the hyrax, disciplined like the locust, and perhaps cunning like the lizard.[64] But this approach does not take the heading seriously enough as the focus of all four images. The point is not found in particular attributes but rather in the unifying pattern whereby these small creatures succeed by living in keeping with their inherent wisdom despite their obvious weaknesses. These creatures do not grasp for what is not theirs but embrace their shortcomings and find success. "By extension," writes Perdue (2000, 265), "humans, not through arrogant pride but through wisdom that is God-given, have the capacity to survive and dwell secure." As Katharine Dell (2000, 281) reflects, it is "a lesson for humans on lowliness."[65] We might properly term their unifying quality humility. In his whole collection, this is the only thing that Agur sees fit to dub "wisdom."[66]

Although there is no moral or application drawn within the stanza, setting this saying within the broader collection draws out its import. These small creatures procure, despite deprivations, provision (ant), protection (hyrax), power (locust), and position (lizard). This amounts to a great reversal, albeit on a small scale. Agur's presentation of four small beasts hinges on the same kind of irony that has powered the other numerical sayings in the chapter. As in 30:18–19, appearances can be deceiving and as in verses 21–23 low creatures of the earth (ארץ) have received great rewards (30:21, 24). The ants are not undeservedly sated (vv. 9a, 22b), nor destitute (v. 9b), nor yet bottomless devourers (vv. 15–16, 20), but dutifully gather "their food" (v. 8). The hyrax is not vulnerable to predators (vv. 14, 17), but enjoys protection expressed in metaphors similar to the protective benefits Agur attributes to God's word (30:5). The locust plague, while surely a terrifying prospect, is typically mobilized by the deity against the enemies of God, most famously in order to deliver Israel (Exod 10:12–14). Finally, the lizard has infiltrated the royal court without resorting to slander (v. 10) or overturning the created order (v. 22a). The verbal connections here are not tight, but conceptually these four creatures present

---

64. There is a tendency to moralize these images, almost to the point of allegory (see Weinberger and Ginsburg 2007, 638–39; cf. Bridges 1847, 519–20; Waltke 2005, 496–98).

65. Rabbinic sources emphasize humility in their exegesis of this passage (Weinberger and Ginsburg 2007, 636).

66. Apart from Agur's apparent disavowal of wisdom in 30:3, this is the only use of √חכם in the chapter.

something of an antithesis to the way pride and greed have been pictured throughout the collection (Waltke 2005, 495; Ansberry 2011, 173). These small animals know how to succeed where humans have only figured out how to devour each other like animals. Agur exhibits a winking cheekiness in presenting four humble creatures as paragons of wisdom.

5.3.2.4. Four Ridiculous Swaggering Beasts: Proverbs 30:29–31

If the saying in 30:24–28 brought us face to face with small creatures whose great wisdom outstrips their size, the final saying in the collection considers four great creatures whose wisdom is perhaps questionable. As in the other numerical sayings, a title line introduces the unifying feature and returns to synonymous parallelism, but the list itself is less orderly. We find no anaphora or syntactic parallelism as in the lists of 30:19, 22–24, and 25–28, nor do we find tight poetic structures as in 30:16. Instead the list of four creatures—the lion, rooster, goat, and king—is uneven, with the lion and king receiving descriptive expansions, while the rooster and goat are simply named. But we must tread carefully, because 30:31 has more textual challenges than any portion other than 30:1. Therefore, our analysis cannot be focused primarily on poetics and close reading but must take account of the broader strokes of the imagery and ideas. Even so, this opaque saying stands near the climax of Agur's collection and contributes to its meaning in important ways. As I read it, this final numerical saying functions as a backhanded compliment to the king—perhaps meant to lampoon all who are tempted to think too highly of themselves.

When the title line tells us these creatures "march well" (מיטיבי צעד) and "walk well" (מיטבי לכת), this may already be a bit tongue in cheek. When used adverbially, √יטב means to do something well or excellently and the combination of "march" (צעד) and "walk" (הלך) often describes holistic success (Jer 10:23; Prov 4:12; and see appendix at 30:29: מיטיבי צעד). But there is no other example of "to do well" (יטב) with צעד or הלך in the Hebrew Bible, nor is there further description of how the lion, rooster, or goat succeeds marvelously beyond the lion's unflinching courage.[67] Cer-

---

67. The image of "walking well" could project courage, but could also be somewhat absurd, because walking—unlike other complements of adverbial √יטב (1 Sam 16:17; Isa 23:16; Jer 1:12; Ezek 33:32; Ps 33:3; Prov 15:2)—is not something that requires a particular level of skill.

tainly, when one thinks of the lion, rooster, and goat it is easy to picture a bit of a swagger. In the case of the lion, this swagger is backed up by the fact that he is "champion among the beasts" and fears no natural enemies (Isa 31:4; Prov 28:1; Job 39:22). Reading the saying at face value, the lion is the "paragon of courage" and his confident gait embodies this definitional trait (Forti 2008, 120–21). But when we turn to the rooster and the goat there may be an amusing incongruity (Sæbø 2012, 374). Although they strut as well as the lion, they lack real muscle to back it up. Their walk may also embody courage, but it suggests delusions of grandeur rather than unstoppable power.

In fact, concerning G Proverbs, James Aitken (2007, 199) argues that collocating these three creatures with the king may amount to "an implied criticism" since there is a "diminuendo" from the lion to the rooster and the goat.[68] According to Aitken (2007, 200–201), the Greek words for rooster (ἀλέκτωρ) and goat (τράγος) are freighted with negative connotations.[69] We may be able to bolster Aitken's suggestion with the imagery of the Hebrew Bible by comparing to Ezekiel's vision. In Ezek 1:10, the "living creatures" that bear up YHWH's chariot-throne each have four faces: the face of a human (אדם) on the front, as well as the faces of three beasts that are the most powerful creatures in their respective realms, the lion among the wild animals (אריה), the ox among the domesticated animals (שור), and eagle among the birds (נשר). As Exod. Rab. 23:13 comments with reference to Ezek 1:10, "The most exalted of all living creatures is man; of birds, the eagle; of cattle, the ox; and of wild beasts, the lion. All of these received royalty and had greatness bestowed upon them, and they are set under the chariot of God" (Lehrman 1951, 291). Thus these composite creatures symbolize kingship and YHWH's power and position as king over all (Greenberg 1983, 56; Allen 1994, 31; Block 1997, 96). The four creatures in Prov 30:29–31 represent the same four domains that we find

---

68. Although Aitken's argument is rooted in the Hellenistic conceptual world and applies to the Greek, the connotations he notes in G's translation represent a compelling early interpretation of the saying in MT Prov 30:29–31.

69. Aitken (2007, 199) points to Aeschylus's *Agamemnon* (1671), among other texts, where the pompous King Aegisthus is pictured just before his death as "a bold cock parading up close to the hen" (κόμπασον θαρσῶν, ἀλέκτωρ ὥστε θηλείας πέλας). "As for the goat," writes Aitken (200), "it is of course associated, irrespective of the historical truth behind it, with the origins of tragedy … and by the Hellenistic period a 'tragic' performance could have negative connotations, representing pomp and pride that are out of step with reality."

in Ezekiel's vision, but in place of the bull we find a goat and in place of the soaring eagle, a strutting rooster.[70] A list of four stately creatures featuring the king and the lion ought to include the bull and the eagle—this would suit the royal iconography of the ancient Near East more broadly and of Proverbs in particular (Prov 19:12; 20:2).[71] The rooster and the goat, then, may be functioning as surprising foils transitioning from the lion to the king. The king imagines himself the lion who is afraid of nothing, but is he perhaps strutting at the head of the hens in the barnyard and suffering from comical arrogance?[72]

In this light, the king could look more ridiculous than grand. Unfortunately the text of Prov 30:31b is uncertain. My preferred reading is "let there be no rising against him" (see appendix at 30:31: אלקום [אל־קום] עמו).

---

70. For reflections on the identification of these animals, see appendix at 30:31: תיש and זרזיר מתנים. Symbolically, the profile of the goat is similar to the bull although less developed and less distinguished. The goat is characterized as "destructive to cultivated areas" with an "overbearing temper and aggressiveness" representing "power and belligerence" (Vancil 1992, 1040). Although goats sometimes represent deities, it is rarely the chief deity of the pantheon as with the bull (Caubet 2002, 221–22). If the deity/king is associated with the bull then the "chief" or "prince" (שר) is the goat (Isa 14:9; Ezek 17:13). When the Hebrew Bible depicts rulers as goats (typically איל or עתוד), it is often in the context of defeat and domination (2 Kgs 24:15; Isa 14:9; Jer 51:40; Ezek 39:18; Zech 10:3). As for the rooster, it is difficult to establish symbolic associations because this is the only verse that mentions this animal (Peters 1914). We do, however, possess a seal (ca. 600 BCE) that pictures a rooster in fighting pose and is inscribed in epigraphic Hebrew, "Belonging to Jaazaniah, servant of the king" (LY'ZNYHW 'BD MLK; Badé 1933). For a broader discussion of the attestation and symbolism of the rooster in ancient Mesopotamia, see Ehrenberg (2002); and for the symbolism of the rooster in Greco-Roman Judaism, see Goodenough (1958, 59–70). Common trends include association with fighting prowess, fertility, and light/the sunrise. The representation of the rooster as pugnacious, which was connected to sexual prowess, resonates with the characterization of the lion and the goat.

71. Proverbs is somewhat distinctive in the Hebrew Bible for representing the king as a lion since this imagery is more frequently applied to YHWH (Strawn 2005, 54–58). The definitive study on lion imagery in the Hebrew Bible remains Strawn 2005. For the lion and the bull as royal images in the ancient Near East more broadly, see Watanabe 2002, 42–64. For associations between eagles and royalty, see Caubet 2002, 225–26; cf. 2 Sam 1:23; Ezek 17:2–7.

72. It is worth remembering that the lion can be a negative image depicting the king's potential for destructive rage (Prov 19:12; 20:2; Pss 7:2; 17:12; 22:13; cf. Keel 1997, 86). In the context of Prov 30 we might draw a line back to verses 13–15 where the proud and greedy generation was depicted as a devouring animal.

In light of the warnings against self-promotion and insubordination in the broader collection (30:6, 10, 21–23, 32), we might read the line as a genuine injunction against confronting the king while the humorous juxtapositions simultaneously mock royal authority (cf. Forti 2008, 123). Is the king more like the lion or the rooster and the goat? Perhaps the latter, but best to steer clear. The saying is underdetermined and does not draw out an explicit joke at the king's expense making it possible to read the saying as both honoring and mocking kings.[73] Such ambiguity enhances incongruity and was a distinctive feature of humor in ancient Jewish contexts (Gruen 2016, 434–36; cf. Aitken 2007, 199). In the context of Prov 30, however, I do not think we can make too much of the contrasting sketches in the final two numerical sayings. Here we have a stark contrast between the most weak and vulnerable animals (to whom we would not want to be compared) and animals that are confident, powerful, and even regal (to whom we might long to be compared). But the powerful animals merely look good, while the weak animals possess goods and are named wise. There is a subversive humor to all of this. The king was unnecessary in 30:27, and 30:22 implies striving to rule is destructive. Now, in 30:31 the king appears slightly ridiculous. In this way the imagery continues to deepen the theme—present throughout the whole collection—that pride and greed are absurd and off-putting, thus implicitly commending humility and contentment.

5.3.2.5. Summary of Proverbs 30:18–31

The four numerical sayings in 30:18–31 present images of how one might live in the world. In contrast to those who have said the numerical saying is primarily a record of natural observation, or it is devised merely for entertainment, I have attempted to show that a coherent ethical theme emerges when we ponder these images in context and consider the subject matter. While it is reductive to repackage each vignette in terms of a moral, these sayings serve to order the readers' perceptions and promote

---

73. Commentaries tend toward a royal interpretation, which reads the saying as unironic praise of the king (e.g., McKane 1970, 664; Waltke 2005, 499; Ansberry 2011, 174). Some commentators, however, seem unwilling to adopt a particular interpretation due to the obscurity of the text (e.g., Fox 2009, 880; O'Dowd 2018, 410). In my opinion, the context of the broader collection helps guide our reading here.

self-reflection. In 30:18–20, a bawdy joke underscores the deceptive and incomprehensible nature of greed. In 30:21–23, a series of clever images urge reflection on the grave distress caused when social conventions are disordered. In 30:24–28, four insignificant creatures subvert our expectations by finding success despite their shortcomings. Finally, in 30:29–31 four strong creatures come off looking silly by contrast.

In short, the effects of pride and greed are presented as disgusting, incomprehensible, destructive, and laughable while those humble animals who content themselves to work within their limits are successful and wise. As we saw in 30:11–17, elements of irony, disgust, wit, and mockery suffuse the material with a subversive and amusing tone. None of these verses come forward and state an ethical principle, but the numerical saying allows Agur to develop his theme by illustrating patterns of behavior with playful verbal expression, evocative imagery, and underdetermined meaning.

5.3.3. Churning Pride: Proverbs 30:32–33

אם־נבלת בהתנשא / ואם־זמות יד לפה:
כי מיץ חלב יוציא חמאה / ומיץ־אף יוציא דם
ומיץ אפים יוציא ריב:

32 If you have been destructive by exalting yourself,
or if you have been scheming—hand to mouth.
33 Because churning milk produces butter,
and churning a nose produces blood,
and churning anger produces strife. (Prov 30:32–33)

In 30:32–33, two notable formal features mark a shift in tone that signals the end of the collection. The form of the numerical saying, which had dominated 30:15–31, disappears, and second-person speech reemerges. Together these verses—which are tightly joined by כי in verse 33—present the moral or application of the whole collection and ground it in a vivid, closing aphorism (Perdue 2000, 267). The message in short: scheming and self-promotion are destructive and uncontrollable.

Proverbs 30:32 is structured as a double conditional clause with second-person verbs: "If you have been destructive [נבלת] ... / or if you have been scheming [זמות]." As discussed formerly, נבל recalls verse 22 and is a morally loaded term denoting extremely destructive antisocial behaviors (see appendix at 30:32: נבלת). The specific way one might be destructive is "by exalting yourself" (בההתנשא).⁷⁴ Elsewhere in the Hebrew Bible the *hithpael* of נשא describes "lifting oneself up" figuratively with strong connotations of pride; as in Num 16:3 when the elders accuse Moses and Aaron of "exalting yourselves" (תתנשאו) over the assembly of YHWH; or in Ezek 17:14 where "not exalting oneself" (לבלתי התנשא) is compared to being humble (שפלה) and keeping covenant. Perhaps most notable, against the broader themes of this chapter, is 1 Kgs 1:5, where Adonijah "exalted himself, saying, 'I will be king'" (מתנשא לאמר אני אמלך). The plot that unfolds over the next several chapters surely falls under the rubric of what the present verse calls "scheming" (זמות) and results in the blood of Adonijah and his conspirators (1 Kgs 2:25, 34).⁷⁵ Agur has singled out such behavior from the beginning of the collection (Waltke 2005, 500). As I suggested in the previous chapter, slandering a servant (30:10) could occur in a context where a subordinate was scheming to exalt themselves and such subversions are the express concern of Prov 30:21–23 where the √נבל features prominently. Likewise, the verb נשא (v. 13) is emblematic of the proud and greedy generation in 30:13. Perhaps unexpectedly, some of the weightiest moral language of the collection is here turned on the reader urging soul-searching and an appropriate response.

The proscribed response is encapsulated in the expression "hand to mouth" (יד לפה), which pictures clapping the hand over the mouth in a gesture of "awe, fear, or humility." These words take the force of a command that lands like a slap in the face (Jones 2019, 143). It is an elided rendition of an idiom that appears some half-dozen times in the Hebrew Bible with variations in cognate literatures as well.⁷⁶ According to Jordan W. Jones (2019, 127–28; cf. Gruber 1980, 289 n. 1), the gesture "connotes, as its most basic inference, silence," but other connotations can accrue to

---

74. The caution against exalting oneself here resonates with the reconstructed prohibition against rising against the king in 30:31 (Ginsburg and Weinberger 2007, 643).

75. The canonical examples of זמם ("to consider, purpose, devise;" BDB, s.v. "זמם") are not necessarily negative and זמם is sometimes predicated of God (Jer 4:28; 51:12; Zech 8:15; Prov 31:16). However, the preponderance of occurrences run toward planning evil or disaster (Gen 11:6; Pss 31:14 [13 ET]; 37:12; 140:9 [8 ET]), even with God as subject (Zech 1:6; 8:14; Lam 2:17). The evidence from Qumran tips the balance sufficiently to warrant the gloss "devise, plot (evil)" in *DCH* (3, s.v. "זמם"). Likewise the related noun זמה is nearly always negative (Prov 10:23; 21:27; 24:9).

76. Judges 18:19: "And they said to him, 'Shut up—put your hand over your mouth [שים ידך על פיך] and come with us;'" cf. Mic 7:16; Job 21:5; 29:9; 40:4; Sir 5:12. See Jones 2019, 126–46 for an enlightening and thorough treatment.

the gesture in context, such as avoidance of shame and expressions of awe or humility. Perhaps the most famous instance of this gesture comes in Job 40:4 where, at the end of YHWH's first speech, Job responds, "Behold, I am insignificant [קלתי]. How can I respond to you? / I put my hand to my mouth [ידי שמתי למו־פי]." How precisely Job's response is meant to be understood is a significant crux in the book (see Glazov 2002), but Job's gesture of silence in 40:4 stands in contrast to 3:1, which opens the speeches: "Job opened his mouth [פתח איוב את־פיהו] and cursed his birthday." Both verses use a verbal form of קלל ("to be small, insignificant" [*qal*], "to curse" [*piel*]). Norman Habel (1985, 549; cf. Clines 2011, 1139) comments: "'I am small' implies: I am reduced to smallness, I am humbled by the speeches of God, just as I was humbled by his afflictions (cf. 7:1–6) and sought to escape by employing a curse (3:1).... By clapping his hand on his mouth (v. 4b), Job not only cuts off any further claim or refutation on his part (cf. 29:9) but also expresses his amazement at the way Yahweh has responded (cf. 21:5)." The staccato nature of this idiom, which stands as the unmarked apodosis to the double protasis introduced by "if" (אם) previously in the verse, is delivered in the same manner in which the gesture is meant to be followed. It embodies an appropriate, humble response to a startling realization accompanied by emotions like awe, fear, and shame (Perdue 2000, 267). Silencing oneself with hand over mouth embodies the opposite reaction to exalting oneself.[77]

If Prov 30:32 calls for a halt to pride and greed—the motives behind much of the disgusting, destructive, and laughable behavior in the chapter—then verse 33 illustrates the consequences of such behavior when indulged. This saying delivers the collection's grand finale of verbal wit—a final sardonic flourish to drive home its warning (Van Leeuwen 1997b, 255). Anaphora again anchors this three-line aphorism which is structured around the verbal sequence of "churning ... produces" (see appendix at 30:33: מיץ). The tight parallelism of the lines differs only in alternating nouns that stand as objects of these verbs, a device that manipulates polysemy to intensify meaning. The first line of the verse lays the concrete foundation for puns to follow by presenting an inevitable cause and effect from home economics: "Churning milk produces butter." The next line presents an equally inevitable image but ups the ante: "Churning a nose produces

---

77. The commentaries tend to emphasize pragmatic silence (e.g., Plöger 1985, 367; Clifford 1999, 268), but in context it also entails emotions such as humility, fear, and awe.

blood." Potentially now, a conflict is introduced and we are dealing with different modes of "churning" even if the concrete meaning has not changed. The third line raises the stakes again and encourages the reader to reprocess the whole. Perhaps at first glance it reads, "Churning nostrils produces strife." But the variation between the singular "nose" (אַף) and dual "nostrils" (אַפִּים) hints that wordplay is afoot (Fox 2009, 881–82).[78] In addition to their concrete referents, both lexemes denote anger (see appendix at 30:33: אַף ... אַפִּים). This polysemy is ambiguous enough that it could cause a reader to puzzle over the intended sense, cueing them to reconsider the lines more broadly. In fact, nearly all the nouns are polysemous. "Blood" (דָּם) can mean literal blood or, by metonymy, "murder" (Gen 42:22; Hos 4:2). The word רִיב can denote general strife (Gen 13:7; Ps 18:44), but its uses run toward the technical sense of legal contention or lawsuit (Deut 17:8; Ezek 44:24). Once we enter the semantic field of anger, we note the aural similarity between חֶמְאָה (ḥemʾâ, "butter") and חֵמָה (ḥēmâ, "wrath"). As surely as churning milk produces butter, and churning a nose produces blood, churning up anger (by scheming and exalting oneself) will produce violence and strife. The polysemy encoded in the lines implies that the consequences of such churning can range from minor injuries to murder and from contention to lawsuits. But churning will have its effect. The poetics of the aphorism spiral out of semantic control, instantiating the chaotic unpredictability of conflict and illustrating with vivid, concrete images the consequences that pertain if one plays the destructive role of the נבל.

In sum, Prov 30:32 lands with scathing intensity. Verbs like נבל, התנשא, and זמם encode serious actions and the abrupt return to the second person in 30:32a combined with the terse command "[put] hand to mouth" in 32b forcefully press the application on the reader. As a conclusion these verses effectively draw out the main themes of 30:11–33 and underline their significance (Ansberry 2011, 174–75). Exalting oneself and scheming are destructive behaviors that are the outworking of deeper issues with pride and greed, themes shot through the material from 30:11–31. As we had cause to note many times, this material drew no explicit applications or morals, but the command drawn here serves to focus all the affective imagery into one point: *be humble*.

---

78. This verse sometimes features as a flagship example of intricate wordplay, e.g., Noegel 2021, 321; Schökel 1988, 29.

5.4. Satirizing Pride and Greed:
Tone, Ethics, and Coherence in Proverbs 30:11–33

In this chapter, I developed a reading of Prov 30:11–33 at some length. In contrast to how these verses have usually been treated, my reading was designed to argue through close analysis that they share both a unifying theme and tone. Proverbs 30:11–17 paint a scathing portrait of a human generation characterized by pride and greed. They are characterized as oblivious, unfeeling predators who live only to consume. In an ironic twist they are themselves consumed by carrion birds. Proverbs 30:18–31 feature four numerical sayings that use striking imagery and clever comparisons to present the effects of pride and greed as disgusting, incomprehensible, destructive, and laughable while those humble animals who content themselves to work within their limits are successful and wise. Finally, 30:32–33 uses strong language replete with verbal wit to press home the need for humble contentment on the audience. Now, not every verse surfaces themes of pride and greed or humility and contentment, but these themes are the undercurrent throughout the collection.

The thing that pulls all of this apparently diverse material together and gives it a common goal is Agur's wry tone, which he adopts to satirize pride and greed. According to William R. Jones (2012, 1255) in *The Princeton Encyclopedia of Poetry and Poetics*, "Satire is both a mode and a genre of verse and prose lit. that adopts a critical attitude toward its target with the goal of censuring human folly." Likewise, the *Oxford English Dictionary*: "A poem or (in later use) a novel, film, or other work of art which uses humour, irony, exaggeration, or ridicule to expose and criticize prevailing immorality or foolishness, esp. as a form of social or political commentary." There are no formal features that define satire, but rather a set of literary traits orbiting around a rhetorical purpose like a constellation. As Jones (2012, 1255) writes, "there are few if any genres that the satiric mode cannot adopt with effects that range from the richly comic to the devastatingly tragic." In his study of antiprophetic satire in the Hebrew Bible, Marcus (1995, 9) points to the following "essential attributes" of satire: the absurd, fantastic, grotesque and other "unbelievable elements," irony, ridicule, parody, and rhetorical features such as metaphor, hyperbole, and word play. Based on the preceding close reading, "satirical" seems an apt description for the tone of this collection.

But why adopt a satirical tone? Because humor *does* things. Where a plain proposition or prohibition might not be compelling, humor can be memorable and affective. Humor can pull apart our norms and expectations to reveal something hidden about human experience. It can soften us toward vice or virtue and make us more readily persuadable (Perks 2012, 125–26). The ancients understood that humor is a Trojan horse—it smuggles enemy soldiers inside the fortress of your mind. Humor can make the way things *truly* are, or *ought* to be, or the way we *wish* things were, emerge momentarily at the top of our psyche in a flash of clarity (Carroll 2014, 60). In short, humor changes minds and wins hearts. In Prov 30:11–33, the wry and satirical tone functions to make the sayings ethical. As I had occasion to point out many times, none of the material between 30:11 and 31 explicitly casts a judgment or draws a moral. Yet the tone of the material leaves us little doubt about the message when it presents its subjects as absurd, disgusting, laughable. Perhaps scholars have denied the ethical intent and common themes in this material in part because they have missed the humor.

In conclusion, 30:11–33 is not a miscellaneous collection of material gathered together here because they happen to share the same external form. These verses are unified by Agur's wry tone toward the purpose of satirizing pride and greed while commending humble contentment. To a greater or lesser extent, every saying in the collection shares this tone and contributes to this message. So, while the numerical sayings have often been treated as the occasion for the unity of the chapter, I want to suggest that they are rather incidental to the tone and theme of the collection. The same goes for the animal imagery, which has been studied less, although it is no less significant. In other words, Agur's words make abundant use of animal imagery and the numerical saying because these rhetorical features were appropriate vehicles for satirizing pride and greed. While I recognize that my reading of this chapter will not satisfy all readers on all points, I have endeavored at least to make it difficult to maintain the assertion that no common theme or design unites these sayings.

6
Agur in His Own Words:
Coherence, Genre, and Philology in Proverbs 30

6.1. Aspects of Coherence in Proverbs 30

This study has argued that MT Prov 30, "The Words of Agur," is best read as a coherent collection animated by the voice of Agur that mocks pride and greed while it commends humility and contentment, thus deepening the presentation of wisdom in Proverbs by subverting its misappropriation and orienting it toward a proper relationship with God. It remains now to say a few words about the collection as a whole within Proverbs. In conclusion, I will highlight four aspects of coherence that unify the chapter; I will consider the question of genre in relation to my reading as well as how Agur's collection relates to the book of Proverbs and wisdom theology more broadly; and I will offer a concluding reflection on philological reading.

The first aspect of coherence is thematic. As I endeavored to show in chapters 4 and 5, the collection centers on a fundamental contrast between humility and pride. Humility is first modeled by Agur when he diminishes his own wisdom before the God who alone encompasses creation yet speaks to humankind (30:1b–5). Agur builds on this theological epistemology by safeguarding relationship with God through a prayer and prohibitions (30:6–10). The remainder of the chapter offers impressionistic object lessons on the characteristics and effects of pride and greed on the one hand and humility and contentment on the other. These vignettes are affective and complex without resolving into neat and clean morals. However, themes of pride and humility are at play throughout, particularly in the climactic diptych of four small creatures and four bold strutters. The fact that the closing saying in 30:32 overtly raises the themes of pride and greed, enjoins humility, and does so with a key term from the numerical sayings ("being destructive," √נבל, v. 22), reinforces the likelihood that it is indeed the unifying theme throughout the chapter.

The second aspect of coherence has to do with tone. In chapter 3, I argued that designating the collection as a "burden" (משא) carries prophetic overtones and suggests it functions as a warning or a rebuke, often with a sardonic or satirical edge. In chapter 2, I noted that many commentators found humor in one saying or another. I explored the possibility that an element of dark humor characterizes Agur's discourse by pervading the whole. We saw this already in 30:1b-4 as Agur begins his speech on a note of exasperation that slides into a hyperbolic confession of ignorance. Yet I suggested that Agur's tone need not be construed as a categorical or po-faced denial of knowledge but might better be read as both pious and playful. He is being ironic—self-deprecating but not insincere. Such language only increases after 30:10 as the wicked generation is lambasted in 30:11-14 and skewered in 30:17. Bawdy comparisons, witty juxtapositions, and clever twists follow in 30:18-31 and the collection resolves in wordplay and wit at 30:33. This is not to say the collection as whole is a joke, much less that every line is intended to get a chuckle, but a certain wry tone is part and parcel of Agur's instruction. Humor is often subversive and Agur's tone serves his rhetorical purposes of exalting the small and self-effacing things over and above arrogant claims and proud gaits.

A third noteworthy aspect of coherence that contributes to tone is Agur's use of animal imagery and subtle animal metaphors. In a remarkable image, Agur begins his instruction by comparing himself to a beast (30:2). This is not an incidental comparison. Hints of the bestial metaphor reemerge at the heart of the prayer in verse 8 with the phrase "tear me off my portion of food." The wicked are also characterized with animalistic, predatory language, particularly in verses 12-17. And, after 30:15, Agur guides us through a poetic menagerie. Given the metaphors implicit in verses 2-14 and the use of animals elsewhere in Proverbs, these beasts seem to function analogically for human types. Even the arrangement of the numerical sayings may contribute to this effect. In 30:18-19 we find a list that blends human and animal elements (vulture, snake, ship, man, and woman). In verses 21-23, it is a list of four human types, while in verses 24-28 it is a list of four animals. In 30:29-31 we again find a list that blends humans and animals (lion, rooster, goat, king). Such mingling of human and animal images suggests we are meant to see the one in light of the other. Surprisingly, Agur characterizes all people—both the proud and the humble—as animals. You can either self-consciously associate with the small creatures, or you can obliviously strut around heading toward a vicious end. Agur's confession that he is "more of a beast than a man" (30:2) connects to the vignette of the four small but inherently wise creatures (30:24–28). This ironic reversal, where true wisdom is found with the small beasts and with those who deny having it, gets at the heart of Agur's collection. The truly wise will heed Agur's comparisons and imitate his example by counting themselves among the lowliest creatures.

The fourth aspect of coherence returns us once again to Agur's voice. In light of the thematic coherence in the chapter and the coherence of tone, it seems all the more compelling to imagine Agur as the animating persona behind the whole collection. Unquestionably, the discourse begins in the first person in 30:2–3. As I argued in chapter 4, I find no compelling reason to posit a change of speaker in the first ten verses. Agur speaks throughout but he is speaking to instruct and as such there are rhetorical questions (30:4), prohibitions with motivational clauses (vv. 6, 10), and a model prayer (vv. 7–9). Such discourse implies an addressee. Some scholars have found an addressee in 30:1b, but this is not the best reading. Instead, the reader is positioned as the *son*, which is how Proverbs refers to the student of wisdom throughout. Proverbs 30:11–31 takes up illustrations and object lessons in pride and humility, greed and contentment, but the voice of the instructor and the presence of his pupil are not lost. In 30:18 the first-person "I" reappears (ידעתים, ממני; Clifford 1999, 266), and in verse 28 the speaking voice addresses his student in the second person (תתפש). Finally, in 30:32 the concluding warning brings the whole discourse home to the student directly. Closing with an application in the second person loops back to 30:1–9, especially 6 and 10. The reader has been the student of wisdom throughout, but if Agur's voice does not animate verse 32, whose does?

Finally, I offer a brief word on the Greek version of Prov 30. My goal in this study has not been to compare MT Proverbs to the Greek, nor has it been to sort out the priority of the versions, nor even to tease out all variants at the text-critical level (philological notes notwithstanding). However, I hope my study has shown that MT Prov 30 ought to be treated as a collection—an anthological literary composition—in its own right. While we will likely never know who the authors or editors of this material were, or the precise nature of the relationship between MT Proverbs and G Proverbs, each text is an intentional composition. Reconstructing a text that lay behind both compositions seems an impossible task, although the Greek is often our best tool for getting behind particularly tricky passages in the

Hebrew (as in vv. 1b or 31b). In Greek, the material in Prov 30 is arranged with a different cast and subsumed under the authority of Solomon. From a redactional perspective, that move makes a good deal of sense given what we know about legendary sages and authorial attribution. It is far more curious and perplexing that MT Prov 30 is attributed to an unknown sage and bears an eccentric character. I have attempted to read Prov 30 as a coherent collection, and my hope is that others will soon develop readings of the Greek version of Prov 30 that treat it similarly.

6.2. Agur's Words and the Question of Genre

Having highlighted four aspects of coherence across the chapter, I wish briefly to address the issue of genre in relation to the collection as a whole. As I described in chapter 2, wisdom literature, as a genre category, and form criticism, as a method of literary analysis, have largely precluded reading Agur's words as a coherent text. Speaking broadly for a moment, both wisdom literature and form criticism have tended to adopt a taxonomic or idealist approach to genre, which understands genres as immutable abstract categories to which texts belong in full (Weeks 2013, 19–20; Kynes 2019, 108–9; Judd 2024, 80).[1] Since genre is irreducible, all the distinct forms that are found in Agur's words—such as confessions, prayers, aphorisms, and numerical sayings—can and should be studied in isolation to understand their true meaning (Weeks 2015, 173). On such a view, correctly identifying the genre of a text is an essential first step toward sound interpretation. Since Prov 30 incorporates many simple genres and does not clearly conform to any one genre as a whole, the chapter becomes less than the sum of its parts.

Modern genre theory, however, has moved away from classification toward a more nuanced understanding of genres as conventions in which both authors and readers participate to create meaning (Judd 2024, 72–75).[2] This shift has led to a focus on the social effects of genres.[3]

---

1. For an authoritative discussion of classical genre theory in relationship to more recent developments, see Frow 2015, 55–78.

2. As Judd (2024, 78) quips, "Genre theory in biblical studies has developed largely parallel to literary genre theory, with only occasional communication of ideas in either direction." A burgeoning literature, however, particularly in relationship to wisdom literature, is beginning to correct this. Consider, e.g., Newsom 2005, 2010; Brown 2008; Weeks 2013, 2015; Cheung 2015; Sneed 2015; Kynes 2019; Judd 2024; and Millar 2022.

3. The landmark essay here is Miller 1984. For a survey of additional developments with reference to biblical studies see Judd 2024, 76–82.

Leading genre theorist, John Frow (2015, 2), describes genres as a form of symbolic action: "the generic organization of language, images, gestures, and sound makes things happen by actively shaping the way we understand the world." If genres are not immutable abstract forms, then texts can have multiple, nonexclusive genre relationships. To use Jacques Derrida's (1980, 65) influential formulation, texts *participate* in genres rather than *belonging* to them. Readers can and do—whether by accident or intentionally—read the same texts according to the conventions of different genres to quite different effects; and writers—who never stop being readers themselves—craft texts that participate in one or more genres to a greater or lesser extent (Kynes 2019, 116). Most of the time decisions about genre take place subconsciously or intuitively, but skilled writers often blend, play with, and even subvert genres toward particular communicative goals. In thinking about the genre of a text, then, the question is not so much, "What are the formal features?" or even, "What ideas are being asserted?" but perhaps more fundamentally, "What is this text meant to *do* to you if you read it?" One way to test a genre designation is by asking whether it produces a compelling or constructive reading of the text in its own social and literary contexts.

Reading without genre is impossible, but for hermeneutical purposes one can adopt a broad, working genre designation, such as "ancient Israelite poetry," so as not to preclude certain readings prematurely. By bracketing scholarly assumptions about wisdom literature and form criticism, I essentially set more narrow genre labels to one side in order to conduct my close reading of Prov 30. In adopting this approach I attempted to take my cues from the text itself. Thus, in chapter 3, I explored the resonance of משא (*maśśāʾ*, i.e., "burden") as a possible emic genre term in 30:1. The term משא becomes a link that creates a constellation of texts, which, when read together, seem to find their common denominator in their tone, purpose, and effect rather than their form or content. On analogy with Isa 13–14 and other משא texts, I argued that characterizing Agur's words as a משא might suggest they are in some manner a warning or a rebuke, perhaps with weighty themes and shades of dark humor. Now that I have developed my interpretation of Agur's words at length, I will endeavor to sum up what reading the chapter as a משא might entail.

The first thing we ought to note in this regard is that Prov 30 as a whole can be read as a mocking rebuke of pride and selfish ambition. This is apparent from Agur's wry tone in his opening lines as well as the imperatives that frame the core of the collection in verses 6, 10, and, most significantly, 32. Second, Prov 30 uses shocking and affective language to deliver its rebuke in unsettling terms. Again, we see this from the start in Agur's startling claims and it is carried through with vivid and grotesque imagery, particularly in 30:11–20, and 29–33. Commenting on verses 11–17, Davis (2000, 143) writes, "The tone of this passage is similar to that of the prophets, who identify in urgent and, indeed, violent terms the sins of the present generation and their punishment." Third, Prov 30 makes liberal use of animal imagery and the world-upside-down motif to help readers grasp the subversive power of humility over against pride. This is foregrounded in 30:21–23 as well as in the juxtaposition of verses 24–28 with 29–31, particularly when we connect these images back to Agur's arresting opening statement, "I am more of a beast than a man" (v. 2). Finally, Prov 30 depicts vivid consequences for those who ignore its wisdom. These consequences are forecast in the heading of verse 21 and come to a climax with the fistfight in 30:33, but they are initially presented as a breakdown of relationship with God through the "lest" (פֶּן) clauses of verses 6, 9, and 10. The most dramatic and conclusive consequences, however, befall the disrespectful child of 30:17, whose exposed corpse is defiled by carrion birds. When we take note of these four aspects of the text, Agur's words can be read as a warning or rebuke that places a responsibility, or "burden," on the addressee in order to stop them short and help them correct their misunderstandings about wisdom before it is too late.

In terms of its *function* as a text, then, Prov 30 has many things in common with Isa 13–14, and other משא texts. Unlike the משאות in Isa 13–30, however, Agur's משא is not addressed to a wicked king or an enemy nation but rather to the implied reader of the book of Proverbs who is perhaps in danger of letting her wisdom go to her head or failing to perceive that human wisdom is found within limits and subordinates itself to God. If we want a specific genre designation for the chapter as a discrete collection, I do not think we can improve on משא, the discourse term with which the text self-identifies. But, having said that, I rush to add three qualifications. First, saying Prov 30 is a משא does not in any way preclude other ways of reading the chapter. For instance, it might be read fruitfully alongside of other anthological poetic texts, Egyptian instructions, or certain psalms, such as the so-called wisdom psalms or psalms of confession and confidence. Second, saying that Prov 30 is a משא does not mean to ignore the simple genres that comprise it, such as prayers, aphorisms, or numerical sayings. These genres retain their own logic but that logic has been taken up to become a part of a larger and more complex whole (Frow 2015, 43–44). Finally, even though the term משא is native to the text, we must remain circumspect about its significance because our understanding of the term is still constructed by us as readers. We do not have an intuitive, native understanding of what a משא entails; instead, we have some eighteen or nineteen examples of ancient texts that carry the heading, which we can study to discern their common features. What I find significant in these texts is based on my perspective as a reader and would likely change if I had hundreds of texts to survey. A native reader might well construe the essence of the genre differently. As such, we may not be able to discern all the nuances with which Prov 30 takes up the term. To the extent that Prov 30 participates in the משא genre, its distinctiveness may well be the most interesting thing about it.

Rather than being the first thing an interpreter establishes, genre may sometimes be, somewhat counterintuitively, the last thing an interpreter should decide on. After all, classifying the genre of a text is a powerful interpretive move (Frow 2015, 110–12; Kynes 2019, 111). If we assign a genre label too early in the process we may well shut down productive readings. When we understand a genre natively, we intuitively read with the grain, as it were, and this shapes our experience of the text as we read it. When we are not native to the texture of the genre, then we are in danger of reading against the grain. Or, to shift the metaphor, when we do not intuit the genre at play in a text, we may well find ourselves playing the wrong game as we read and develop an interpretation that does not make the best sense of the text as we have it. If we are at all concerned with what a text might have meant to its authors or earliest readers, we often have to proceed cautiously with quite a broad genre category in mind while developing a nuanced close reading with careful attention to comparative and analogous texts (Kynes 2019, 140). Once we discern what a text is doing and which texts it seems to relate to the most, then we can tentatively locate it within a genre and further refine our reading.[4] As Kynes (2019, 138) has reminded the guild, genres are descriptive not prescriptive: "They should inform, not norm, lest they deform." This is particularly true of challenging or contested texts like Prov 30 that may be doing creative or unusual things with genre. If we misunderstand how genre is working in these texts our ability to hear them speak in their own words will be impeded substantially.

---

4. Weeks's (2013, 21–24) discussion of Ps 34 offers a helpful analogous example.

6.3. Reading Agur's Words as Wisdom Literature within Proverbs

The question of genre in relationship to Prov 30 inevitably returns to the wisdom literature classification. Having developed my understanding of Agur's theology, this study would be incomplete without considering Agur's relationship to the book of Proverbs and the theology of wisdom literature more broadly. As the leading exposition of Proverbs currently available, Fox's two-volume Anchor Bible commentary makes a notable dialogue partner. Although Fox (2009, 850) considers 30:1–9 "a cohesive first-person meditation," it is at odds with its theological context. "Though now joined to the book of Proverbs," he writes, "Agur's oracle is really a reaction to it.... It was appended as a cautionary response to the exaltation of wisdom that characterizes the rest of the book" (956). "In fact," he believes, "Agur's oracle would not be reckoned as wisdom if it were not attached to Proverbs" (861). Fox asserts this categorically based on his view that wisdom thought and revelation are mutually exclusive categories (946–50). The marked absence of divine revelation is, in fact, one of wisdom's defining characteristics: "wisdom is human in its particulars and in its workings.... it treats the powers of the human mind as adequate to the attainment of all sorts of knowledge" (946–47).[5] On Fox's reading, Agur rejects wisdom in favor of revelation when he denies having human understanding, wisdom, and knowledge of the Holy One in 30:2–3. The rhetorical questions in verse 4 emphasize human ignorance; "No one, of course," is their intended response. The scriptural invocations in verses 5–6, then, assert that "far superior to human wisdom is God's revealed word" (858). Even Agur's prayer stands at odds with the worldview of the rest of the book: "The other sages of Proverbs are well aware of temptation, but they believe that the character strength that comes from the discipline of the teachings is a safeguard against temptation. Agur would have us turn directly to God for such a safeguard" (862). In short, Agur's "attitude toward wisdom differs profoundly from what we see elsewhere in Proverbs" (861).

In contrast to Fox, I will argue that Agur's words might rather be understood as a fuller flowering of ideas that have been present more

---

5. Fox (2009, 950) defines revelation narrowly as referring to God's actual speech, either spoken *en plein air* or recorded in a text and argues such "verbal revelation is not part of Proverbs's religious system."

subtly throughout Proverbs.⁶ Although no other passage in Proverbs appears to reject wisdom the way Prov 30:2–3 does, these two verses can be read as part of an undercurrent in the book that acknowledges certain pitfalls inherent to wisdom, suggests it can be misused, and ultimately relegates human wisdom to divine revelation and the knowledge of God. Agur's denial of wisdom can be read, for example, against the "be not wise in your own eyes" passages (Sneed 2021, 26). Roland Murphy (1998, 201) says such verses amount to an exploration of the danger of wisdom (see also O'Dowd 2009, 132). Again, this theme gets its start in Prov 1–9 but extends throughout the book.

בטח אל־יהוה בכל־לבך / ואל־בינתך אל־תשען:
בכל־דרכיך דעהו / והוא יישר ארחתיך:
אל־תהי חכם בעיניך / ירא את־יהוה וסור מרע:

Trust in YHWH with your whole heart, / and do not lean on your understanding.
In all your ways, know him, / and he will make your paths straight.
Do not be wise in your eyes; / fear YHWH and turn from evil.
(Prov 3:5–7)

These verses are couched within an exhortation to cling to the "teaching" (תורה) and "commandments" (מצות) of the parental instructor (Prov 3:3). In this context, trusting in YHWH is exhorted in contrast to leaning on one's own understanding. Understanding, then, is only as strong as its source. The chiastic structure of these three verses pairs leaning on your own understanding with being wise in your own eyes (Schipper 2019, 132). There is a type of understanding that is fragile and potentially untrustworthy, and the instructor links *this* type of understanding with the student's unaided faculties. The instructor is not denying that the student has understanding or wisdom but instead suggesting that considering oneself wise such that one leans on one's understanding is fraught. Pride and overweening confidence in one's own abilities can sneak in to sabotage wisdom. In contrast to this the student can strive to know YHWH and to depend on him for direction and protection in life. These

---

6. It is part and parcel of Proverbs's pedagogy to set ambiguous and paradoxical statements side by side, forcing the reader to wrestle with them toward a deeper resolution (e.g., Prov 26:4–5; or 10:15 and 18:11; see further Alter 1985, 164, 175–78, 184; O'Dowd 2009, 130–35; and Schwáb 2013).

three couplets center around knowing God and the direction he gives. Such knowledge is achieved through trusting in and fearing YHWH, which necessarily entails *not* leaning on one's own understanding and *not* being wise in one's own eyes.

Throughout Proverbs, being wise in one's own eyes presents a real danger. Proverbs 12:15 offers the first example of the theme in the sayings collections:

דרך אויל ישר בעיניו / ושמע לעצה חכם:
The way of a fool is straight in his eyes, / but the one listening to counsel is wise.

The one who takes advice is wise in part because he is willing to question the way things appear to him. Schipper (2019, 428) comments that this verse "illustrates a fundamental insight of sapiential thought: whoever regards oneself as wise will learn otherwise." Such sentiments suggest that fundamental to wisdom is a willingness to question yourself, to take advice, and *not* to count yourself among the wise (14:12 // 16:25; 26:5, 12, 16; 28:11). This idea perhaps comes to a head in 28:26.

בוטח בלבו הוא כסיל / והולך בחכמה הוא ימלט:
The one trusting in his heart, he is a fool, / but the one walking in wisdom, he will be delivered.

Being wise in one's own eyes, then, comes close to another way of saying someone is foolish. But Proverbs makes a more subtle point. Consider 26:12:

ראית איש חכם בעיניו / תקוה לכסיל ממנו:
You have seen a man wise in his own eyes: / the fool has more hope than he.

Remarkably, this verse casts the fool and the person "wise in his own eyes" in different camps. It is even more dangerous to be wise in your own eyes than to be a fool. The way this verse is phrased does not exclude the person "who might have a deserved reputation for their wisdom" (Murphy 1998, 201). Wisdom, although overwhelmingly celebrated and extolled, is not an unqualified good because it can tip over into pride. At this point wisdom turns back on itself and becomes foolishness.⁷ It seems insufficient to argue that being wise in one's own eyes is *merely* the same as being a fool, because Proverbs would seem to have a category for people who truly are knowledgeable and skillful at life, but whose self-awareness of their knowledge and their skill opens them up to pride and subsequent disaster (16:18).

But not only does wisdom pose this subtle danger, it is also fundamentally limited. No matter how successful human wisdom may be, it is relegated by divine sovereignty. The cluster of sayings in 16:1–9 makes this point as forcefully as any passage in the book, but there are other notable texts as well. In a manner we might more readily associate with Ecclesiastes, Prov 20:24 suggests there is simply a limit to humanity's powers of discernment:

מיהוה מצעדי־גבר / ואדם מה־יבין דרכו׃
The steps of a man are from YHWH; / How will a human discern his way?

Likewise when wisdom confronts God there is no contest:

אין חכמה ואין תבונה / ואין עצה לנגד יהוה׃
There is no wisdom and there is no understanding / and there is no council against YHWH. (Prov 21:30)

Ultimately, in Proverbs each person's way is weighed by God (21:2). Thus the emphasis throughout the book on the relationship between wisdom, humility, and the fear of YHWH (3:34; 6:16–19; 8:13; 11:2; 15:33; 18:12; 22:4). This emphasis is captured most poignantly in 15:33.

יראת יהוה מוסר חכמה / ולפני כבוד ענוה׃
The fear of YHWH is wisdom's instruction, / and before honor is humility.

As I read this verse, it suggests humility precedes honor in the same way wisdom's instruction precedes the fear of YHWH. Thus, one might say, humility and wisdom's instruction are aligned in the sense that they are

---

7. Murphy (1998, 201, 228) connects Prov 26:12 and 30:2–3 to Eccl 7:23–24. Commenting on Qohelet's admission that he failed to attain wisdom, Murphy (201) writes, "In view of Prov 26:12 he cannot be accused of folly!" I would say the same of Agur.

foundational qualities that lead to rewards (Weeks 2010a, 121). This might even be taken to suggest they are fundamentally similar—to be humble is to heed wisdom's instruction. The connection 15:33 draws between humility, fear of YHWH, and wisdom brings us full circle to Prov 3:5–7 where knowing God includes not being proud but trusting and fearing him. This way of framing things connects also to 9:10.

תחלת חכמה יראת יהוה / ודעת קדשים בינה:
The beginning of wisdom is the fear of YHWH / and knowledge of the Holy is understanding.

This nexus of 3:5–7; 9:10; and 15:33 brings together humility, wisdom, and the fear of/knowledge of God in a striking manner that should inform our reading of Agur's confession in 30:2–3. Human wisdom is only truly wisdom when it is relegated by the divine.

In this light—although no other verse in Proverbs explicitly mentions "God's word"—the concept of revelation is present in the book such that Prov 30:1–9 could be read as extending it and drawing it out rather than contradicting it. After all, alongside the rest of the wisdom books, Proverbs insists wisdom comes from God (Schellenberg 2021a, 32, 38–39; Prov 1:20–21; 3:19–20; 8:2–3, 22; 20:12; 29:13).[8] The key text is Prov 2:6:

כי־יהוה יתן חכמה / מפיו דעת ותבונה:
For YHWH gives wisdom / knowledge and understanding [are] from his mouth.

Although this verse does not invoke Scripture, per se, it does source knowledge and understanding to YHWH's mouth (מפיו). This significant detail suggests these qualities are dispensed through speech and thus carry some content—they are not to be imagined merely as intellectual faculties whose natural operations produce wisdom (Waltke 2004, 223–24;

---

8. Schellenberg cites the following extra-Proverbial texts sourcing wisdom to God: Ps 94:10; Job 32:8–9; Eccl 2:26; Dan 2:21; Sir 1:10, 26; 6:37; 17:7, 11; 39:6; 43:33; Wis 9:17. Although some of the most explicit formulations are considered later, Schellenberg (2021a, 38) cautions, "the latter formulations are explicit articulations of assumptions that implicitly were present for a long time." Neither should we overlook the intertextual connection between Prov 1:1; 10:1; 25:1 and 1 Kgs 3, where Solomon's wisdom is depicted as divine inspiration granted by YHWH (see Sneed 2021, 21–22).

pace Fox 2000, 113). In her work on epistemology, revelation, and wisdom, Annette Schellenberg (2021b, 164) draws attention to the way Lady Wisdom's speech is marked by the vocabulary of revelation. Proverbs 1:23 offers a vivid example:

הנה אביעה לכם רוחי / אודיעה דברי אתכם:
Look! My spirit will flow over you / and I will reveal my words to you.

While Lady Wisdom's words are not depicted as YHWH's words, they are nevertheless supernatural and derived from her special knowledge of YHWH's creative processes (8:2–3; 22–31).[9] Similarly, Prov 16:1 says,

לאדם מערכי־לב / ומיהוה מענה לשון:
The plans of the heart belong to humankind, / but the answer of the tongue is from YHWH.

This text does not have divine speech in view, but it does suggest God determines the words humans utter out loud—perhaps containing wisdom, advice, or rebuke. God speaks indirectly through the wise and even the unwise. It is not obvious that the ancients would have made a sharp distinction between the ideas in Prov 2:6 and 16:1 (Schellenberg 2021b, 158; Weeks 2010a, 115). Finally, one verse in Proverbs mentions "a vision" (חזון) positively and sets the concept in parallel with "instruction" or *torah* (Delitzsch 1875, 252).

באין חזון יפרע עם / ושמר תורה אשרהו:
Without a vision people run wild, / but keeping instruction is its prosperity. (Prov 29:18)

Even Fox (2009, 840–41, cf. 949) acknowledges that this verse refers to prophecy, but he considers it something of an outlier. The sages and scribes who wrote and transmitted Proverbs, however, had a worldview capable of appropriating Prov 29:18 within the rest of the book (Schellenberg 2021b, 165; Weeks 2010a, 115).

---

9. For consideration of Lady Wisdom's role in relationship to epistemology, see O'Dowd 2009, 120–26.

Moreover, there is a case to be made that Proverbs assumes revelation in the way it alludes to Deuteronomy and the Torah. Weeks (2007, 96–127) has argued this case by drawing out a thick web of imagery in Prov 3. In a manner strongly reminiscent of Deuteronomy, Prov 3:11–12 connects "the discipline of YHWH" (מוסר יהוה) to the image of a father reproving a beloved son (Weeks 2007, 102–3; Deut 8:5; 11:2; cf. 1:31; 32:6). In Prov 3:3 the father enjoins the son to write the preeminent covenant virtues of "devotion and faithfulness" (חסד ואמת) "on the tablet of your heart" (כתבם על לוח לבך), a phrase that evokes the tablets of the law (Weeks 2007, 105; Deut 9:9; Exod 31:18; 1 Kgs 8:9; and again in Prov 7:3). Finally, consider the beginning of the parental instruction in 3:1:

בני תורתי אל־תשכח / ומצותי יצר לבך:
My son, may you not forsake my teaching / and may your heart guard my commandments.

Such terminology, which is not isolated in Proverbs but invoked often, could hardly have failed to raise associations with Torah for ancient Jewish audiences (Weeks 2007, 104–5; Schipper 2019, 128).[10] "If the writer intended no such allusion," muses Weeks (2007, 105), "then his close packing of such terms, in the vicinity of references to YHWH, can have done nothing to allay the misapprehension." Thus it is hard to imagine an ancient Jewish reader who, when approaching the book of Proverbs, would make the kind of mental distinctions between human wisdom on the one hand and revealed Torah on the other that Fox is making. Rather, wisdom may be understood as the way Prov 1–9 characterizes "those who have internalized the Law" (Weeks 2007, 113).

When Prov 30 subordinates wisdom to revelation, it may be distinctive, but we ought not to characterize it as opposed to the thought of the rest of the book (Sneed 2021, 25). Ecclesiastes and Job certainly make more of the limits of wisdom, but the theme is not entirely absent from Proverbs. The book acknowledges that wisdom will always carry its dangers and ultimately bottom out because humans are fallible (Prov 20:9).

---

10. The word *tôrāh* or "instruction" (תורה) is used thirteen times in Proverbs and "command" (מצוה) is used ten times; these terms are often in close proximity (Prov 1:8; 2:1; 3:1; 4:2, 4; 6:20, 23; 7:1–2; 10:8; 13:13–14; 19:16; 28:4, 7, 9; 29:18; 31:26). On allusions to Torah in Prov 28:4, 7, 9 and 29:18, see Fishbane 1985, 288 n. 20; O'Dowd 2017, 376; and Schipper 2021, 265–68.

As commentators have sometimes noted, the words of Agur represent the most developed and pointed exploration of this theme. Agur's denial of the false wisdom that masquerades for pride can be read as constitutive of true wisdom that embodies humility. Reading the whole chapter as a coherent collection can help draw this out, since the traditional wisdom elements in 30:11–33, especially the juxtaposition of humble and proud beasts in 30:24–31, serve as illustrations of the theology described in verses 1–10. Within the book of Proverbs, chapter 30 deepens the presentation of wisdom by cautioning that there is a type of wisdom that is nonwisdom (cf. 3:5–7; 28:26). This nonwisdom is a sort of overconfident intelligence that does not humble itself before YHWH. True wisdom, according to Proverbs, is wrapped up with the fear of YHWH and the knowledge of God. Agur's move to disparage his own wisdom in comparison with the knowledge of the Holy is *not* being wise in his own eyes—it is the better part of wisdom. Agur's words, then, stand as a sort of counterintuitive demonstration or model of wisdom placed toward the climax of the book (see Yoder 2009a).

I doubt whether Agur's words would seriously worry an interpreter who came to them without the modern wisdom literature category in place, at least as it is articulated by Fox and many other scholars. The presence of Prov 30:1–10 within Proverbs might rather serve as a check against Fox's understanding of wisdom as a genre. Lest readers think wisdom is something that can be sourced entirely in the human mind and attributed only indirectly to God, Agur makes the role of divine revelation more fundamental. When our understanding of wisdom literature requires relegating portions of books that are definitional to the category in order to retain its theological purity, one has to wonder whether the generic cart has gotten in front of the proverbial horse.

6.4. Philology, Reading, and Hermeneutics

In conclusion, I offer a reflection on how we approach texts. Describing eighteenth-century hermeneutics, Michael Legaspi (2010, 26) wrote, "Instead of looking *through* the Bible in order to understand *the truth about the world*, eighteenth-century scholars looked directly at the text, endeavoring to find new, ever more satisfactory frames of cultural and historical reference by which to understand *the meaning of the text*" (emphasis original). As Legaspi tells it, this eighteenth-century impulse created the "academic bible" and calcified in the nineteenth-century into a historicism that was concerned primarily with looking *through* the Bible to understand *the world behind the text*. Somewhere along the way, Scripture died. While I am undeniably reading Legaspi's academic bible, my goal has been to look again *at the text* in order to hear it speaking in its own words. If my reading is not yet scriptural as such, my hope is that it is resuscitative.

Throughout this study I have attempted to prioritize close reading of the text as a culturally and linguistically situated historical artifact while eschewing specific historical-critical methodologies (e.g., form criticism) or reconstructions of the history of ideas (e.g., wisdom literature). Rather than reconstructing a history of ideas within the chapter or asking questions about its compositional history, I have asked, "How does this text present itself?" "What is Agur doing in his own words?" Such an approach could be termed *philological*. In his landmark 1936 essay, "Beowulf: The Monsters and the Critics," J. R. R. Tolkien, arguably the most famous philologist of the last century, presents a moving plea for this kind of reading in his allegory of the tower:

> A man inherited a field in which was an accumulation of old stone, part of an older hall. Of the old stone some had already been used in building the house in which he actually lived, not far from the old house of his fathers. Of the rest he took some and built a tower. But his friends coming perceived at once (without troubling to climb the steps) that these stones had formerly belonged to a more ancient building. So they pushed the tower over, with no little labour, in order to look for hidden carvings and inscriptions, or to discover whence the man's distant forefathers had obtained their building material. Some suspecting a deposit of coal under the soil began to dig for it, and forgot even the stones. They all said: "This tower is most interesting." But they also said (after pushing it over): "What a muddle it is in!" And even the man's own descendants, who might have been expected to consider what he had been about, were heard to murmur: "He is such an odd fellow! Imagine his using these old stones just to build a nonsensical tower! Why did not he restore the old house? He had no sense of proportion." But from the top of that tower the man had been able to look out upon the sea. (1997, 7–8)

Though some would argue that philology is now such an outdated and amorphous term that we ought to abandon it, I believe its very breadth and heritage allows it to function evocatively for revitalizing the task of biblical studies.[11] If the designation feels like a throwback, this intention-

---

11. Philology is currently undergoing a renaissance in biblical studies, but the value and appropriate reference of the term remains contested. For a cross section

ally highlights the emphasis on retrieving several hallmarks of biblical studies from our venerable past.

First, a philological approach is textual. It takes its warrant from the warp and woof of the text. Thus at its root, philology still encompasses the breadth of technical skills that form the basis of the analysis of texts: epigraphy, lexicography, grammar and syntax, comparative and historical linguistics, and, of course, text criticism. The renovation of philology as a term in the modern academy is, at one level, a self-conscious reinvestment in the techne of lower criticism for the sake of reading texts afresh (Orlemanski 2015, 159–60). Closely tied to the employ of these tools is an emphasis on close reading—attention to the way the text goes from the smallest details to the highest level of literary analysis.

Second, a philological approach is comparative and self-conscious. It responsibly situates the text in its context as a historical artifact and asks questions about it in relation to other artifacts and ourselves. In his landmark intellectual history, James Turner summarizes:

> What needs emphasis is that common methods, a common mode of knowledge, survive in all disciplines within the philological family. All are interpretive in method; all deploy comparison in making their interpretations; all are sensitive to contexts, cultural or textual or visual; all believe historical lineages of some sort essential to understanding; all think that ideas, texts, paintings, institutions, artifacts, languages are products of history, shaped by their historical contexts. (2014, 383)

Philologists always remember the located nature of texts as well as their locations as readers. Such a comparative and self-reflective stance can and should occasionally become metacritical, critiquing the history of scholarship from the perspective of the text and the reader.[12]

Third, a philological approach is humanistic. It seeks to plumb the depths of what makes us human and draws us forward toward better

---

of approaches consider Hendel 2015; Lambert 2016; Najman 2017a; and Holmstedt 2021a and 2021b. For the wider movement in the humanities known as *new philology*, see the excellent analysis in Orlemanski 2015; and the programmatic essays Pollock 2009 and 2014. With reference to Judaism, Christianity, the classical tradition, and theology, see the essays in Lied and Lundhaug 2017; and Conybeare and Goldhill 2020.

12. This kind of metacriticism is exemplified by Tolkien's essay. Weeks 2013; Kynes 2019; and Vayntrub 2019 are examples of metacriticism in biblical studies.

versions of ourselves. This is indeed how Sheldon Pollock wants to characterize the term:

> Philology is, or should be, the discipline of making sense of texts. It is not the theory of language—that's linguistics—or the theory of meaning or truth—that's philosophy—but the theory of textuality as well as the history of textualized meaning. If philosophy is thought critically reflecting upon itself, as Kant put it, then philology may be seen as the critical self-reflection of language. Or to put this in a Vichean idiom: if mathematics is the language of the book of nature, as Galileo taught, philology is the language of the book of humanity. (2009, 934)

One of the most widely agreed upon features of philology is in fact this *humanistic* character. Philology is not deductive or systematizing—like philosophy or physics—but rather inductive, empirical, and interpretive, attending to what is distinctive (Turner 2014, 381).[13] Philology is not a discipline or a method. Philology is a metonymy for the field of biblical studies that seeks to capture, as a former professor of mine once put it, a particular stance toward texts.[14]

My reading of Prov 30 has attempted to model such a philological stance toward texts. Where texts are controverted and seemingly convoluted, such an approach has the potential to produce constructive readings. Counterintuitively, a constructive reading stands to have more historical value than some of the historically motivated readings of the nineteenth

---

13. So, e.g., in contrast to the science of linguistics that studies the theory of language in abstracted systems, philology looks at specific manifestations of language in texts (Naudé and Miller-Naudé 2020, 13; cf. Lied and Lundhaug 2017, 16). In contrast to philosophy, which strives to be logical and deductive, philology is fundamentally inductive and interpretive. See further the helpful formulations of this idea solicited from leading scholars of Hebrew and biblical literature by Miller-Naudé and Naudé (2020, 15 n. 50). Compare with Holmstedt's favorable quotation from Michael O'Connor (Holmstedt 2021a, 3; quoting O'Connor 2002, 42), sub "philology" for "reading": "Linguistics is, in fact, a science and therefore committed to a modern horizon, involving verifiability, falsifiability, or comparable criteria for proceeding; it is also, unlike biblical studies, oriented away from the unique. Reading, in contrast, is devoted to the unique. Reading, as an act or an endeavor can be modern in that sense, but it can also be pre-modern or pre-critical or it can be post-modern. It can be, as linguistics cannot be, naive or canny."

14. I have adopted the language of philology as metonymy from Orlemanski (2015, 174).

and twentieth centuries. In terms of Prov 30, historically motivated reading has bequeathed assumptions about a worldview associated with the wisdom tradition, form-critical attempts to tease out the numerical sayings, and the search for Agur's origins in the illusive land of *Maśśā'*. The extent to which these assumptions are inaccurate becomes the extent to which we misconstrue the text. Agur's voice becomes convoluted, incapable of speaking a better word. A constructive approach, by contrast, invests in the coherence of the text on the working assumption that the ancients put *this* text together in *this* way. Would they have done so if it was a genuine cacophony, a bundle of irreconcilable contradictions? It is possible. However, if the tradents and redactors behind the text *did* see coherence in what they crafted, then the more historical reading appreciates that. But beyond their historical value, constructive readings stand to speak to the present with a clear voice from the past. They stand as a sort of prolegomena to reading as Scripture—a stairway to the top of the tower where we can look out on the sea.

Appendix: Translation and Philological Notes

Translation of Proverbs 30

1 The words of Agur Bin-Yaqeh, the burden,
  the oracle of the man:
  "{I am weary and powerless.}[1]
2 Though I am more of a beast than a man,
  and I do not have the understanding of humankind,
3 and I have not learned wisdom,
  yet knowledge of the Holy I know.
4 Who ascended to heaven and then descended?
  Who gathered wind in his palms?
  Who bound waters in a robe?
  Who established all the ends of the earth?
  What is his name and what is the name of his son?
  Surely you know!
5 All the speech of Eloah is refined;
  he is a shield for those taking refuge in him.
6 Do not add to his words,
  lest he rebuke you and you are shown to be false.
7 Two things I ask from you;
  do not withhold them from me before I die:
8 Emptiness and falsehood remove from me,
  poverty and riches do not give me,
  tear me off my portion of food.
9 Lest I am sated and deny,
  and I say, 'Who is YHWH?'
  Or lest I am destitute and steal,

---

1. The braces, here and in verse 31, indicate places where the text I translate deviates from MT. Proverbs 30:1 is discussed in §3.4; verse 31 is discussed below.

and I grasp the name of my God.
10 Speak not against a servant to his lord,
    lest he curse you and you are punished.
11 A generation curses its father
    and does not bless its mother.
12 A generation is pure in its own eyes,
    but it is not washed of its excrement.
13 A generation—how high are its eyes!—
    and its eyelids are raised up.
14 A generation—its teeth are swords,
    and its fangs are knives
    for devouring the poor from the land
    and the needy from humankind.
15 The leech has two daughters—give, give!
    There are three things that will never be sated;
    four that never say, 'Too much!':
16 Sheol and a sealed womb,
    land that is never sated with water,
    and fire that never says, 'Too much!'
17 An eye that derides a father
    and despises obeying a mother—
    ravens of the wadi will carve it out,
    and fledgling vultures will devour it.
18 There are three things that are too difficult for me,
    and four that I do not know:
19 The way of the vulture in the sky,
    the way of a snake on a rock,
    the way of a ship in the heart of the sea,
    and the way of a man in a girl.
20 Thus is the way of a woman who commits adultery.
    She eats and wipes her mouth,
    then she says, 'I have not done wrong.'
21 Under three things a land quakes,
    and under four it cannot endure:
22 Under a servant if he becomes king,
    or a destructive man if he is sated with food;
23 under a loathsome woman if she gets married,
    or a maidservant if she disinherits her mistress.
24 There are four insignificant things in a land,

but they are inherently wise:
25 The ants are not a powerful people,
and yet they prepared their food in the summer.
26 Rock hyraxes are not a mighty people,
and yet they put their house in the cliff.
27 The locust swarm does not have a king,
and yet it went out—the whole thing by divisions.
28 A lizard you can grasp with the hands,
and yet she is in kingly palaces.
29 There are three things that march well,
and four that walk well:
30 A lion—champion among the beasts—
he will not turn back before anything,
31 a strapping rooster or a he-goat,
and a king—{let there be no rising against him.}
32 If you have been destructive by exalting yourself,
or if you have been scheming—hand to mouth.
33 Because churning milk produces butter,
and churning a nose produces blood,
and churning anger produces strife."

Philological Notes

Verse 3

ולא ... אדע | The Greek completely lacks a negative: θεὸς δεδίδαχέν με σοφίαν, καὶ γνῶσιν ἁγίων ἔγνωκα ("God has taught me wisdom, and I have gained knowledge of holy things," NETS). If this reading accurately reflects a Hebrew *Vorlage*, it suggests ואל ("but God") in place of ולא and למדני ("taught me," 3ms *piel qatal* + 1cs object suffix) in place of למדתי ("I learned," 1cs *qal qatal*). However, there is no additional evidence in the manuscript tradition to support G's reading (Field 1875; and Kennicott 1780 have no data). Moreover, were G's reading original it is difficult to imagine what would have resulted in MT, particularly since it requires not one but two scribal errors. Alternatively, G's rendering may have occurred through exegetical metathesis for theologically motivated reasons (de Waard 1993, 257). Since Solomon is presented as the author of Prov 30 in G, the translator may have avoided ascribing ignorance or foolishness to him (Fox 2014a, 10). Still, it is worth pointing out that such exegetical metathesis could have occurred in intralingual transmission of manuscripts. The Greek reading tells us little-to-nothing, then, about how the translator understood the syntactic relationship of the two lines, but it does support reading verse 3 as an affirmation of learning rather than a further denial.

קדשים | The singular קדוש refers to God far more often than the plural, usually, in the construct phrase "the Holy One of Israel" (קדוש ישראל, e.g., 2 Kgs 19:22; Isa 1:4; 5:19; 47:4; Jer 50:29; 51:5; Pss 71:22; 78:41; 89:19). In the Hebrew Bible, as in cognate traditions of the ancient Near East, √$qdš$ often refers to divine beings or angels more generally (e.g., Zech 14:5; Ps 89:6–7; Job 5:1; see Parker 1999, 718–20; Costecalde 1985), but it can be applied to humans as well (e.g., Num 15:40; Pss 16:3; 34:10; 2 Chr 35:3). In the Second Temple period, √קדש refers to angelic/human figures with greater frequency. The War Scroll (1QM), to pick one of many examples, uses קדושים to refer to heavenly beings (1QM XXII, 1, 7; XV, 14–15; see Heiser 2004, 194) but also to humans (III, 4–5; X, 9–10). Aramaic usage in the book of Daniel follows this pattern (Dan 4:5–6, 14–15; 5:11; 7:18, 21–22, 25, 27; for extensive discussion see Heiser 2004; Collins 1993, Goldingay 1988; Noth 1984; Dequeker 1973; and Brekelmans 1965). The one example of √קדש in Ben Sira points to heavenly beings in the context of wisdom (Sir 42:17, 21). But the construct of √קדש + דעת only occurs at Qumran in one highly fragmentary text (4Q402 [4QShirShabb^c] 4, 6). As Carol Newsom (Eshel et al. 1998, 228–29) reconstructs the line, it may read [דעת קדו]שי קדושים, that is, "knowledge of the [most] hol[y ones]." Further down in line 12, we find the phrase "the God of knowledge" (אלוהי דעת), which associates דעת with God, although the context is too fragmentary to suggest a reference for line 6. Scholars who read Agur as a reactionary against "traditional wisdom" find in קדשים a reference to "esoteric, heavenly, eschatologically-oriented wisdom," that is, the knowledge angelic beings possess (Sandoval 2020a, 89). While this is certainly possible, it falls afoul of Occam's razor when close analogs for קדשים are available in Prov 30:5, 9; and 9:10. As I argue throughout this study, I do not think Agur's words are in conflict with traditional wisdom, and קדשים certainly does not demand that explanation. *Pace* Sandoval (2020a), I find the use of קדשים insufficient to establish the presence of apocalyptic wisdom in Prov 30 or a concordantly late date for verses 1–4 (cf. Hos 12:1).

Verse 4

כי תדע | The Greek reads ἵνα γνῷς ("that you may know"), but this line is missing from the Vaticanus and Sinaiticus manuscripts (see R-H, *BHS*). This omission suggests the line was missing from the Old Greek, which in turn suggests it may have been missing from proto-MT as well (Fox 2015, 381). Some commentators excise the line on this basis, suggesting it is probably an editorial intercalation from Job 38:5 (Oesterly 1929, 270; Clifford 1999, 260). Nevertheless, the reading is part of MT, and G, V, S, and T witness to it.

Verse 5

כל אמרת | Verse 5 is a close parallel to Ps 18:31 [30 ET] // 2 Sam 22:31b.

2 Sam 22:31b–32a

אמרת יהוה צרופה / מגן הוא לכל החסים בו: / כי מי אל מבלעדי יהוה

Ps 18:31–32a [30–31a ET]

אמרת יהוה צרופה / מגן הוא לכל החסים בו: / כי מי אלוה מבלעדי יהוה

Prov 30:5

כל אמרת אלוה צרופה / מגן הוא לחסים בו:

It is easy to imagine a process of working memory whereby the adjective כל was misplaced either intentionally or unintentionally in the line (Screnock 2017, 86–88). This shift has little effect on the meaning since the implication of both statements applies to *all* words and refuge-seekers implicitly. The direction of quotation is typically assumed to be from 2 Sam 22:31 to Ps 18:31 and then to Prov 30:5 (Gunneweg 1992, 257). This is based on the antiquity of the poems imbedded in the primary history, the later date of the Psalter, and the yet later date of Proverbs (or so the usual line of thinking goes). Indeed, the next verse will allude to Deuteronomy suggesting Prov 30 is the more allusive text, which in turn suggests it is the borrower (Ben-Porat 1976, 111). Moreover, it seems likely that the composer of Prov 30 had his eye on Ps 18 rather than 2 Sam 22 because this could explain the inspiration for his rare use of the name אלוה.

אלוה | This relatively rare designation for God is the singular form of the Northwest Semitic root √'lh from which the more common plural form אלהים ("God") is also derived. This word became the primary word for god(s) in Aramaic (Pardee 1999, 286; Jastrow 1903, s.v. "אֱלָהּ"; Sokoloff 2002, s.v. "אֱלָהּ"; 2009, s.v. "ܐܰܠܳܗܳܐ"), and in Ugaritic the singular 'lh and the plural 'lhm are both used as divine names (Pardee 1999, 285; *DULAT*, s.v. "aliyn"; *DNWSI*, s.v. "'lh₁"). In Biblical Hebrew the name is used with shades of difference in three types of contexts: archaic/archaizing poetry (ten times), the book of Job (forty-one times), and postexilic texts (six times). In archaic/archaizing poetry אלוה is normally used in distancing the God of Israel from the gods of the nations and describing his incomparability (Deut 32:15, 17; Isa 44:8; Hab 1:11; 3:3; Pss 18:32; 50:22; 114:7; 139:19). In Job 3–41 the divine names Elohim and YHWH are suppressed in favor of designations that are rare elsewhere, for example, "Almighty" (שדי), "God/El" (אל), and אלוה. This pervasive switch probably reflects a literary agenda to characterize the speakers as foreign and ancient, if it does not bear on the provenance of the book in some way. In the incontestably postexilic texts, אלוה seems to be used in a way that is indistinguishable from the use of אלהים throughout the Hebrew Bible, perhaps under the influence of Aramaic (Dan 11:37–39; Neh 9:17; 2 Chr 32:15). Proverbs 30:5 is most similar to verses in archaizing poems like Ps 50:22 and 139:19 that use אלוה as a divine name. However, like Deut 32; Ps 18; and Isa 44, Prov 30 follows the pattern of setting four or five different names for God together in just a few verses. Perhaps this is the reflex of Biblical Hebrew poetry to use synonyms across parallel lines, but it is also possible a more significant point is intended. The use of אלוה could, as in Job, be part of characterizing Agur. But these texts may also be making a theological statement by blending names for God that come from different contexts and smack of different languages in order to underline the sovereignty and incomparability of the God of Israel.

Verse 6

אל־תוסף | Some would call verse 6 a quotation of the so-called canon formula found in Deut 4:2 (cf. Deut 13:1; 11Q19 [11QTemple[a]] LIV, 6). The language is quite close, but it might be better termed a periphrastic allusion than a direct citation.

Deut 4:2: לא תספו על־הדבר

Prov 30:6: אל־תוסף על־דבריו

First, in Proverbs we find אל + jussive, which breaks subtly from the stronger לא + *yiqtol* in Deuteronomy (*BHRG* §19.5.2.1; Joüon §114i). Second, note that Proverbs's text has been adapted to reflect the singular addressee of the collection (cf. 30:4, 10, 32), while Deuteronomy's plural assumes the gathered people of Israel. Third, Deuteronomy can say "the word" (הדבר), which relates to the entirety of Moses's message on the plains of Moab. Finally, Proverbs has "his words" (דבריו). The pronominal suffix can only refer back to Eloah in 30:5 and the content of "his words" is more mysterious. Finally, the masora alerts us to the unique pointing of the jussive תּוֹסְףְּ. We might expect תּוֹסֵףְ, which is in fact the reading of one manuscript from the Cairo Geniza (*BHS*; see GKC §§10k and 69v; and cf. discussion in Delitzsch [1875, 279] and Fox [2009, 859]).

יוכיח בך | The only other place where יכח takes a complement with the preposition ב is 2 Kgs 19:4 // Isa 37:4. This use of the preposition is figurative of contact (*BHRG* §39.6.1.b.ii; cf. *IBHS* §11.2.5f) and has an analog in passages where יכח parallels words in the semantic field of striking (Ps 141:5; Prov 19:25).

Verse 9

מי יהוה | The Greek has τίς με ὁρᾷ; ("Who sees me?") in place of מי יהוה ("Who is YHWH?"). This reflects a Hebrew text מי יחזה (Num 24:4). The other versions align with MT, but Fox speculates G could preserve an older reading (2015, 382). The Greek reflects a Hebrew text that could plausibly lead to graphic confusion for יהוה (cf. G Isa 2:2), and a scribe could well have been influenced by pharaoh's scoffing question in Exod 5:2 and texts where the wicked think they escape unobserved (Isa 29:15; Ps 64:6).

Verse 10

K: אדנו Q: אדניו | The *qere* is plural where the *ketiv* is ambiguous. The Greek, T, and V have the singular, while S agrees with the *qere*. The *ketiv* is preferable—it opens up more interpretive options since either עבד or אדנו could be the subject of קללך, and it is not clear whom the referent of plural "masters" would be.

Verse 11

דור ... דור | Proverbs 30:11–14 is a poetic stanza that is held together by theme and topic through anaphora, the repetition of דור at the head of each couplet. Most translators have used a predication of existence or a presentative construction assuming an unmarked relative clause, that is, "*There are* those *who* curse their father" (e.g., NRSV). According to Fox (2009, 865; also Toy 1899, 527), the epigram "is a series of complex noun phrases with no expressed predicate. The one-member sentence implies a predication of existence." However, if the Hebrew intended this, one could imagine the use of יש (Delitzsch 1875, 285). As it stands, reading a series of relative clauses, that is, "A generation [that] curses its father," results in incomplete sentences. Moreover, 30:13 cannot be a relative clause (see below). Waltke, however, takes all four instances of דור as examples of left-dislocation (i.e., nominative absolutes or *casus pendens*; BHRG §48; *IBHS* §4.7.b–c): "A generation—they curse their fathers" (Waltke 2005, 458 and n. 39). But left-dislocation is not a natural reading for 30:11 and 12 (see below), and on this analysis דור remains unspecified in the discourse. The Greek avoids these difficulties by reading ἔκγονον κακόν ("bad offspring") in place of דור. The addition of the word κακόν eliminates the problem of an unspecified generation and the use of the singular noun ἔκγονον, which is not a collective noun like דור, makes the saying individual. In G the sense is clear—it is a description of how a *bad* child acts. If this correctly captures the intent of the Hebrew then it is an unparalleled use of דור in the Hebrew Bible to refer to a gnomic individual, that is, a type of child or offspring. Anaphora is a poetic device not a syntactic structure. Just because the poet made a decision to start each line with דור does not mean that the lines must therefore exhibit grammatical parallelism. I take a flexible approach to the syntax that attempts to reflect what is the same in each couplet while accepting the differences. As it stands, 30:11 is a simple finite clause. The subject is דור, which has been raised to the front of the clause because it is a new topic in the discourse.

Verse 12

דור טהור | This verse uses nominal clauses or null copulas. The poet perpetuates the anaphora with ease and no particular emphasis, since subject-predicate word order is unmarked for nominal clauses (*BHRG* §46.2.3.1).

Verse 13

דּוֹר מָה־רָמוּ עֵינָיו | Because the interrogative מה is an exclamative adverbial interjection in this verse (*IBHS* §18.3f; Joüon §144e), it breaks the grammatical sequence and forces us to read דור as a case of left-dislocation, commonly called a nominative absolute or *casus pendens* (Holmstedt 2014, 121; cf. *IBHS* §4.7). Here the poet is using left-dislocation to serve the device of anaphora and keep the stanza laser focused on his topic, the particular type of generation he has been describing. The noun phrase עיניו is the subject of the clause and its third-person masculine singular possessive pronoun is coreferential with left-dislocated דור.

Verse 14

דּוֹר חֲרָבוֹת שִׁנָּיו | As in verse 13, דור is left-dislocated, specifying the antecedent of the third-person masculine singular clitic suffixes on שניו and מתלעתיו. The function of this syntactic structure is poetic, perpetuating the anaphora of the stanza as it builds toward its climactic description of the wicked generation.

מאדם | *BHS* proposed emending מאדם ("from humankind") to מאדמה ("from the ground"), presumably on the logic that אדמה ("ground") formed a better parallel to ארץ ("earth"). There is, however, no textual evidence that anything is amiss here and ארץ is often a synecdoche for "humanity" (Isa 14:9, 16; Ps 99:1).

Verse 15

לעלוקה | Although עלוקה is a *hapax legomenon*, its meaning is clearly "leech." The versions all render with better-attested words (e.g., βδέλλα, LSJ, s.v.), and Aramaic and Syriac provide strong cognate evidence (Jastrow 1903, s.v. "עֲלוּקָה"; Sokoloff 2009, s.v. "ܥܠܘܩܐ"; T Ps 12:9; T Prov 30:15; b. Avod. Zar. 12b). The root עלק has the sense "hang, be suspended, cleave, adhere" (BDB, sv. "עלק"; Delitzsch 1875, 288 n. 1). Other meanings have been suggested, such as a proper name or title (Toy 1899, 528–29; Vattioni 1965; cf. comments in Delitzsch 1875, 287), "vampire-like demon" (BDB, s.v. "עלק"; Oesterley 1929, 275; see comments in Glück 1964, 367 n. 2), and even "erotic passions" (Glück 1964, 369), but such explanations are unnecessary and too creative by half (see North 1965).

הב הב | The phrase הב הב is morphologically unprecedented in the Hebrew Bible and syntactically it has no obvious relationship to the rest of the line. The Greek reads ἀγαπήσει ἀγαπώμεναι ("lovingly beloved," NETS), apparently having analyzed the form as derived from √אהב or possibly √חבב (Fox 2015, 383). The Syriac seems to follow G by rendering ܚܒܝܒ̈ܐ (concretely "burning," but metaphorically "beloved;" Sokoloff 2009, s.v. "ܚܒܒ"). The targum splits the difference between MT and S by preserving the consonants of MT but approximating the meaning of S (מהבהבן, "burning, parched" [Sokoloff 1990, s.v. "הבהב"; Waard 2008, 56*], but metaphorically "lusty" or possibly "greedy" [Jastrow 1903, s.v. "הַבְהֵב"329; Fox 2009, 1062; Healey 1991, 60]). There are likely other examples of the versions misunderstanding forms of √יהב and rendering with √אהב (see Ps 55:23; and Hos 8:13 with discussion in Thomas 1939, 63; and Barr 1968, 233–34).

Against the versions, most modern interpreters believe this form is a second-person masculine singular *qal* imperative from √יהב ("to give"), although, elsewhere in the Hebrew Bible we find הָבָה (GKC §69o). The root is more common in Aramaic, attested in many forms and dialects, where it covers much of the semantic range of √נתן (Sokoloff 1990, s.v. "יהב"; 2002, s.v. "ܝܗܒ"). Here we do find הַב (e.g., Dan 5:17; Tg. Onq. Gen 30:1, 26; Tg. Neof. Num 11:13; T Prov 23:25). It is speculative, but when one considers that עלוקה ("leech") is a *hapax legomenon* in the Hebrew Bible, although it is present in Aramaic, and that the form of הב conforms to Aramaic usage, it seems plausible that this saying has a foreign tint.

In the Hebrew Bible, √יהב only occurs in direct speech as an imperative. Usually it means "give," but five times it is an exclamation paired with a first-person volitive; normally glossed "come, let us" (Gen 11:3, 7; 38:16; Exod 1:10; *IBHS* §40.2.5c; cf. Joüon §§75k and 105e). It is unlikely the exclamation is intended in this verse because we have no related volitive or context, and exclamations can only derive meaning from the broader discourse. What we have in the MT, then, is a drastically elided, arresting poetic expression that *names* the daughters for what they *say*. As an imperative, the morphology implies direct speech, thus the reader mentally supplies the elided element אמרו or תאמרנה. However, syntactically the relationship appears appositional, which would demand nouns implying proper names. Thus the reader would supply a pair of short null copulas such as שם האחת ... ושם השנית (cf. Gen 4:19; Ruth 1:4). The cryptic ambiguity of this line probably intends for us to be able to read הב הב both as names and direct speech.

Verse 16

וְעֹצֶר רָחַם | The nominal form of √עצר occurs just three times (Isa 53:8; Ps 107:39; and Prov 30:16; cf. Judg 18:7; 1 Sam 9:17; and Jer 20:9). Although there has been considerable speculation (e.g., Kutsch 1952; Thomas 1960, 290; Meek 1960, 328), the other two instances of the noun are generally translated "oppression" (*DCH* 6, s.v. "עֹצֶר") or "restraint, coercion" (BDB, s.v. "עֹצֶר"). The verb means "to stop," "hold back," or "bind up" (e.g., Num 17:13–15; Judg 13:15–16; 2 Chr 22:9). A notable idiom describes infertility, for example, Gen 16:2: "YHWH has held me back from childbearing" (עצרני יהוה מלדת; cf. Gen 20:18; Isa 66:9; Sir 42:10; cf. Deut 11:17; 2 Chr 7:13). The present construct phrase seems to depend on this idiom and is best understood as an epexegetical genitive, that is, the noun in construct modifies the absolute noun adjectivally (*IBHS* §9.5.3c). The Syriac and T reflect this understanding.

The Greek, however, departs significantly from MT with ἔρως γυναικός ("love of a woman"). De Waard (2008, *56) offers a clever explanation whereby an aural metathesis of *'ōṭer* to *er'ōṭ* was transcribed phonetically as *erōs*. *Womb* might then be taken as a metonymy for woman in order to get γυναικός (Toy 1899, 532). Alternatively, G may have interpreted the root רחם according to the Aramaic, "love, passion" (Fox 2015, 384; cf. G Prov 28:13 and G^A-Judg 5:20 where the same association is made). This would make γυναικός an epexegetical gloss for עצר. Perhaps G simply rewrote the phrase to capture the sense, taking the physical reality (a barren womb) to its likely result (a woman begging for children, cf. Gen 30:1). Vladimir Olivero (2021), however, makes a compelling argument that the translator of G Proverbs freely adapts 30:16 in order to weave in an allusion to Hesiod's *Theogony* (lines 116–122) by making reference to Chaos/Hades (Χάος/ᾄδης), Gai/Earth, (Γαῖ'/γῆ), Tartarus (Τάρταρος), and Eros ("Ερος). For a Hellenistic Jewish audience, this allusion evokes an ontological genealogy of insatiability: "After the topological principles [Hades, Earth, Tartaros], Eros appears, the logical principle, the force that enables generation, the incessant thrust to reproduction" (Olivero 2021, 34). Olivero (32 n. 19) notes that his argument does not necessarily preclude Fox or de Waard's explanations in so far as they describe exegetical techniques at the translator's disposal. The expansions and alterations to 30:16 in the Greek seem to be the work of the translator's creative reworking of the text for his cultural milieu.

Verse 17

לִיקֲהַת | This noun occurs only here and in Gen 49:10 but most likely means *obedience* (Delitzsch 1875, 294–95; Fox 2015, 385). The versions, however, have rendered the word *old age* (G: γῆρας, likely followed by S and T). Accordingly, scholars have suggested alternate explanations, taking the root to be either זקן (Toy 1899, 532) or להק (from an Ethiopic root meaning "to be old;" see Driver 1928, 394; Thomas 1941, 154–55; Greenfield 1958, 212–14; de Waard 1993, 258). Both suggestions would require several emendations reflecting either a different reading in the *Vorlage* or scribal errors. But there is nothing wrong with the sense of יקהה in the verse, despite the rarity of the word. The versions are probably the result of lexical ignorance with subsequent harmonization toward the use of זקן in Prov 23:22 (Barr 1968, 271 n. 1; Fox 2015, 385). The expected vocalization is לְיִקֲהַת, which was preferred by Ben Asher and is witnessed to in Codex Erfurt 1 (GKC §20h n. 2; see Fox 2015, 385).

בני־נשר | Although נשר clearly refers to a bird of prey, it is not clear which bird of prey is intended. The two options normally put forward are the eagle (i.e., the golden eagle, *Aquila chrysaetos*) and the vulture (i.e., the griffon vulture, *Gyps fulvus*). Both of these birds are massive, powerful, and majestic. Most translators—ancient and modern—have opted for eagle (Healey 1991, 61 n. 8), but the context pictures a carrion bird. The Greeks, followed by the Romans, had a cultural prejudice against the vulture in favor of the eagle, which likely influenced the reading in G (ἀετός) and in V (*aquila*). This prejudice and translation have persisted to the present, while in the ancient Near East the prestige and cult of the vulture had some prominence (Kronholm 1999, 80; Borowski 1998, 150). Based on analysis of "habits and habitat" in context, G. R. Driver (1955a, 8) concludes נשר is "without doubt primarily the vulture." "At the same time," he admits, "the [נשר] undoubtedly includes the eagle as it is often translated in the ancient Versions" (9). Whether any given occurrence of נשר in the Hebrew Bible fits the eagle or the vulture better is debatable (e.g., Ezek 17:3, 7; but Mic 1:16; cf. Driver 1955b, 1958; Kronholm 1999; Forti 2008, 30–31). Clearly the ancient Hebrews did not use this word to differentiate between these animals (Fisher 1980, 606–7; Fox 2009, 869). Modern interpreters can make a cautious judgement based on the context or opt for something more general, such as "bird of prey."

The expression בני נשר probably refers to the actual young of the animal. Expressions with the bound form of בן usually refer to a class or type, but with designations for specific animals the expression is most often literal, not classifying or metaphorical (*pace* Toy 1899, 530). So "sons of rebellion" are rebels (Num 17:25) but "sons of a dove" are young doves (Lev 5:7, 11); or "sons of death" are men as good as dead (1 Sam 26:16), but "sons of cattle" are calves (1 Sam 14:32); and even "sons of the flock" are lambs (Ps 114:4, 6), but "sons of goats" are kids (2 Chr 35:7). See especially Ps 147:9; Job 4:11; Ezra 6:9. Therefore *fledgling* raptors are pictured rather than the class *raptor* generally (see NJPS; *pace* NRSV and others).

Verse 18

K: וארבע Q: וארבעה | The *qere* agrees in gender with the third-person masculine plural resumptive object pronoun in ידעתים and with דרך in the list to follow (Joüon §152g). Moreover, Benjamin Kennicott records far more manuscripts attesting to the *qere* than the *ketiv* (1780, 475). The *ketiv* is perhaps original for being "incorrect" and therefore the more difficult reading (Fox 2015, 384–85). Alternatively the *ketiv* could be adjusted toward ארבע in 30:15b (Waltke 2005, 460 n. 52).

Verse 19

דרך | The Greek uses three different words to render the four occurrences of דרך in this verse: ἴχνη ("tracks"), ὁδούς ("ways"), and τρίβους ("paths"). Perhaps this is intended as an improvement of literary style (Fox 2014a, 14–16), but it could also reflect the play between the concrete and figurative sense of דרך. It is a marked departure from G's preservation of anaphora in verses 11–14 with דור.

עלי | This form of the preposition על with a final י is relatively rare, occurring some thirty-six times in the Hebrew Bible. Over two-thirds of these examples are in Psalms and Job and nearly all are in poetry. As this preposition is most likely derived historically from עלי/√עלה (GKC §103o; *IBHS* §11.2.13a), this form may be hanger-on from Old Canaanite dialects where the preposition still ended in a vowel (*HALOT*, s.v. "II עַל"; Joüon §103m). For the older Canaanite form עלי in Phoenician, see *KAI* 1.2 and Charles Krahmalkov (2001, 251–52) and for Ugaritic, see Cyrus Gordon

(1965, §10:13) and John Huehnergard (2012, 75). It may be used as an archaism, for euphony, or both.

בעלמה | Although עלמה is a notorious theological crux in Isa 7:14 (see Kamesar 1990 for a survey of historical exegesis), the present context does not demand a precise definition. The related nominals עֶלֶם (1 Sam 17:56; 20:22) and עֲלוּמִים (Job 20:11; 33:25; Ps 89:46; Isa 54:4) appear to mean "young man" and "youth" respectively. Our word clearly pictures a young woman and probably has some allure and a connotation of innocence, but we cannot be too precise about her age, marital status, or sexual history (Gen 24:43; Exod 2:8; Ps 68:26; Song 1:3; 6:8; Sutcliffe 1960, 126–28). As Fox (2009, 871) points out, the use of עלמה, whether or not it is taken to connote virginity, certainly connotes an uneven and possibly illicit sexual rendezvous, since we might expect "the way of a man in his wife" (ודרך גבר באשתו) if a marital liaison was imagined (also Delitzsch 1874, 297–98; cf. Waltke 2005, 492).

The preposition ב in the fourth line seems intentionally ambiguous (Fox 2009, 872). There are perhaps three options for reading this ב. The instrumental ב (*BHRG* §39.6.[3].[a]; *IBHS* §11.2.5d, nos. 15–16; GKC §119o), the comitative ב (*BHRG* §39.6.(3).(e); *IBHS* §11.2.5d, nos. 10–12), or the locative ב (*BHRG* §39.6.[1].[a]; *IBHS* §11.2.5b). The instrumental sense would emphasize the way of the man as he uses the woman toward his own purposes ("he had his way with her"). The comitative sense would suggest the way of a man together *with* a girl. This is the common romantic interpretation (Scott 1965, 181; Murphy 1998, 235). The locative sense would make the woman a place onto or into which the man moves. Some verbs, especially verbs of "extending, touching, and fastening," take ב with their object complement while most other verbs take ב phrases as adverbial adjuncts (*IBHS* §11.2.6f; GKC §119k). The challenge here is that no verb governs the preposition within the clause.

This ambiguity may account for the versions. T is very close to MT with עלימתא ("young woman," cf. Tg. Onq. Gen 24:43; Tg. Ong. Exod 2:8; Tg. Isa 7:14). The Greek, however, has παρθένος for עלמה twice (Gen 24:43; Isa 7:14), and νεᾶνις four times (Exod 2:8; Ps 68:26; Song 1:3; 6:8), but only here does G change the sense to read ἐν νεότητι ("in youth"). The Vulgate is similar and may be following G (thus de Waard 2008). As Chrisophe Rico (2007, 274–75), however, has pointed out, S, the Old Latin, and important witnesses to V all have a possessive pronoun: "in *his* youth." These witnesses suggest a consonantal Hebrew text reading עלמיו, with עֲלוּמִים

spelled defectively. Rico (2007, 276–77) argues that "in his youth" makes better sense than "in a girl" as the climax of the sequence in Prov 30:18–19 and graphic confusion between ה and י is responsible for the reading in MT. The evidence Rico highlights is significant, and it does suggest there was a Hebrew *Vorlage* with the reading עלמיו. I am not convinced, however, that this Hebrew *Vorlage* contains the better reading. As I argue in §5.3.2.1, I believe עלמה is in keeping with the tone of the collection as a whole and is not ill-suited to the context, but rather forces the interpreter toward a more sardonic interpretation. In fact, the incongruity of עלמה when combined with the graphic similarity of ה and י may have motivated a scribe, whether intentionally or not, to render עלמה as עלמיו. Thus Fox (2015, 385) suggests G (followed by V and S) avoids the graphic sexual image for the sake of propriety. It could also be that the interplay between דרך and ב misled the translator so that he went searching for a gloss of עלמה that seemed a better fit with the preposition. If he connected עלמה with the abstract concept of youth, he may have thought of νεότητος (G Prov 2:17; 5:18). The Greek Prov 2:17a reads διδασκαλίαν νεότητος ("teaching of youth") for MT אלוף נעוריה ("companion of her youth"). Coming to the puzzling expression in 30:19, a translator may have redacted the sense toward G Prov 2:17a, understanding "the way of a man in his youth" to be a reference to keeping covenant (2:17b). The adulterous woman of 30:20 might then be understood as a reference to Lady Folly of the prologue, thus interpreting 30:19–20 allegorically and flattening out the play on דרך to boot.

Verse 20

כן | The use of the adverb כן in the first position links verse 20 closely to 30:18–19. Syntactically, כן derives its meaning from its reference in context (deixis). In the vast majority of cases it points backward in the discourse to an element that precedes it (i.e., it is anaphoric; *BHRG* §40.30.[1]). Thus Delitzsch (1875, 298) quips, "where is there a proverb … that begins with כֵּן?" While this is not the only possible analysis of the syntax of כן, it seems the most plausible one, particularly when one notes the repetition of דרך and the sexual innuendos in verses 18–20. The implication, then, is that the *way* of the woman in verse 20 is somehow explained by the four *ways* in 18–19.

Verse 22

כי ... כי | Syntactically, verses 21–23 are one clause. Proverbs 30:21 is the compound main clause and verses 22–23 contain a list of four items in apposition to ארבע in 22b. These four items (שפחה, עב, נבל, שנואה) are each modified by a כי clause. Though we may be tempted to treat these כי clauses as relatives (e.g., NIV), this is not the best analysis because כי never introduces relative clauses (Holmstedt 2016). Rather, the whole stanza should be analyzed as a complex conditional clause where the apodosis precedes the protasis (GKC §159*aa–bb*): "*If* a servant becomes king, etc., *then* the earth will not be able to bear it." Conditional כי is often indistinguishable from the temporal use so *when* would also be an acceptable gloss (*BHRG* §40.29.1.[1]; BDB, s.v. "כִּי"). We are not dealing with types of servants or types of fools but with unrealized, potential situations (*irrealis* clauses).

נבל | Many translations and interpreters gloss נבל as *fool* (e.g., NRSV; Scott 1965, 179; Murphy 1998, 236). But this is a weak gloss for a grave term (Phillips 1975, 241). There are two common words for fool in Biblical Hebrew (כסיל and אויל), and נבל is distinguished from both of these terms by its usage and distribution (Donald 1963, 286–89). The root occurs more often in the Torah and prophetic books than in wisdom literature and cognates belong more to the semantic field of sin and shame than folly (see Donald 1963): נָבֵל (verb, six times), נְבָלָה (noun, thirteen times), נְבָלוּת (noun, once), נָבָל (adjective, eighteen times). The verb נבל means "to shame" or "disgrace publicly" such that the relationship is broken, usually in covenantal or familial contexts (Deut 32:15; Jer 14:21; Mic 7:6; Nah 3:6; Sir 9:7). Nine out of thirteen times the noun occurs in the expression "he did a *nəbālāh* in Israel" (עשׂה נבלה בישראל), and most of these examples refer to extreme forms of sexual violence or sexually deviant behavior (Gen 34:7; Deut 22:21; Judg 19:23, 24; 20:6, 10; 2 Sam 13:12; Jer 29:23). Not all examples are sexually explicit, for example, the sin of Achan (Josh 7:15). In all examples, however, נבלה "is a general expression for serious disorderly and unruly action resulting in the break up of an existing relationship whether between tribes, within the family, in a business arrangement, in marriage or with God" (Phillips 1975, 241). But more than this, נבלה seems to denote actions that incur shame and bring dishonor on the whole population so that the offending party has to be summarily eliminated, ejected, or atoned for to restore the honor of the community as a whole (Deut

22:21; Josh 7:15; Judg 20:6–10; 1 Sam 25:23–27; Job 42:8). The adjective נבל is associated with lacking wisdom (חכם, Deut 32:6), "shame" (חרפה, 2 Sam 13:13), "iniquity" (און, Isa 32:6), "transgressions" (פשע, Ps 39:8), and doing "corrupt" and "abominable" deeds (שחת and תעב, Pss 14:1; 53:2). The נבל is someone who is characterized by the kind of disgraceful and shameful behavior referred to by נבלה, as Abigail's pun in 1 Sam 25:23 makes clear: "for according to his name thus he is: *Nābāl* is his name and *nabālāh* is with him" (*pace* Barr 1968, 7). The kind of behavior designated by √נבל lacks consideration for social values, norms, and the well-being of others through reckless and arrogant violence that threatens the stability of the whole community and brings shame and disgrace on it. This is beyond foolishness, this is destructive, antisocial behavior. See further Roth (1960) and Gerleman (1974).

Verse 23

שנואה כי תבעל | The basic form and meaning of שנואה is clear, but the precise connotation presents a conundrum. The word is a feminine singular *qal* passive participle from √שנא ("to hate"), thus the common gloss "hated woman." According to many scholars the hated woman is an "unattractive unmarried woman" (Delitzsch 1875, 300; Toy 1899, 533; Oesterly 1929, 278), perhaps drawing connections to Gen 29:31 and 33 where Leah is called שנואה (cf. Deut 21:15–17). On another view the שנואה is a divorcee. This view is not grounded in Hebrew texts but in ancient Aramaic Jewish marriage contracts from Elephantine, which enshrine provisions for divorce that utilize √שנא as a technical term:

ענניה בעדה ויאמר שנית לאנתתי יהוישמע לא תהוה לי אנתת כסף שנ[א]ה בראשה

Should Ananiah stand up in an assembly and say: "I hated my wife Jehoishma; she shall not be to me a wife," silver of ha[tr]ed is on his head. (Porten and Yardeni 1989, 78, 82; B3.8:21–22; with analysis in Yaron 1958, 10–28)

Despite the apparent strength of this parallel text, later Aramaic usage does not preserve this technical sense (Sokoloff 1990, s.v. "סני"; 2002, s.v. "هعر"), the versions have literal glosses suggesting they infer no special situation or technical sense, and שנואה never names a divorcee. What is more, there is no provision, legal or otherwise, against a divorcee getting remarried in ancient Israel, therefore, it is hard to see how this could be earth-shaking (Fox 2009, 876). "Hated woman" seems best.

The question of precisely what earth-shaking thing this woman does to incur hate remains, and it turns on the sense of the verb תבעל. The *qal* of √בעל means "to marry" or "take as a wife" (Deut 21:13; 24:1; Isa 54:5; 62:5; Mal 2:11) with the related sense of "to rule, master" (Isa 26:3; Jer 3:14; 31:32). These senses are difficult to differentiate in metaphorical contexts, which probably indicates intentional ambiguity rooted in the cognitive overlap of the two ideas (Fox 2009, 876–77; *DCH* 2, s.v. "בעל I"). The feminine singular *qal* passive participle √בעל means "married" (Gen 20:3; Deut 22:22; Isa 54:1; 62:4a). Pointed as we have it in the MT, תִּבָּעֵל is a *niphal yiqtol* meaning "to be married" (Isa 62:4b). If one understands שנואה to mean a spurned wife, the verse becomes "a tautology to a fault" (Waltke 2005, 460–61 n. 61). Therefore, Van Leeuwen (1986, 608) favors repointing תבעל as a third-person feminine singular *qal yiqtol*: תִּבְעַל "to marry, rule, master." But a feminine subject is never the semantic agent of √בעל, which could be the problem: "The hateful woman plays the husband's role and lords it over the household" (Fox 2009, 877). However, Waltke (2005, 461) objects to repointing תבעל, because the verb is bivalent in the *qal* (Deut 21:13; 24:1; Isa 26:13; 62:5; Jer 3:14; 31:32; Mal 2:11; 1 Chr 4:22). In support of Waltke, all the versions adopt a translation that indicates they understand תבעל means "to be married."

But what is wrong with a hated woman getting married? Context rather than philology must decide. In Prov 30:22, the שנואה is the female counterpart of the נבל, which strongly suggests this woman is culpable. She is hated because she *is* hateful, that is, "loathsome." The verb תבעל parallels ישבע and represent an undeserved reward for a wicked person. The Greek renders כי תבעל with the phrase ἐὰν τύχῃ ἀνδρὸς ἀγαθοῦ ("if she obtains a good man"). Adding ἀγαθοῦ reveals G's interpretation—it is not that a woman "lords it over" anyone but rather that a *bad* woman gets a *good* man. "Hated" need not imply fault (Gen 29:31, 33; Deut 21:15–17), but here fault is implied. What the sage considers earth-shaking is an unrighteous woman being rewarded.

Verse 24

קטני־ארץ | Many commentators instinctively read קטני־ארץ as a superlative ("the smallest on earth," Murphy 1998, 233; Fox 2009, 878; GKC §133g). Supporting this instinct, G, S, and T all preserve superlatives and the only

Appendix: Translation and Philological Notes   239

other example of the bound form of קטנים is a superlative: אנכי מקטני שבטי ישראל ("I am from *the least* of the tribes of Israel," 1 Sam 9:21). But, as this comparison makes clear, a superlative would require a definite noun (GKC §133.3; *IBHS* §14.5). Isaiah 23:8 might make a better analogy: כנעניה נכבדי־ ארץ, "Her [Tyre's] traders were honored on earth" (Delitzsch 1875, 310).

והמה חכמים מחכמים | The second line of Prov 30:24 has a straight-forward verbless clause (והמה חכמים) with puzzling modifier (מחכמים). As pointed in the MT, מְחֻכָּמִים is a rare masculine plural *pual* participle. In fact, there is only one other *pual* participle from √חכם in ancient Hebrew (Ps 58:6 [5 ET]). The *piel* participle shows up twice as often (Pss 105:22; 119:8; Job 35:11; Sir 6:37), and seems to mean "to make wise, wisen" or "to instruct" (BDB, s.v. "חָכַם" 314; *HALOT*, s.v. "חכם"; *DCH* 3, s.v. "חכם"). By deduction, then, more than attestation, the *pual* means "to be made wise" or "instructed" (Fox 2009, 879).

The rarity of this form probably led G to read σοφώτερα τῶν σοφῶν ("wiser than the wise," NETS). Apparently, the translator read a comparative מ + the adjective חכמים (מֵחֲכָמִים), which is a natural reading for the consonants as they stand. The Syriac agrees with G and most modern commentators and translations adopt this reading (Murphy 1998, 233 n. 24a; Scott 1965, 180; NIV, NRSV). But with a superlative we would expect the article instead of מ, the bound form of הכמים, or both. Theodotion, however, testifies to MT with the reading σοφίᾳ σεσοφισμένα ("having been made wise by wisdom," Field 1875, 372)—a dative noun and a passive participle. Theodotion's reading is supported by T: והינון חכימין ומחכמין ("and they are wise and made wise"). The ו shows that T understands both חכימין and מחכמין to be coordinated predicates modifying הינון. This strongly suggests T is reading a participle, either *pael* or *aphel*, rather than a comparative מ + adjective. It remains a question of vocalization, but it seems easier to explain how the reading of G, S, and their modern followers arose from the rarer reading in Theodotion, T, and MT than the other way around.

The *pual* participle is occasionally used in an adjectival capacity with a noun or adjective of the same root in order to intensify the quality at issue (Delitzsch 1875, 301). This is analogous to the infinitive absolute (*BHRG* §20.2.4). For example: "Do not eat it raw nor boiled boiling [וּבָשֵׁל מְבֻשָּׁל, i.e., totally boiled] in water" (Exod 12:9); "We have finished a searched search [חֵפֶשׂ מְחֻפָּשׂ, i.e., a thorough search]" (Ps 64:7); "a precious cornerstone of a founded foundation [מוּסָד מוּסָּד, i.e., a secure foundation]" (Isa

28:16). The only other example of the *pual* participle √חכם is also used adjectivally and the meaning "made wise" or "trained" is appropriate:

אשר לא־ישמע לקול מלחשים / חובר חברים מחכם:
Who does not listen to the voice of the charmers— / the spell-caster trained in spells (Ps 58:6 [5 ET]).

A wooden reading of our phrase, might be something like: "They are wise being made wise." Thus Eliezer Ginsburg and Yosef Weinberger (2007, 636) follow Metzudos and translate, "Who are wise, having been made wise [by the Creator]." Fox (2009, 879) cites Sa'adia who explains this means "stamped with the wisdom of nature" or "instructed by instinct." These animals are wise because they were made that way—it is in their nature.

Verse 25

הנמלים | The identification of נמלה as "ant" is undisputed despite the fact that it occurs only twice in ancient Hebrew, here and Prov 6:6. Cognates are well-attested in Semitic languages, for example, Akkadian *lamattu* (*CAD* 9:67) and *namalu* (*CAD* 11.1:208), which is treated as a West Semitic loanword (it occurs notably in the El-Amarna tablets, see *DNWSI*, s.v. "nmr₁"; *HALOT*, s.v. "נְמָלָה"). Likewise, the versions are univocal in rendering "ant" (G: μύρμηξ; T: שושמני; S: ܫܘܫܡܢܐ; V: *formicae*).

Verse 26

שפנים | The שפן appears in four passages (Lev 11:5; Deut 14:7; Ps 104:18; and Prov 30:26) and has been variously glossed as "coney" (KJV) or "badger" (NRSV, NJPS). In the Torah, this animal is unclean because it chews the cud but lacks a cloven hoof and is listed alongside the ארנבת (typically understood to be the hare; see BDB, s.v. "אַרְנֶבֶת"; *HALOT*, s.v. "אַרְנֶבֶת"; *DCH* 1, s.v. "אַרְנֶבֶת"). Both G and S gloss שפן with specialized words that are not attested apart from the passages in question (G: χοιρογρύλλιοι, "hare," LEH, s.v. "χοιρογρύλλιος"; S: ܫܦܢܝܢ, "hyrax," Sokoloff 2009, s.v. "ܫܦܢܝܢ"). Targum Prov 30:26 has a transliteration of S: חנסי (probably in error for חגסי, "rabbit, or coney," Jastrow 1903, s.v. "חָגָס"). This suggests the ancient translators knew what animal they were dealing with and used the specific term. Based on the description of its habitat and behavior, scholars unanimously identify it as the hyrax (*Procavia capen-*

sis), a small ungulate more closely related to aardvarks and antelopes than rabbits (Gesenius 1854, 1103, s.v. "שָׁפָן"; Tristram 2013 [1884], 1–2; Firmage 1992, 1143; 1157 n. 31; Gilbert 2002, 21).

Verse 27

חֹצֵץ כֻּלּוֹ | The verb חצץ only occurs two other times in Biblical Hebrew (Judg 5:11; Job 21:21), but derives from a family of words having to do with separating or cutting: "arrow" (חֵץ), "half" (חֲצִי), "to divide" (חצה), and "gravel" (חָצָץ). In both rabbinic Hebrew and Aramaic חצץ can mean "to drive a wedge, cut off," that is, "to divide, partition, interpose" (Jastrow 1903, s.v. "חָצַץ"; Sokoloff 2002, s.v. "חצץ"). The closest parallel to our verse is the challenging Judg 5:11: מקול מחצצים בין משאבים ("from a sound of divisions between watering places"). The word משאבים is itself a *hapax legomena* (BDB, s.v. "מַשְׁאָב") and various construals of מחצצים are available (Block 1999, 228–29; Butler 2009, 118 n. 11a; Webb 2012, 196). But Rashi can help. In his commentary, he draws on the lexical work of Mahberet Menachem and concludes "the meaning is 'battle formations,'" which he connects to Prov 30:27. Indeed, "divisions"—in the military sense—works quite nicely in Judg 5:11. Elsewhere in Judges the verb חצה refers to the division of men into fighting units (Judg 7:16; 9:43; cf. Gen 32:8; 33:1; Num 31:27).

It seems best to understand חצץ in Prov 30:27 similarly, meaning something like "dividing" or "forming divisions." Certainly, our couplet has a military flavor, which comports well with imagery used of locusts elsewhere in the Hebrew Bible (Joel 2). Long ago, Thomas (1965, 276) pointed out יצא itself often has the sense of "go out to battle, march" (cf. Judg 2:15; 2 Kgs 18:7; Deut 28:25). Although it is periphrastic and does not clearly indicate how to translate חצץ, G supports this interpretation: καὶ ἐκστρατεύει ἀφ' ἑνὸς κελεύσματος εὐτάκτως ("yet they march orderly at the command of one," NETS). The words ἐκστρατεύει (LSJ, s.v. "ἐκστρατεύω") and εὐτάκτως (LSJ, s.v. "εὐτάκτως," mng. II. [sic] Adv.) carry militaristic connotations.

In terms of syntax, in all nine Biblical Hebrew clauses with כל + third-person masculine singular pronominal suffix and a participle, כל + pronoun is the subject and the participle is the predicate (Jer 6:13; 8:6, 10; 15:10; 20:7; Ps 29:9; Prov 30:27). When the expression כֻּלּוֹ ("all of him/it") has a collective noun as the antecedent (in this case ארבה, "the locust swarm") it refers to the whole collective (*BHRG* §24.3.2.[3]; Young 2013,

478; von Siebenthal 2009, 77). The participial clause, "the whole thing," that is, the locust swarm, "was dividing," modifies the main clause (ויצא) as an adjunct (*BHRG* §20.3.2.2 [2]).

Verse 28

שממית | The versions translate as "lizard": G: καλαβώτης ("spotted lizard, gecko," LSJ, s.v.); S: ܐܡܩܗ ("lizard," Sokoloff 2009, s.v. "ܐܡܩܬܐ"); V: *stellio*. The targum, no doubt following S, has אקמה, generally believed to be in error for אמקה (Waard 2008, 56*; Díez Merino 1984, 107). Notably, the only other place that καλαβώτης and ܐܡܩܗ/אמקה occur in G, S, and T is Lev 11:30, where the Hebrew is אנקה. This is also a *hapax legomenon*, although it appears to be a cognate to the Syriac and Aramaic. But S and T may be transliterating because ܐܡܩܗ/אמקה are not clearly attested apart from Lev 11:30 and Prov 30:28. Despite this, a later rabbinic tradition associates שממית with the spider (e.g., b. Shabb. 77b; b. Sanh. 103b; Fox 2009, 879; Forti 2008, 116). However, these references too are inconclusive and can nearly all be rendered "lizard" or "gecko" equally well (see Healey 1991, 61; Hess 1915, 128; and Delitzsch 1875, 303–5, who lands on "lizard" but has a thorough discussion). The fact that the versions draw together two *hapax legomena*, שממית and אנקה, with the same translation, and the latter appears in a list of unclean reptiles, leans toward a broad identification as "lizard." This is a serviceable gloss in context, but we ought not to imagine we have accurately identified this mysterious critter.

תתפש | As pointed in the MT, תְּתַפֵּשׂ is a third-person feminine singular/second-person masculine singular *piel yiqtol*: "The lizard grasps with two hands" (3fs); or "You grasp the lizard with two hands" (2ms). However, the *piel* of √תפש is unattested. Elsewhere, when the verb √תפש takes the preposition ב plus "hand" (יד) or "palm" (כף) as an adjunct, ב is always instrumental and the sense of תפש is "to catch" or "seize" (Delitzsch 1875, 305; cf. Ezek 21:16, 24; 29:7; Jer 38:23). Even more significantly, every other example of the verb √תפש takes an object complement, that is, the verb is bivalent; not "lizards grasp," but "lizards grasp *walls.*" Moreover, the third-person feminine singular reading describes the lizard's distinctive ability to scale walls, but the context demands a weakness in line with the other small creatures (Plöger 1984, 366; Forti 2008, 117). Finally, the form of ידים here is dual, suggesting a pair of human hands rather than the lizard's four feet. Reading in context, it seems best to understand תתפש

as a second-person masculine singular form addressed to an "indefinite personal subject" (GKC §144h), that is, the reader.

But G has a double translation: χερσὶν ἐρειδόμενος καὶ εὐάλωτος ὤν ("holds (itself) fast with its hands and is easily caught"). Fox (2015, 387; 2009, 878–79) reasons G's readings assume a third-person feminine singular/second-person masculine singular *niphal* and that we should follow suit. One strength of this approach is it yields an attested form (תִּתָּפֵשׂ; Jer 34:3; 51:41). However, while the thesis that G is reading a *niphal* is certainly plausible, it is not necessary. The first reading in G (χερσὶν ἐρειδόμενος) could readily reflect תתפש as an active third-person feminine singular form. The second option (καὶ εὐάλωτος ὤν) captures the sense of תתפש as an active second-person masculine singular form even though G uses a passive expression to do so (a predicate adjective, cf. MT and G at Prov 19:25). Notably, S and T preserve active meanings and take שממית as the subject, although they have their own textual difficulties (see de Waard 2008, 56*; Díez Merino 1984, 107). The Greek simply appears to be wrestling with an unvocalized text, unsure of whether the lizard is the subject or the object. We do well to preserve the pointing as MT has it—in part *because* we do not understand it.

Verse 29

מיטיבי צעד | Here we have a masculine plural *hiphil* participle in construct with a noun. In the next line we have the same construction except that לכת is an infinitive (*BHRG* §20.1.3.[1]). This participle phrase is an unmarked relative clause that is an adjunct modifying the preceding nominal clause—G, S, and T all use relative pronouns or particles in rendering this verse. While there is no exact parallel for the phrase מיטיבי צעד in Biblical Hebrew, there are five verses where the *hiphil* of √יטב takes an infinitive as its object complement (1 Sam 16:17; Isa 23:16; Jer 1:12; Ezek 33:32; Ps 33:3; and cf. Prov 15:2). Based on these parallels the nature of the construct relationship here is probably best described as adverbial (Waltke 2005, 462 n. 73; *BHRG* §25.4.5; and cf. Deut 9:21; 13:15; 17:4; 19:18; 2 Kgs 11:18). The sense of מיטיבי, then, is to do something well or skillfully (*DCH* 4, s.v. "יטב"; *HALOT*, s.v. "יטב"). The noun צעד is usually glossed "step," but it probably means something closer to "stride" or "march." In several places צעד is in synonymous parallelism with דרך (Jer 10:23; 31:4; 34:21; Prov 16:9) and even with עבר (Prov 7:8) but never with פעם ("footstep," "beat"). Of twenty-five occurrences in ancient Hebrew, only two are concrete (2 Sam 6:13; Sir 45:9) and the rest are metaphorical denoting a person's manner of living (e.g., Prov 4:12; 5:5; 16:9; Sir 37:15).

Verse 30

ליש | Avot R. Nat. 39:2 lists ליש among the six names by which the lion (האריה) is called, but this rare moniker occurs just three times in the Hebrew Bible (Isa 30:6; Job 4:11). The versions form a broad consensus that ליש refers to a young lion (T Isa 30:6; G Isa 30:6; Prov 30:30; and S Isa 30:6; and Prov 30:30), but all Strawn (2005, 326) will say with certainty is that ליש is male. Other Semitic languages have cognates (e.g., Arm. ליתא and possibly Akkadian *nēšu*; Firmage 1992, 1153; *HALOT*, s.v. "לַיִשׁ"; Strawn 2005, 325; Jastrow 1903, s.v. "לֵישׁ"), but these cognates shed no light on a narrow nuance. In lieu of any precise identification, Waltke (2005, 499) suggests that ליש was selected for its assonance with תיש.

Verse 31

זרזיר מתנים | The identity of the זרזיר מתנים is confounding. Since it is the less problematic word, I will treat מתנים first. Normally glossed "loins" or "waist," מתנים occurs forty-seven times in Biblical Hebrew and refers to the middle of the body around the groin and buttocks (*HALOT*, s.v. "מָתְנַיִם"; for cognates see *CAD* 10:412; *DULAT*, s.v. "mtn I"; Sokoloff 2002, "מָתְנָיָא"; 2009, s.v. "ܚܨܐ"). The מתנים are dual, suggesting a pair, but it is difficult to be anatomically precise. They are the place where a solider straps on his sword (2 Sam 20:8; Neh 4:18). When מתנים are "bound," "girded," or "strengthened" it pictures someone prepared for physical action, particularly war or feats of strength (1 Kgs 18:46 [שנס]; Jer 1:17 [אזר]; Nah 2:2 [חזק]; 1Q28a [1QSa] 1:17 [חזק]; cf. Prov 31:17 [חגר]). But מתנים also has a sexual shading, connoting virility, and possibly encoding a euphemism for the genitals (Exod 28:42; Deut 33:11; 1 Kgs 12:10; Isa 45:1; Ezek 21:11; Nah 2:11; Ps 69:24; and Job 12:18). Victor Hamilton (1980, 536–37) brings these observations together, "The loins are the seat of strength (Job 40:16; Nah 2:2), especially of the male as connected with virility.... To damage the loins is to weaken or render helpless (Deut 33:11; Ps 69:24)."

Now, concerning the *hapax legomenon* זרזיר, no less a luminary than Rashi simply concluded, "I do no know what it is" (לא ידעתי מה הוא). Indeed, proposals are many and varied (see Forti 2008, 119). It seems safe to assume the זרזיר is an animal, but what animal? One path derives זרזיר

Appendix: Translation and Philological Notes   245

from √זרר ("squeeze, flow," *DCH* 3, s.v. "זרר") or √זור ("to press down and out," BDB, s.v. "זור III"). Scholars taking this path imagine a beast with a narrow waist as if cinched by a belt and fit for sprinting (e.g., Rashi and Ibn Ezra on this verse). Arriving at an etymological gloss for זרזיר, they define it as "girded, girt … that which is girt" (Peters 1914, 154; *HALOT*, s.v. "זַרְזִיר"; cf. BDB, s.v. "זַרְזִיר"; *DCH* 3, s.v. "זַרְזִיר"). The zebra, leopard, and war horse have all been suggested, but the greyhound has been the most enduring identification (Delitzsch 1875, 308–9). This path, however, proves a road to nowhere—the versions are against it and the etymological method is suspect, not least because √זור and √זרר are themselves tenuous and poorly attested.

Another path identifies זרזיר by following the vast majority of ancient interpreters. The versions unanimously gloss "rooster" (G=ἀλέκτωρ; S=ܐܟܒܪ; T=ואבכא; V=*gallus*). There are plenty of *hapax legomena* the versions struggle with; it is remarkable that on זרזיר they speak univocally (although it remains possible they are all blindly following G). Rabbinic sources largely support this identification (Midr. Lam. 5:1; Gen. Rab. 100:75). Yet this route still has challenges. In other rabbinic and Aramaic sources זרזיר means "starling" (Jastrow 1903, s.v. "זַרְזִיר II"; Sokoloff 2009, s.v. "ܙܪܙܝܪܐ"). In Gen. Rab. 65:3 the זרזיר is classified as an unclean bird by close comparison to the raven, but the rooster is clean (Fox 2009, 880). Yet *rooster* remains the best guess following the versions (Peters 1914, 154–56; Bewer 1948, 61). Whether or not this is precisely correct, some kind of male bird fits the context.

But what on earth is "a rooster of loins?" Because זרזיר מתנים is such a puzzle, many scholars suggest a text-critical solution. Some suggest מתנים או is a corruption of מתנשא ו (Bewer 1948, 61; Clifford 1999, 265); the original line perhaps having read זרזיר מתנשא ותיש ("a rooster exalting himself and a he-goat"). This reading makes a certain amount of sense, but there is no evidence for it. I suggest מתנים is here modifying זרזיר attributively bearing the connotation of masculine strength and virility (Waltke 2005, 462 n. 76). It is worth noting, this is how G, α', and θ' seem to have understood מתנה in Eccl 7:7 (εὐτονίας, "vigor"), where it is possible their *Vorlage* read מתניו (Weeks 2021, 170–71; cf. V: *robur*, "hardness"). One textual tradition, following G, expands the phrase as it does the rest of the verse—G: καὶ ἀλέκτωρ ἐμπεριπατῶν θηλείαις εὔψυχος ("also a cock strutting courageously among the hens," NETS); S: ܘܬܪܢܓܠܐ ܕܡܗܠܟ ܒܝܬ ܬܪܢܓܠܬܐ ("and a rooster who struts between the hens"); Old Latin: *gallus inter gallinas* ("a rooster among the hens"). If strength and virility are indeed the connotations, then the versions capture the sense by providing the rooster with a flock of hens. G's εὔψυχος ("courageously") could be a gloss of מתנים given its martial connotations and idioms like Job 40:16 and Nah 2:2 (cf. Waltke 2005, 499 n. 221). The addition of a phrase about walking is fully warranted from 30:29, especially if there was a desire to make the description of the rooster match the description of the lion and the king. Such an expansion could have originated with G or his *Vorlage*.

I gloss "strapping rooster" because it connects strength and virility with the idea of being girded or prepared for action (cf. the iconography of a fighting cock on the seal of Jaazaniah; Badè 1933).

או | The conjunction או ("or") may seem jarring. Some speculate 30:30–31 contains a list of three items with תיש as a gloss of זרזיר מתנים (Fox 2009, 880–81; Thomas 1960, 291). But several medieval Jewish commentators used Prov 30:31 as evidence that או can have a simple conjunctive sense (see Ibn Ezra and Bachya ben Asher on Lev 4:23). Likewise, Delitzsch maintains a list of four items making a comparison with Song 2:9 and suggesting או merely creates a sharp distinction between figures (1875, 310; cf. Waltke 2005, 462 n. 78; *BHRG* §40.3).

תיש | The תיש is a male goat (Gen 30:35; 32:14; 2 Chr 17:11). Neither T nor S translates the word because תיש appears to be a more common word for goat in both Aramaic and Syriac (Jastrow 1903, s.v. "תַּיִשׁ"; Sokoloff 1990, s.v. "תייש"; 2009, s.v. "ܬܝܫܐ"; Firmage 1992, 1152; 1Q23 [1QEnGiants[a]] 1 in Barthélemy and Milik 1955, 97; b. Ber. 63a). Given the low number of occurrences in Biblical Hebrew and its striking distribution against Aramaic-speaking social contexts, תיש may well be an Aramaic loanword. It may be used in the Hebrew Bible to color the narrative with an appropriate dialect, to refer to a specific breed of goat known in Syria, or both.

אלקום [אל־קום] עמו | In the first half of verse 31 the text is secure despite its obscurity, but here all acknowledge the text is corrupt since אלקום represents no known Biblical Hebrew lexeme or lexical pattern.

A few older interpreters balked at a human figure in a list of animals and argue the original probably had a fourth beast rather than "king" (מלך; Toy 1899, 537; Thomas 1960, 291). However, Agur persistently blends human and animal imagery, and "king" is secure in the versions. Attempts to read אלקום as the name of a deity (Toy 1899, 536; Feigin 1925, 138–39) or an Arabic expression (BDB, s.v. "אַלְקוּם"; Delitzsch 1875, 311–12; Peters

1914, 155) are speculative and not convincing (GKC §35m; Waltke 2005, 462 n. 79; Fox 2009, 881).

More plausible are the attempts of scholars to suggest variant readings or conjectural emendations that might lie behind the versions.

G: καὶ βασιλεὺς δημηγορῶν ἐν ἔθνει
and a king making a speech in a nation (NETS)
S: ܘܡܠܟܐ ܕܡܡܠܠ ܒܝܢ ܥܡܡܐ
and the king who speaks among the people
T: ומלכא דקאים וממליל בית עממי
and the king who rises and speaks among his people
V: nec est rex qui resistat ei
and a king, whom none can resist (Douay-Rheims)

Setting aside V for the moment, I make four observations. First, the choice between relative clause (S, T) or participle clause (G) to modify king is inconsequential. This choice merely reflects the style of the target language and represents the consistent pattern each text has taken with the four creatures in verses 30–31. Second, G, S, and T all include the idea of speaking. Third, G, S, and T all read עַמּוֹ "his people" rather than the MT pointing עִמּוֹ "with him." Finally, T preserves a double translation, maintaining both the idea of speaking and adding rising (perhaps reflecting √קום). I think there is a fairly straightforward story to tell here and T holds the key. Since, no retroversion of G, S, or T arrives at anything clearly derived from MT, one might imagine the versions had a substantially different *Vorlage* (creative possibilities are available in Bewer 1948, 61–62; and Thomas 1960, 291). However, the text in front of the translator may have been closer to MT, perhaps something like קם אל עמו ("rising toward his people," see Driver 1951, 194; McKane 1970, 664; Clifford 1999, 264). In what context might a king "rise toward" his people? One answer is in order to speak to them. If this is correct, then T draws out the logic of the versions for us by including both √קום and the idea of speaking.

Sadly, there is no Hebrew manuscript evidence to directly support this reconstruction. Instead, the brackets in the text above indicate that I adopt the reading of the Oriental manuscript tradition against the Leningrad Codex (Fox 2015, 387; *BHS*). The subtle but significant difference is the word division, yielding אַל־קוּם in place of אַלְקוּם (Tov 2015, 128–31). Many commentators reject this reading on syntactic grounds. Delitzsch (1875, 311) wrote, "אַל with the infin. is not Heb." (also Toy 1899, 536). However, although there are no exact parallels, this syntax is not impossible. The particle אל is a clause-level negator (*BHRG* §41.3). As part of a nominal clause or null copula it appears to negate nominals, especially when there is an "added volitional nuance" (Joüon §§160oa; 114h-k). Since the infinitive is a verbal noun that expresses action without reference to time or person, אל + infinitive should be considered equivalent to אל + noun (*BHRG* §20.1.1; Fox 2009, 881). There are many examples of this construction (Judg 19:23; 2 Sam 1:21; 13:16; Prov 12:28; 27:2; 31:4). Analyzed this way אל־קום עמו is a nominal clause (null copula) in apposition to מלך. The adverb אל negates the null being-verb and קום עמו is its predicate (for the infinitive as the predicate of a null copula see *BHRG* §20.1.3.[1]). In this context, עם + קום bears the nuance "against" (Ps 94:16; *HALOT*, s.v. "עם" mng. 1; Fox 2009, 881). Thus the whole clause is, "and a king—[let there be] no rising with (i.e., against) him."

If the versions had ומלך אל־קום עמו or ומלך עמו אלקום in front of them, they may have arrived at their readings through a process similar to the one outlined above. It is likely the translator first zeroed in on the items he could easily process: ומלך and עמו. Reading without vowels in context with a king, עמו was understood as עַמּוֹ ("his people"). Once this decision was made, it constrained possible readings of אל־קום/אלקום—the king must do something in relationship to his people. Searching for an interpretation of אל־קום/אלקום the translator could have identified √קום, as T seems to have done (Tov 2015, 119–20). Once √קום is settled on, it is possible to arrive at the versions' readings. Fox (2015, 387) and de Waard (2008) suggest exegetical metathesis of קום and אל. Perhaps also plausible is that the translator read לקום and ignored א as erroneous (Tov 2015, 195). In support of reading √קום, V clearly aligns with the Oriental manuscript tradition, showing either that Jerome had the same word division in his *Vorlage*, or he read MT in the way I am suggesting. Rabbinic sources appear to read the text similarly. Commenting on Isa 24:20, Ibn Ezra cites Prov 30:31 as an example of the infinitive of √קום (see also b. Sanh. 82b).

Verse 32

נבלת | This verb is unique in the *qal*, as indicated by the masora. In contrast to the *piel* (Deut 32:15; Jer 14:21; Mic 7:6; Nah 3:6), in the *qal* נבל has no object (i.e., it is intransitive), so it seems best to understand it as a stative verb. Stative verbs were perhaps originally "conjugated adjectives" (Joüon §41b). Therefore we ought to associate the *qal* verb closely with the adjective (Delitzsch 1875, 313), meaning "to be highly destructive, antisocial" (see also the note at v. 22: נבל).

Verse 33

מִיץ | All three occurrences of this word are in this verse. Nevertheless, the Akkadian cognate *mâṣu* and the context here (doing something to milk to produce butter or perhaps curds) make the meaning "churning" fairly secure (*CAD* 10.1, s.v. "mâṣu B"; Held 1958, 171 n. 45; 1985). Historically, this may relate to √מצץ and/or √מצה and carry the idea of pressure (cf. Judg 6:38; Ps 73:10; Isa 16:4; 66:11). In rabbinic Hebrew the word appears a number of times meaning something like "squeezing" or perhaps "wringing out" (Jastrow 1903, s.v. "מִצּוּי").

אפים ... אף | Concretely, אף (singular) and אפים (dual) mean "nose" and "nostrils" respectively, but by metaphorical extension both words picture anger (*HALOT*, s.v. "אַף II" mng. 4.c). When אף means anger the most common expression uses it as the subject of the verb חרה ("to burn") or one of its synonyms (e.g., Gen 30:2; 39:19; Isa 5:25; 30:27). But אף also means anger in other contexts (e.g., Gen 27:45; 49:6; Isa 10:5; 13:3). Except for the famous idiom of Exod 34:6 and passages that echo it, אפים nearly always means "nostrils" (Dan 11:20 and Prov 14:17 are the exceptions; Fox 2009, 882; *pace* Bauer 1999). These broader usage patterns *might* suggest אפים more naturally reads concretely while אף pictures anger more often. But in the second line of this verse אף goes with דם creating a concrete picture (a bloody nose), while in the third line אפים goes with ריב creating a more abstract concept (contentious feuds). The Hebrew poet probably alternated אף and אפים for the sake of the parallelism and poetic style, but perhaps this subtly flags the pun by making the lines sound slightly unnatural. It is not till the third line, then, that the pun lands and the reader reprocesses the whole. Like us, the ancient versions wrestle with how to render these lines. The targum glosses אף as רוגזא ("anger") and אפים as חורינא דאפי ("contentiousness of the face"). The Greek resolves the metaphor by replacing אפים with ἐξέλκης λόγους ("extort words," see Fox 2014a, 11). The need to translate one occurrence of אף or אפים as "anger" and the other as "nose" to get at the sense forces us to flatten out the poetic potential of the text.

Bibliography

Abegg, Martin G., Jr., with James E. Bowley, and Edward M. Cook. 2003. *The Non-biblical Texts from Qumran*. Vol. 1 of *The Dead Sea Scrolls Concordance*. Leiden: Brill.

Adams, Samuel L., and Matthew Goff, eds. 2020. *The Wiley Blackwell Companion to Wisdom Literature*. Wiley-Blackwell Companions to Religion. Chichester: Wiley & Sons.

Aejmelaeus, Anneli. 1986. "The Function and Interpretation of כי in Biblical Hebrew." *JBL* 2:193–209.

Aitken, James K. 2007. "Poet and Critic: Royal Ideology and the Greek Translator of Proverbs." Pages 190–204 in *Jewish Perspectives on Hellenistic Rulers*. Edited by Tessa Rajak, Sarah Pearce, James K. Aitken, and Jennifer Mary Dines. HCS 50. Berkeley: University of California Press.

Aitken, James K., and Lorenzo Cuppi. 2015. "Proverbs." Pages 341–55 in *The T&T Clark Companion to the Septuagint*. Edited by James K. Aitken. London: Bloomsbury.

Albright, William F. 1956. "The Biblical Tribe of Massa' and Some Congeners." Pages 1–14 in *Studi orientalistici in onore di Giorgio Levi della Vida*. Vol. 1. Pubblicazioni dell'Istituto per l'Oriente 52. Rome: Istituto per l'Oriente.

Allegro, John M. 1968. *Qumran Cave 4.I (4Q158–4Q186)*. DJD V. Oxford: Clarendon.

Allen, Leslie C. 1994. *Ezekiel 1–19*. WBC 28. Dallas: Word.

Alster, Bendt. 1975a. "Paradoxical Proverbs and Satire in Sumerian Literature." *JCS* 27:201–30.

———. 1975b. *Studies in Sumerian Proverbs*. Mesopotamia 3. Copenhagen: Akademisk Forlag.

———. 1997. *Proverbs of Ancient Sumer: The World's Earliest Proverb Collections*. 2 vols. Bethesda, MD: CDL.

———. 2005. *Wisdom of Ancient Sumer*. Bethesda, MD: CDL.

Alter, Robert. 1985. *The Art of Biblical Poetry*. New York: Basic Books.
———. 2019. *The Hebrew Bible: A Translation with Commentary*. 3 vols. New York: Norton.
Ansberry, Christopher B. 2011. *Be Wise, My Son, and Make My Heart Glad: An Exploration of the Courtly Nature of the Book of Proverbs*. BZAW 422. Berlin: de Gruyter.
Assmann, Jan. 1983. "Königsdogma und Heilserwartung: Politische und kultische Chaosbeschreibungen in ägyptischen Texten." Pages 345–77 in *Apocalypticism in the Mediterranean World and the Near East: Proceedings of the International Colloquium on Apocalypticism, Uppsala, August 12–17, 1979*. Edited by David Hellholm. Tübingen: Mohr.
Avrahami, Yael. 2012. *The Senses of Scripture: Sensory Perception in the Hebrew Bible*. LHBOTS 545. New York: T&T Clark.
Babcock, Barbara A., ed. 1978. *The Reversible World: Symbolic Inversion in Art and Society*. Symbol, Myth, and Ritual Series. Ithaca, NY: Cornell University Press.
Badé, William Frederic. 1933. "The Seal of Jaazaniah." *ZAW* 51:150–56.
Balentine, Samuel E. 2006. *Job*. SHBC 10. Macon, GA: Smyth & Helwys.
———. 2021. "Proverbs." Pages 495–514 in *The Oxford Handbook of Wisdom and the Bible*. Edited by Will Kynes. Oxford: Oxford University Press.
Barr, James. 1968. *Comparative Philology and the Text of the Old Testament*. Oxford: Clarendon.
———. 1969. "The Symbolism of Names in the Old Testament." *BJRL* 52:11–29.
———. 1989. *The Variable Spellings of the Hebrew Bible*. Schweich Lectures 1986. Oxford: Oxford University Press.
Barthélemy, Dominique. 2015. *Job, Proverbes, Qohélet et Cantique des Cantiques*. Vol. 5 of *Critique textuelle de l'Ancien Testament*. OBO 50.5. Fribourg: Academic Press; Göttingen: Vandenhoeck & Ruprecht.
Barthélemy, Dominique, and Józef T. Milik. 1955. *Qumran Cave 1*. DJD I. Oxford: Clarendon.
Bauer, Johannes Baptist. 1999. "Wann heißt 'appayim 'Zorn'? Ex 15,8; Prov 30,33; Dan 11,20." *ZAW* 111:92–94.
Beattie, James. 1778. *Essays: On Poetry and Music as They Affect the Mind; on Laughter, and Ludicrous Composition; on the Utility of Classical Learning*. New ed. Edinburgh: Creech; London: Dilly.
Bekins, Peter, and Alexander T. Kirk. 2017. "A Thorny Text: The Use of את and the Subversion of Form in Ezek 2:6." *VT* 67:357–71.

Ben-Porat, Ziva. 1976. "The Poetics of Literary Allusion." *PTL: A Journal for Descriptive Poetics and Theory of Literature* 1:105–28.
Berger, Peter L. 2014. *Redeeming Laughter: The Comic Dimension of Human Experience*. 2nd ed. Berlin: de Gruyter.
Berman, Samuel B. 1996. *Midrash Tanhuma-Yelammedenu: An English Translation of Genesis and Exodus from Printed Version of Tanhuma-Yelammedenu with an Introduction, Notes and Indexes*. Hoboken, NJ: KTAV.
Beverly, Jared. 2020. "Nebuchadnezzar and the Animal Mind (Daniel 4)." *JSOT* 45:145–57.
Bewer, Julius A. 1948. "Two Suggestions on Prov 30:31 and Zech 9:16." *JBL* 67:61–62.
Bickell, G. 1891. "Kritische Bearbeitung der Proverbien: Mit einem Anhange über die Strophik des Ecclesiasticus." *WZKM* 5:79–102.
Biddle, Mark E. 2013. *A Time to Laugh: Humor in the Bible*. Macon, GA: Smyth & Helwys.
Bledsoe, Seth A. 2013. "Can *Ahiqar* Tell Us Anything about Personified Wisdom?" *JBL* 132:119–37.
Blenkinsopp, Joseph. 1995. *Sage, Priest, Prophet: Religious and Intellectual Leadership in Ancient Israel*. Louisville: Westminster John Knox.
Bloch-Smith, Elizabeth. 1992. *Judahite Burial Practices and Beliefs about the Dead*. JSOTSup 123. Sheffield: Sheffield Academic.
Block, Daniel I. 1997. *The Book of Ezekiel: Chapters 1–24*. NICOT. Grand Rapids: Eerdmans.
———. 1999. *Judges, Ruth*. NAC 6. Nashville: Broadman & Holman.
Böck, Barbara. 2009. "Proverbs 30:18–19 in the Light of Ancient Mesopotamian Cuneiform Texts." *Sef* 69:263–79.
Boda, Mark J. 2006. "Freeing the Burden of Prophecy: *Maśśā'* and the Legitimacy of Prophecy in Zech 9–14." *Bib* 87:338–57.
Bodi, Daniel. 2013. "The Numerical Sequence x/x+1 in Aramaic Ahiqar Proverbs and in Ancient Near Eastern Literature." *Aliento* 4:17–43.
Boer, P. A. H. de. 1948. "An Enquiry into the Meaning of the Term משא." *OtSt* 5:197–214.
Bordjadze, Karlo V. 2017. *Darkness Visible: A Study of Isaiah 14:3–23 as Christian Scripture*. PTMS 228. Eugene, OR: Wipf & Stock.
Borowski, Oded. 1998. *Every Living Thing: Daily Use of Animals in Ancient Israel*. AltaMira: Walnut Creek, CA.

———. 2002. "Animals in the Literature of Syria-Palestine." Pages 289–306 in *A History of the Animal World in the Ancient Near East*. Edited by Billie Jean Collins. HdO 64. Leiden: Brill.
Brekelmans, C. H. W. 1965. "The Saints of the Most High and Their Kingdom." Pages 305–29 in *Kaf-Hē: 1940–1965*. Edited by P. A. H de Boer. OTS 14. Leiden: Brill.
Brenner, Athalya. 2003. *Are We Amused? Humour about Women in the Biblical Worlds*. JSOTSup 383. London: T&T Clark.
Brettler, Marc Z. 2010. "The 'Coherence' of Ancient Texts." Pages 411–19 in *Gazing on the Deep: Ancient Near Eastern and Other Studies in Honor of Tzvi Abusch*. Edited by Jeffery Stackert, Barbara Nevling Porter, and David P. Wright. Bethesda, MD: CDL.
Bridges, Charles. 1847. *An Exposition of the Book of Proverbs*. 2nd ed. London: Seeleys.
Briggs, Richard S. 2021. *The Lord Is My Shepherd: Psalm 23 for the Life of the Church*. Touchstone Texts. Grand Rapids: Baker Academic.
Brown, Jeannine K. 2008. "Genre Criticism and the Bible." Pages 111–50 in *Words and the Word: Explorations in Biblical Interpretation and Literary Theory*. Edited by David G. Firth and Jamie A. Grant. Nottingham: Apollos.
Brown, William P. 2002. "The Pedagogy of Proverbs 10:1–31:9." Pages 150–82 in *Character and Scripture: Moral Formation, Community, and Biblical Interpretation*. Edited by William P. Brown. Grand Rapids: Eerdmans.
———. 2014. *Wisdom's Wonder: Character, Creation, and Crisis in the Bible's Wisdom Literature*. Grand Rapids: Eerdmans.
Bruch, Johann Friedrich. 1851. *Weisheits-Lehre der Hebräer: Ein Beitrag zur Geschichte der Philosophie*. Strasbourg: Treuttel & Würtz.
Brunner-Traut, E. 1977. "Der Katzmäusekrieg—Folge von Rauschgift." *GöMisz* 25:47–51.
Budde, K. 1882. "Das hebräische Klagelied." *ZAW* 2:1–52.
Bunson, Margaret R. 2012. "Satirical Papyrus." Pages 355 in *Encyclopedia of Ancient Egypt*. Edited by Margaret R. Bunson. 3rd ed. New York: Facts On File.
Buss, Martin J. 1999. *Biblical Form Criticism in Its Context*. JSOTSup 274. Sheffield: Sheffield Academic.
Butler, Trent C. 2009. *Judges*. WBC 8. Nashville: Nelson.
Byargeon, Rick W. 1998. "Echoes of Wisdom in the Lord's Prayer (Matt 6:9–13)." *JETS* 41:353–65.

Carr, David M. 2005. *Writing on the Tablet of the Heart: Origins of Scripture and Literature*. Oxford: Oxford University Press.

Carroll, Nöel. 2014. *Humour: A Very Short Introduction*. Oxford: Oxford University Press.

Caubet, Annie. 2002. "Animals in Syro-Palestinian Art." Pages 211–34 in *A History of the Animal World in the Ancient Near East*. Edited by Billie Jean Collins. HdO 64. Leiden: Brill.

Cheung, Simon Chi-chung. 2015. *Wisdom Intoned: A Reappraisal of the Genre "Wisdom Psalms."* LHBOTS 613. London: T&T Clark.

Childs, Brevard S. 1979. *Introduction to the Old Testament as Scripture*. Philadelphia: Fortress.

———. 2001 *Isaiah: A Commentary*. OTL. Louisville: Westminster John Knox.

Clifford, Richard J. 1999. *Proverbs: A Commentary*. OTL. Louisville: Westminster John Knox.

Clines, David J. A. 2004. "Job's Fifth Friend: An Ethical Critique of the Book of Job." *BibInt* 12:233–50.

———. 2011. *Job 38–42*. WBC 18b. Nashville: Nelson.

———. 2013. "The Worth of Animals in the Divine Speeches of the Book of Job." Pages 101–13 in *Where the Wild Ox Roams: Biblical Essays in Honour of Norman C. Habel*. Edited by Alan H. Cadwallader and Peter L. Trudiger. HBM 59. Sheffield: Sheffield Phoenix.

———. 2021. "Alleged Basic Meanings of the Hebrew Verb *qdš* 'Be Holy': An Exercise in Comparative Hebrew Lexicography." *VT* 71:481–502.

Cohen, Abraham, trans. 1951. *Midrash Rabbah: Ecclesiastes*. Edited by Harry Freedman and Maurice Simon. London: Soncino.

Collins, John J. 1993. *Daniel: A Commentary on the Book of Daniel*. Hermeneia. Philadelphia: Fortress.

Conybeare, Catherine, and Simon Goldhill, eds. 2020. *Classical Philology and Theology: Entanglement, Disavowal, and the Godlike Scholar*. Cambridge: Cambridge University Press.

Cook, Johann. 1997. *The Septuagint of Proverbs: Jewish and/or Hellenistic Proverbs? Concerning the Hellenistic Colouring of LXX Proverbs*. VTSup 69. Leiden: Brill.

Cook, John A. 2005. "Genericity, Tense, and Verbal Patterns in the Sentence Literature of Proverbs." Pages 117–34 in *Seeking Out the Wisdom of the Ancients: Essays Offered to Honor Michael V. Fox on the Occasion of His Sixty-Fifth Birthday*. Edited by Ronald L. Troxel, Kelvin G. Friebel, and Dennis R. Magary. Winona Lake, IN: Eisenbrauns.

Costecalde, C.-B. 1985. "La racine qdš et ses dérivés en milieu ouest-sémitique et dans les cunéformes." *DBSup* 10:1346–93.

Crenshaw, James L. 1995. "Clanging Symbols." Pages 371–82 in *Urgent Advice and Probing Questions: Collected Writings on Old Testament Wisdom*. Macon, GA: Mercer University Press.

———. 2010. *Old Testament Wisdom: An Introduction*. 3rd ed. Louisville: Westminster John Knox.

Cuppi, Lorenzo. 2011. "Long Doublets in the Septuagint of the Book of Proverbs, with a History of the Research on the Greek Translations." PhD. diss., Durham University.

———. 2012. "The Treatment of Personal Names in the Book of Proverbs From the Septuagint to the Masoretic Text." Pages 19–39 in *Greek Scripture and the Rabbis*. Edited by Timothy Michael Law and Alison Salvison. CBET 66. Leuven: Peeters.

D'Agostino, Franco. 1998. "Some Considerations on Humour in Mesopotamia." *RSO* 72:273–78.

Dahood, Mitchell. 1963. *Proverbs and Northwest Semitic Philology*. SPIB 113. Rome: Pontificium Institutum Biblicum.

Davis, Ellen F. 2000. *Proverbs, Ecclesiastes, and the Song of Song*. WeBC. Louisville: Westminster John Knox.

Day, John, Robert P. Gordon, and H. G. M. Williamson, eds. 1995. *Wisdom in Ancient Israel: Essays in Honour of J. A. Emerton*. Cambridge: Cambridge University Press.

Deist, Ferdinand. 1997. "Boundaries and Humour: A Case Study from the Ancient Near East." *Scriptura* 63:415–24.

Delitzsch, Franz. 1874. *Biblical Commentary on the Proverbs of Solomon*. Vol. 1. Translated by M. G. Easton. Clark's Foreign Theological Library 43. Edinburgh: T&T Clark.

———. 1875. *Biblical Commentary on the Proverbs of Solomon*. Vol. 2. Translated by M. G. Easton. Clark's Foreign Theological Library 47. Edinburgh: T&T Clark.

Dell, Katharine J. 2000. "The Use of Animal Imagery in the Psalms and Wisdom Literature of Ancient Israel." *SJT* 53:275–91.

Derrida, Jacques. 1980. "The Law of Genre." Translated by Avital Ronell. *Critical Inquiry* 7:55–81.

Dequeker, L. 1973. "The Saints of the Most High." Pages 108–87 in *Syntax and Meaning: Studies in Hebrew Syntax and Biblical Exegesis*. Edited by M. J. Labuschagne. OTS 18. Leiden: Brill.

Díez Merino, Luis. 1984. *Targum de Proverbios: Edición Príncipe del Ms. Villa-Amil no. 5 de Alfonso de Zamora.* BHBib 11. Madrid: Consejo Superior de Investigaciones Científicas.
Dijkstra, Meindert. 1995. "Is Balaam Also among the Prophets?" *JBL* 114:43-64.
Dillon, E. J. 1895. *The Sceptics of the Old Testament: Job, Koheleth, and Agur.* London: Isbister.
Donald, Trevor. 1963. "The Semantic Field of 'Folly' in Proverbs, Job, Psalms, and Ecclesiastes." *VT* 13:285-92.
Driver, G. R. 1928. "Some Hebrew Words." *JTS* 29:390-96.
———. 1951. "Problems in the Hebrew Text of Proverbs." *Bib* 32:173-97.
———. 1955a. "Birds in the Old Testament: I. Birds in Law." *PEQ* 87:5-20.
———. 1955b. "Birds in the Old Testament: II. Birds in Life." *PEQ* 87:129-40.
———. 1958. "Once Again: Birds in the Bible." *PEQ* 90:56-58.
Ehrenberg, Erica. 2002. "The Rooster in Mesopotamia." Pages 53-62 in *Leaving No Stones Unturned: Essays on the Ancient Near East and Egypt in Honor of Donald P. Hansen.* Edited by Erica Ehrenberg. Winona Lake, IN: Eisenbrauns.
Eising, Hermann. 1997. "נאם." *TDOT* 9:109-13.
Eissfeldt, Otto. 1913. *Der Maschal im Alten Testament.* BZAW 24. Giessen: Töpelmann.
———. 1964. *Einleitung in Das Alte Testament: Unter Einschluß der Apokryphen und Pseudepigraphen sowie der apokryphen- und pseudepigraphenartigen Qumrān-Schriften; Entstehungsgeschichte Des Alten Testaments.* 3rd rev. ed. NTG. Tübingen: Mohr.
———. 1965. *The Old Testament: An Introduction, including the Apocrypha and Pseudepigrapha, and Also the Works of Similar Type from Qumran; The History of the Formation of the Old Testament.* Translated by Peter R. Ackroyd. Oxford: Blackwell.
Elgvin, Torleif, et al. 1997. *Qumran Cave 4.XV: Sapiential Texts, Part 1.* DJD XX. Oxford: Clarendon.
Emerton, J. A. 2001. "The Teaching of Amenemope and Proverbs XXII 17-XXIV 22: Further Reflections on a Long-Standing Problem." *VT* 51:431-65.
Erlandsson, Seth. 1970. *The Burden of Babylon: A Study of Isaiah 13.2-14.23.* ConBOT 4. Lund: CWK Gleerup.

Erman, Adolf. 1924. *Eine ägyptische Quelle der "Sprüche Salomos."* Sitzungsberichte der Preussischen Akademie der Wissenschaften 15. Berlin: Akademie der Wissenschaften.

Eshel, Esther, et al. 1998. *Qumran Cave 4.VI: Poetical and Liturgical Texts, Part 1.* DJD XI. Oxford: Clarendon.

Ewald, Heinrich A. 1836–1839. *Die poetischen Bücher des Alten Bundes.* 4 vols. Göttingen: Vandenhoeck & Ruprecht.

———. 1837. *Sprüche Salomo's: Kohélet; Zusätze zu den früheren Theilen und Schluss.* Die poetischen Bücher des Alten Bundes 4. Göttingen: Vandenhoeck & Ruprecht.

———. 1848. "Über die volks-und geistesfreiheit Israel's zur zeit der großen Propheten bis zur ersten zerstörung Jerusalems." *JBW* 1:95–113.

Feigin, S. 1925. "וּמֶלֶךְ אַלְקוּם עִמּוֹ (Proverbs 30:31)." *AJSL* 41:138–39.

Fernández Marcos, Natalio. 2001. "On the Borderline of Translation Greek Lexicography: The Proper Names." *JNSL* 27:1–22.

———. 2003. "On Double Readings, Pseudo-Variants and Ghost-Names in the Historical Books." Pages 591–604 in *Emanuel: Studies in the Hebrew Bible, Septuagint, and Dead Sea Scrolls in Honor of Emanuel Tov.* Edited by Shalom M. Paul, Robert A. Kraft, Lawrence H. Schiffman, and Weston W. Fields. VTSup 94. Leiden: Brill.

Field, Frederick. 1875. *Origenis Hexaplorum.* Vol 2. Oxford: Clarendon.

Firmage, Edwin. 1992. "Zoology (Fauna)." *ABD* 6:1109–67.

Fishbane, Michael. 1985. *Biblical Interpretation in Ancient Israel.* Oxford: Oxford University Press.

Fisher, Milton C. 1980. "נשׂר." *TWOT* 2:606–7.

Floyd, Michael H. 2002. "The מַשָּׂא (*maśśā'*) as a Type of Prophetic Book." *JBL* 121:401–22.

———. 2018. "The Meaning of *Maśśā'* as a Prophetic Term in Isaiah." *JHS* 18:9. https://doi.org/10.5508/jhs.2018.v18.a9.

Forti, Tova L. 2008. *Animal Imagery in the Book of Proverbs.* VTSupp 118. Leiden: Brill.

———. 2017. "Septuagint." Pages 253–59 in *The Hebrew Bible: Writings.* Edited by Armin Lang and Emanuel Tov. THB 1C. Leiden: Brill.

———. 2018. *"Like a Lone Bird on a Roof": Animal Imagery in the Structure of the Psalms.* CrStHB 10. University Park, PA: Eisenbrauns.

Foster, Benjamin R. 1974. "Humor and Cuneiform Literature." *JANES* 6:69–85.

———. 1992. "Humor and Wit: Mesopotamia." *ABD* 3:328–30.

———. 1995. "Humor and Wit in the Ancient Near East." Pages 2459–69 in vol. 4 of *Civilizations of the Ancient Near East*. Edited by Jack M. Sasson. New York: Scribner's Sons.
Fox, Michael V. 1977. "Frame-Narrative and Composition in the Book of Qohelet." *HUCA* 48:83–106.
———. 1981. "Job 38 and God's Rhetoric." *Semeia* 19:53–61.
———. 1985. *The Song of Songs and the Ancient Egyptian Love Songs*. Madison: University of Wisconsin Press.
———. 2000. *Proverbs 1–9: A New Translation with Introduction and Commentary*. AB 18A. New York: Doubleday.
———. 2009. *Proverbs 10–31: A New Translation with Introduction and Commentary*. AB 18B. New York: Doubleday.
———. 2013. "How the Peshitta of Proverbs Uses the Septuagint." *JNSL* 39:37–56.
———. 2014a. "A Profile of the Septuagint Proverbs." Pages 3–17 in *Wisdom for Life: Essays Offered to Honor Prof. Maurice Gilbert SJ on the Occasion of His Eightieth Birthday*. Edited by Nuria Calduch-Benages. BZAW 445. Berlin: de Gruyter.
———. 2014b. "From Amenemope to Proverbs: Editorial Art in Proverbs 22,17–23,11." *ZAW* 126:76–91.
———. 2015. *Proverbs: An Eclectic Edition with Introduction and Commentary*. HBCE 1. Atlanta: Society of Biblical Literature.
———. 2018. "The Meanings of the Book of Job." *JBL* 137:7–18.
Franklyn, Paul. 1983. "The Sayings of Agur in Proverbs 30: Piety or Scepticism?" *ZAW* 95:238–52.
Freedman, Harry, trans. 1951. *Midrash Rabbah: Genesis*. Vol. 1. Edited by Harry Freedman and Maurice Simon. London: Soncino.
Fritsch, Charles T., and Rolland Schloerb. 1955. "The Book of Proverbs." *IB* 4:767–957.
Frow, John. 2015. *Genre*. 2nd ed. New Critical Idiom. New York: Routledge.
Gehman, Henry S. 1940. "The 'Burden' of the Prophets." *JQR* 31:107–21.
Gemser, Berend. 1963. *Sprüche Salomos*. 2nd ed. HAT 16. Tübingen: Mohr Siebeck.
George, A. R. 1993. "Ninurta-Pāqidāt's Dog Bite, and Notes on Other Comic Tales." *Iraq* 55:63–75.
Gerleman, Gillis. 1974. "Der Nicht-Mensch: Erwägungen zur hebräischen Wurzel *N B L*." *VT* 24:147–58.

Gese, Hartmut. 1958. *Lehre und Wirklichkeit in der alten Weisheit: Studien zu den Sprüchen Salomos und zu dem Buche Hiob*. Tübingen: Mohr.

Gesenius, Wilhelm. 1854. *A Hebrew and English Lexicon of the Old Testament, Including the Biblical Chaldee*. Translated by Edward Robinson. 5th rev. ed. Boston: Crocker & Brewster.

Gilbert, Allan S. 2002. "The Native Fauna of the Ancient Near East." Pages 3–75 in *A History of the Animal World in the Ancient Near East*. Edited by Billie Jean Collins. HdO 64. Leiden: Brill.

Ginsburg, Eliezer, and Yosef Weinberger. 2007. *Mishlei/Proverbs: A New Translation with a Commentary Anthologized from Talmudic, Midrashic, and Rabbinic Sources*. Vol. 2. 6th ed. Artscroll Tanach. Rahway, NJ: Mesorah Publications.

Glazov, Gregory Yuri. 2002. "The Significance of the 'Hand on the Mouth' Gesture in Job Xl 4." *VT* 52:30–41.

Glück, J. J. 1964. "Proverbs 30:15a." *VT* 14:367–70.

Goff, Matthew J. 2007. *Discerning Wisdom: The Sapiential Literature of the Dead Sea Scrolls*. VTSup 116. Leiden: Brill.

———. 2013. *4QInstruction*. WLAW 2. Atlanta: Society of Biblical Literature.

———. 2019. "Wisdom." Pages 449–58 in *T&T Clark Companion to the Dead Sea Scrolls*. Edited by George J. Brooke and Charlotte Hempel. London: T&T Clark.

Goldingay, John. 1988. "'Holy Ones on High' in Daniel 7:18." *JBL* 107:495–97.

Good, Edwin M. 1965. *Irony in the Old Testament*. London: SPCK.

Goodenough, Erwin R. 1958. *Pagan Symbols in Judaism*. Vol. 8.2 in *Jewish Symbols in the Greco-Roman Period*. Bollingen Series 37. New York: Pantheon.

Gordon, Cyrus H. 1930. "Rabbinic Exegesis in the Vulgate of Proverbs." *JBL* 49:384–416.

———. 1965. *Ugaritic Textbook: Grammar, Texts in Transliteration, Cuneiform Selections, Glossary, Indices*. 3 vols. AnOr 38. Rome: Pontifical Biblical Institute.

Gordon, Edmund I. 1959. *Sumerian Proverbs: Glimpses of Everyday Life in Ancient Mesopotamia*. University Museum Monographs 19. Philadelphia: University Museum, University of Pennsylvania.

Graf, Karl Heinrich. 1862. *Der prophet Jeremia erklärt*. Leigzig: Weigel.

Greenberg, Moshe. 1983. *Ezekiel 1–20: A New Translation with Introduction and Commentary*. AB 22. Garden City, NY: Doubleday.

Greenfield, Jonas C. 1958. "Lexicographical Notes I." *HUCA* 29:203–28.
Greenspahn, Frederich. E. 1994. "A Mesopotamian Proverb and Its Biblical Reverberations." *JAOS* 114:33–38.
Greenstein, Edward L. 1992. "Humor and Wit: Old Testament." *ABD* 3:330–33.
———. 2003. "The Poem on Wisdom in Job 28 in Its Conceptual and Literary Contexts." Pages 253–80 in *Job 28: Cognition in Context*. Edited by Ellen van Wolde. BibInt 64. Leiden: Brill.
———. 2007. "Sages with a Sense of Humor: The Babylonian Dialogue between the Master and His Servant and the Book of Qoheleth." Pages 55–66 in *Wisdom Literature in Mesopotamia and Israel*. Edited by Richard J. Clifford. SymS 36. Atlanta: Society of Biblical Literature.
———. 2015. "Finding One's Way in Proverbs 30:18–19." Pages 261–68 in *Marbeh Hokmah: Studies in the Bible and the Ancient Near East in Loving Memory of Victor Avigdor Hurowitz*. Edited by Shamir Yonah, Edward L. Greenstein, Mayer I. Gruber, Peter Machinist, and Shalom M. Paul. 2 vols. Winona Lake, IN: Eisenbrauns.
Gruber, Mayer I. 1980. *Aspects of Nonverbal Communication in the Ancient Near East*. 2 vols. StPohl 12. Rome: Biblical Institute Press.
Gruen, Erich S. 2002. *Diaspora: Jews amidst Greeks and Romans*. Cambridge: Harvard University Press.
———. 2016. *Constructs of Identity in Hellenistic Judaism: Essays on Early Jewish Literature and History*. DCLS 29. Berlin: de Gruyter.
Gunkel, Hermann. 1906. "Die israelitische Literatur." Pages 51–102 in *Die Orientalischen Literaturen*. Vol. 1 of *Kultur der Gegenwart*. Edited by Paul Hinneberg. Berlin: Teubner.
Gunneweg, A. H. J. 1992. "Weisheit, Prophetie und Kanonformel: Erwägungen zu Proverbia 30,1–9." Pages 253–60 in *Alttestamentlicher Glaube und Biblische Theologie: Festschrift für Horst Dietrich Preuß zum 65. Geburtstag*. Edited by Jutta Hausmann and Hans-Jürgen Zobel. Stuttgart: Kohlhammer.
Habel, Norman C. 1985. *The Book of Job: A Commentary*. OTL. Philadelphia: Westminster.
Hackett, Jo Ann. 1984. "The Dialect of the Plaster Text from Tell Deir 'Alla." *Or* 53:57–65.
Ham, T. C. 2013. "The Gentle Voice of God in Job 38." *JBL* 132:527–41.
Hamilton, Victor P. 1980. "מתן." *TWOT* 1:536–37.
Haran, Menahem. 1972. "The Graded Numerical Sequence and the Phenomenon of 'Automatism' in Biblical Poetry." Pages 238–67 in *Inter-

national *Organization for the Study of the Old Testament: Congress Volume.* VTSup 22. Leiden: Brill.

Harding, G. Lankester. 1971. *An Index and Concordance of Pre-Islamic Arabian Names and Inscriptions.* NMES 8. Toronto: University of Toronto.

Hays, Christopher B. 2007. "Chirps from the Dust: The Affliction of Nebuchadnezzar in Daniel 4:30 in Its Ancient Near Eastern Context." *JBL* 126:305–25.

Healey, John F. 1991. *The Targum of Proverbs.* ArBib 15. Collegeville, MN: Liturgical Press.

Heim, Knut M. 2008. "A Closer Look at the Pig in Proverbs XI 22." *VT* 58:13–27.

———. 2001. *Like Grapes of Gold Set in Silver: An Interpretation of Proverbial Clusters in the Book of Proverbs.* BZAW 273. Berlin: de Gruyter.

Heiser, Michael S. 2004. "The Divine Council in Late Canonical and Noncanonical Second Temple Jewish Literature." PhD diss., University of Wisconsin-Madison.

Held, Moshe. 1958. "mḫṣ/*mḫš in Ugaritic and Other Semitic Languages: A Study in Comparative Lexicography." *JAOS* 79:169–76.

———. 1985. "Marginal Notes to the Biblical Lexicon." Pages 97–103 in *Biblical and Related Studies Presented to Samuel Iwry.* Edited by Ann Kort and Scott Morschauser. Winona Lake, IN: Eisenbrauns.

Hendel, Ronald. 2015. "The Untimeliness of Biblical Philology." *Philology* 1:9–28.

Herder, Hans-Peter. 1787. *Vom Geist der Ebräischen Poesie: Eine Anleitung für die Liebhaber derselben und der ältesten Geschichte des menschlichen Geistes.* Leipzig: Haug.

Hess, Johann Jacob. 1915. "Beduinisches zum Alten und Neuen Testament." *ZAW* 35:120–31.

Hoftijzer, Jacob, and Gerrit van der Kooij. 1976. *Aramaic Texts from Deir 'Alla.* DMOA 19. Leiden: Brill.

———, eds. 1991. *The Balaam Text from Deir 'Alla Re-Evaluated: Proceedings of the International Symposium Held at Leiden 21–24 August, 1989.* Leiden: Brill.

Holmes, R., and J. Parsons. 1823. *Vetus Testamentum Graecum cum Variis Lectionibus.* Vol. 3. Oxford: Clarendon.

Holmstedt, Robert D. 2014. "Critical at the Margins: Edge Constituents in Biblical Hebrew." *KUSATU* 17:109–56.

———. 2016. *The Relative Clause in Biblical Hebrew.* LSAWS 10. Winona Lake, IN: Eisenbrauns.

———. 2021a. "Introduction: Linguistic Theory and Philology in the Study of Biblical Hebrew." Pages 1–8 in *Linguistic Studies on Biblical Hebrew*. Edited by Robert D. Holmstedt. SStLL 102. Leiden: Brill.

———. 2021b. "Linguistics, Philology, and the Text of the Old Testament." Pages 21–45 in *James Barr Assessed: Evaluating His Legacy over the Last Sixty Years*. Edited by Stanley E. Porter. BibInt 192. Leiden: Brill.

Houlihan, Patrick F. 2001. *Wit and Humour in Ancient Egypt*. London: Rubicon.

Huehnergard, John. 2012. *An Introduction to Ugaritic*. Peabody, MA: Hendrickson.

Imes, Carmen Joy. 2018. *Bearing YHWH's Name at Sinai: A Reexamination of the Name Command of the Decalogue*. BBRSup 19. University Park, PA: Eisenbrauns.

Izenberg, Oren. 2012. "Persona." Pages 1024–25 in *The Princeton Encyclopedia of Poetry and Poetics*. Edited by Roland Greene. 4th ed. Princeton: Princeton University Press.

Jackson, Melissa A. 2012. *Comedy and Feminist Interpretation of the Hebrew Bible: A Subversive Collaboration*. OTM. Oxford: Oxford University Press.

Jahnow, Hedwig. 1923. *Das hebräische Leichenlied im Rahmen der Völkerdichtung*. BZAW 36. Gießen: Töpelmann.

Jarick, John. 2016a. "Ecclesiastes among the Comedians." Pages 176–88 in *Reading Ecclesiastes Intertextually*. Edited by Katharine J. Dell and Will Kynes. LHBOTS 587. London: T&T Clark.

———, ed. 2016b. *Perspectives on Israelite Wisdom: Proceedings of the Oxford Old Testament Seminar*. LHBOTS 618. London: T&T Clark.

Jasnow, Richard. 2001. "'And Pharaoh Laughed…' Reflections on Humor in Setne I and Late Period Egyptian Literature." *Enchoria* 27:62–81.

Jastrow, Marcus. 1903. *A Dictionary of the Targumim, the Talmud Babli and Yerushalmi, and the Midrashic Literature*. 2 vols. New York: Putnam.

Johnson, Benjamin J. M. 2022. "Humor in the Midst of Tragedy: The Comic Vision of 1 Samuel 4–6." *JBL* 141:65–82.

Johnston, Philip S. 2002. *Shades of Sheol: Death and Afterlife in the Old Testament*. Downers Grove, IL: IVP Academic.

Jones, Jordan W. 2019. *She Opens Her Hand to the Poor: Gestures and Social Values in Proverbs*. PHSC 30. Piscataway, NJ: Gorgias.

Jones, Scott C. 2011. "Lions, Serpents, and Lion-serpents in Job 28:8 and Beyond." *JBL* 130:663–86.

Jones, William R. 2012. "Satire." Pages 1255–58 in *The Princeton Encyclopedia of Poetry and Poetics*. Edited by Roland Greene. 4th ed. Princeton: Princeton University Press.

Judd, Andrew. 2024. *Playing with Scripture: Reading Contested Biblical Texts with Gadamer and Genre Theory*. Routledge Interdisciplinary Perspectives on Biblical Criticism. New York: Routledge.

Kamesar, Adam. 1990. "The Virgin of Isaiah 7:14: The Philological Argument from the Second to the Fifth Century." *JTS* 41:51–75.

Kaminsky, Joel S. 2000. "Humor and the Theology of Hope: Isaac as a Humorous Figure." *Int* 54: 363–75.

Keefer, Arthur J. 2016. "The Use of the Book of Proverbs in Systematic Theology." *BTB* 46:35–44.

Keel, Othmar. 1997. *The Symbolism of the Biblical World: Ancient Near Eastern Iconography and the Book of Psalms*. Translated by Timothy J. Hallett. Winona Lake, IN: Eisenbrauns.

Kennicott, Benjamin. 1780. *Vetus Testamentum Hebraicum cum variis lectionibus*. Oxford: Clarendon.

Kidner, Derek. 2008. *Proverbs: An Introduction and Commentary*. TOTC. Downers Grove, IL: InterVarsity Press.

Kim, Hyun Chul Paul. 2021. "The Oracles against the Nations." Pages 59–78 in *The Oxford Handbook of Isaiah*. Edited by Lena-Sofia Tiemeyer. Oxford: Oxford University Press.

Kister, Menahem. 2004. "Wisdom Literature and Its Relation to Other Genres: From Ben Sira to Mysteries." Pages 13–47 in *Sapiential Perspectives: Wisdom Literature in Light of the Dead Sea Scrolls; Proceedings of the Sixth International Symposium of the Orion Center for the Study of the Dead Sea Scrolls and Associated Literature, 20–22 May, 2001*. Edited by John J. Collins, Gregory E. Sterling, and Ruth A. Clements. STDJ 51. Leiden: Brill.

Kline, Joanna Greenlee. 2021. "Agur's Prayer (Proverbs 30:7–9): An Everyday Response to Extraordinary Revelation." Pages 238–52 in *Speaking with God: Probing Old Testament Prayers for Contemporary Significance*. Edited by Phillip G. Camp and Elaine A. Phillips. McMaster Biblical Studies 8. Eugene, OR: Wipf & Stock.

Krahmalkov, Charles R. 2000. *A Phoenician-Punic Grammar*. HdO 54. Leiden: Brill.

Kramer, Samuel N. 1947. "Gilgamesh and the Land of the Living." *JCS* 1:3–46.

Kronholm, Tryggve. 1999. "נָשַׁר." *TDOT* 10:77–85.

Kruger, Paul A. 2012. "A World Turned on Its Head in Ancient Near Eastern Prophetic Literature: A Powerful Strategy to Depict Chaotic Scenarios." *VT* 62:58–76.

Kuntz, J. Kenneth. 2001. "Sighting the Stern: The Impact of Chs. 30–31 on the Book of Proverbs as a Canonical Whole." *Proceedings of the Central States Society of Biblical Literature and the American Schools of Oriental Research* 4:121–41.

Kutsch, Ernst. 1952. "Die Wurzel עצר im Hebräischen." *VT* 2:57–69.

Kynes, Will. 2019. *An Obituary for "Wisdom Literature": The Birth, Death, and Intertextual Reintegration of a Biblical Corpus*. Oxford: Oxford University Press.

———, ed. 2021a. *The Oxford Handbook of Wisdom and the Bible*. Oxford: Oxford University Press.

———. 2021b. "Wisdom and Wisdom Literature: Past, Present, and Future." Pages 1–14 in *The Oxford Handbook of Wisdom and the Bible*. Edited by Will Kynes. Oxford: Oxford University Press.

Lakoff, George, and Mark Turner. 1989. *More Than Cool Reason: A Field Guide to Poetic Metaphor*. Chicago: University of Chicago Press.

Lambert, David A. 2016. "Refreshing Philology: James Barr, Supersessionism, and the State of Biblical Words." *BibInt* 24:332–56.

Lambert, Wilfred G. 1996. *Babylonian Wisdom Literature*. Winona Lake, IN: Eisenbrauns.

Lazaridis, Nikolaos. 2012. "Humor and Satire, Pharaonic Egypt." Pages 3338–41 in *The Encyclopedia of Ancient History*. Edited by Roger S. Bagnall, Kai Brodersen, Craige B. Champion, Andrew Erskine, and Sabine R. Huebner. 13 vols. Chichester: Wiley-Blackwell.

Lee, Jin Tae. 1973. "The Ugaritic Numeral and Its Use as a Literary Device." PhD. diss., Brandeis University.

Legaspi, Michael C. 2010. *The Death of Scripture and the Rise of Biblical Studies*. OSHT. Oxford: Oxford University Press.

Lehrman, S. R., trans. 1951. *Midrash Rabbah: Exodus*. Vol. 3. Edited by Harry Freedman and Maurice Simon. London: Soncino.

Lella, Alexander A. di, J. A. Emerton, and D. J. Lane, eds. 1979. *Proverbs, Wisdom of Solomon, Ecclesiastes, Song of Songs*. The Old Testament in Syriac according to the Peshitta Version 2.5. Leiden: Brill.

Levine, Baruch A. 1989. *Leviticus: The Traditional Hebrew Text with the New JPS Translation*. JPS Torah Commentary. Philadelphia: Jewish Publication Society.

Levine, Étan. 1990. "Qohelet's Fool: A Composite Portrait." Pages 277–94 in *On Humour and the Comic in the Hebrew Bible*. Edited by Yehuda T. Radday and Athalya Brenner. BLS 23. Sheffield: Almond Press.

———. 1997. "The Humor in Qohelet." *ZAW* 109:71–83.

Lichtheim, Miriam. 2006a. *The Late Period*. Vol. 3 of *Ancient Egyptian Literature: A Book of Readings*. Berkley: University of California Press.

———. 2006b. *The New Kingdom*. Vol. 2 of *Ancient Egyptian Literature: A Book of Readings*. Berkley: University of California Press.

———. 2006a. *The Old and Middle Kingdoms*. Vol. 1 of *Ancient Egyptian Literature: A Book of Readings*. Berkley: University of California Press.

Lied, Liv Ingeborg, and Hugo Lundhaug, eds. 2017. *Snapshots of Evolving Traditions: Jewish and Christian Manuscript Culture, Textual Fluidity, and New Philology*. TUGAL 175. Berlin: de Gruyter.

Lindenberger, J. M. 1985. "Ahiqar: A New Translation and Introduction." *OTP* 2:479–507.

Lipiński, Edward. 1994. *Studies in Aramaic Inscriptions and Onomastics II*. OLA 57. Leuven: Peeters.

Longman, Tremper, III. 2003. "Israelite Genres in Their Ancient Near Eastern Context." Pages 177–195 in *The Changing Face of Form Criticism for the Twenty-first Century*. Edited by Marvin A. Sweeney and Ehud Ben Zvi. Grand Rapids: Eerdmans.

Lovejoy, Arthur O. 1936. *The Great Chain of Being: A Study of the History of an Idea*. Cambridge: Harvard University Press.

Luria, S. 1929. "Die Ersten werden die Letzten sein." *Klio* 22:405–31.

Lyon, David G. 1920. "Crawford Howell Toy." *HTR* 13:1–22.

Machinist, Peter. 1983. "Assyria and Its Image in the First Isaiah." *JAOS* 103:719–37.

Marcus, David. 1995. *From Balaam to Jonah: Anti-Prophetic Satire in the Hebrew Bible*. BJS 301. Atlanta: Scholars Press.

Marno, David. 2012. "Tone." Pages 1441–42 in *The Princeton Encyclopedia of Poetry and Poetics*. Edited by Roland Greene. 4th ed. Princeton: Princeton University Press.

Maxwell, Nathan Dean. 2007. "The Psalmist in the Psalm: A Persona-Critical Reading of Book IV of the Psalter." PhD diss., Baylor University.

McKane, William. 1970. *Proverbs: A New Approach*. OTL. Philadelphia: Westminster.

———. 1980. "משא in Jeremiah 23 33–40." Pages 35–54 in *Prophecy: Essays Presented to Georg Fohrer on His Sixty-Fifth Birthday, 6 September 1980*. Edited by J. A. Emerton. BZAW 150. Berlin: de Gruyter.

Meade, John. 2017. "Hexaplaric Greek Translations." Pages 267–70 in *The Hebrew Bible: Writings*. Edited by Armin Lang and Emanuel Tov. THB 1C. Leiden: Brill.

Meek, Theophile James. 1960. "Translating the Hebrew Bible." *JBL* 79:328–35.

Meltzer, Edmund S. 1992. "Humor and Wit: Ancient Egypt." *ABD* 3:326–28.

Milgrom, Jacob. 2000. *Leviticus 17–22: A New Translation with Introduction and Commentary*. AB 3A. New York: Doubleday.

Millar, Suzanna R. 2020. "Openness, Closure, and Transformation in Proverb Translation." *BT* 71:79–100.

———. 2022. "The Multiple Genres of Wisdom." Pages 34–56 in *The Cambridge Companion to Biblical Wisdom Literature*. Edited by Katharine J. Dell, Suzanna R. Millar, and Arthur Jan Keefer. Cambridge: Cambridge University Press.

Miller, Carolyn R. 1984. "Genre as Social Action." *Quarterly Journal of Speech* 70: 151–67.

Miller, Cynthia L. 2005. "Ellipsis Involving Negation in Biblical Poetry." Pages 37–52 in *Seeking Out the Wisdom of the Ancients: Essays Offered to Honor Michael V. Fox on the Occasion of His Sixty-Fifth Birthday*. Edited by Ronald L. Troxel, Kelvin G. Friebel, and Dennis R. Magary. Winona Lake, IN: Eisenbrauns.

Moberly, R. W. L. 2013. *Old Testament Theology: Reading the Hebrew Bible as Christian Scripture*. Grand Rapids: Baker Academic.

Montanari, Franco. 2015. *The Brill Dictionary of Ancient Greek*. Edited by Madeleine Goh and Chad Schroeder. Leiden: Brill.

Montgomery. James A. 1934. *Arabia and the Bible*. Philadelphia: University of Pennsylvania.

Moore, Rick D. 1994. "A Home for the Alien: Worldly Wisdom and Covenantal Confession in Proverbs 30, 1–9." *ZAW* 106:96–107.

Morreall, John. 2009. "Humor as Cognitive Play." *Journal of Literary Theory* 3:241–60.

———. 2020. "Philosophy of Humor." In *The Stanford Encyclopedia of Philosophy*. Edited by Edward N. Zalta. https://tinyurl.com/SBL2653a.

Müller, Hans-Peter. 1970. "Der Begriff 'Rätsel' im Alten Testament." *VT* 20:465–89.

———. 1998. "מָשָׁא." *TDOT* 9:20–24.

Murphy, Roland E. 1998. *Proverbs*. WBC 22. Waco, TX: Word.

Najman, Hindy. 2017a. "Ethical Reading: The Transformation of the Text and the Self." *JTS* 68:507–29.

———. 2017b. "Jewish Wisdom in the Hellenistic Period: Towards the Study of a Semantic Constellation." Pages 459–72 in *Is There a Text in This Cave? Studies in the Textuality of the Dead Sea Scrolls in Honour of George J. Brooke*. Edited by Ariel Feldman, Maria Cioată, and Charlotte Hempel. STDJ 119. Leiden: Brill.

Najman, Hindy, Jean-Sébastien Rey, and Eibert J. C. Tigchelaar, eds. 2017. *Tracing Sapiential Traditions in Ancient Judaism*. JSJSup 174. Leiden: Brill.

Naudé, J. A. (Cobus). 1969. "*Maśśā'* in the Old Testament with Special Reference to the Prophets." *OTWSA* 12:91–100.

Naudé, Jacobus A, and Cynthia Miller-Naudé. 2020. "Linguistics and Philology—Separate, Overlapping or Subordinate/Superordinate Disciplines? Linguistic and Philological Perspectives: Papers Forming Part of the 2017 and 2018 SBL Linguistics and Biblical Hebrew Seminar." *JSem* 29. https://doi.org/10.25159/2663-6573/8573.

Newsom, Carol A. 1994. "The Moral Sense of Nature: Ethics in the Light of God's Speech to Job." *PSB* 15:9–27.

———. 2005. "Spying Out the Land: A Report from Genology." Pages 437–50 in *Seeking Out the Wisdom of the Ancients: Essays Offered to Honor Michael V. Fox on the Occasion of His Sixty-Fifth Birthday*. Edited by Ronald L. Troxel, Kelvin G. Friebel, and Dennis R. Magary. Winona Lake, IN: Eisenbrauns.

———. 2010. "Pairing Research Questions and Theories of Genre: A Case Study of the Hodayot." *DSD* 17:241–59.

Noegel, Scott B. 2021. *"Wordplay" in Ancient Near Eastern Texts*. ANEM 26. Atlanta: Society of Biblical Literature.

North, Francis Sparling. 1965. "The Four Insatiables." *VT* 15:281–82.

Noth, Martin. 1984. "The Holy Ones of the Most High." Pages 215–28 in *The Laws of the Pentateuch and Other Essays*. London: SCM.

Novenson, Matthew V. 2019. "Whose Son Is the Messiah?" Pages 72–84 in *Son of God: Divine Sonship in Jewish and Christian Antiquity*. Edited by Garrick V. Allen, Kai Akagi, Paul Sloan, and Madhavi Nevader. University Park, PA: Eisenbrauns.

O'Connor, Michael P. 2002. "Discourse Linguistics and the Study of Biblical Hebrew." Pages 17–42 in *Congress Volume Basel 2001*. Edited by André Lemaire. VTSup 92. Leiden: Brill.

O'Dowd, Ryan P. 2009. *The Wisdom of Torah: Epistemology in Deuteronomy and the Wisdom Literature*. FRLANT 225. Göttingen: Vandenhoeck & Ruprecht.

———. 2017. *Proverbs*. Story of God Bible Commentary 15. Grand Rapids: Zondervan.

———. 2018. "Poetic Allusions in Agur's Oracle in Proverbs 30.1–9." Pages 103–119 in *Inner Biblical Allusion in the Poetry of Psalms and Wisdom*. Edited by Kevin Chau, Mark Boda, and Beth Laneel Tanner. LHBOTS 659. London: T&T Clark.

Oesterly, W. O. E. 1927. *The Wisdom of Egypt and the Old Testament in the Light of the Newly Discovered 'Teaching of Amen-em-ope'*. London: SPCK.

———. 1929. *The Book of Proverbs: With Introduction and Notes*. London: Methuen & Co.

Olivero, Vladimir. 2021. "A Genealogy of Lust: The Use of Hesiod's Theogony in the LXX Translation of the Book of Proverbs." *Text* 30:28–42.

Orlemanski, Julie. 2015. "Philology and the Turn Away from the Linguistic Turn." *Florilegium* 32: 157–81.

Pardee, Dennis. 1999. "Eloah אלה." *DDD* 285–88.

Parker, Simon B. 1999. "Saints קדושים." *DDD* 718–20.

Passaro, Angelo. 2014. "The Words of Agur (Prov 30:1–9) and the Book of Proverbs: Some Historico-Anthropological Considerations." Pages 50–57 in *Wisdom for Life: Essays Offered to Honor Prof. Maurice Gilbert SJ on the Occasion of His Eightieth Birthday*. Edited by Nuria Calduch-Benages. BZAW 445. Berlin: de Gruyter.

Patton, Kimberley C. 2000. "'He Who Sits in the Heavens Laughs': Recovering Animal Theology in the Abrahamic Traditions." *HTR* 93:401–34.

Penar, Tadeusz. 1975. *Northwest Semitic Philology and the Hebrew Fragments of Ben Sira*. BibOr 28. Rome: Biblical Institute Press.

Perdue, Leo G. 2000. *Proverbs*. IBC. Louisville: John Knox.

Perks, Lisa Glebatis. 2012. "The Ancient Roots of Humor Theory." *Humor* 25:119–32.

Perry, T. Anthony. 2008. "Wisdom Begins in Wonder: The Riddle of Proverbs 30:18–20." Pages 157–73 in *God's Twilight Zone: Wisdom in the Hebrew Bible*. Peabody, MA: Hendrickson.

Peters, John P. 1914. "The Cock in the Old Testament." *JBL* 33:152–56.

Phillips, Anthony. 1975. "Nebalah: A Term for Serious Disorderly and Unruly Conduct." *VT* 25:237–42.

Plöger, Otto. 1984. *Sprüche Salomos (Proverbia)*. BKAT 17. Neukirchen-Vluyn: Neukirchener Verlag.
Polk, Timothy. 1983. "Paradigms, Parables and *Mĕšālîm*: on Reading the *Māšāl* in Scripture." *CBQ* 45:564–83.
———. 1984. *The Prophetic Persona: Jeremiah and the Language of the Self*. JSOTSup 32. Sheffield: JSOT Press.
Pollock, Sheldon. 2009. "Future Philology? The Fate of a Soft Science in a Hard World." *Critical Inquiry* 35:931–61.
———. 2014. "Philology in Three Dimensions." *postmedieval* 5:398–413.
Porten, Bezalel, and Ada Yardeni. 1989. *Contracts*. Vol. 2 of *Textbook of Aramaic Documents from Egypt*. Jerusalem: Hebrew University, Department of the History of the Jewish People.
———. 1993. *Literature, Accounts, Lists*. Vol. 3 of *Textbook of Aramaic Documents from Egypt*. Jerusalem: Hebrew University, Department of the History of the Jewish People.
Quick, Laura. 2019. "Clothed in Curses: Ritual, Curse and Story in the Deir 'Alla Plaster Inscription." Pages 95–109 in *To Gaul, to Greece and into Noah's Ark: Essays in Honour of Kevin J. Cathcart on the Occasion of His Eightieth Birthday*. Edited by Laura Quick, Ekaterina E. Kozlova, Sonja Noll, and Philip Y. Yoo. JSSSup 44. Oxford: Oxford University Press.
Rad, Gerhard von. 1970. *Weisheit in Israel*. Neukirchen-Vluyn: Neukirchener Verlag.
———. 1972. *Wisdom in Israel*. Translated by James D. Martin. London: SCM.
Radday, Yehuda T. 1990. "Esther with Humor." Pages 295–313 in *On Humour and the Comic in the Hebrew Bible*. Edited by Yehuda T. Radday and Athalya Brenner. BLS 23. Sheffield: Almond Press.
Radday, Yehuda T., and Athalya Brenner eds. 2003. *On Humour and the Comic in the Hebrew Bible*. BLS 23. Sheffield: Almond Press.
Richards, Eliza. 2012. "Voice." Pages 1525–27 in *The Princeton Encyclopedia of Poetry and Poetics*. Edited by Roland Greene. 4th ed. Princeton: Princeton University Press.
Richter, Hans-Friedemann. 2001. "Hielt Agur sich für den Dümmsten aller Menschen? (Zu Prov 30,1–4)." *ZAW* 113:419–21.
Rico, Christophe. 2007. "L'énigme aux chemins effacés: Pr 30,18–20." *RB* 114:273–77.
Ricoeur, Paul. 1976. *Interpretation Theory: Discourse and the Surplus of Meaning*. Fort Worth: Texas Christian University Press.

Riede, Peter. 2002. *Spiegel der Tiere: Studien zum Verhältnis von Mensch und Tier im alten Israel.* OBO 187. Fribourg: Academic Press; Göttingen: Vandenhoeck & Ruprecht.
Ringgren, Helmer. 1977. "בער." *TDOT* 2:201–5.
Roberts, J. J. M. 2015. *First Isaiah: A Commentary.* Hermeneia. Minneapolis: Fortress.
Rochettes, Jacqueline des. 1996. "Qohélet ou l'humour noir à la recherche de Dieu dans un contexte hébraïco-hellénique." Pages 49–71 in *L'Évangile exploré: Mélanges offerts à Simon Légasse à l'occasion de ses soixante-dix ans.* Edited by A. Marchadour. LD 166. Paris: Cerf.
Rogerson, John W. 1984. *Old Testament Criticism in the Nineteenth Century: England and Germany.* London: SPCK.
———. 2012. "Delitzsch, Franz Julius." *EBR* 6:497.
Roth, Wolfgang M. W. 1960. "NBL." *VT* 10:394–409.
———. 1962. "The Numerical Sequence x/x+1 in the Old Testament." *VT* 12:300–311.
———. 1965. *Numerical Sayings in the Old Testament.* VTSup 13. Leiden: Brill.
Rüger, Hans Peter. 1981. "Die gestaffelten Zahlensprüche des Alten Testaments und aram. Achikar 92." *VT* 31:229–34.
Sæbø, Magne. 2012. *Sprüche.* ATD 16.1. Göttingen: Vandenhoeck & Ruprecht.
Sallaberger, Walther. 2018. "Updating Primeval Wisdom: the Instructions of Šuruppak in Its Early Dynastic and Old Babylonian Contexts." Pages vii–xxviii in *In the Lands of Sumer and Akkad: New Studies; A Conference in Honor of Jacob Klein on the Occasion of His Eightieth Birthday.* Edited by Mordechai Cogan. Jerusalem: Israel Academy of Sciences and Humanities.
Samely, Alexander. 2013. "A New Framework for the Description of Ancient Jewish Literature." Pages 3–28 in *Profiling Jewish Literature in Antiquity: An Inventory, from Second Temple Texts to the Talmuds.* Edited by Alexander Samely, Philip Alexander, Rocco Bernasconi, and Robert Hayward. Oxford: Oxford University Press.
Samely, Alexander, Philip Alexander, Rocco Bernasconi, and Robert Hayward, eds. 2013. *Profiling Jewish Literature in Antiquity: An Inventory, from Second Temple Texts to the Talmuds.* Oxford: Oxford University Press.

Samet, Nili. 2011. "'The Tallest Man Cannot Reach Heaven; the Broadest Man Cannot Cover Earth': Reconsidering the Proverb and Its Biblical Parallels." *JHS* 10. https://doi.org/10.5508/jhs.2010.v10.a18.

———. 2021. "Redaction Patterns in Biblical Wisdom Literature in Light of the Instructions of Shuruppak." *ZAW* 133:208–24.

Sandoval, Timothy J. 2020a. "Agur's Words to God in Proverbs 30 and Prayerful Study in the Second Temple Period." Pages 83–114 in *Petitioners, Penitents, and Poets: On Prayer and Praying in Second Temple Judaism*. Edited by Timothy J. Sandoval and Ariel Feldman. BZAW 524. Berlin: de Gruyter.

———. 2020b. "Text and Intertexts: A Proposal for Understanding Proverbs 30.1b." *JSOT* 45:158–177.

Sauer, Georg. 1963. *Die Sprüche Agurs: Untersuchungen zur Herkunft, Verbreitung und Bedeutung einer biblischen Stilform unter besonderer Berücksichtigung von Proverbia c. 30*. BWANT 5.4. Stuttgart: Kohlhammer.

Saur, Markus. 2014. "Prophetie, Weisheit und Gebet: Überlegungen zu den Worten Agurs in Prov 30,1–9." *ZAW* 126:570–83.

Schellenberg, Annette. 2021a. "Epistemology: Wisdom, Knowledge, and Revelation." Pages 29–44 in *The Oxford Handbook of Wisdom and the Bible*. Edited by Will Kynes. Oxford: Oxford University Press.

———. 2021b. "'Wisdom Cries Out in the Street' (Prov 1:20): On the Role of Revelation in Wisdom Literature and the Relatedness and Differences between Sapiential and Prophetic Epistemologies." Pages 157–73 in *Scribes as Sages and Prophets: Scribal Traditions in Biblical Wisdom Literature and in the Book of the Twelve*. Edited by Jutta Krispenz. BZAW 496. Berlin: de Gruyter.

Schipper, Bernd U. 2013. "When Wisdom Is Not Enough! The Discourse on Wisdom and Torah and the Composition of the Book of Proverbs." Pages 55–79 in *Wisdom and Torah: The Reception of "Torah" in the Wisdom Literature of the Second Temple Period*. Edited by Bernd U. Schipper and D. Andrew Teeter. JSJSup 163. Leiden: Brill.

———. 2019. *Proverbs 1–15: A Commentary on the Book of Proverbs 1:1–15:33*. Translated by Stephen Germany. Hermeneia. Minneapolis: Fortress.

———. 2021. *The Hermeneutics of Torah: Proverbs 2, Deuteronomy, and the Composition of Proverbs 1–9*. Rev. ed. AIL 43. Atlanta: Society of Biblical Literature.

Schipper, Jeremy. 2009. *Parables and Conflict in the Hebrew Bible.* New York: Cambridge University Press.
Schneider, Heinrich. 1961. "Die Töchter des Blutgels in Spr 30,15." Pages 257–64 in *Lex Tua Veritas: Festschrift für Hubert Junker zur Vollendung des siebzigsten Lebensjahres am 8. August 1961, dargeboten von Kollegen, Freunden und Schülern.* Edited by Heinrich Gross and Franz Mussner. Trier: Paulinus.
Schneiders, Sandra M. 1999. *The Revelatory Text: Interpreting the New Testament as Sacred Scripture.* 2nd ed. Collegeville, MN: Liturgical Press.
Schökel, Luis Alonso. 1988. *A Manual of Hebrew Poetics.* SubBi 11. Rome: Pontifical Biblical Institute.
Schwáb, Zoltán. 2013. "Is Fear of the Lord the Source of Wisdom or Vice Versa?" *VT* 63:652–62.
Scott, R. B. Y. 1965. *Proverbs, Ecclesiastes: Introduction, Translation, and Notes.* AB 18. Garden City, NY: Doubleday.
Screnock, John. 2017. *Traductor Scriptor: The Old Greek Translation of Exodus 1–14 as Scribal Activity.* VTSup 174. Leiden: Brill.
Seitz, Christopher R. 1993. *Isaiah 1–39.* IBC. Louisville: John Knox.
———. 2005. "Canonical Approach." Pages 100–102 in *Dictionary for Theological Interpretation of the Bible.* Edited by Kevin J. Vanhoozer, Craig G. Bartholomew, Daniel J. Treier, and N. T. Wright. London: SPCK; Downers Grove, IN: IVP Academic.
Sherman, Phillip. 2020. "The Hebrew Bible and the 'Animal Turn.'" *CurBR* 19:36–63.
Shupak, Nili. 2005. "The Instruction of Amenemope and Proverbs 22:17–24:22 from the Perspective of Contemporary Research." Pages 203–20 in *Seeking Out the Wisdom of the Ancients: Essays Offered to Honor Michael V. Fox on the Occasion of His Sixty-Fifth Birthday.* Edited by Ronald L. Troxel, Kelvin G. Friebel, and Dennis R. Magary. Winona Lake, IN: Eisenbrauns.
Siebenthal, Heinrich von. 2009. "'Collectives' in Ancient Hebrew: A Closer Look at the Semantics of an Intriguing Noun Category." *KUSATU* 10:67–81.
Siedlecki, Armin. 2003. "The Literature of Ancient Israel by Hermann Gunkel." Pages 26–83 in *Relating to the Text: Interdisciplinary and Form-Critical Insights on the Bible.* Edited by Timothy Sandoval and Carleen Mandolfo. JSOTSup 384. London: T&T Clark.
Sjöberg, Åke W. 1972. "'He Is a Good Seed of a Dog' and 'Engardu the Fool.'" *JCS* 24:107–19.

Skehan, Patrick W. 1971. *Studies in Israelite Poetry and Wisdom*. CBQMS 1. Washington, DC: Catholic Biblical Association of America.

Skehan, Patrick W., and Alexander A. Di Lella. 1987. *The Wisdom of Ben Sira*. AB 39. New York: Doubleday.

Smend, Rudolf. 1995. "The Interpretation of Wisdom in Nineteenth-Century Scholarship." Pages 257–68 in *Wisdom in Ancient Israel: Essays in Honour of J. A. Emerton*. Edited by John Day, Robert P. Gordon, and H. G. M. Williamson. Cambridge: Cambridge University Press.

———. 2007. *From Astruc to Zimmerli*. Translated by Margaret Kohl. Tübingen: Mohr Siebeck.

———. 2014. "Ewald, Georg Heinrich August." *EBR* 8:360.

Smith, Mark S., and Wayne T. Pitard. 2009. *Introduction with Text, Translation and Commentary of KTU/CAT 1.3–1.4*. Vol. 2 of *The Ugaritic Baal Cycle*. VTSup 114. Leiden: Brill.

Sneed, Mark R. 2011. "Was There a Wisdom Tradition?" *CBQ* 73:50–71.

———, ed. 2015. *Was There a Wisdom Tradition? New Prospects in Israelite Wisdom Studies*. AIL 23. Atlanta: SBL Press.

———. 2018. "Methods, Muddles, and Modes of Literature: The Question of Influence between Wisdom and Prophecy." Pages 30–44 in *Riddles and Revelations: Explorations in the Relationship between Wisdom and Prophecy in the Hebrew Bible*. Edited by Mark J. Boda, Russell L. Meek, and William R. Osborne. LHBOTS 634. London: T&T Clark.

———. 2021. "Inspired Sages: *Massaʾ* and the Confluence of Wisdom and Prophecy." Pages 15–32 in *Scribes as Sages and Prophets: Scribal Traditions in Biblical Wisdom Literature and in the Book of the Twelve*. Edited by Jutta Krispenz. BZAW 496. Berlin: de Gruyter.

Sokoloff, Michael. 1990. *A Dictionary of Jewish Palestinian Aramaic of the Byzantine Period*. Ramat-Gan: Bar-Ilan University Press.

———. 2002. *A Dictionary of Jewish Babylonian Aramaic of the Talmudic and Geonic Periods*. Ramat-Gan: Bar-Ilan University Press; Baltimore: Johns Hopkins University Press.

———. 2009. *A Syriac Lexicon: A Translation from the Latin, Correction, Expansion, and Update of C. Brockelmann's "Lexicon Syriacum."* Winona Lake, IN: Eisenbrauns; Piscataway, NJ: Gorgias.

Southwood, Katherine E. 2021. *Job's Body and the Dramatised Comedy of Moralising*. Routledge Studies in the Biblical World. London: Routledge.

———. 2022. "Comical Moments and Comical Characterisations in Tobit: The Undermining of Self-righteous Piety, Simplistic Retribution, and Limited Yahwism." *JSOT* 46:443–59.
Staubli, Thomas. 2019. "Feces: The Primary Disgust Elicitor in the Hebrew Bible and the Ancient Near East." Pages 119–43 in *Sounding Sensory Profiles in the Ancient Near East*. Edited by Annette Schellenberg and Thomas Krüger. ANEM 25. Atlanta: SBL Press.
Steinberg, Julius. 2018. "Reading Proverbs as a Book in the Writings." Pages 181–98 in *The Oxford Handbook of the Writings of the Hebrew Bible*. Edited by Donn F. Morgan. Oxford: Oxford University Press.
Steiner, Richard S. 1997. "The Aramaic Text in Demotic Script (1.99)." *COS* 1:309–27.
Steinmann, Andrew E. 1995. "The Graded Numerical Saying in Job." Pages 288–97 in *Fortunate the Eyes That See: Essays in Honor of David Noel Freedman in Celebration of His Seventieth Birthday*. Edited by Astrid B. Beck, Andrew H. Bartelt, Paul R. Raabe, and Chris A. Franke. Grand Rapids: Eerdmans.
———. 2001. "Three Things … Four Things … Seven Things: The Coherence of Proverbs 30:11–33 and the Unity of Proverbs 30." *HS* 42:59–66.
———. 2009. *Proverbs*. ConcC. Saint Louis: Concordia.
Stewart, Anne W. 2016. *Poetic Ethics in Proverbs: Wisdom Literature and the Shaping of the Moral Self*. Cambridge: Cambridge University Press.
Stier, Rudolf. 1850. *Die Politik der Weisheit in den Worten Agur's und Lemuel's Sprüchwörter Kap. 30 und 31*. Barmen: Langewiesche.
Stolz, F. 1997. "נשׂא." *TLOT* 2:769–74.
Strawn, Brent A. 2005. *What Is Stronger Than a Lion? Leonine Image and Metaphor in the Hebrew Bible and the Ancient Near East*. OBO 212. Fribourg: Academic Press; Göttingen: Vandenhoeck & Ruprecht.
Strugnell, John, Daniel J. Harrington, and Torleif Elgvin. 1999. *Sapiential Texts, Part 2: Cave 4.XXIV*. DJD XXXIV. Oxford: Clarendon.
Sutcliffe, Edmund F. 1960. "The Meaning of Proverbs 30:18–20." *ITQ* 27:125–31.
Sweeney, Marvin A. 1996. *Isaiah 1–39: With an Introduction to Prophetic Literature*. FOTL. Grand Rapids: Eerdmans.
Sweeney, Marvin A., and Ehud Ben Zvi, eds. 2003. *The Changing Face of Form Criticism for the Twenty-First Century*. Grand Rapids: Eerdmans.
Swete, Henry Barclay. 1891. *The Old Testament in Greek according to the Septuagint*. Cambridge: Cambridge University Press.

Talmon, Shemaryahu. 1960. "Double Readings in the Masoretic Text." *Text* 1:144–84.
Teeter, D. Andrew, and William A. Tooman. 2020. "Standards of (In)coherence in Ancient Jewish Literature." *HBAI* 9:94–129.
Thomas, D. Winton. 1939. "The Root אָהֵב 'Love' in Hebrew." *ZAW* 57:57–64.
———. 1941. "A Note on לִיקְּהַת in Proverbs xxx. 17." *JTS* 42:154–55.
———. 1960. "Textual and Philological Notes on Some Passages in the Book of Proverbs." Pages 280–92 in *Wisdom in Israel and in the Ancient Near East: Presented to Harold Henry Rowley by the Society for Old Testament Study in Association with the Editorial Board of Vetus Testamentum, in Celebration of His Sixty-Fifth Birthday, 24 March 1955*. Edited by D. Winton Thomas and Martin Noth. VTSup 3. Leiden: Brill.
———. 1965. "Notes on Some Passages in the Book of Proverbs." *VT* 15:271–79.
Thomas, Samuel I. 2019. "Mysteries." Pages 329–31 in *T&T Clark Companion to the Dead Sea Scrolls*. Edited by George J. Brooke and Charlotte Hempel. London: T&T Clark.
Tolkien, J. R. R. 1997. "Beowulf: The Monsters and the Critics." Pages 5–48 in *The Monsters and the Critics and Other Essays*. Edited by Christopher Tolkien. London: HarperCollins.
Toorn, Karel van der. 2007. *Scribal Culture and the Making of the Hebrew Bible*. Cambridge: Harvard University Press.
Torczyner, Harry (N. H. Tur-Sinai). 1924. "The Riddle in the Bible." *HUCA* 1:125–49.
Torrey, Charles C. 1954. "Proverbs, Chapter 30." *JBL* 73:93–96.
Tov, Emanuel. 1990. "Recensional Differences between the Masoretic Text and the Septuagint of Proverbs." Pages 43–56 in *Of Scribes and Scrolls: Studies on the Hebrew Bible, Intertestamental Judaism, and Christian Origins, Presented to John Strugnell on the Occasion of His Sixtieth Birthday*. Edited by Harold W. Attridge, John J. Collins, and Thomas H. Tobin. Resources in Religion 5. Lanham, MD: University Press of America.
———. 2015. *The Text-Critical Use of the Septuagint in Biblical Research*. 3rd ed. Winona Lake, IN: Eisenbrauns.
Toy, Crawford H. 1899. *A Critical and Exegetical Commentary on the Book of Proverbs*. ICC. Edinburgh: T&T Clark.
Tristram, Henry Baker. 1867. *The Natural History of the Bible: Being a Review of the Physical Geography, Geology, and Meteorology of the Holy*

Land, with a Description of Every Animal and Plant Mentioned in Holy Scripture. London: Society for Promoting Christian Knowledge.

———. 2013. *The Fauna and Flora of Palestine*. Cambridge: Cambridge University Press, 1884. Repr., Cambridge: Cambridge University Press.

Turner, James. 2014. *Philology: The Forgotten Origins of the Modern Humanities*. Princeton: Princeton University Press.

Ullendorff, Edward. 1979. "The Bawdy Bible." *BSOAS* 42:425–56.

Van Leeuwen, Raymond C. 1986. "Proverbs 30:21–23 and the Biblical World Upside Down." *JBL* 105:599–610.

———. 1997a. "The Background to Proverbs 30:4aα." Pages 102–21 in *Wisdom, You Are My Sister: Studies in Honor of Roland E. Murphy, O. Carm., on the Occasion of His Eightieth Birthday*. Edited by Michael L. Barré. CBQMS 29. Washington, DC: Catholic Biblical Association of America.

———. 1997b. "The Book of Proverbs: Introduction, Commentary, and Reflections." *NIB* 5:17–264.

———. 2003. "Form Criticism, Wisdom, and Psalms 111–112." Pages 65–84 in *The Changing Face of Form Criticism for the Twenty-First Century*. Edited by Marvin A. Sweeney and Ehud Ben Zvi. Grand Rapids: Eerdmans.

Vancil, Jack W. 1992. "Goat, Goatherd." *ABD* 2:1040–41.

Vattioni, Francesco. 1965. "Proverbes, XXX, 15–16." *RB* 72:515–19.

Vayntrub, Jacqueline E. 2016. "'To Take Up a Parable': The History of Translating a Biblical Idiom." *VT* 66:627–45.

———. 2019. *Beyond Orality: Biblical Poetry on Its Own Terms*. Ancient World. London: Routledge.

Veenker, Ronald A. 1999–2000. "Forbidden Fruit: Ancient Near Eastern Sexual Metaphors." *HUCA* 70/71:57–73.

Visotzky, Burton L. 1992. *The Midrash on Proverbs*. YJS 27. New Haven: Yale University Press.

Vycichl, W. 1983. "Histoire de chats et de souris: Un Problème de la littérature égyptienne." *Bulletin de la Société de Égyptologie de Genève* 8:101–8.

Waard, Jan de. 1993. "Metathesis as a Translation Technique?" Pages 249–60 in *Traducere navem: Festschrift für Katharina Reiss Zum 70. Geburtstag*. Edited by Justa Holz-Mänttäri and Christiane Nord. Studia Translatologica 3. Tampere: University of Tampere Press.

———, ed. 2008. *Proverbs*. BHQ 17. Stuttgart: Deutsche Bibelgesellschaft,.

Waltke, Bruce K. 2004. *The Book of Proverbs: Chapters 1–15*. NICOT. Grand Rapids: Eerdmans.

———. 2005. *The Book of Proverbs: Chapters 15–31*. NICOT. Grand Rapids: Eerdmans.

Watanabe, Chikako E. 2002. *Animal Symbolism in Mesopotamia: A Contextual Approach*. WOO 1. Vienna: Institut für Orientalistik der Universität Wien.

Watson, Wilfred G. E. 1984. *Classical Hebrew Poetry: A Guide to Its Techniques*. JSOTSup 26. Sheffield: JSOT Press.

———. 1990. "Ugaritic Onomastics (1)." *AuOr* 8:113–27.

———. 2003. "Ugaritic Onomastics (7)." *AuOr* 21:243–48.

Webb, Barry G. 2012. *The Book of Judges*. NICOT. Grand Rapids: Eerdmans.

Weber, Robert, and Roger Gryson. 2007. *Biblia Sacra Iuxta Vulgatum*. 5th ed. Stuttgart: Deutsche Bibelgesellschaft.

Weeks, Stuart. 1994. *Early Israelite Wisdom*. OTM. Oxford: Oxford University Press.

———. 2007. *Instruction and Imagery in Proverbs 1–9*. Oxford: Oxford University Press.

———. 2010a. *An Introduction to the Study of Wisdom*. T&T Clark Approaches to Biblical Studies. London: T&T Clark.

———. 2010b. "Predictive and Prophetic Literature: Can *Neferti* Help Us Read the Bible?" Pages 25–46 in *Prophecy and the Prophets in Ancient Israel: Proceedings of the Oxford Old Testament Seminar*. Edited by John Day. LHBOTS 531. London: T&T Clark.

———. 2012. *Ecclesiastes and Scepticism*. LHBOTS 541. London: T&T Clark.

———. 2013. "The Limits of Form Criticism in the Study of Literature, with Reflections on Psalm 34." Pages 15–25 in *Biblical Interpretation and Method: Essays in Honour of John Barton*. Edited by Katharine J. Dell and Paul M. Joyce. Oxford: Oxford University Press.

———. 2015. "Wisdom, Form and Genre." Pages 161–177 in *Was There a Wisdom Tradition? New Prospects in Israelite Wisdom Studies*. AIL 23. Edited by Mark R. Sneed. Atlanta: SBL Press.

———. 2016. "Is 'Wisdom Literature' a Useful Category?" Pages 3–23 in *Tracing Sapiential Traditions in Ancient Judaism*. Edited by Hindy Najman, Jean-Sébastien Rey, and Eibert J. C. Tigchelaar. JSJSup 174. Leiden: Brill.

———. 2020. *Ecclesiastes 1–5: A Critical and Exegetical Commentary*. ICC. London: T&T Clark.
———. 2021. *Ecclesiastes 5–12: A Critical and Exegetical Commentary*. Vol. 2. ICC. London: T&T Clark.
Weis, Richard. 1986. "A Definition of the Genre Maśśā' in the Hebrew Bible." PhD diss., Claremont Graduate School.
Westermann, Claus. 1995. *Roots of Wisdom: The Oldest Proverbs of Israel and Other Peoples*. Louisville: Westminster John Knox.
Whedbee, William. 1998. *The Bible and the Comic Vision*. Cambridge: Cambridge University Press.
Whitekettle, Richard. 2012. "The Leech Sisters: Greed and Sibling Conflict in Proverbs 30,15a." *BZ* 56:93–95.
Whybray, R. N. 1974. *The Intellectual Tradition in the Old Testament*. BZAW 135. Berlin: de Gruyter.
———. 1994a. *Proverbs*. NCB. Grand Rapids: Eerdmans.
———. 1994b. *The Composition of the Book of Proverbs*. JSOTSup 168. Sheffield: JSOT Press.
———. 1998. *Job*. Readings. Sheffield: Sheffield Academic.
Williamson, H. G. M. 1994. *The Book Called Isaiah: Deutero-Isaiah's Role in Composition and Redaction*. Oxford: Oxford University Press.
———. 2020. "Animals or Demons in Isaiah 13:21–22." Pages 227–35 in *Fortgeschriebenes Gotteswort: Studien zu Geschichte, Theologie und Auslegung des Alten Testaments: Festschrift für Christoph Levin zum 70. Geburtstag*. Edited by Reinhard Müller, Urmas Nõmmik, and Juha Pakkala. Tübingen: Mohr Siebeck.
Wise, Michael O., Martin G. Abegg, and Edward M. Cook. 2005. *The Dead Sea Scrolls: A New Translation*. Rev. ed. New York: Harper Collins.
Wolff, Hans Walter. 1974. *Hosea: A Commentary on the Book of the Prophet Hosea*. Hermeneia. Philadelphia: Fortress.
Wright, Benjamin G., III. 1989. *No Small Difference: Sirach's Relationship to Its Hebrew Parent Text*. SCS 26. Atlanta: Scholars Press.
———. 2011. "Translation Greek in Sirach in Light of the Grandson's Prologue." Pages 73–94 in *The Texts and Versions of the Book of Ben Sira: Transmission and Interpretation*. Edited by Jean-Sébastien Rey and Jan Joosten. JSJSup 150. Leiden: Brill.
Yaron, Reuven. 1958. "Aramaic Marriage Contracts from Elephantine." *JSS* 3:1–39.
Yee, Gale A. 1988. "The Anatomy of Biblical Parody: The Dirge Form in 2 Samuel 1 and Isaiah 14." *CBQ* 50:565–86.

Yoder, Christine R. 2009a. "On the Threshold of Kingship: A Study of Agur (Proverbs 30)." *Int* 63:254–63.

———. 2009b. *Proverbs*. AOTC. Nashville: Abingdon.

Young, Ian. 2013. "Collectives: Biblical Hebrew." Pages 477–79 in vol. 1 of *Encyclopedia of Hebrew Language and Linguistics*. Edited by Geoffrey Khan. 4 vols. Leiden: Brill.

Zimmerli, Walther. 1933. "Zur Struktur der alttestamentlichen Weisheit." *ZAW* 51:177–204.

———. 1964. "The Place and Limit of Wisdom in the Framework of Old Testament Theology." *SJT* 17:146–158.

Ancient Sources Index

Hebrew Bible/Old Testament		29:33	183, 237–38
		30:1	171, 230
Genesis		30:2	249
1:1–2:3	56	30:26	230
1:27	155	30:35	246
2	155	31:39	138
2–3	56	32:8	241
4:19	230	32:14	246
5:1–2	128	32:28–30	127
5:24	118	33:1	241
7:2	168	34:7	236
8:6	173	37:33	155
11:3	230	28:16	230
11:4–5	118	38:33	138
11:6	195	39:12	137
13:7	197, 230	39:19	249
16:2	231	42:16	124
16:9	183	42:22	197
18:14	177	42:30	85
19:11	107	44:28	138
20:3	238	45:17	113
20:18	231	45:28	134
22:3	155	47:21	140
22:6	169	48:5–6	128
22:10	169	48:16	128
24:19	155	49:6	249
24:43	234	49:10	63
25:14	35, 70–72		
25:25–26	127	Exodus	
27:4	134	1:9	188
27:36	127	1:10	230
27:45	249	2:8	234
28:12–13	6	3:13	127
28:12–15	119–20	3:20	177
29:31	183, 237–38	4:22	65, 128–29

Ancient Sources Index

Exodus (cont.)		19	11
5:2	137, 227	19:3	167
7:18	107	20:9	172
9:8	120–21	22:28	155
10:12–14	189	25:2–7	155
12:9	239		
12:34	120–21	Numbers	79–80
15:8	180	4	74
15:11	177	11:11	75–76
19:4	173	11:13	230
19:11	118–19	11:17	75–76
19:18	118–19	11:25	119
19:20	118–19	11:28	128
20:1–17	119	12:5	119
20:7	135	12:13	100
20:12	167	13:28	187
20:24	127	15:40	224
21:17	172	16:14	173
21:27	169	17:13–15	231
22:4	113	17:25	128, 233
24:43	234	20:4	113
28:42	244	21:6	179
29:4	168	22–24	82
31:18	214	22:6	188
33:18–19	127	22:19–29	82
34:5	119	23:7	85
34:6–7	127	23:9	179
34:6	249	23:18	85
34:10	177	24:2–3	85–86
39:32	100	24:4	227
		24:15–16	85–87
Leviticus		24:20	85
4:23	246	24:21	85, 188
5:7	23	24:23	85
5:11	23	31:27	241
7:24	138		
10:6	112	Deuteronomy	49, 225
10:10	168	1:12	75–76
11	155	1:31	214
11:5	240	4	144
11:13	172	4:1	141
11:15	172	4:1–2	143
11:30	242	4:1–8	141, 143
14:8	168	4:2	6, 110, 141, 143, 226
16:2	120	4:3–6	141

4:8	141	30:10	119
5:11	135	30:11	177
5:16	167	30:12	119
6:1–2	143	30:14	119
6:11	136	31:20	137
8:5	129, 214	32:5–6	128
8:10	137	32:6	128, 214, 237
8:12	137	32:15	226, 236, 248
8:15	179	32:17	226
9:7	137	32:19	65
9:9	214	32:27	65
9:21	243	32:31	112
11:2	214	33:11	244
11:15	137	33:29	137
11:17	231		
13:1	141	Joshua	
13:15	243	7:15	236–37
14:1	128	9:9	127
14:7	240		
14:12	172	Judges	
14:14	172	2:15	241
14:29	137	5:11	241
15:11	169	5:20	231
17:4	243	6:5	188
17:8	197	6:38	249
19:18	243	7:16	241
21:13	238	9:43	241
21:15–17	237–38	13:15–16	231
21:18–21	172	13:17–18	127
21:23	172	14:14	149
22:6–7	155	14:18	149, 187
22:10	155	16:21	173
22:21	236–37	18:7	231
22:22	238	18:19	195
22:28	137	19:23	236, 248
23:13–14	168	19:24	236
23:16	140	19:29	169
24:1	238	20:6–10	236–37
24:14	169		
25:2	64	Ruth	
25:6	128	1:4	230
26:12	137	1:20	127
28:25	241	2:14	136
28:39	63	4:10	128
28:58	127		

1 Samuel		4:29–34	67
2:10	121	4:30	64
3	82	5:10	71–72, 107
3:14–17	81	5:13	43
9:17	231	8:9	214
9:21	239	8:37	188
11:2	173	8:41–45	127
14:32	233	10:1	149
14:33	104	11:8	137
14:52	128	12:10	244
16:17	190, 243	15:22	104–5
17:56	234	17:6	173
20:22	234	18:40	137
25:17	64	18:46	244
25:23–27	237	20:35	128
25:25	127	21:19–21	76
26:16	233	21:24	172
2 Samuel		2 Kings	
1:19–27	91	2:1	118
1:21	248	2:11	118
1:23	192	5:17	74
6:13	244	9	81, 83
13:12	236	9:25–26	75–76, 87
13:13	237	11:18	243
13:16	248	14:7	137
15:33	75–76	16:7	128
16:1–4	140	18:7	241
19:26–28	140	19:4	227
19:36	75	19:22	168, 224
20:8	244	24:15	192
21:10	172		
22:10	118	1 Chronicles	
22:31	6, 109–10, 225	1:30	35, 70–71
22:31–32	225	4:22	238
22:45	137	9:30	128
23:1	86–87, 100	15:22	70
23:1–2	87	15:27	70
1 Kings		2 Chronicles	
1:5	195	7:13	231
2:25	195	17:11	70, 78, 246
2:34	195	19:7	70, 78
3	212	22:9	231
3:12–13	136	24:27	75–76

32:15	226	21:21	241
35:3	224	25:4–6	113
35:7	233	25:6	155
		26:8	120
Ezra		27:1	85
4:16	97	28	14
5:17	97	28–41	38, 123
6:9	233	28:38	43
		29:1	85
Nehemiah		29:9	195–96
4:18	244	29:17	139, 169
9:13	119	30:1	155
9:17	226	30:8	183
11:7	66, 95, 97, 105	30:29	155
13:15	79	31:23	96, 107
13:19	79	32:8–9	212
		33	151
Esther		33:14–29	149
7:3–8:2	140	33:21	100
7:9–10	140	33:25	234
		35:11	239
Job 4, 14, 30, 38, 54, 67, 125, 156, 164,		37:5	177
177, 214, 226		38	56, 121, 123–26, 144
1:1	71	38–41	44, 124
2:11	71–72	38:4–5	124
3:1	196	38:4–11	120–21
4	107	38:4	124–25
4:2	100–101, 107	38:5	123, 225
4:5	107	38:8	125
4:11	233, 244	38:18–19	125
5	151	38:33	125
5:1	224	38:37	125
5:9	177	38–39	156–57
5:19–22	149	39:22	191
7:1–6	196	39:27–30	179
7:20	76	39:28	188
9:10	177	40:4	45, 125, 195–96
11:7–12	157	40:16	244, 246
12:7–10	157	42:1–6	126
12:18	244	42:3	125, 177
16:8	137	42:5	125
18:3	155	42:8	237
20:4–7	118		
20:11	234	Psalms	17, 54, 145
21:5	195	2:7	128

Psalms (cont.)

2:8	121	50:8	112
7:2	192	50:10–11	156
8:6–8	155	50:22	226
12:2	135	52:6	173
12:9	170, 229	52:9	136
14:1	237	53:2	237
14:4	169	55:23	230
16:3	224	56:5	169
17:12	192	58:6	239–40
18	132, 144	58:7	169
18:3	188	59:7	155
18:9	118	62:12–13	148
18:18	187	64:6	227
18:28	168	64:7	239
18:30	6, 132	66:3	137
18:31	109–10, 225	68:26	234
18:31–32	225	69:24	244
18:32	226	71:22	224
18:44	137, 197	72:8	121
15:50	127	73	42, 44, 113–15, 117, 144, 184
19	17	73:1	114
20	15	73:2–3	114–15, 186
22:7	113, 155	73:10	249
22:13	192	73:12–13	114
23	68, 115	73:18–28	114
23:4	111	73:22	100, 113, 115, 155
24:4	135	73:23–28	115
27:4	134	74:14	187
28:1	91	77:19	183
29:6	157	78:12	177
31:14	195	78:15	179
32:1	66, 84	78:41	224
33:3	190, 243	78:48	113
34	17, 207	78:52	157
34:10	224	83:2	100
37:12	195	89:6–7	224
37:13	173	89:19	224
38:5	85	89:24	234
39:8	237	92:7	113
46:2	180	94:8	113
49:7	136	94:10	212
49:11	113	94:16	248
49:13	91, 113	99:1	186, 229
49:21	91	101:4–5	139
		101:5	96, 107

103:13	128	1:25	122
104	155	1:26	173
104:2–6	120	2:1	129, 214
104:14	157	2:1–4	116
104:17–20	155	2:5–6	116
104:18	188, 240	2:6	212–13
104:21	156	2:8	122
104:25–26	179	2:13	122
104:27	157	2:15	122
105:22	239	2:17	235
105:41	179	2:19–21	122
106:7	177	3:1	129, 214
107:39	231	3:3	209, 214
109:23	188	3:5–7	209, 212, 215
109:24	137	3:6	122
111:5	138	3:11–12	129, 214
112:3	136	3:16	136
114:4	233	3:19–20	212
114:6	233	3:34	211
114:7	226	4:2	214
118:12	155	4:4	214
119:8	239	4:12	190, 244
123:2	183	4:19	122
131:1	168, 177, 182	5:3	181
139:6	107	5:5	244
139:14	177	5:15	181
139:19	226	5:18–19	157, 235
139:20	135	6:1–19	153
140:9	195	6:5	157
141:5	227	6:6	157, 187, 240
144:5	118	6:6–8	187
145–150	56	6:8	63
147:9	156–57, 233	6:11	136
		6:12	154
Proverbs		6:16	44
1:1	8, 14, 67, 69, 212	6:16–19	34, 148, 152–53, 211
1:2	116	6:17	153, 168
1:6	149	6:18–19	153
1:7	143	6:20	129, 214
1:8	214	6:23	214
1:10	129	7	19
1:12	171	7:1–3	214
1:17	157–58	7:8	243
1:20–21	212	7:22–23	157
1:23	122, 213	8	36

Proverbs (cont.)

8:2–3	212–13	19:10	183
8:13	211	19:12	157, 192
8:14	121	19:16	214
8:18	136	19:20–21	122
8:22–31	212–13	19:25	227
9:9	122	19:26	167
9:10	116, 143, 212, 224	20:2	157, 192
9:17	181	20:9	168, 214
10:1	8, 19, 67, 69, 167, 212	20:12	212
10:1–22:16	9–10, 19	20:13	183
10:5	63	20:20	167
10:8	214	20:24	211
10:9	122	21:2	168, 211
10:15	136, 209	21:9	185
10:23	195	21:14	187
11:2	211	21:19	185
11:22	157, 163	21:27	195
11:28	136	21:30	211
12:1	113	22–24	40
12:9–14	69	22:1	136
12:10	157	22:4	136, 211
12:11	183	22:13	157–58
12:15	122, 168, 210	22:17	8, 19
12:28	248	22:17–24:24	8–11, 71, 122
13:13–14	214	22:19	122
13:18	136	22:20	10
14:12	122, 210	22:21	122
14:14	157	23:5	157, 179
14:17	249	23:19	129
14:24	136	23:22	232
15:2	190, 243	23:25	167, 230
15:7	157	23:32	157
15:17	158	23:34	180
15:33	211–12	24:9	195
16:1	213	24:21	129
16:1–9	211	24:22	22
16:2	168	24:23	8, 69
16:8	89	24:23–34	22, 24
16:9	243–44	24:34	136
16:18	211	25:1	8, 67, 69, 212
16:25	210	25:1–29:27	9, 22
17:12	157–58	25:24	185
18:11	209	26:2–3	157–58
18:12	211	26:4–5	209
		26:5	210

26:8	120	30:1-9	6, 13, 23, 48, 144, 203, 208, 212
26:11	157		
26:12	210-11	30:1-10	115, 147, 215
26:13	157-58	30:1-14	4, 22-24, 33-35, 42
26:13-16	164	30:1-33	9, 24-25
26:14	164	30:2	111, 113-14, 138-39, 202-3
26:16	168, 210	30:2-3	5, 35, 45, 111, 115, 117, 122, 126, 143-44, 176, 182, 203, 208-9, 211
26:17	157		
26:20	172		
27:2	248	30:2-4	5, 12, 34, 38, 44, 54
27:8	157-58	30:2-5	144
27:9	122	30:2-10	26, 110, 143, 160
27:11	129	30:2-14	202
27:20	171	30:3	10, 111-12, 116, 128, 138, 189, 223-24
27:23	157		
27:23-27	158	30:4	4-5, 12-13, 36-37, 45, 54, 65, 117, 120-21, 123-27, 138, 143-44, 174, 203, 225, 227
27:26-27	157-58		
28:1	157, 191		
28:4	214	30:5	12, 109-10, 130-33, 136, 141, 189, 224-6
28:7	214		
28:9	214	30:5-6	5, 34, 51, 53-54, 132, 208
28:11	210	30:5-17	46
28:13	231	30:6	11-13, 46, 133-34, 139, 141-42, 144-45, 193, 203, 205-6, 226-27
28:15	157		
28:18	122, 214	30:6-9	45
28:19	136, 183	30:6-10	132-43, 186, 201
28:26	215	30:7	100, 133, 138
29:13	212	30:7-9	5, 12-13, 34, 36, 44, 53-54, 110, 114, 142, 145, 182, 203
29:18	213-14		
29:27	122	30:7-33	45-47
30	2-6, 8-13, 22-26, 33-39, 42-48, 51, 53-54, 57, 61-108, 110-15, 116-17, 119, 121-22, 126, 128, 132-45, 147-49, 150, 154, 157, 160, 165-99, 201-4, 206, 208-9, 211-12, 215, 221, 224, 228, 235-36, 246-47	30:8	42, 133-36, 138-39, 142, 189, 202
		30:8-9	185
		30:9	6, 10-11, 53, 128, 132, 134, 136-39, 142, 174, 181, 185, 189, 206, 224, 227
		30:10	12-13, 46, 53, 110, 133-34, 139, 142, 144-45, 189, 193, 195, 202-3, 205-7, 227
30:1	5, 6, 8, 11-13, 33, 45, 53, 61-108, 110-11, 119, 145, 183, 190, 203-4, 221		
		30:10-12	150
30:1-2	69	30:10-33	5-6, 48
30:1-3	42	30:11	10, 54, 166-69, 199, 228
30:1-4	36, 38, 45-47, 57, 202, 224	30:11-14	5, 53, 166-74, 202, 228
30:1-5	142, 201	30:11-17	12, 23, 54, 165-70, 173-74, 182, 186, 194, 198, 206
30:1-6	5, 37		

Proverbs (cont.)
30:11–20   206
30:11–31   13, 197, 203
30:11–33   26, 54, 110, 147–48, 154, 165–99, 215
30:12   5, 121, 166–69, 173, 181, 228
30:12–13   167–68, 172
30:12–14   167
30:12–17   202
30:13   55, 166, 168, 195, 228–29
30:13–14   121
30:13–15   192
30:14   10, 24, 38, 57, 168–70, 172, 173, 181, 185, 189, 229
30:14–17   137
30:15   4–5, 10–11, 24, 38, 45–46, 157, 160, 167, 170, 173, 202, 229
30:15–16   36, 39, 47, 53, 148, 166–67, 170–73, 176, 181, 185, 189
30:15–31   36, 194
30:15–33   22–24, 34, 42–43, 148
30:16   10, 190, 231, 231
30:17   5, 39, 53–54, 63, 157, 166–67, 171–75, 189, 202, 206, 232
30:18   12–13, 174–76, 182, 203, 233
30:18–19   5, 39, 53, 148, 172, 176–77, 179–81, 189, 202, 235
30:18–20   176–82, 194, 235
30:18–31   173–76, 193–94, 198, 202
30:18–33   54
30:19   157, 174, 177, 180–81, 235
30:19–20   160, 235
30:19–31   12
30:20   5, 10, 46, 53, 137, 174, 176–77, 179, 181–82, 185–86, 189–90, 235
32:21   189, 206
30:21–23   5, 57, 148, 160, 182–86, 189, 193, 195, 202, 206, 236
30:22   10, 137, 174, 183, 185, 189, 193–94, 202, 236, 238
30:22–23   53, 185–86, 236
30:22–24   190
30:23   183, 237
30:24   5, 10, 187, 189, 238–39

30:24–28   5, 39, 53, 148, 187–90, 194, 202–3, 206
30:24–31   215
30:25   187, 240
30:25–26   187
30:25–28   157, 190
30:26   188, 240
30:27   188, 193, 241
30:28   4, 188, 203, 242
30:29   190, 243
30:29–31   5, 39, 53, 149, 160, 190–94, 202, 206
30:29–33   206
30:30   244
30:30–31   157, 246–47
30:31   4, 190, 192–93, 199, 204, 221, 244–48
30:32–33   12, 47, 53, 57, 160, 194–97, 198
30:32   5, 10, 13, 45, 174–75, 193–94, 196–97, 201, 203, 206, 227, 248
30:33   5, 194, 196–97, 202, 206
31:1   8, 11, 33, 35, 69–73, 82, 94
31:1–9   22
31:2–3   72
31:4   248
31:7   136
31:10–31   22
31:15   138
31:16   195
31:17   244
31:26   214

Ecclesiastes   7, 14, 17–19, 30, 56, 67–69, 164, 184, 211, 214
1:1   64, 67
1:1–13   17
1:2   17
1:8   137, 171
1:12–2:26   17
2:21   186
2:26   212
3:9–22   17
4:8   136–37, 171
5:9   137, 171

Ancient Sources Index 291

5:14	136	13:1–14:27	88		
6:2	136	13:2–22	88		
6:3	137, 171	13:3	249,		
7:1–12	17	13:6–22	89		
7:7	245	14:1–23	90–91		
7:15	186	14:4–5	93		
7:23–24	211	14:4–21	88, 94		
9:11	186	14:9	155, 186, 192, 229		
9:17–11:4	17	14:10–13	90, 92–94		
10:4–7	186	14:13	118		
12:1–14	17	14:15	93		
		14:16	186, 229		
Song of Songs	68	14:16–17	92		
1:3	234	14:22–23	88		
2:9	246	14:23	90		
4:16	181	14:28	75, 88		
5:1	181	15:1	75, 88		
6:8	234	16:2	102		
		16:4	249		
Isaiah	4, 75, 79–80, 82	16:6	89		
1:2	157	16:12	100–101, 107		
1:2–4	128	16:14	89		
1:3	155–56	17:1	75, 88		
1:4	224	17:4	89		
1:13	135	19:1	75, 88		
1:13–14	107	21:1	75, 88		
1:14	107	21:2	85		
2:2	227	21:11	75, 88		
2:21	179	21:13	75, 88		
4:4	168	22:1	75, 88		
5:14	171	23:1	75, 88		
5:19	224	23:8	239		
5:25	249	23:9	89		
7:13	107	23:16	191, 243		
7:14	233–34	24:14	89		
9:5	177	24:20	248		
9:19	171	25:1	177		
10:5	249	25:3	187		
10:12	89	26:13	238		
11:2	116	28:8	168		
11:6–9	155	28:16	239–40		
13	88–89	28:29	177		
13–14	88, 90, 94–95, 205–6	29:14	177		
13–30	206	29:15	227		
13:1	75, 81, 83, 88	30:6	75, 88, 244		

Isaiah (cont.)		9:23–24	31
30:17	127	10:23	190, 243
30:27	249	12:5	107
31:4	191	14:12	111
32:6	237	14:21	236, 248
33:24	66, 84, 92	15:10	241
37:4	227	16:19	121
37:23–29	89	17:21	76
40	56, 121–22, 126, 144	17:21–22	79
40:1–9	122–23	17:27	76
40:12	120–21	18:15	135
40:12–14	43, 121–22	20:7	241
40:18–31	123	20:9	96, 100–102, 107, 231
43:6	128	23	78
44:8	226	23:33–34	75
45:1	244	23:36	75
45:11	128	23:38	75
45:22	121	23:31–40	77, 79
47:4	224	29:23	236
47:13	107	31:4	243
48:21	179	31:20	128
52:10	121	31:29	169
53:8	231	31:32	238
54:1	238	34:3	243
54:4	234	34:21	243
54:5	238	38:23	242
62:4–5	238	46:23	188
63:16	128	49:7	72
64:8	128	50:29	224
66:9	231	51:5	224
66:11	249	51:12	195
		51:40	192
Jeremiah	86	51:41	243
1:12	190, 243	51:53	118
1:17	244		
2:8	137	Lamentations	
3:4	128	2:14	75, 81, 83, 135
3:14	238	2:17	195
3:19	128		
4:28	195	Ezekiel	86, 192
6:13	241	1:10	155, 191
7:33	172	4:12	168
8:6	241	4:14	138
8:7	156	10:2	120
8:10	241	10:7	120

12:10	75	7:25	224		
13:1–23	142	7:27	224		
13:6–9	135	8:2–8	155		
13:23	135	11:20	249		
14:5	137	11:37–39	226		
16	56	12:6	177		
17:2–7	192				
17:3	232	Hosea			
17:7	232	2:1	128		
17:13	192	4:2	197		
17:14	195	8:10	70		
19:3	138	8:13	230		
19:6	138	9:2	137		
21:11	244	11:1	128		
21:16	242	12:1	115, 224		
21:24	242				
21:28	135	Joel			
22:23–29	142	1:6	169, 188		
22:27	138–39, 142	2	241		
22:28	135, 142	2:1	186		
27:4	180	2:2	187–88		
27:25–27	180	2:7–8	188		
27:33	171	2:10	183		
28:2	180	2:25	188		
28:8	180	2:26	171		
29:7	242				
32:2	155	Amos			
33:32	190, 243	1:3	148		
37:14	86	1:6	148		
38:13	155	4:1	155		
39:18	192	4:8	171		
44:24	197	5:8	127		
		8:8	183		
Daniel	16	9:6	127		
2:10	106				
2:21	212	Obadiah			
4:5–6	224	4	179		
4:14–15	224				
5:11	224	Jonah			
5:16	106	2:9	135		
5:17	230	2:11	65		
6:24	140	4:10	64		
7:2–12	155	4:11	155		
7:18	224				
7:21–22	224				

Micah		187–88	148, 152
1:16	232		
5:2	121	Babylonian Theodicy	
6:14	171	24.256–257	118
7:1–6	184		
7:6	236, 248	Complaints of Khakheperre-Sonb	184
7:15	177		
7:16	195	Deir 'Alla Balaam text	82, 94, 184
Nahum		Dialogue of Pessimism	54, 118
1:1	75, 81, 83		
2:2	244, 246	El-Amarna Tablets	240
2:11	244		
2:14	155	Gilgamesh and the Land of the Living	
3:6	236, 248	Lines 28–29	118–19
Habakkuk		Instruction of Amenemhet	
1:1	75, 83	I, 1	14
1:11	226		
2:5	171	Instruction of Amenemope	10, 14, 40,
3:3	226	49, 71	
3:14	169	II, 11–13	14
3:17	137		
		Instruction of Ankhsheshonq	
Zechariah		18.6	162
1:6	195		
3:3	168	Instruction of Any	
8:14–15	195	9, 10–15	14
9:1	75–76		
9:10	121	Instruction of Ptahhotep	13
10:3	192		
12:1	75–76, 87	Instructions of Šuruppak	13, 24–25
14:5	224		
		KTU 1.4 (Baal epics)	151–54
Malachi		iii.12–14	151
1:1	75–76	iii.12–16	152
2:10	128	iii.14–22	151
2:11	238	iii.17–21	148
3:10	138	iii.21–22	152
Ancient Near Eastern Texts		Ludlul Bel Nemeqi	118
Ahiqar	14, 152–54, 158	Myth of the Sun's Eye	161
86	159		
121–122	159		

Ancient Sources Index 295

Papyrus Amherst 63	15	6:22–31	77
11.11–19	15	6:35	77
17.5–22.9	15	6:37	77, 212, 239
		9:7	236
Papyrus Insinger	15, 19	9:18	79
5.12	16	15:7–8	136
6.17	16	17:7	212
7.16–17	16	17:11	212
8.21	16	20:18	163
		23:16–17	149
Poem of the Righteous Sufferer		25:1–2	149
2.36–37	118	25:7–11	149
		26:5–6	149
Prophecies of Neferti	184	33:24	77
		36:22	121
Satirical Papyrus	161	37:15	244
		38:2	78–79
Sumerian Proverbs	15, 118	39:6	212
2.92	163	42:10	231
5.15	158	42:17	224
		42:21	224
Ugaritic literature	43–45, 47, 58	43:33	212
		44:21	121
Deuterocanonical Texts		50:25–26	149
		51:26	77–79, 94
Tobit			
3:2–6	16	Baruch	71
4:3–21	14, 16, 17	1:1–4	14
		3:22–23	72
Wisdom of Solomon	16, 30, 178	3:29–4:4	43
2:13	129	3:36	129
2:18	129	4:8	129
5:9–11	178–79		
5:14	178–79	1 Esdras	
9:17	212	3–5	149–50
18:13	128	3:5	150
		3:12	150
Ben Sira	16, 30, 70, 74, 80, 83, 136	4:35–41	150
Prologue	14		
1:2–8	43	Dead Sea Scrolls	
1:10	212		
1:26	212	1Q/4QMysteries	16, 80, 83, 9
5:12	195		
6:18–37	77	1Q23 (1QEnGiants^a)	246
6:21	77, 79, 94		

1Q27	80	Hebrews	
		1:4	36
1Q28 (1QSa)			
1:17	244	Rabbinic Texts	
1QM (War Scroll)	224	Abot de-Rabbi Nathan	
		39.2	244
4Q174 (4QFlor)	138		
		b. Avodah Zarah	229
4Q160 (4QVision of Samuel)	81–83		
		b. Berakhot	
4Q402 (4QShirShabb^c)	224	63a	246
4Q416 (4QInstruction^b)	88	b. Ketubot	
		64b	181
4Q417 (4QInstruction^c)	139		
		b. Menahot	
4Q418 (4QInstruction^d)	88	98a	181
11Q19 (11QTemple^a)		b. Pesahim	
LIV, 6	226	87b	140
		b. Qiddushin	
		2b	180

Ancient Jewish Texts

Aquila 96–97, 99, 100–101, 103, 105, 245			
		b. Sanhedrin	
Josephus, *Jewish Antiquities*		70b	64
8.3	149	82b	248
8.5	149	100a	181
		103b	242
Letter of Aristeas	149		
		b. Shabbat	
Septuagint 4, 7–8, 9, 11, 21–25, 42, 45,		56a	140
47, 65–66, 97–98, 104, 140, 168, 191,		77b	242
203–4			
		Ecclesiastes Rabbah	
Theodotion 96–101, 103, 105, 239, 245		1.1.2	64

New Testament

		Exodus Rabbah	
		23:13	191
Matthew			
6:9–13	142	Genesis Rabbah	
		44:6	85
Luke		65:3	245
3:38	128	100:75	245

Midrash Lamentations 5:1	245	3.7	56
Midrash Mishle	23, 64, 98, 129, 178, 185	Hesiod, *Theogony* 116–122	231
Midrash Tanhuma	65, 98, 100	Old Latin	234, 245
Vaera 5	23		
Vaera 5.2	64, 98	Vulgate	65–66, 234

Peshitta   67, 105, 140, 229–31, 239, 242

Vedic/Sanskrit Texts

Rigveda   36, 41

Song of Songs Rabbah
  1.1.10   64
  1.6.1   140

Targums   67, 169, 229, 230, 242, 249

Targum Onqelos
  Gen 24:43   234
  Gen 30:1   230
  Gen 30:26   230
  Exod 2:8   234

Targum Neofiti
  Num 11:13   230

Tg. Psalms
  12:9   170, 229
  30:15   229

Tg. Proverbs
  23:25   230
  30:26   240

Tg. Isaiah
  7:14   234
  30:6   244

Greco-Roman Texts

Aeschylus, *Agamemnon*   191

Aristotle, *Rhetoric*   91, 160
  3.1   56

Modern Authors Index

Abegg, Martin G., Jr., 80
Adams, Samuel L., 48
Aejmelaeus, Anneli, 124
Aitken, James K., 21–22, 66, 191, 193
Albright, William F., 63, 71
Alexander, Philip, 20–21
Allegro, John M., 138
Allen, Leslie C., 191
Alster, Bendt, 13, 15, 24–25, 118–19, 158, 161, 163
Alter, Robert, 73, 92–93, 163, 209
Ansberry, Christopher B., 25, 128, 184, 190, 193, 197
Assmann, Jan, 184
Avrahami, Yael, 181
Babcock, Barbara A., 184
Badé, William Frederic, 192, 246
Balentine, Samuel E., 9, 126
Barr, James, 97, 102, 127, 230, 232, 237
Barthélemy, Dominique, 65, 80, 85, 98, 100–101, 246
Bauer, Johannes Baptist, 249
Beattie, James, 160
Bekins, Peter, 111
Ben-Porat, Ziva, 225
Ben Zvi, Ehud, 41
Berger, Peter L., 160
Berman, Samuel B., 23
Bernasconi, Rocco, 20–21
Beverly, Jared, 156
Bewer, Julius A., 245, 247
Bickell, G., 102
Biddle, Mark E., 163
Bledsoe, Seth A., 152
Blenkinsopp, Joseph, 32

Bloch-Smith, Elizabeth, 173
Block, Daniel I., 191, 241
Böck, Barbara, 178
Boda, Mark J., 75
Bodi, Daniel, 149
Boer, P. A. H. de, 75
Bordjadze, Karlo V., 89–92, 173
Borowski, Oded, 179, 232
Bowley, James E., 80
Brekelmans, C. H. W., 224
Brenner, Athalya, 163
Brettler, Marc Z., 19
Bridges, Charles, 51, 172, 178, 184, 189
Briggs, Richard S., 68
Brown, Jeannine K., 204
Brown, William P., 9, 11
Bruch, Johann Friedrich, 30, 49
Brunner-Traut, E., 162
Budde, K., 91
Bunson, Margaret R., 162
Buss, Martin J., 41
Butler, Trent C., 241
Byargeon, Rick W., 142
Carr, David M., 49
Carroll, Nöel, 160–1, 199
Caubet, Annie, 192
Cheung, Simon Chi-Chung, 204
Childs, Brevard S., 21, 51, 88, 93, 132
Clifford, Richard J., 61, 71, 113, 116, 127, 134, 168–69, 178, 183–84, 196, 225, 245, 247
Clines, David J. A., 115, 123–24, 156, 196
Cohen, Abaraham, 64, 178
Collins, John J., 224
Conybeare, Catherine, 217

Cook, Edward M., 80
Cook, Johann, 23, 66, 84
Cook, John A., 80, 112
Costecalde, C.-B., 224
Crenshaw, James L., 22, 32, 63, 73, 110, 116, 144
Cuppi, Lorenzo, 21-23, 66-67, 84, 97-100
D'Agostino, Franco, 161
Dahood, Mitchell, 140
Davis, Ellen F., 23, 25, 51-55, 57-58, 160, 168, 181, 184, 206
Day, John, 48
Deist, Ferdinand, 161
Delitzsch, Franz, 6, 31-32, 35-40, 48-49, 55, 57, 63, 71, 73, 94, 97, 109, 112, 139, 170, 172, 178-80, 184, 213, 227-29, 232, 234-35, 237, 239, 242, 245-47, 249
Dell, Katharine J., 157, 189
Dequeker, L., 224
Derrida, Jacques, 205
Díez Merino, Luis, 242-43
Dijkstra, Meindert, 82
Dillon, E. J., 144-45
Donald, Trevor, 113, 236
Driver, G. R., 232, 247
Ehrenberg, Erica, 192
Eising, Hermann, 86
Eissfeldt, Otto, 44, 91, 149-50, 154
Elgvin, Torleif, 80, 139
Erlandsson, Seth, 88
Emerton, J. A., 10
Erman, Adolf, 40
Eshel, Esther, 224
Ewald, Heinrich A., 31-35, 38-40, 48, 55, 57, 109, 145, 171, 178
Feigin, S., 246
Fernández Marcos, Natalio, 104-5
Field, Frederick, 223, 239
Firmage, Edwin, 188, 241, 244, 246
Fishbane, Michael, 214
Fisher, Milton C., 232
Floyd, Michael H., 75
Forti, Tova L., 65, 172, 176, 178-79, 181, 187-88, 191, 193, 232, 242, 244

Foster, Benjamin R., 161-3, 16
Fox, Michael V., 3, 6, 8, 10, 22-24, 27, 48, 58, 65-66, 68, 72-73, 79, 84, 95-100, 112, 116, 118, 123-24, 126-27, 129, 134, 138, 140, 144, 154, 168-71, 177-78, 180-82, 184, 186, 188, 193, 197, 208, 213, 223, 225, 227-28, 230-35, 238-40, 242-43, 245-49
Franklyn, Paul, 3, 23, 57, 63, 97, 110, 113, 115, 124, 127, 134, 141
Freedman, Harry, 8
Fritsch, Charles T., 51
Frow, John, 204-5, 207
Gehman, Henry S., 75
Gemser, Berend, 4, 22, 42-43, 46, 55, 57
George, A. R., 161
Gerleman, Gillis, 23
Gese, Hartmut, 32
Gesenius, Wilhelm, 241
Gilbert, Allan S., 188, 241
Ginsburg, Eliezer, 116, 169, 178, 186, 189, 195, 240
Glazov, Gregory Yuri, 196
Glück, J. J., 229
Goff, Matthew J., 48, 80, 139
Goldhill, Simon, 217
Goldingay, John, 224
Good, Edwin M., 163-64
Goodenough, Erwin R., 192
Gordon, Cyrus H., 64-65, 98, 233-34
Gordon, Edmund I., 163
Gordon, Robert P., 48,
Graf, Karl Heinrich, 75
Greenberg, Moshe, 191
Greenfield, Jonas C., 232
Greenspahn, Frederick E., 118-19
Greenstein, Edward L., 119, 163-64, 17
Gruber, Mayer I., 195
Gruen, Erich S., 163, 193
Gunkel, Hermann, 32, 41, 50
Gunneweg, A. H. J., 110, 113, 131-32, 225
Habel, Norman C., 124, 196
Hackett, Jo Ann, 82
Ham, T. C., 123-24

Hamilton, Victor P., 244
Haran, Menahem, 148
Harding, G. Lankester, 63
Harrington, Daniel J., 139
Hays, Christopher B., 169–70
Hayward, Robert, 20–21
Healey, John F., 230, 232, 242
Heim, Knut M., 9, 164
Heiser, Michael S., 224
Held, Moshe, 249
Hendel, Ronald, 217
Herder, Johann Gottfried, 148–49
Hess, Johann Jacob, 242
Hoftijzer, Jacob, 82
Holmes, R., 97
Holmstedt, Robert D., 217–18, 229, 236
Houlihan, Patrick F., 161
Huehnergard, John, 234
Imes, Carmen Joy, 127
Izenberg, Oren, 68
Jackson, Melissa A., 163
Jahnow, Hedwig, 91
Jarick, John, 48, 164
Jasnow, Richard, 161
Jastrow, Marcus, 63, 66, 79, 137, 140, 169, 226, 229, 240–41, 244–46, 249
Johnson, Benjamin J. M., 163
Johnston, Philip S., 173
Jones, Jordan W., 195
Jones, Scott C., 179
Jones, William R, 198
Joüon, Paul, 63, 74, 111, 227, 229–30, 233, 248
Judd, Andrew, 41, 204
Kamesar, Adam, 234
Kaminsky, Joel S., 163
Keefer, Arthur J., 127
Keel, Othmar, 192
Kennicott, Benjamin, 96, 106, 223, 233
Kidner, Derek, 51, 160
Kim, Hyun Chul Paul, 89
Kirk, Alexander T., 111
Kister, Menahem, 80
Kline, Joanna Greenlee, 114
Kooij, Gerrit van der, 82

Krahmalkov, Charles R., 233
Kramer, Samuel N., 119
Kronholm, Tryggve, 172, 232
Kruger, Paul A., 184
Kuntz, J. Kenneth, 9
Kutsch, Ernst, 231
Kynes, Will, 30–33, 48–50, 73–74, 145, 204–5, 207, 217
Lakoff, George, 155
Lambert, David A., 217
Lambert, Wilfred G., 15, 118–19, 170
Lazaridis, Nikolaos, 161–65,
Lee, Jin Tae, 154
Legaspi, Michael C., 2151–6
Lehrman, S. R., 191
Lella, Alexander A. di, 77
Levine, Baruch A., 11
Levine, Étan, 164
Lichtheim, Miriam, 10, 14–16, 162, 184
Lied, Liv Ingeborg, 217
Lindenberger, J. M., 152, 159
Lipiński, Edward, 82
Longman, Tremper, III, 41
Lovejoy, Arthur O., 155
Luria, S., 184
Lundhaug, Hugo, 217
Lyon, David G., 37–38
Machinist, Peter, 92
Marcus, David, 92, 163, 198
Marno, David, 56
Maxwell, Nathan Dean, 68
McKane, William, 3, 42, 45–47, 50, 52, 55, 57, 61, 75, 77, 91, 111, 113, 116, 132, 160, 173, 178–79, 184, 186–87, 193, 247
Meade, John, 99
Meek, Theophile James, 231
Meltzer, Edmund S., 161–62
Milgrom, Jacob, 11
Milik, Józef T., 80, 246
Millar, Suzanna R., 164, 204
Miller, Carolyn R., 204
Miller, Cynthia L., 112
Miller-Naudé, Cynthia, 75–76, 218
Moberly, R. W. L., 37

Montanari, Franco, 67
Montgomery, James A., 63
Moore, Rick D., 3, 23, 110, 128
Morreall, John, 160-61
Müller, Hans-Peter, 74-75, 149, 151
Murphy, Roland E., 3-4, 22, 65, 71, 99, 112, 135, 167, 173, 176, 181-82, 184, 187-88, 209-11, 234, 236, 238-39
Najman, Hindy, 48, 74, 217
Naudé, Jacobus, 218
Newsom, Carol A., 74, 179, 204, 224
Noegel, Scott B., 197
North, Francis Sparling, 229
Noth, Martin, 224
Novenson, Matthew V., 127
O'Connor, Michael P., 218
O'Dowd, Ryan P., 23, 25, 58, 65, 110, 116, 128-29, 167, 178-79, 184, 193, 209, 213-14
Oesterly, W. O. E., 40, 181, 184, 225, 229, 237
Olivero, Vladimir, 171, 231
Orlemanski, Julie, 217-18
Pardee, Dennis, 226
Parker, Simon B., 115, 224
Parsons, J., 97
Passaro, Angelo, 110
Patton, Kimberley C., 155
Penar, Tadeusz, 78
Perdue, Leo G., 3-4, 51-55, 58, 111, 172, 178, 184, 189, 194, 196
Perks, Lisa Glebatis, 160, 199
Perry, T. Anthony, 181
Peters, John P., 192, 245-47
Phillips, Anthony, 236
Pitard, Wayne T., 151
Plöger, Otto, 22, 62, 95, 106, 116, 166-67, 172, 178, 181, 184, 196, 242
Polk, Timothy, 68, 91
Pollock, Sheldon, 217-18
Porten, Bezalel, 14, 152, 159, 237
Quick, Laura, 15
Rad, Gerhard von, 4, 22, 31, 123, 149-50, 154
Radday, Yehuda T., 163

Rey, Jean-Sébastien, 48
Richards, Eliza, 12
Richter, Hans-Friedemann, 111
Rico, Christophe, 179, 181, 234-35
Ricoeur, Paul, 37
Riede, Peter, 155-56, 187
Ringgren, Helmer, 113
Roberts, J. J. M., 92
Rochettes, Jacqueline des, 164
Rogerson, John W., 33, 35
Roth, Wolfgang, 46, 148, 176, 178, 184, 186, 237
Rüger, Hans Peter, 149
Sæbø, Magne, 95, 106, 160, 167, 171, 184, 191
Sallaberger, Walther, 25
Samely, Alexander, 8, 11, 20-21
Samet, Nili, 24-25, 118
Sandoval, Timothy J., 99, 224
Sauer, Georg, 6, 25, 42-47, 55, 57, 63, 148, 167
Saur, Markur, 23, 73, 110, 113, 115
Schellenberg, Annette, 212-13
Schipper, Bernd U., 8-9, 16, 22-23, 32, 49, 91, 111, 112, 126-27, 141, 167, 209-10, 214
Schipper, Jeremy, 91
Schloerb, Rolland, 51
Schneider, Heinrich, 171
Schneiders, Sandra M., 37
Schökel, Luis Alonso, 197
Schwáb, Zoltán, 209
Scott, R. B. Y., 3, 99, 181, 234, 236, 239
Screnock, John, 103-4, 225
Seitz, Christpher R., 21, 51, 88-89
Sherman, Phillip, 155
Shupak, Nili, 10
Siebenthal, Heinrich von, 242
Siedlecki, Armin, 41
Sjöberg, Åke W, 161
Skehan, Patrick W., 65, 77, 128
Smend, Rudolf, 9, 33, 41, 49
Smith, Mark S., 151
Sneed, Mark R., 48-49, 73, 83, 204, 209, 212, 214

Sokoloff, Michael, 137, 140, 169, 226, 229-30, 237, 240-42, 244-46
Southwood, Katharine E., 163-64
Staubli, Thomas, 168
Steinberg, Julius, 11
Steiner, Richard S., 15
Steinmann, Andrew E., 25, 58, 147, 149
Stewart, Anne W., 9
Stier, Rudolf, 6
Stolz, F., 75
Strawn, Brent A., 192, 244
Strugnell, John, 139
Sutcliffe, Edmund F., 176, 178, 234
Sweeney, Mavin A., 41, 91
Swete, Henry Barclay, 97
Talmon, Shemaryahu, 105-6
Teeter, D. Andrew, 18-21
Thomas, D. Winton, 40, 230, 231-32, 241, 246
Thomas, Samuel I., 16,
Tigchelaar, Eibert J. C., 48
Tolkein, J. R. R., 216
Tooman, William A., 18-21
Toorn, Karel van der, 49
Torczyner, Harry (N. H. Tur-Sinai), 149, 178
Torrey, Charles C., 98-99
Tov, Emanuel, 21, 23-24, 66, 84, 103, 247-48
Toy, Crawford H., 31, 37-40, 46, 55, 57, 64, 67, 87, 95, 109, 112-13, 116, 118, 132, 135, 154, 159, 167, 169, 173, 178, 184, 228-29, 231-32, 237, 246-47
Tristram, Henry Baker, 187-88, 241
Turner, James, 36, 73, 155, 217-18
Turner, Mark, 73, 155
Ullendorff, Edward, 168
Van Leeuwen, Raymond C., 4, 23, 41, 113, 119, 145, 168, 171, 176, 178, 184, 196, 238
Vancil, Jack W., 192
Vattioni, Francesco, 229
Vayntrub, Jacqueline E., 14-15, 21, 33, 50-51, 74-75, 88, 90-91, 94, 217
Veenker, Ronald A., 181

Visotzky, Burton L., 23, 65, 98, 129, 178, 185
Vycichl, W., 162
Waard, Jan de, 22, 99, 105, 140, 223, 230-32, 234, 242-43, 248
Waltke, Bruce K., 6, 10, 23, 25, 48, 58, 66, 84, 106, 112, 129, 134-35, 138, 147, 167, 169, 171, 180, 184-85, 187-90, 193, 195, 212, 228, 233-34, 238, 243-47
Watanabe, Chikako E., 192
Watson, Wilfred, 63, 148
Webb, Barry G., 241
Weeks, Stuart, 9, 13, 16-18, 41, 48, 69, 74, 77, 129, 141, 164, 168, 184-86, 204, 207, 212-14, 217, 245
Weinberger, Yosef, 116, 169, 178, 186, 189, 195, 240
Weis, Richard, 63, 71-72, 75
Westermann, Claus, 50
Whedbee, William, 163-64
Whitekettle, Richard, 170-71
Whybray, R. N., 3, 11, 23, 32, 71, 123, 148, 154, 184
Williamson, H. G. M., 88, 90
Wise, Michael O., 80
Wolff, Hans Walter, 128
Wright, Benjamin D., III, 78
Yardeni, Ada, 14, 152, 159, 237
Yaron, Reuven, 237
Yee, Gale A., 91-94, 163
Yoder, Christine R., 9, 25, 58, 129, 170, 173, 176, 178, 184-85, 215
Young, Ian, 241-42
Zimmerli, Walther, 32

www.ingramcontent.com/pod-product-compliance
Lightning Source LLC
Chambersburg PA
CBHW021935290426
44108CB00012B/842